MANUS RELIGION

PLATE I

THE RETURN HOME

Manus Religion

An Ethnological Study of the Manus Natives of the Admiralty Islands

BY

R. F. FORTUNE

UNIVERSITY OF NEBRASKA PRESS · Lincoln

Library of Congress Catalog Card Number 36–2179
Manufactured in the United States of America

First Bison Book printing: February, 1965
Second Bison Book printing: August, 1969

Bison Book edition printed by arrangement with the American Philosophical Society.

MANUS RELIGION

PREFACE

This book, resulting from my field work amongst the Manus fisher folk of the Admiralty Islands, runs true to title. It is about the spiritualistic cult of these people, and about their system of morals which the oracles, representing the ghosts, enforce and sanction. "Manus Religion," unlike "Sorcerers of Dobu,"[1] my previous record of my first field work under the Australian National Research Council, is not an account of social organisation, trade and economics, mythology and dance songs, but an account only of the supernatural cult and moral system of a people. The reason for this is that I stand responsible for an account of only a part of Manus culture, another part of it being accounted for in the writings of my wife, Dr. Margaret Mead,[2] who accompanied me on the Admiralty Island expedition, while much of the Manus mythology has been published with texts by Father P. J. Meier.[3] An early account of the Admiralty Islanders with some specific material on the Manus tribe is that of R. Parkinson.[4] I published in 1931 a summary account of the Manus Religion.[5] I have yet to write of Manus rituals of

[1] "Sorcerers of Dobu. The Social Anthropology of the Dobu Islanders of the Western Pacific." London, George Routledge and Sons, Ltd., 1932; New York, E. P. Dutton and Company, 1932.

[2] Mead, Margaret, "Growing up in New Guinea"; New York, William Morrow and Company, 1930; London, George Routledge and Sons, Ltd., 1931. "An Investigation of the Thought of Primitive Children with Special Reference to Animism," *Journal of the Royal Anthropological Institute of Great Britain and Ireland*, vol. 62, pp. 173–190, London, 1932. "Melanesian Middlemen," *Natural History*, vol. 30, pp. 115–130, New York, 1930. "Kinship in the Admiralty Islands," *Anthropological Papers of the American Museum of Natural History*, vol. XXXIV, Part II, New York, 1934. This study of Dr. Mead's was written after the completion of the first draft of this manuscript and presuming upon its early publication, contains a number of detailed references to it. This expected order of publication was reversed and I have made some rearrangements of this study. For all references in Dr. Mead's paper which cite Chapter V, read Chapter IV.

[3] Meier, P. J., S.M., "Mythen und Sagen der Admiralitätinsulaner," *Anthropos*, vols. 2 to 4.

[4] Parkinson, R., "Dreisig Jahre in Südsee."

[5] Fortune, R. F., "Manus Religion," *Oceania*, vol. 2, no. 1, pp. 74–108, Sydney, 1931.

life crises, of Manus economics, and an account of the Manus language and grammar. The diary of spiritualistic events from day to day, which is published in this study as Chapter IV, is taken from complete texts in the Manus language[6] which are not published here.

The Manus are fishermen who live in houses on stilts in the sea lagoons, between the reef and the shore-lines of several islands of the Admiralty group. This book deals with the imponderable aspects of their lives, with their religion (from which they will be converted), and with their morals (what will happen to these remains to be seen). The material setting, which is somewhat irrelevant to the imponderable stuff of this study, is an island group between 1°50′ and 3°10″ south latitude, and between longitudes 146° and 148° east. From an account given by the naturalist aboard H.M.S. *Challenger*, which visited the group in 1875, I learn that "the group forms the northwesterly germination of the long curved chain of large islands and groups of islands, which stretching roughly N.E. and S.W. is composed of New Ireland, Solomons and New Hebrides groups. The Great Admiralty is distant from New Hanover, the nearest large island of the chain, about one hundred and thirty miles, and from the nearest point of the mainland of New Guinea, to the southwest, about one hundred and fifty miles."

Manus natives used to sail these two named distances in their dugout canoes; the open Pacific runs with only a single uninhabited land break in each. They used no seafaring magic, being better sailors than magicians, and they are today highly valued as schooner crews. Their own long-distance canoe runs are forbidden by the Government at the present time, as being attended by too great a risk of life. They are enterprising and intelligent and upright beyond the

[6] It so happens that the Manus language and our own are very similarly oriented in matters of morality. I have therefore freely used the translations, *good* and *bad*, *sin* and *shame*, without further explanation. The reader will be safe in understanding all such translations in the connotation characteristic of English puritanism, with the moral values of which the Manus values are in very marked accord. In this respect Manus contrasts with Dobu, for the Dobuan language is not oriented in questions of morality as our own and the Manus language are.

average of natives of New Guinea, or the New Guinea littoral, and are agreed to be such by most observers. They have earned a recent reputation for enthusiasm in pleading cases in the local courts. Their cultural emphases are not very different from our own. They fish, trade and work hard, and they are kept to work and to good morals by authority—in their case not secular, but remarkably efficient none the less. They earned a name for treachery years ago when they killed whites in order to secure rifles, but that phase is well over, and was reasonable in its motives while it lasted.

The writer lived among the Manus for six months, during most of which time he spoke the Manus language and understood it. He had an interpreter lent him through the kind offices of Mr. E. P. W. Chinnery, Director of District Services, and Government Anthropologist, of Rabaul. The interpreter was useful for the first three months for formal linguistic work. He had left home as an orphan to go to school, then entered Government employ, and therefore did not know his own culture; he knew the language however but without appreciating any reason for my learning it. Many of the natives of Peri village entered into the ethnological spirit with zest, rare among the natives of the wider area. The Manus delight in facts and argument. They will, for instance, carry a useless fish jaw for months, in the hope of meeting a man with whom they had an argument about the number of teeth in the jaw of that particular species. They debate heatedly whether or not a report (received by one man from a geologist) that New Guinea was once joined by a land bridge to Australia is true. The night before I left, the village argued over the water from house to house as to whether a lad who had died ten years before was older or younger than another still living. They debate questions about entirely useless matters for the love of truth. They deserve credit for their ready help in the collection of facts about their own lives and culture.

To my wife, Dr. Margaret Mead, I owe all the many advantages of a collaboration in the field, as well as specific criticism of this work in manuscript.

I wish to thank Professor A. Radcliffe-Brown, Dr. R. C. Chapman, and all the executive officers of the Australian National Research Council, for their ready kindness to me. I owe my privilege of working in the Admiralty Islands, and with the Manus tribe there, to the generous financial support of that Council, a body which financed first my work in Dobu in 1927–28, and subsequently my work in Manus in 1928–29. In between these two expeditions I spent three months in New Zealand, where I was joined by Dr. Mead, who was working under the auspices of a different Foundation, shortly before we proceeded to the Admiralty Islands.

I wish to express my deepest thanks also to Brigadier General E. A. Wisdom, Administrator of the Mandated Territory of New Guinea, to His Honour Judge F. B. Phillips, and to Mr. E. P. W. Chinnery, Government Anthropologist, for their courtesy and assistance in the Mandated Territory. In the Admiralties I was most hospitably received by Mr. F. W. Mantle, Mr. and Mrs. F. MacDonnel, Mr. J. Kramer, and Mr. and Mrs. Burrows of Lorengau. I have rendered my thanks to those who assisted me so generously in Papua in my separate work on Dobu of that Territory. I am also deeply indebted to Mr. Melrose of the New Guinea Service, whom I was fortunate to meet in Sydney, and who advised me that the Admiralty Islands comprise an area which sheltered native cultures of a character unparalleled in New Guinea, and natives with whom work would be profitable—an excellent judgment founded on a close acquaintance, and one shared by my courteous hosts and helpers in Rabaul when I met them not long afterward.

I wish to express my deep appreciation to The American Philosophical Society for undertaking the publication of this study. I wish to thank Dr. Ruth Benedict and Miss Marie Eichelberger for reading this work in manuscript and for suggestions offered. I am most indebted further to Dr. Margaret Mead and to Dr. Ruth Benedict for their kindness in supervising this work through the press and assuming responsibility for any necessary rearrangements or condensations which I will have no opportunity to check, owing to my absence in New Guinea.

November, 1934.

TABLE OF CONTENTS

LIST OF ILLUSTRATIONS

CHAPTER I

MANUS RELIGIOUS SENTIMENT

1

EACH Manus[1] man worships his Father, not in Heaven, but in his house front rafters, not one Father for all, but each man his own. The skull of the father of the house owner has an honoured place in a finely carved wooden bowl hung high above, and just inside, the entry at the front of the house. The spiritual presence, of which the skull is the material relic, guards the house and supervises the morals of its people.

This supervision is no empty formula. When misfortune visits a house with illness[2] or failure in fishing,[3] this is understood to be due to the righteous anger of the ghostly father, and oracles state the acts that have aroused it. The oracle, being possessed, expresses the just wrath of the Sir Ghost, *Moen palit* (as the ghostly father is called), secures confession of sin, or, if it is foreknown, makes indictment of it. Then, that the evil which is upon the house may be averted, expiation must be made.

The name of Sir Ghost is hallowed. The house owner often talks to his father's ghost, and honours the name of his father in his manner of speech. When he, in his turn, dies, his son or heir will honour him similarly, but not the ghost of the grandfather. The Manus honour a ghostly father, never a ghostly grandfather, saying that Sir Ghosts deserve to become anonymous and dishonoured when they fail to protect their sons from death. Then their skulls are cast out of the houses into the lagoons, in the house-breaking that follows a house owner's death. Their ghosts then wander the lagoon and open sea spaces of the "middle seas" between

[1] See Preface for geographical location of these people.

[2] See Chapter IV, passim.

[3] See Chapter IV, Sections 31, 34, and 40.

the Manus villages. No one gives them shelter in a house. They are "washed by all rains, burned by all suns." No one hallows their names. The recent and more beloved and respected dead is newly installed in the place of honour in the newly erected house front.

The will of Sir Ghost is done in these lagoon villages according to the traditional code. Although the Father is not one, but many, the moral code enforced by the oracles, who represent the ghostly presences on earth, is one and undivided.[4] The oracles who apply this social will to the exigencies of individual cases secure obedience by virtue of their ghostly authority, and by fear of the literally deadly consequences of defiance. The ghosts wield capital punishment. On rare occasions a man defies an oracle's ruling, stating that the oracle has not given a judgment derived from the will of Sir Ghost, but rather one derived from the oracle's too clearly evident human capacity.[5] There is a well-defined code from which no oracle who values his or her authority can afford to depart too widely.

Sir Ghost gives a man his daily fishing upon which he depends for his existence. To punish sin a Sir Ghost may either bring illness in his ward's house, or remove the potency, or soul stuff, for catching fish from his ward's nets and traps. Again when the fish come over the reef in shoals to spawn in the lagoons, as different species do in different lunar months with each high tide, it is the Sir Ghosts of the village who are understood to drive them inshore so conveniently.

Although Sir Ghost punishes trespassers, he is expected to forgive them. He is expected to inflict sickness, never death,[6] and to remove the sickness immediately when expiation is offered. Illness always brings about seances, indictments of sins and expiations for them. If, then, illness is followed by death, the death is not attributed to the now expiated sins of the house people or to the visitation of the wrath of their Sir Ghost upon them. Forgiveness is most

[4] See Chapter V.
[5] See Chapter IV, Section 13.
[6] See Chapter IV, Sections 12 and 13.

absolutely affirmed and assumed. Some other explanation of death must be offered. Here the fact that Sir Ghosts are many fathers, not one All Father, comes into play. Death is attributed by the oracles to the malice of the Sir Ghost of a distant house of unrelated people, usually members of the same village. While a Sir Ghost is a moral presence within his own house, punishing trespass most justly, always forgiving trespass that has been expiated, he sometimes plays the part of a malicious ghost towards the unrelated persons of other houses. He has a dual capacity: as Sir Ghost, he is just and good towards his own kindred; as a malicious ghost, he is a scatterer of death unmerited by trespass or sin amongst others not his kindred. In relation to his kindred he is *Moen palit*, Sir Ghost; in relation to others he is merely *palit*, ghost, and the two native terms express his dual role. Each house owner trusts his Sir Ghost to protect him and his household from death by preventing his fellow ghosts, if possible, from malice, or at least by warding off malicious attack from ghosts. When death occurs, it is this trust which is felt to be betrayed, and for betrayal of this trust it is said the old Sir Ghost is thrown out with his skull, preparatory to the installation of the new. Sir Ghost does not fail to forgive trespass, but he may fail to ward off malicious attack. This is the dogma upon which the oracles work. The members of the household whose Sir Ghost is oracularly indicated as having acted as malicious ghost in causing death in an unrelated household do not relish this verdict. In a private and entirely unoracular capacity, they often challenge the entire dogma. They would have the dead to have died from his own sins, or the sins of his kin, and from the wrath of his own Sir Ghost. An entirely unoracular murmur to this effect goes about after a death, and becomes popular belief to a large extent. If the oracles hear that this has been spoken of, they treat such speech as a sin to be expiated next time an illness falls anywhere near the too outspoken person who has attributed a death to immorality.[7] The kin of the dead and the kin whose Sir Ghost has been oracularly indicted as a

[7] See Chapter IV, Section 14.

malicious ghost avoid each other for a considerable time after a death. This avoidance is said to be sanctioned by the fear that the ghost of the dead may take reprisals upon the living whose Sir Ghost has acted as malicious ghost in causing the death. It is an avoidance also warranted by the difference between the oracular judgment, which is in comfort of the bereaved, and the judgment of that group whose Sir Ghost was oracularly indicted as a malicious ghost responsible.[8]

The fact that Sir Ghost is expected to punish, and also to forgive trespass, reflects Manus behaviour toward their fellows. Offended natives condone an offence against them once it is expiated, as they themselves would be condoned under like circumstances. The fact that Sir Ghost may act as a malicious ghost in causing death in an unrelated household is too strong to be a reflection of human fact. There is no human malice to match this ghostly terror. But often the oracles follow the lines of petty malice between one house and another, or between themselves and another in determining the identity of the Sir Ghost who has acted as a malicious ghost in causing a death. They also follow some accidental facts like gossip of unaccountable blood having been seen on someone's house floor. A mixture of accidental gossip and the following of lines of petty malice may raise malevolence to a great height in terms of the religion. It becomes too serious for the human beings concerned to countenance it, transcends the human plane of behaviour, and is finally given ghostly place in a more terrible aspect.[9]

Sir Ghost is understood to play a part in keeping his ward from temptation, not so much positively as by force of deterrent punishment. Nevertheless, a man in doubt between two courses will appeal to his Sir Ghost through an oracle for the right decision.

Sir Ghost keeps his ward from evil. In time of a canoe wreck at sea, or in time of severe illness, a man prays directly to his ghostly Father.[10]

[8] See Chapter IV, Section 13.
[9] See Chapter IV, Section 13.
[10] Chapter IV, Section 19.

Finally, the power of Sir Ghost is absolute and submission is made to it. If Sir Ghost gives life, a man lives; if Sir Ghost withholds life, a man dies. This is repeatedly said to Sir Ghost when a man addresses him. All of a man's material estate he calls not his, but his Sir Ghost's, and this he does even when he gives a feast from his own resources to his fellows.

The forms of the sacred in human societies are very old, and have much in common that overleaps the differences in social structures between continents, even between the civilisations of Europe on the one hand and the civilisations of primitive peoples on the other. This fact was overlooked by theorists such as Sir Edward Tylor, who, on the grounds that monotheistic religion alone gave efficient sanction to the moral structure in society, concluded that ancestor cult and polytheistic religions were "lower" forms of religion than monotheism. That this stand is quite untenable will become obvious in the course of the following study of Manus religion; for Manus religion not only sanctions the moral structure, but sanctions the moral structure in terms of a piety that finds ready expression in the terminology of our own forms of piety. The practices of the expiation and the remission of sins, and of seances held by mediums in cover of darkness through their "controls" are regular Manus practices, as also is the practice of filial piety to a Spiritual Father enlisted in the interest of a moral system.

The sentiment of Manus religion is not unlike the sentiment of our own religion. It is a patrilineal cult widely removed from all matrilineal sentiment. It is a sentiment of submission to the Higher Powers widely removed from the vesting of man with higher powers in magic. But still the underlying postulates of Manus religion are very different from those of our own. The most striking difference is in the attitude towards belief. The Manus native regards belief pragmatically for its social uses much more than we do.

Manus children are not subjected to religious pressure. Faith and belief are taken for granted. The children are taught by their parents respect for property, prudery in the natural functions and habits of motor co-ordination. These things are held of first importance, and cannot be taken for granted. Only in his or her adult life does the Manus native become subject to social pressure that is not entirely secular. He is taught by his ghostly father respect for property, prudery and fidelity in his marriage. The non-religious teachings of the living father are continued in the religious teachings enforced by the ghostly father. From the point of view of a Manus native his childhood is secular in government while his maturity is religious in government—this difference being rooted in the death of his father. Men die young in Manus, so that the transition usually occurs at a natural stage between childhood and early manhood.

The immortality of the soul is not in Manus a source of comfort to a human being in trying to face his possible obliteration. In fact, obliteration does follow in Manus belief. A dead man does his duty to his descendants as their ghostly father. Then he fails in it when he allows his son to die. He then becomes a ghost of the island edges, then a nameless ghost of the middle sea spaces for a time, but finally turns to a sea-slug.

The Manus system of belief runs upon its unformulated cardinal tenet that a ghost is no more than its social worth to the living. This cardinal postulate is somewhat foreign to our way of thinking, which tends to set up scientific committees to investigate psychic phenomena, and to take religious belief as an individual mental solace, or as an opportunity for a crusade, or a missionary adventure, or as a target for a Huxley. Where we tend to take belief or lack of it earnestly for its own sake, the Manus native takes it earnestly for what it is worth socially. The Manus have a social purpose for ghosts, but they have little respect for ghosts except for this purpose.

The Manus like ourselves are apt to regard morality even outside the religious sanction. But the fact that they possess a religious sanction gives them a socially established way of keeping their moral sentiments quick, of bringing offenders to book without seeming to be personal. That is what a religious sanction does. It provides an impersonal law with an impersonal instrument, the will of God as with us, or the will of the ancestor's ghost in the house rafters as with the Manus. Then human sternness to a sinner is the best kindness to him. It is putting him right with the impersonal Law, which otherwise will wreck him most disastrously. I do not, of course, intend that God or the ancestor is conceived as impersonal, rather the contrary, but what I do intend is the truth that the Law is really impersonal in the sense that a priest, or a primitive moralist and communer with the ancestor, who interposes to correct a sin, does not appear to be a rude and a meddlesome interferer with the sinner's private affairs, provided always that the sinner believes in the priest, or in the primitive communer with the ancestor, as the case may be. The sacred person in correcting the sinner saves him from a worse damnation, whether it be death as in Manus, or punishment in the future life as with us. The difference between an impersonal sanction in a religious system and a personal sanction in a magical system will be apparent to present readers who may read in my book, "Sorcerers of Dobu," an account of the use of a personally executed sanction in a magical system.

It is clear then that Manus religion is only partially a matter of belief. It is a belief in a personal guardian from death and disaster, and in a moral governor who administers an impersonal government. Yet it is also a belief that this supernatural being becomes a sea-slug. The Manus are very self-conscious of the human uses of belief, so that they carry it no further than its usefulness. They have talked favourably of the prospect of throwing all the ancestral skulls into the sea, thus throwing out all their Sir Ghosts, and adopting instead the Christian God. The advantage stated for the prospect is the substitution of private confession and private expiation of sin for public confession, public indictment and public expiation of sin. The present impediment when I was in Manus was that no priest was yet available as a substitute for the more searching and relentless native oracles, and the community were not prepared to face numerous deaths due to the fact that sinners were unshriven.

The Manus are not aware that modern Christianity challenges their most fundamental postulate—that unexpiated sin causes death. They are not aware of any secular attitude towards the health or the illness of the body. They suffer much from malaria and have supplies of quinine given them by the Government. Yet, in cases of malaria, they always have recourse to their oracles to shrive them of their sins, never to the quinine. The Government quinine supply is poured into the sea, and application put in for more on occasion in order to please the Government.

The Manus believe in a personal guardian from death and disaster and in a moral governor who administers an impersonal government through their Sir Ghost. But they quail in belief whenever a death occurs. Then the personal guardian has failed to guard. The sins have all been shriven and expiated, the moral government has been honoured and appeased, but the death has occurred nevertheless. So out with Sir Ghost! His skull may be battered to powder, and the powder thrown into flames, or it may merely be hurled into the sea. Sir Ghost becomes a vague lurking danger of the middle seas, not very seriously regarded—then a sea-slug. But the system goes on. A new skull is bleached from the corpse of the recently dead. It is installed in the house front with the women wailing at the reminder of the death. Long live Sir Ghost—but no longer than his son and heir whom he protects.

This repeated affirmation and repeated repudiation of one Sir Ghost after another depends upon the fact that there is no secular attitude towards the life and death of the body or towards the body's ills. Death is regarded as punishment of sin. It is not accepted as impersonal. From this fact flows the Manus pragmatism in belief. A Manus man in a semi-delirious state with a temperature of 104° to 105° will still talk in terms of a dogma of expectation of immediate punishment for sin in this life, and, like Job, he may cry out against his punishment, protesting his freedom from sin.[11]

[11] See, *e.g.*, Section 30 in Chapter IV.

CHAPTER II

GENERAL SKETCH OF THE RELIGION

1

MANUS religion draws upon much of the formal supernatural dogma and technique that are widely distributed in the world, although the design in which these are used is distinctive. The Manus have the familiar concept of the ghosts of the dead, of a certain kind of soul or vital essence in the living, the concept of ghostly control of this soul or vital essence in the living, the concept that in trance or in swoon this soul or essence approaches the ghosts. They have also a little magic with spells, familiars and herbs. A less widely distributed concept, also important in Manus, is the idea of oracular inspiration in the form of diviners and mediums who have "controls," properly constituted persons who can interpret ghostly intention to their fellows, without trance or swoon, however, or any abnormal manifestation, without "materialisations" but soberly and in an easy manner quite natural in appearance.

A Manus village shelters not only the mortal natives, but also the ghosts of natives who were recently mortal. The names of ghosts are on the lips of the living almost as often as the names of their mortal comrades. These ghosts are not far off in some distant abode of their own. They share the houses of the village with the mortals.

Moreover each ghost has its own house or abode, often the house where it lived as a mortal. Personality survives death in Manus. A man's house is still his after death. If he is a member of the native constabulary appointed by the Australian Administration, he is still a policeman among the ghosts after his death. There he receives the periodic visits of a ghostly white District Officer of a ghostly Administration and collects the ghostly taxes paid by his fellow ghosts, taxes from which he, by virtue of his office, is exempt as mortal and as ghost. If he cut a notable figure as a mortal, he cuts a notable figure as a ghost. His mortal interests are his ghostly interests. In the minds of mortals surviving him nothing of him is lost except his visible presence, his corporeal part. To his relatives he is kinder as a ghost than he is to persons not related to him, or but distantly related. As a ghost he is severe to those of his mortal kin who flout the traditional ways of his people, just as he was as a mortal. There is but one difference. As a ghost he knows the secrets of his mortal kin, not with omniscience, it is true, but at least with multiscience. Little secret sin is hidden from him. He has lost one disadvantage of mortality.

As dogma this is believed. Ostensibly, oracles know more than other men by communication with the multiscient ghosts. Actually they are good detectives as mortals. Belief in the dogma prevents too much sophisticated attention to the oracles' private detective work, even by the oracles themselves.

Each ghost accompanies the surviving head man of his house everywhere by land or sea unless instructed otherwise. Although he possesses multiscience, he does not possess multipresence, far less omnipresence. The companion ghost protects his mortal house-mate from the attacks of ghosts of other houses, of other families, when, as often occurs, such protection is necessary.

Within each mortal is *mwelolo*, soul stuff. It is divisible into many parts, and therefore semi-material. If a ghost wishes ill to a mortal, he takes the soul stuff from the mortal. Loss of soul stuff renders a mortal unwell, or if the loss is permanent, dead. A ghost takes the soul stuff from one of his mortal kin only in disapproval of secret sin or laxity amongst that kin, and if that trouble is repaired by the mortals the ghost will normally restore the soul stuff to the body from which he took it, before a permanent loss of soul stuff stiffens that body in death.

To repair the secret sin or laxity it must first be discovered by the mortals. They do not usually know what it is as they lack the greater knowledge that is believed to be peculiar to ghosts. An oracular channel of communication between ghosts and mortal reveals what the ghost has disapproved. This oracular judgment was perhaps originally made by swoon or trance taking the subsequently oracular person close to the ghosts; but such an oracle may initiate others who have had no such experience, but who, once initiated, may act equally well.

Ghosts, who are kind to their mortal kin, in taking soul stuff from them only temporarily and for the just purposes of correction, may, and do, deal more harshly with mortals not their kin. They may kill them out of sheer malice. Hence it is necessary to a mortal that the ghosts of his kin defend him from ghosts in general, and accompany him to that end wherever he goes.

From the mortal point of view security from illness and death is found by binding ghosts of kinsmen firmly in defence, and by avoiding secret sin or such laxity as is certain to bring down the anger of these ghosts of kinsmen. Cure of illness is effected by expiating secret sin or laxity.

It is also effected by exorcism of evil magic in certain cases. The boundary between cure by expiation brought to the attention of offended ghosts, and cure by exorcism of black magic by an offended magician, is one difficult to delimit. The ills of unweaned infants are generally attributed to black magic, and also the ills of women incident to child birth. But for others the ill is attributed to black magic only where theft from another man's palms is diagnosed by the oracles and confessed by the sinner. Furthermore the ills of child-bearing women are not exclusively attributed to black magic, as the ills of unweaned infants tend to be.

Generally speaking, for all persons past the weaning stage, expiation to offended ghosts is the primary way of curing their ills, and exorcism of magic is secondary. In case the sickness is long continued, both methods are usually employed.

For the present the social implication of the religion is not apparent. We must first see the oracles at work rebuking sinners and effecting expiation in particular cases before it can be realised how dynamically the system infuses the Manus code with strength and vitality, and how, moreover, its elasticity has allowed the ready incorporation of a few facets of the European code enforced originally by the German or the Australian Administration.

2

Each adult Manus male has his own individual ghost and that ghost has him. The relationship between the two is peculiar, but the verb of possession which I have used is the parallel of the Manus way of reference. Ghosts are frequently referred to, not only by name, but also as "Sir Ghost of mine," "Sir Ghost of thine," or "Sir Ghost of his." It is known everywhere that X's Sir Ghost is his dead brother Y, who died under such and such circumstances so many years ago; and so the charting of the separate associations between individual mortals and individual ghosts into so many pairs is common knowledge.

A better way to describe the yoked relationship between an individual mortal and his own individual Sir Ghost is to state that the two are close relatives who preserve a compact between them for their mutual advantage. In this sense they own each other and one of them by breaking the terms of the compact can cause the other to disown him.

I shall have to use translations of the special terms which the Manus use to distinguish the two parties to the compact. A ghost which has entered into a compact with a man is Sir Ghost to that man; the man is ward or mortal ward to his Sir Ghost. Thus I shall use Sir Ghost as a term radically different from ghost, in implying always a relationship to a certain ward. Sir Ghost is Sir Ghost to one man only; to other men he is a ghost merely.

Sir Ghost may be father and his ward, son; [1] or Sir Ghost may be son, and his ward, father; or they may be brothers; they may stand in the mother's brother-sister's son relation-

[1] This is the most common form, and patterns the religious sentiment for the ghostly father.

ship. A few men have taken dead white men as their Sir Ghosts, but this is plainly a new development and not general. Only the ghost of a male can be a Sir Ghost.

The terms of the compact between ward and Sir Ghost include first that ward take part in the rites over the mortal remains which Sir Ghost left behind him. It may seem at first that this action might be prompted by sufficiently natural motives of familial piety and sorrow. So it is, but that does not prevent it from being rationalized later as being a part of a compact. It is a common feeling in Melanesia that a mourner deserves payment.

I shall not detail the last rites in full. Let it suffice here that the ward, in common with a large number of mourners, lays strings of native currency on the corpse, and further is present at the final disposal of the corpse later. When the currency is laid on the corpse, Sir Ghost is told that this is the wherewithal with which he must purchase him a wife from the ghostly women about him. He must divert his best energies to his marriage on that plane, and avoid thinking of his kin left behind him (lest he think to such purpose as to take one or more of them with him). At the final disposal of the corpse a magical exorcism is used in like spirit, which protects the dead's kin from danger of the dead's continued attachment to them.

We now come to the ward's special activities that are his individual part in the compact. Although practically all that the ward does may be viewed as done for his own protection, he does not view it in that way. He views it as solicitude for Sir Ghost, when it is actually only in part solicitude for the dead, but more considerably solicitude for himself. Thus it comes about that the element of self-solicitude which we have singled out from the rites over the corpse does not prevent the ward from describing his part in those rites as a favour done to Sir Ghost for which he expects a return from Sir Ghost; and that even although he was but one participant amongst many. Accordingly he views his purely individual activities, now to be detailed, as placing Sir Ghost even more considerably in debt to him.

The ward preserves the skull from the body of his Sir Ghost, hangs it in an honoured place in the house front within a finely carved wooden bowl, and adorns the bowl with pendant ovalum shells also—this last only if he is a man of rank and has the right to that privilege. Into the bowl on occasión he puts devotional offerings of aromatic herbs.

On public occasions when a feast is brought to the verandah of his house, the ward addresses Sir Ghost in front of the assembly. He tells Sir Ghost that the feast is given in Sir Ghost's honour. Similarly any property given away or received by the ward, the latter refers to as given away or received by Sir Ghost.[2] The ward tells Sir Ghost that whereas he is a mortal of no great importance, Sir Ghost formerly as mortal was a man of great importance. Finally the ward takes up a rolled handful of food and robustly concluding his speech with, "Food offering to you this," hurls the food at the outer thatch, inside of which the skull bowl hangs.

The ward keeps a vigilant eye on the skull. There are outsiders to whom his Sir Ghost is a ghost merely. They are not in compact with that ghost, and they may feel annoyed with it, crediting it with causing deaths amongst themselves. In such a case their unavowed but secret desire is to capture that ghost's skull, and by shattering the skull and burning the pieces, extinguish that ghost as easily and readily as a candle may be extinguished. The ward keeps watch in such cases to prevent the extinction of Sir Ghost. Nowadays he may even keep Sir Ghost's skull in safety under lock and key until local feeling against his Sir Ghost subsides.

Sir Ghost and ghost in general are all invisible and incorporeal. But the skull is conceived as a corporeal necessity to the incorporeal. This gives mortals a way in which they can honour or dishonour, or even extinguish, a ghost. The ward by sheltering the skull in his house shelters his Sir Ghost from inclement weather. If, owing to the circumstances of death, the skull is lost, a coconut is used instead of it, and

[2] An heir takes his legator as Sir Ghost, so that this terminology refers to inheritance of property.

equally well.[3] On occasion the ward speaks to Sir Ghost, pointing out that he is giving Sir Ghost shelter and house room from the ills of the weather, food and warmth, an honoured place in the front of the house, and his own deep respect. In return Sir Ghost will give him and his household good health, or good luck in fishing, or a fair wind for a canoe voyage; the request varies according to the most urgent need at the moment.

If at any time Sir Ghost appears not to be giving what had been asked of him, his ward will easily be fired to anger. He will then threaten Sir Ghost with a final breaking of their compact. Does Sir Ghost wish to be thrown out of the house into the open, "to be washed by all rains, scorched by all suns," to have his name called upon by no one, to be homeless and forgotten? If Sir Ghost continues to withhold good fortune from him, then out Sir Ghost must go. (Manipulation of the skull is, of course, manipulation of Sir Ghost, and the skull is the corporeal handle that places the incorporeal ghost in the power of mortals.)

Such threats are not carried out unless Sir Ghost fails signally in his part of the compact, of which we shall speak later. To understand fully the normal part played in the compact by Sir Ghost we have first to consider the part played by ghosts in general. All ghosts are conceived as being dangerous to mortals. They are conceived as being angry and outraged at finding themselves suddenly translated from their corporeal form and into a bare, cold and lonely immateriality. This is especially so when they are still new to it. The most feared ghosts are the ghosts of important men who have died suddenly very recently, before or in their prime, and for someone else's sin. A ghost of a man who died because his daughter or his son committed a sex offence, for example, will be specially vicious toward anyone anywhere who subsequently commits a similar offence. It often happens thus that the general malice of ghosts is pointed also with a particular malice. A ghost is likely to pick upon an old enemy who survives him, or upon a mortal who had been

[3] Cross-cousins may joke about the substitution, however.

in debt to him and who had not paid up at the time of his death, or upon a man who is now about to obtain an honour which he was on the point of obtaining when he was suddenly cut off from the mortal plane, or upon a man who has had the temerity to marry his widow.

On the purely human plane it is not felt that it is wrong to aspire to attain an honour that another was prevented from by his death, or to marry a widow. It is felt to be dangerous. From such danger Sir Ghost is trusted to protect his ward. That is, he is expected to fend off ghosts who wish to take the *mwelolo*, soul stuff, from his ward or from one of his ward's kin. Ghosts in general, acting maliciously as they do, are not credited with attempt at mild temporary taking of soul stuff, but with attempt to take it finally, irretrievably leaving its possessor a corpse, and the corpse's former soul stuff a ghost like themselves, and in their own unpleasant and angry predicament.

Although soul stuff, so wrested finally from the body, becomes a single indivisible ghost, it is divisible before the body becomes a corpse; so that several different angry ghosts can, and often do, each possess a piece of the same mortal's soul stuff. How sick that mortal becomes under the treatment depends on how much of his soul stuff is kidnapped in this way, how far away from him it is taken, whether or not when taken away it is hacked or treated violently by the kidnapping ghost, and finally upon how long a time any piece of it is kept. Recovery from sickness is due to the kidnapping ghost or ghosts returning the soul stuff in response to mortal measures that have yet to be fully described. Death is due to relentlessness on the part of the ghosts, and their retention of the soul stuff, the retention of even one small piece of it by one relentless ghost being sufficient. A small piece outstanding, even after many pieces have been returned, will attract the entire soul stuff to itself. That is, even though mortal measures are successful in many ghostly quarters, one failure brings death. On account of the complexities of the situation, the arts of dealing with ghosts are not to be despised even if deaths occur despite them.

It is an important part in the compact driven between Sir Ghost and his ward that the Sir Ghost shall never vent upon the house of his ward this vicarious spite and maliciousness at merely being a ghost. He must keep such feelings for houses which are not related to him, houses to which he is ghost, not Sir Ghost.

The second count in Sir Ghost's obligations we have already touched upon. He must keep sentinel watch over his ward's household and protect it from ghosts which are trying to vent on other houses the general malice that they are compacted not to vent in their own houses where they are Sir Ghosts. When his ward goes abroad Sir Ghost must accompany him to the same end.

In point of act it is usually accepted that Sir Ghost keeps to the letter the former of his two obligations. It is in the second of his obligations that Sir Ghost periodically fails. If there is a death in his ward's house one of two alternative explanations is offered: (1) some one member of the house has committed a deep sin, and refused to confess and expiate it; in this case Sir Ghost made a member of his ward's household ill hoping for confession and expiation to follow. This did not follow, so the illness passed into death at Sir Ghost's hands. (2) Ghostly malice killed a person of Sir Ghost's ward's household. This explanation is the one generally put forward. It charges Sir Ghost with failure to keep to his obligation in effectually guarding his ward's household against ghosts. Sir Ghost has broken his side of the compact.[4]

What follows now depends on which member of the household died. If the ward himself dies the skull of his Sir Ghost may be thrown into the sea. Sir Ghost is no one's Sir Ghost any longer, so he has no one to call his name or to honour it. Any threats that his ward may have made to him in vexation have now come true—he is "washed by all rains, scorched by all suns." He wanders, homeless, the open seas between the villages. There he constitutes a mild and anonymous

[4] The second explanation is usually the preferred oracular one; the first explanation may be preferred by popular opinion, despite the oracles, however. This difference will be discussed below

danger to sea voyagers. Anonymity for a ghost is a great fall in Manus, where every ghostly individual of importance is named, and where practically all benefits and mishaps are ascribed to certain ghosts (determined in each case, and named), who are Sir Ghosts each in his own house.

It is this continual throwing out of a Sir Ghost at his ward's death that ensures the cult as a cult of the recently deceased only. The former ward is now Sir Ghost to his heir.

If the skull of the former faithless Sir Ghost is not thrown into the sea, it is ground to pieces and burnt by the children of its dead ward. So as a ghost it is extinguished utterly.

In many households there are two skulls kept; two Sir Ghosts. In such cases one Sir Ghost may have as ward the father of the household, the other may have as ward the young son of the house. In such cases the father usually has the skull of the more recent death as his, the ghost from that death as his Sir Ghost, since newness in a ghost is conceived as potency. If now the son of the house dies, the son's Sir Ghost will be cast out. If a woman or a younger child dies, one or more Sir Ghosts may, or may not, be thrown out of the house. As a rule no Sir Ghost is thrown out for such a death, or the succession of skulls would be broken, since a woman's or a young child's skull cannot serve as a man's or an elder male child's skull can; a female ghost, or a younger male, cannot be a Sir Ghost competent to protect a household.

In a few cases the Sir Ghost or Sir Ghosts are hurled out for a woman's or an infant's death but the presence of adult skulls in the great majority of houses proves such cases exceptional. In such cases a different method of installing a new Sir Ghost is followed from that by which the heir simply installs the skull of the man whom he succeeds at his succession. It will be recalled that every ghost is married off, or rather encouraged to do so during the last rites over the corpse. News of marriages consummated between particular named ghosts is frequently announced by the mediums. At fitting periods thereafter, corresponding roughly to the periods within which such things occur to mortals, news of births to ghosts so married comes from the oracles, news of the sex of the infants, later news of the names given to them, and still later news of how they are progressing.

A man who has broken his succession of Sir Ghosts normally begs from a friend one of the children born to his friend's Sir Ghost on the other plane. This ghostly born child he installs as his new Sir Ghost. He has no skull with which to deal with the new Sir Ghost, but trusts to be able to deal with it by speech only.

When the Sir Ghost and his skull are retained following the death of a woman or an infant of the ward's household there is considerable bitterness between ward and Sir Ghost over the poor way in which the latter is keeping the compact. He is retained *faut de mieux* only, and under threat of his being thrown out.

As a note concerning the compact, it must be put on record that a ward's care for his Sir Ghost does not cost him any self-sacrifice whatever. The currency that is laid on the corpse is recovered again. The food offerings are of little value; they are made only when the ward is the chief giver or chief recipient of an important economic exchange, which does not occur often except in the case of the eight or nine wealthiest men in a hundred. Even to such a man the occasion arises probably not more than four or five times a year. The attention given to Sir Ghost is sporadic, and without continuity. It is sustained continuously only when illness or very bad luck in fishing falls to the lot of a house. And such attention lapses as soon as all goes well again.

I speak now of the normal situation obtaining between a ward and a Sir Ghost of two or three years' standing. Between a ward and a Sir Ghost that is the ghost of a son, father, brother or mother's brother very recently dead, there is more real feeling. But it goes away rapidly.

The Manus dramatise death as Sir Ghost's final betrayal of his compact, in spite of all his ward's great benefits to him. Into this dramatisation are fitted acts of propitiation of a pattern found commonly in other parts of the world; and there conceptualised more frankly as self-preservative measures, undertaken in self-solicitude. The Manus devotion to Sir Ghost in practice is so slight, except when trouble has already come, that it wears a very definite aspect of self-solicitude. Only it is conceptualised as solicitude for Sir Ghost. Return solicitude from Sir Ghost is expected, of course. Love should repay love.

This local aspect, reared upon an old structure of more widespread belief, is made possible by the special Manus differentiation between Sir Ghost and ghost merely by the concept of the compact that Sir Ghost enters into to differentiate him from ghost, by the fact that Sir Ghost and his ward are near relatives. All of this permits an altruistic view of the propitiation.

Manus religion may be regarded, in this respect, as a result of a fusion of two attitudes. On the one hand is the fear of the ghosts. On the other hand is the love of one's own who are dead. So we get ghost on the one hand, Sir Ghost on the other.[5]

The lack of any really self-sacrificing devotion to Sir Ghost is most reasonable, considering the way in which one Sir Ghost after another fails his ward. The Manus put a price upon their devotion to their dead; but it is an impossible price. They want life, long life, and no accidents. Their demands inhibit such a deep devotion to, and full religious solicitude for, their family dead, as that of a Chinese household, for example. It is theoretically possible that they might nevertheless give a much more intense service and sacrifice to Sir Ghost, and suffer a much more well-founded feeling of betrayal than they actually do. It is not in their character, however, to spend great reserves religiously. They act as if they were conscious of the traps in their religious pattern.

[5] There is a surface analogy in the Manus relationship to the Usiai, the inland, enemy tribe, and in the Manus relationship to the Manus ghosts. Thus each Manus man has his Sir Usiai, whom he called "my Sir Usiai" and with whom he has the greatest solidarity. A man's Sir Usiai is his especial trading partner. Apart from a special relationship between a Manus man and his Sir Usiai, a Manus man is in inimical relationship to all Usiai men. The term "Sir" is used in Manus speech to indicate an Usiai partner or a ghostly partner who is one singled out from a general class which is otherwise entirely inimical. Any member of the general class, other than the partner, is never given the benefit of the term.

They have a deep and very fundamental distaste for ghosts, which cannot but infect somewhat their feelings towards Sir Ghost. In other words they realise very clearly that too optimistic demands from life are not always met. It is well to persist in such demands, for they may work to some extent. It is well to be outraged when that extent proves to be limited. And it is also well to keep that feeling of outrage sufficiently to the fore to inhibit any too great personal expenditures in making one's demands.

The above is not what they say, but it is what they act out. Nevertheless, the feeling that Sir Ghost is somewhat infected with the distastefulness of ghosts generally is clearly evident in occasional speech as well as in action. Such speech is a slip of the tongue. It is not regarded as proper to be outright in saying that a Sir Ghost is a necessary protection, only valued because of the greater danger from ghosts without him. In dreams a deeper attitude sometimes appears, as when one man I knew dreamt of his Sir Ghost saying to another, "Now let's kill a good man," and both laughed at the project.

3

The concept of the compact between a ward and his Sir Ghost does not, as we have said, cover the full relationship between the two. The compact is the organisation for defence of ward against ghosts. It does not denature Sir Ghost of all ghostly qualities, but only of the malicious qualities. Sir Ghost is not normally berated if he take the soul stuff of a member of his ward's family temporarily with intent to restore it in case expiation is made of the sin or error which he is justly objecting to. That is his prerogative. It is understood that he takes action for just and worthy reasons only.

On the whole most of the illness within a house is accredited to action taken by the Sir Ghost of the head of that house. But much illness is also accredited to the action of ghosts (of other houses) who have penetrated Sir Ghost's defence of his house, the latter never being omnipresent. When a death results and is attributed to ghosts, Sir Ghost is blamed for his weak defence, occasionally even with a slight suspicion as to his possible complicity, so great is the revulsion from the more ordinary attitude. But when mere sickness occurs, attributed not to Sir Ghost, but to ghosts, Sir Ghost is not blamed viciously for his weak defence. The excuse of his being able to be in only one place at a time is generally accepted. For he has to defend not only his ward but his ward's family, who scatter every day, only gathering by night.

There is no rigid rule to constrain the oracles in deciding whether a particular case of illness is Sir Ghost caused, or ghost caused. The oracles depend upon a kind of private detective work. If any sin or error of commission or omission of the kind traditionally associated with Sir Ghostly wrath is suspected, or privately discovered to have been committed by any member of a family in which illness subsequently strikes any member, then an oracular judgment of Sir Ghostly wrath is the first to be made. Preferably the sin should be recent, but if it is old it will do, provided that it has not been discovered and expiated before. If, however, there is no oracular knowledge of available unexpiated sin, or no suspicion of it, then the oracles must perforce fall back upon the theory of ghost causation, with all its unreasonableness and malice, compared with the satisfying explanation of sin, and reasonable just offence taken by the Sir Ghost (satisfying to the oracles).

There is a tendency to do nothing to counteract malice by ghosts. That is, since Sir Ghost only enforces a moral code, it is always possible to cure Sir Ghost caused illness by expiating the offence against the code. But since ghost caused illness is typically from malice, from a stain on the ghostly character, not on the mortal character, less can be done about it. Sometimes an offering is made to the angry ghost, sometimes not. When made, it is made reluctantly and tardily, compared with the speed and readiness with which offence against the code is repaired.

For this reason the oracles prefer the indictment of mortal sin to the indictment of ghostly malice, at least when the sufferer is still ill and efforts at curing him are in progress. If the oracle sees that cure is hopeless, he or she is likely to shift quickly from an indictment of mortal sin to an indictment of ghostly malice. In this way the system of curing by expiation of sin is not put rashly to such uses as are bound to weaken belief in it.[6] The oracles do not perceive this point as far as I know. They merely separate punishment for sin from an act of malice. According to usual rule, punishment is administered by Sir Ghost, malice by ghosts. An oracle is usually employed only by more or less friendly persons, and it is natural enough that she should prefer not to press the burden of sin too heavily upon the sinner.

While an oracle proceeds in this way, releasing sinner and Sir Ghost together from the guilt of causing death in their common family, public opinion accepts the oracular version only for the time. Deaths of persons long dead are generally attributed to their own sin, or to sin by a member of their intimate family or relationship group, this attribution coming from other such groups, of course.[7] The group itself, on the contrary, continues to believe in the alibi of ghostly malice given it at the time of the death, and so in the comparative justness of its Sir Ghost or Sir Ghosts; whereas outside groups to whom those Sir Ghosts are ghosts and therefore malicious to them, do not acquit the said Sir Ghosts of executing capital punishment in the Sir Ghost's own group; all this, of course, without thinking that their own Sir Ghosts are like that.

On some occasions the oracles do not keep clear the distinction between Sir Ghost's comparatively gentle correction of sin, and the ghosts' comparatively harsh venting of malice. Sir Ghost may act as maliciously as any ghost; but it would be a great error to suppose that this manner of diagnosis is general. It is not. The average oracle is very discreet in not accusing the Sir Ghostly dead of a family with malice towards the living of the family to the latters' faces.

The oracles, in making new oracular statements, are likely to refer to the reasons for long past deaths. To do so non-

[6] See Isole's mediumship over the death of Popwitch, p. 163.

[7] See Paliau's reaction to the above occasion, p. 174.

oracularly is regarded as dangerous. Why stir up ghosts unnecessarily, angering them by recalling gratuitously that they died for their sins, or, and even more unbearably for ghostly peace of mind, for their relatives' sins? An oracle, of course, that gave a particular death a ghostly and malicious origin, so clearing the bereaved family from overwhelming self-reproach of guilty sin, will hardly take a different view oracularly later. But any other oracle who was one of the outside public may subsequently interpret the death as due to a sin in the bereaved family.

This is often done when a particular type of malice is diagnosed in a ghost. It is said that X died for his wife's sin. Since X's wife is of X's household, this assumes that X's Sir Ghost killed X, an assumption that was probably not put before X's family by the acting oracles at the time of X's death, although the acting oracles may have used it before X was seen to be dying. In such case the sin was expiated, and X's subsequent death attributed to other reason. But popular opinion may have subsequently stuck fast to X's dying because of his wife's sin. An oracle working upon A's illness, and not having been an acting oracle at X's illness and death, may say X died because of his wife's sin; that X, as a ghost, in revenge killed his widow's sister, and the ghost of the widow's sister [8] is now revenging herself on her sister by making ill the widow's son, A. In this diagnosis, all the malice and revenge is from a ghost towards another household, not from a Sir Ghost towards a ward's household. But in making an explanation of a later illness one oracle does not necessarily respect a different oracle's final finding on the cause of a former death, and so such an oracle may impute to a former Sir Ghost a deed of capital punishment executed upon his ward's household. In this way popular opinion becomes standardised, and sin is generally stressed as the cause of death, mortal sin, not ghostly malice, although individual oracles are continually making individual exceptions to try to save sinners' faces, and their own faces also,

[8] Female ghosts on occasion act in damaging mortals; but they are not Sir Ghosts. That is, they have no protective value as a Sir Ghost has.

since their practice is based upon confession of sin and the belief that expiation is necessarily curative.

In radical distinction, an oracle in using bygone history, even of a case where he or she was not acting as oracle, need not subscribe to the popular view of a death as caused by a sin in the bereaved family, but may take up what was a "saving of face" diagnosis of a former acting oracle. Full liberty is used in such matters. It must be stressed that the system is an empirical one. In certain instances the malice of a ghost may be the preferred primary explanation of an illness. It is not necessarily a hypothesis of despair adopted when reparation of sin has been tried and failed. The exigencies of detective work or the accidents of the time and place and personality of the oracle determine much. If a widow has just remarried and immediately her sister falls ill, the malice of the ghost of the widow's former husband lies right at hand, and detective work may have raised no hint of secret sin unexpiated.[9] Similarly infection with the black magic of a sorcerer is not necessarily a hypothesis of despair adopted as a last resort; there may be good grounds for suspecting the sick person of having thieved from another's palms that are protected with black magic. The oracles, also, to a certain extent, may attribute illness to ghostly malice merely because they are not vitally enough concerned with curing the case to wring confession of sin from one reluctant to confess, or because they are not sufficiently well-informed to know what sins to suspect, or because the case is not serious and an oracle friendly to the patient may prefer not to charge sin when there is no apparent necessity.

Even more importantly the case of the illness of a married woman does not necessarily fit the scheme according to which the oracles prefer the indictment of mortal sin to the diagnosis of ghostly malice. This preference may be followed even over a married woman, but on the whole the cult is a man's cult best adjusted to men.

By the Manus system a man's wife is in a far less determinate position than her husband. She has left her own kin

[9] See the death of the wife of Pondramet, p. 328.

and the houses that shelter the ghosts of her ancestors, the Sir Ghosts to whom her brothers are wards. She has gone to the house of a man whose Sir Ghost is not her Sir Ghost, except by extension. Under these circumstances one might expect some cultural solution of the question, Who is Sir Ghost to a married woman?

Actually the Manus have avoided arriving at a solution. Sometimes the husband's Sir Ghost corrects the wife's sin, sometimes the brother's Sir Ghost corrects the sister's sin. No ghost whatever is the special guardian and protector of a woman, unless it is the husband's Sir Ghost (except when marriage is matrilocal, when it is the brother's Sir Ghost who becomes the husband's Sir Ghost also). But this husband's or husband's-cum-brother's Sir Ghost is only thought to protect a woman when she is with her husband or brother. For a man's Sir Ghost goes wherever his ward goes, and is thought not to be responsible for what occurs in his absence. Since every day women go about women's work in female groups, and men about men's work in male groups, women go unprotected spiritually for the greater part of their lives.

This fact of lack of spiritual protection for women is perfectly realised by the Manus, and the men frankly consider it as appropriate. Women are more likely to be killed by malicious ghosts than men, since women lack Sir Ghostly protection. Accordingly women should stay at home with their husbands. But husbands need not stay with their wives. If their wives are killed by ghostly malice in the men's absence, that must not restrain the work of men, which often leads abroad.

This twist is not purely theoretical. The illnesses of women actually are more often ascribed to ghostly malice. The oracles resort to explanation of ills in terms of ghostly malice in time of non-child bearing, and in terms of mortal malice (black magic) in time of child bearing with far greater freedom than in the case of the ills of men.[10] The fact that expiation is not paid to avert ghostly malice, as it is paid to make Sir Ghostly correction cease, is thus in some measure

[10] See the illness of Alupwai and the death of the wife of Pondramet, p. 329.

a comparative disregard of doing anything for women. This remains true, although women play a part in the cult as mediums.

The system is very differently adjusted to the ills of married women and widows on the one hand, and to the ills of men and children (past the weaning stage) on the other. This fact can be realised most fully from the concrete data in Chapter IV.

In case of a woman sinning sexually she and her husband's kin, and also her brother's kin may be punished by the Sir Ghosts of the respective kins. Thus sexual sin by a woman is dangerous to a double range of kin, where sexual or other sin by a man is dangerous only to himself and to his own kin, his wife alone of his affinal kin being added. In case of sexual sin by either man or by woman the kin of the partner in the sin are also in danger from their Sir Ghosts, but, reckoning this fact, a woman's sexual sin provokes three kins, where a man's provokes two only. In brief, brothers-in-law and their kins are united in condemnation of a woman's sexual sin, where sisters-in-law and their kins are not united effectively to chastise a man's equivalent sin. Thus in sexual sin a woman provokes a doubled Sir Ghostly wrath. But where a woman has not sinned sexually her status with any Sir Ghost is doubtful, and the idea of Sir Ghostly correction of a varied category of lesser sins of manifold type does not apply to women as clearly as to men.

The guiding principle here is that women shall have the lower status. They are doubly damned for sexual sin, and for lesser sin they have not the benefit of expiation. Such expiation is made for a male sinner by his kindred. But a married woman is spiritually renounced by her kindred to some extent, and yet not spiritually adopted thoroughly by her husband's kindred. She becomes a target for ghostly malice, and, in time of child bearing, for mortal malice (black magic). But in some cases a woman's spiritual isolation may appear less clearly. Thus matrilocal residence occurs fairly often and the Sir Ghost of the house is now the woman's and her husband's and her brother's. In such case the woman's Sir

Ghost may extend his field of operation to the husband's kin who live patrilocally, since the Manus decline to view a Sir Ghost as other than the husband's Sir Ghost, but insist that the Sir Ghost of a house depends on the gentile and ancestral territory in which a house is placed. Accordingly matrilocal residence makes a tangled theology.

I may add that, despite its believed curative effect, confession of sin is not easily secured from the sinner. The oracles use a kind of "third degree," consisting in profession of information from the multiscient ghosts in pronouncements which are sufficiently vague but sufficiently specific to make the sinner confess. This is not true of all oracular forms however. Others depend on very strong suspicion based on facts, or on knowledge of facts secured by what I have called detective work, which is really a persistent interest in others' affairs, in secret gossip and an eye for appearance of guilt.

It might be thought that in this way confession would be more readily secured. But a great shame is at work to hinder it, and further a great fear of reproach. For if his ward's eldest son sins, Sir Ghost does not necessarily take his ward's eldest son's soul stuff. Sir Ghost takes the soul stuff of the next person in that household to fall ill. By the laws of probability, sin is much more likely to hurt someone else than the sinner. Then the eldest son must confess to secure the cure of one dear to him. If he conceals it, he is assured that a death will likely result from his concealment. He will then commit patricide, fratricide or the like. But if he confesses, the family reproach will fall on him for having caused illness and danger of death to one of those who love him and who care for him. This type of reproach, which is made with the utmost severity, is feared and dreaded by all. So much is this the case, and so great is the shame felt at public exposure of sex offence or theft, for instance, that confession must usually be wrung from the sinner by the oracles against the sinner's great resistance. He or she usually pits an attempt at concealment against the oracles, even although the oracles by virtue of their communications from the ghosts have more than mortal knowledge of secret sin.

In the end the "more than mortal knowledge" usually wins, but the oracles may be hard put to it. They have normally to know enough to appear to be able to substantiate their profession of multiscience.

There are however other sins than sex offence and theft, that are less secret and with which the oracles make easier play. And sometimes sex offence or theft "will out" before any illness occurs; in this case the oracles have only to credit the rumour they have heard, despite the alleged sinner's denial of guilt, if illness occurs subsequently in the sinner's kin group. The sinner's denial may then often be worn down by persistent pressure.

4

A few of the men and of the women of the community form a small, but unorganised collection of diviners and mediums, the men, diviners, the women, mediums. It is any male's privilege to talk to his Sir Ghost at any length. But only the privileged diviners and mediums can receive communications from the other plane. For a complete conversation with a Sir Ghost or with ghosts a diviner or a medium is an absolutely necessary accessory.

The man wishing to be a diviner has first to be granted the power by his Sir Ghost. As the only channel through which the said Sir Ghost can communicate to his ward permission to divine is through an already accredited diviner or medium, this Sir Ghostly permission is, in effect, the permission of one already initiated.

Following the granting of his Sir Ghost's permission, the novice is consecrated by an already established diviner or medium,[11] and he and his Sir Ghost are consecrated to divine together hereafter. The novice pays his consecrator a good round fee for this.

The method of divination is as follows: The diviner takes his divining bones, two short pieces of bone connected by a string, looks at them, and rubs them repeatedly with his hands as he propounds his question to them. For example

[11] In all the cases I know, it was a medium who consecrated a man to be a diviner.

he may ask, "Is this lad ill because his mother did not pay so and so the pots she owes him?" He then throws the bones astride his shoulder, one falling on his chest, one on his back. He then pays attention to his back. If his back itches on the left side the answer to his question is "yes," but if it itches on the right side, the answer is "no." This answer comes from his Sir Ghost. The bones used are from the left lower arm of an old woman who was afraid of ghosts. As the bones in her shook when she was alive, so they still are responsive to ghostly influence. In practice the bones of any old woman will do. Sometimes the left lower arm-bone of a child is used.

It is not conceived that the question was suggested by Sir Ghost or any ghost. Here there is no belief in inspiration. A diviner asks only questions that flow from his own or from popular suspicion, suspicion that is often so well grounded as to be very close neighbour to knowledge.

Men who have been diviners and no longer practice their divining are very often found. The reason for giving up divining is commonly because the divining was used to find out the reasons for an illness of a person of the diviner's own household. Reasons were found and the causes of illness all expiated and removed, but the illness did not abate and the person died nevertheless. The divining was laid aside, sometimes contemporary with the hurling out of a Sir Ghost in the same revulsion.

It is interesting to note that whereas there is a continuous substitution of a new Sir Ghost for each Sir Ghost thrown out, a divining power laid aside is not customarily taken up again. I know of many cases of the customary type. But as I know of none in which divining was resumed again, I do not know from my own observation whether there must be a new consecration and a new fee paid. I was told that such would be necessary, if anyone wanted to take up again a thing for which he was obviously not suited. Some of the disappointed and non-practising diviners say of their former practice, "I thought then communication actually came from the other plane, but it did not; I was only expressing myself."

The practicing diviners not only divine in cases of illness, when issues are in deadly earnest and when they expect strict truth to be revealed oracularly, but they also divine in jest when they expect that the Sir Ghostly inspirer may also act in jest. A man may be chasing a pig. Will he catch the pig before the pig reaches the sandbank there? Quickly two or three diviners who are looking on put the question to their sets of bones, and sling the sets of bones over their respective backs. Two answer "yes," and one answers "no." They watch the chase with zest. The result proves to be "no." The diviner who was correct proceeds to chaff his incorrect comrades, who retaliate by a challenge to divine something else. Such chaffing remarks of "Your divination is a lie" are not seriously taken however; for a diviner's Sir Ghost jests with the diviner at the same time as one diviner jests with another. Three diviners jesting are really three diviners and three Sir Ghosts all in one humour. For if a diviner divines that someone in the house of P stole a piece of calico reported missing from the house of Q it may happen that the diviner is wrong, and if so, P with a great burst of anger may tell the diviner that his divination is a lie. The diviner keeps his dignity and belief in himself in such cases, and no one knows which to believe; the diviner has the greater authority, the protester the greater indignation.

Many men also divine by spitting betel juice on to a pepper (*Piper methysticum*) leaf. If the juice runs to the left side of the midrib the answer is "yes" to the question they have propounded; but if it runs to the right side the answer is "no." This form of divination is unconsecrated, however, and is not used in any serious issue such as illness or determination of theft. The bone-using diviners undertake all serious issues.

The woman wishing to become a medium must obtain permission and grant of power from the Sir Ghost of the house wherein she lives. In effect this works as in the case of a man wishing to become a diviner. Further she must be a woman who has given birth to a male child which died in its childhood.

She pays an established medium a large fee. This medium then consecrates the novice and with her the ghost of her dead child to work together in seances hereafter. The novice is now ready to practice mediumship.

The method of the seance is as follows.

The enquirer into the intentions of his Sir Ghost or of any other ghost says first, "Let X appear" (X being the name of the ghost of the child of the medium). After a short silence the medium emits a staccato series of shrill whistles. This is X speaking through her mouth.

I must pause here to explain the collaboration between the medium and the ghost of her dead male child. The latter is called *mwererang mwerepalit*, "intermediary between mortals and ghosts"—in spiritualistic terminology, the medium's control. The control obeys the medium's wishes and behests. He alone of all the ghosts takes possession of her mouth and whistles through it. The medium believes that the thoughts which occur to her subsequent to each time she whistles, are a translation into mortal speech of the whistles, which are the spirit's speech. She is merely a channel through which her control's speech passes and an interpreter of that speech. There is no code of special whistles with special interpretations. She just whistles; then she just talks in the same general manner as all mediums have talked in all the hundreds of seances, maybe thousands of seances, that she has heard as an uninitiate.

After the whistling is done the medium translates "X is here; he asks what you want." (X, it will be recalled, is the control.) The enquirer may say, "Why is Z (his Sir Ghost) angry with my child and why does he strike him down (the child being ill)?" At this the medium whistles again, and then translates for X. The translation at this point usually is, "I don't know. I'll go and ask Z."

The medium then waits in silence to give X time to ask Z and to come back and report; she then whistles and then translates what X says which is what X has heard from Z. So the seance continues, the control going to ask questions propounded by mortals from any ghost named by the mortals, and coming back to report what the ghost in question says. Or the control may be told to find out himself who the ghosts are that are causing havoc on the mortal plane, to interview them, and to come back and report, re-interview them and so on. The report from a Sir Ghost or from a ghost follows the general lines that we have already discussed.

Since every pronouncement of a diviner or medium expresses in effect personal feelings, we must raise the question as to how far this is understood. In most cases the non-initiate's belief that Sir Ghost causes illness justly within his own household governs the oracle also, and controls the oracular utterance. But when the oracle makes a diagnosis of a ghost-caused death, he or she, in imputing malice to a certain named ghost, is impugning the Sir Ghost of someone else. The ward of that Sir Ghost is never pleased at his own guardian being publicly branded as a malicious murderer. Consequently the oracle may find it best to select the Sir Ghost of a person who is already at odds, in a secular capacity, with the oracle. Then there may follow some hot accusations that the oracle does not represent the ghosts truthfully, but only the oracle's feelings in a private and purely human capacity. Meanwhile the oracle puts up with this, rather than hurt a friend's feelings by a grave charge against a friend's Sir Ghost.

The oracle himself, or herself, is by no means a fraud. It is only necessary to believe that after one is consecrated, whatever itch comes into one's back or whatever comes into one's mind when one sets out to divine or to conduct a seance is suggestion from the ghosts.

The medium may know that she heard privately from Y yesterday that Y saw blood on X's threshold. Today a boy died after a bloody retching in the house of Z. She thinks constantly of that report of blood on X's threshold. She does not like X and knows that she does not like him. That night in a seance she is an oracle from the ghosts. As oracle she does not mention the report of blood on X's threshold. She ascribes a certain motive to the Sir Ghost of X's house for having maliciously killed a boy in the house of Z. Sir

Ghost of X, as a mortal, was cut off just as he was getting ready to make a great economic exchange, made only once in a lifetime, one which Z also is now about to make. Hence his zealous and covetous malice due to his own hurt.

This is an actual case. But the medium is not a fraud, nor does she conceive herself as such. As oracle she follows a humanly obtained clue into its possible spiritual ramifications. Then she delivers a pronouncement of that ramification, if it appears to be consonant with the humanly obtained clue—which she does not mention, as she knows it came from human observation. Her own elaboration of it is so much ratiocination. This ratiocination she believes implicitly is ghostly suggestion. If it agrees with mortally obtained clues, what of it? What mortals see in part, the ghosts see in its wholeness. Naturally what both mortals and ghosts see, one imperfectly, the other more completely, is the same reality. The medium believes as stoutly as Bishop Berkeley in his own variant belief, that truth, which is in part in the minds of one or of many mortals, is in greater measure in the minds of the ghosts. And like a true divine she is in rapport with more than the unconsecrate, and both she and the unconsecrate believe it, except possibly some person whose feelings for the moment may have been rudely outraged by the oracle. Even such a person is greatly daring if he expresses his doubts publicly.

So also of itches in the back. Wherever they may come from at other times, after the divining bones are out and in place, they are from inspiration. And as the medium takes a clue from mortal observation, only her ratiocination over it in the seance being inspired, so the diviner frankly propounds his question from his own observation or report of gossip, only the answer being inspired.

I have discussed the ordinary and most usual way of initiation in the oracular practice. A much less frequent way is by trance experience. Having had a trance a man may begin divining or a woman enter into her mediumship. Such a diviner or such a medium is in fact more highly thought of than the more usual type, and, if a medium, more in demand as a consecrator of novices, male and female, than other mediums.

Many mediums are found who have given up their mediumship just as the diviners did, and for the same reason. And I have heard one exceptionally outspoken ex-medium echo the same plaint as the ex-diviner, "What I then thought came from the ghosts came only from mortals."

As one most important proviso, it should be always understood that the medium does not wield the entire power of the system as a European medium wields the power of European spiritualism. Usually the Manus medium is overshadowed by the diviners. The reason for this is simple. Divining may be done at any time, the seance may only be held at night. The usual course of events is that an alarm of serious illness leads immediately to divining. The diviners look for a "yes" or a "no" reply to their mortal conjectures and suspicions. For example the diviner may say, "Is this child ill because her father did not make the payment he should have made to so and so yesterday?" Then, if the answer is "yes," the payment to so and so is usually made immediately. At night the medium in her seance represents the father's Sir Ghost as reprimanding his ward, and saying that he made the child ill because of the father's business delinquency. What was a diviner's mortal query and suspicion, only the affirmative "yes" (itch on the left side of the back) being inspirational, is now converted *en bloc* by the medium into inspirational or oracular utterance. Since the sin was remedied immediately after the divination, it can usually be pointed out to the angry Sir Ghost at the seance that reparation has already been made. In consideration for it, will he now return to the sick person the soul stuff he has taken? Thus the seance is usually an echo of the preceding divination, and a collection of soul stuff as a *quid pro quo* for expiation or reparation already accomplished. Sometimes expiation or reparation is promised, and the soul stuff asked for in advance, but this is only done under force of circumstances preventing quick expiation before the night seance, or under the condition that entirely new oracular pronouncement be first made at the seance.

Furthermore a medium in the course of a seance may

exhaust the matter of precedent divination, and still doubt whether the sick person's soul stuff is all discovered and expiation made for it. This is common enough when the sick person seems to be sinking visibly. In such a case a medium may defer to the diviners present. She may ask them to divine whether all the soul stuff is returned or not. They may say "yes" or "no" and say whether the expiation already made has or has not influenced the ghostly or Sir Ghostly recipient of expiation sufficiently to lead him to return the soul stuff, or whether some other angry ghost, who has taken soul stuff and has it in his possession, has been overlooked to date. The diviners may supply a part of this information and the medium complete it, or they may supply all of it, and the medium echo it, or the medium may supply it all herself without deferring to the diviners present.

Both divination and mediumship as used by the Manus demand strong intimation or knowledge of facts. But the Manus also employ seers from their neighbours, the Usiai of the Great Admiralty. Usiai seers employ at least two methods. By one method the seer claims knowledge derived from his soul which goes out in sleep and sees past events occur. So he diagnoses theft, sex offence or what not. By another method the seer comes to the sick person, instead of remaining apart and sending his report after sleeping. In the presence of the sick person he goes into an appearance of possession, quietly enough conducted, but with fixity and dilation of the eyes. He then makes a charge of sin. The sick person or one of his kin may then substantiate it, the sinner thinking that he has been discovered. Then the seer, remaining in a state of possession, makes a new charge.

It is characteristic of Usiai seers' results, whichever method is used, that the charges of sin are normally vague, but vaguely specific. As foreigners they are without the benefit of local detective work.[12] But their method does not always suffer thereby. Sometimes it provokes confession of an unsuspected sin. The filling-in of details by the penitent is

[12] There is always some gossip, however, at the morning market between pairs of Manus and Usiai who are trade partners, *i.e.*, between a Manus man and his Sir Usiai.

PLATE II

IN TIME OF THE SPAWNING OF FISH

called *tandridrian*, a different term from that used for confession. Confession is one matter when, after oracular divination, or in anticipation of such, it is secured by pressure exerted by matter of fact urgings by one's cross-cousins, who are, by virtue of the relationship function, one's especial Father Confessors. It is then called *pwareani*. *Tandridrian* is supplying details of a sin to all interested parties when the general fact is known, even if not known in full, from an Usiai seer's supernaturally derived vision.

The Manus diviner gets no pay for using his art for others. The medium gets the native equivalent of four pence a seance. But the Usiai seer demands and gets high fees, the native equivalent of several shillings. He is paid the same type of fee as a magician, Manus or Usiai, for performing an exorcism, although his services are oracular, not magical.

5

For the purpose of the distinction between the treatment given by Sir Ghost to his ward's household and that given by ghosts generally, the term household must not be taken as always including those who live in the one house, although such is generally intended. But in cases where members of one patrilineal family have set up independent households, the Sir Ghost or Sir Ghosts of one of these act as Sir Ghost, not as ghost, to the mortal members of the others. Just as the mortals of such households act always in cooperation, so, it is conceived, do the Sir Ghosts on their plane. This qualification does not make a very extensive range for any one Sir Ghost in practice. He has no classificatory kinship range, but can remain as Sir Ghost over only three or four houses at most. And even so he is preeminently Sir Ghost in the actual house within which his skull is sheltered, for he is most frequently responsible for what occurs to the mortals also sheltered there. On occasion, however, one of his brother Sir Ghosts from such a close kindred house may be held also responsible with him, or even more responsible than he in taking the initiative, he merely conniving. Indeed in some cases there is so much connivance between brother Sir

Ghosts that the medium does not differentiate between them, but reports merely, "All the Talipolalau are angry," which is equivalent to saying, "The ghosts of the brothers of the Robinson family are angry." This may be done despite the fact that the said ghosts and their skulls are distributed separately in the several houses of the present generation.

The ghosts of women of a household, while not Sir Ghosts, and not as important as Sir Ghosts, are sometimes credited with causing illness in the household. These women ghosts are commonly either Sir Ghost's sisters, or else Sir Ghost's wife or wives. Sir Ghost's sisters act either in collaboration with Sir Ghost, or else, if independently, in the same manner as Sir Ghost. Sir Ghost's wives are very rarely indeed credited with power. I know of only two cases, and in those, I am sorry to say, they did not manifest justice towards mortals. One was a case in which Sir Ghost had two wives. They were quarrelling. Whenever a mortal man has two wives, their obscenity and quarrelling trouble the village daily. These two ghost wives, quarrelling between themselves, vented anger on their husband's ward's household, sheer anger that the ward had given no reason to merit. Reference to this case is only a comment on the troubles of keeping two wives.

In another case, a man's wife, dying before him, was taken as ghost wife by the man's Sir Ghost. She did not relish her marriage to a ghost so much her senior. So she killed her mortal husband in order to upset her marriage on the other plane. Unlike Sir Ghost and his sisters, the wives of Sir Ghost act for purely selfish reasons when they act at all.

We must classify a close brother's Sir Ghost functionally as a Sir Ghost, and also a Sir Ghost's sister, whereas a Sir Ghost's wife (or wives) is more like a ghost than a Sir Ghost. Furthermore in three cases that I shall detail later the Sir Ghost of a host punished the moral breach of a guest just after the guest's departure. Here a ghost of another house acted functionally as a Sir Ghost, following a residence under his care, but not maliciously as the ghosts of other houses do. Further I shall detail later five cases of the Sir Ghosts of close affinal relatives who punished breaches of the moral code. Thus a brother's Sir Ghost, a brother-in-law's Sir Ghost and a Sir Ghost's ghostly sister may take the functions of a man's own Sir Ghost.

Computing the major cases of ghostly and Sir Ghostly infliction of ills that came to my attention in six months' observation in a Manus village, I find in fifty-seven cases in all, thirty-seven of Sir Ghost punishing breaches of the moral code. This resulted from a representative and unselected record. As Sir Ghost I include here a man's own Sir Ghost and that of his brother, and in a case or two only, a sister's or brother's Sir Ghost. There were eight cases of other ghosts punishing moral breaches, five being the brother-in-law's Sir Ghost, three being a guest's host's Sir Ghost. There were nine cases of ghosts acting maliciously; then in three cases the Sir Ghost acted maliciously. Over and above this number there occurred two similar actions of Sir Ghost's ghostly wife, or wives. The few actions of Sir Ghost's ghostly sister I have included under the action of Sir Ghost, as in these cases ghostly sister and ghostly brother were conceived as acting in coöperation.

We have discussed extensions of the Sir Ghost concept. We may now discuss some extensions of oracular practice. There are a very few exceptional men who act as mediums and I found one who acted as both medium and diviner. The traditional distinction between diviner and medium is laid aside by these men. They are not initiated by the female mediums, nor by the diviners. According to their own accounts, they believe that, though they are uninitiated, their Sir Ghosts talk through them in a way that they can understand. They are distinctly irregular, but command rather more than less prestige on that account. They take over no other female functions. There are no women diviners.

It should be added that many diviners have two or three sets of divining bones, acquired separately at different times, and each set serving only one specific purpose. Thus, one set may serve for diagnosing ghostly or Sir Ghostly anger, another set may serve for fishing divination, and a third set may serve for divining as to whether or not a woman is disposed to marry. This third type is very much rarer than the two former ones.

6

The first and greatest offence which Sir Ghost punishes is loose sexual conduct. Since practically all girls are betrothed by the time of puberty, and a vast exchange of wealth takes place between the contracting families and their respective helpers, and since the betrothed groom and the betrothed bride are conceived as already married in law, although the marriage is not yet consummated, the concept of adultery is extended to cover any sex affair outside marriage. Girls must be chaste or they sin.

Youths on their part must not seduce a girl of their own village or of a friendly village, or they are also involved in a technical adultery. In the old days they were permitted to keep a female war captive as a prostitute. But apart from the youths' prostitute any sex affair was, and is, sin.

It is not usual that any betrothed girl's lapse is detected certainly, or is self-confessed, without much trouble ensuing. Such an affair cannot be confessed by either youth or girl without bringing down a thunder of angry public disapproval and tremendous shame upon the guilty pair.

It is usual for the all-seeing ghosts to commence their operations before the mortals have more than a vague suspicion, and sometimes not even that. One of three possibilities may happen:

1. The Sir Ghost of the girl's house may make one of her kin or the girl herself ill.

2. The Sir Ghost of the youth's house may make one of his kin or the youth himself ill.

3. The Sir Ghost of the house wherein the sin was committed may make one of that house ill.

The moment such an illness occurs the community is all suspicion. If the oracles have anything to go upon, and being older puritanical persons they are likely to have, they oracularly make the charge. If one of the guilty pair confesses, it will save life. Usually one or both, self-certain of his or her own guilt, cannot stand being suspected for life of being a murderer, and confession ensues. The motives enlisted are so strong that even a vague, diffuse suspicion may elicit confessions from a certain quarter, not especially suspected by the community.

Now, following confession, there is rage in the village. The pair are berated each by his and her respective households, and the youth's future bride's kin and the girl's future groom's kin add to the din of outrage and affront.

The youth's kin make *kano*, expiatory payment, to the kin of his betrothed bride. (He cannot have sinned with his betrothed, for there is a most rigid avoidance that is always respected between them.) The girl's kin make *kano* to the kin of her betrothed groom. Both kins make *kano* to the people of the house within which the sin was committed, if that house is other than one of their own. Then if the Sir Ghost of the youth's kin has produced the illness among his kin which opened all these proceedings, the guilty girl's kin make *kano* to the guilty youth's kin; if the Sir Ghost of the girl's kin opened up proceedings with illness among her kin, the guilty youth's kin make *kano* to the girl's kin.

Kano is never made ostensibly to mortals. As between the guilty pair it goes one way or the other as an expiatory offering to whichever Sir Ghost is infuriated because of the sin and is manifesting his fury by causing illness in his own house. Once these payments of *kano* are all made, the sin is wiped out; so that a future illness in the kin of the other guilty party does not reverse the payment of *kano* between the kins of the two guilty parties. It causes search for a new sin.

Let us take as an example the *kano* paid by the erring girl's relatives to the house of her contracted groom. They put wealth on a canoe and punt it to that house. They put the wealth on the platform of the house. Those within do not appear. They remain inside, too offended to come out. Then the head of the girl's house addresses by name the Sir Ghosts of the house on whose platform he has laid the wealth. He tells them that he offers them this wealth as expiation for the affront laid upon them and he begs that they will be no longer angered. Then he goes away leaving his offering. After he has gone the mortals within the house take the expiatory wealth to themselves.

It may be wooden chests with locks and keys, or axes or knives; it may be a fine canoe or two; it may be even a small child handed over to a stranger house, and so lost finally to its parents.

Note how this expiatory offering, *kano*, is made, never ostensibly to offended mortals, always ostensibly to offended ghosts. To the man making the expiatory offering they are ghosts, to the man who acquires the offering they are Sir Ghosts.

If the betrothed girl's seducer is a married man the *kano* payments are made in the same manner.

Adultery in the full sense, that is from a marriage consummated, leads in theory to the same ghostly and mortal complications as far as *kano* is concerned; and actually does so in fact when the adultery is that of a married man with a betrothed girl. Adultery in which a married woman is concerned remains a theoretical possibility, very rarely confessed and expiated. In Peri village from amongst forty-two women married or widowed, in a village ever suspicious of sex offence and ever watchful, there was only one record of past adultery against any woman. There were several cases on record of married men seducing widows or betrothed girls. In Patusi, the next door village, there was a record of one charge against one married woman. The youth implicated by suspicion, when pressed to confess and save the woman's life as she was ill, resolutely said that there was no truth in the charge, though it was confessed by the woman herself in her last extremity, possibly delirium. The woman died. The village took the youth to the white court and had him gaoled on the charge of adultery. He came out still swearing the charge unjust, and left Patusi village and his kin forever.

The fact remains that married women are not accessible to a seducer, except under certain conditions that transform the seduction into an offer of honourable marriage.

To understand this, let us consider what would be the

situation confronting a married woman who confessed to adultery, let us say, because her brother, actually very ill, was at death's door, in her belief, unless she confessed and saved him. *Kano* payments would be made in regular order. Usually when a woman is flogged by her husband she flees to the houses of her own kin. But in this case her own kin would not receive her, not so much for making them pay heavy expiatory payment as for bringing danger of death amongst them, and for shaming them publicly. In fear of death from her presence no other house would receive her. She would be utterly at her husband's mercy. And mercy in such cases would not be expected. From the island of Lou, neighbour to Manus, I have a responsible report of a husband branding his faithless wife's pubic parts with a red hot iron. That is the type of mercy that would be expected in Manus also. For instance, a brother cleaved open his sister's skull with one of the edges of a great squared faggot, and she was only a girl, betrothed but not married. This was for sex lapse. The girl luckily enough recovered consciousness in about two hours and then the brother spoke publicly in an almost inaudible voice telling how, had she died, he would have committed suicide that day.[13]

It is because of this temper and because a married woman has no refuge in which she can escape it in its worst form—that is from a husband—that adultery by a woman is almost unknown in Manus.

In practice the woman wishing to leave her husband merely goes to her brother's house, where she is always received kindly. Her husband has no right to recover her against her will, and she can set out from her brother's house to a new husband if she wishes, without the ghost or Sir Ghosts causing any trouble attributable to such lawful action, provided always that any debts due by her kin to her former husband's kin in the marriage exchanges are first paid.

Confession of adultery involving a married woman, therefore, is not common in the Manus villages. And if there were such adultery there would be confession. The strain

[13] For the account, see p. 131.

placed on a sinner when the sinner's own kinsman is *in extremis* is tremendous. Also, the man's kinsman might be ill first, not the woman's. In such a case it is certain that the man would not spare the woman he had sinned with. If the sin existed it would most certainly become public knowledge. It is doubly impressive, therefore, that confession of sin with married women hardly ever occurs, although confessions of the seduction of women and girls by married men do occur.

Diagnosis of illness following the remarriage of widows is often that the ghost of the dead husband, angry at his widow's remarriage, has caused it; and this diagnosis is the more likely the more recent the death of the former husband. It should be noted that it is no secular breach of the moral code to marry a widow; whereas adultery or pre-marital lapse is a conspicuous breach. The case that is not a breach of the moral code is never punished by a Sir Ghost of either of the parties; the case that is a breach of the moral code is always so punished. Sir Ghost stands for morality, ghost does not. I must explain this statement before proceeding further.

It is not merely as an aspect of his rôle as guardian and protector of his ward that Sir Ghost punishes immorality. It is true that Sir Ghost protects his ward from the general malice of ghosts. It is true that most immorality in Manus is regarded as an inroad upon the rights of others, an infringement of rights. So it is conceivable that the Sir Ghost of a man whose rights have been infringed might act as a ghost towards the household of the infringer of rights. It is conceivable that sickness as punishment for immorality might be administered by ghosts, not by Sir Ghost. This does not occur in fact, however. Within a close kin group the Sir Ghost of an elder brother may punish someone of the household of his ward's younger brother, or his ward's younger sister, but such a case is an extension of the Sir Ghost concept. The Sir Ghost of the eldest line of a family is the head of the entire family, and as such he is Sir Ghost to more than one household, although the households of the junior lines have also their own less powerful Sir Ghosts. The human allocation of power as between senior and junior kin is thus maintained among the Sir Ghostly kin.

Since according to Manus belief ghosts do not punish immorality, the Manus theory is never that Sir Ghost in punishing immorality in his ward's household is forestalling more serious action against his ward's household by ghosts. There is no shadow of such belief. Sir Ghost protects his ward and the ward's household from what is felt as an unreasonable, or at least an objectionable, malice of ghosts. Sir Ghost protects his ward against action by ghosts that is not consonant with any moral code. But Sir Ghost punishes the ward's household for immorality within it from no pressure exterior to himself. Thus Sir Ghost as protector, guardian and helper is Sir Ghost in one capacity; Sir Ghost as corrector of immorality is Sir Ghost in another and different capacity.

It may be said that Sir Ghost may be conceived of as but one of the human family in a moral community, and all of them are trying to keep up the morals of the house, mortals and Sir Ghosts alike. All are helpers of all others within the family, whether by friendly coöperation, or by severe and unfriendly correction. A brother may lay open his sister's skull with a faggot, or the Sir Ghostly father of both of them may make one of them ill by abstracting soul stuff. Then if it happens, though rarely, that a Sir Ghost behaves really maliciously to a ward, instead of with just correction, he is merely behaving in a rare, but possibly fatherly fashion. It is quite true that the Manus ideas about the ghostly plane are very largely thus a mere shift of human behaviour from mortals to ghosts.

In the same spirit it is often true that the particular malice attributed to a ghost is a reflection of a real malice in the person of another house and kin to whom that ghost is Sir Ghost. But again this is often not so. Even when it does follow, the mortal has often an inactive, small malice, where the same mortal's Sir Ghost, acting as ghost to the unrelated household against which the malice is conceived, is represented as exercising an active death-dealing malice. Sometimes the mortal feels the same ferocity as his Sir Ghost, acting as a ghost, is thought to exercise. Sometimes the mortal feels very little or no ferocity. In such a case the conception that the ghostly plane is but the mortal plane reread breaks down, and such cases occur frequently in Manus practice.

For this reason, and for some others like it, we must consider Manus belief about the ghostly plane in its own right, as something more than a free expression or a reflection of social attitudes of a general nature. To a great extent it is a system that runs in its own laid-down grooves. We have no way of determining whether a brother would lay open his sister's skull for her immorality, for example, if he had not been brought up in the belief that it was good behaviour, and behaviour patterned on Sir Ghostly action. We have no way of determining to what extent the fear of Sir Ghost increases puritanism, and correction of sinners. The general social attitude colours the religion, and the religion colours the general social attitude.

Shame is cultivated in the society, sin is thought of with shame, and sin and disaster are connected. The connection is made in the religion. It is not in any sense a necessary connection, except that once made in Manus it has been maintained. The religion concentrates unpleasant feeling, shame connected with sex, and horror and fear and sorrow connected with illness and death, anger of one relative at another for directly arousing such shame and sorrow, such horror and fear, scorn and contempt of non-relatives who are co-villagers. All this concentration of sentiment feeds the fear of Sir Ghost. No other relative and no human being is regarded in any remotely similar way, except to the extent that the sin of a relative potentially damaging one makes one fear a relative, a situation that arises whenever a relative's sin is uncovered. Here it is doubtful whether the human situation is read into the ghostly plane, so much as a fear properly of Sir Ghost is read into a human relationship.

An illustration may illuminate the fact concretely. Let us suppose that the Manus acted as the Gilbert Islanders do when the kin of a nubile girl find that she has been seduced. They choke her to death by weighting a wooden beam across her throat. Let us suppose further that the Manus objection to sin expressed itself as simply as that at a certain stage in Manus history, an entirely fanciful hypothesis though this is. Then let us suppose further that the human executioners became ghostly executioners by some conjectural process of change. We would then have, as we have not in actual knowledge, a process of a mortal nature reread in ghostly terms. Then however we could not assume that this rereading was a mere reflection of a social attitude. It does not seem that any Gilbert Island woman has anything to fear except the consequences of her own sin. But any Manus native, man or woman, fears that he or she may die for a relative's sin. This element in the religion is an important one, and one that is no rereading of a human situation as such. As I have said, this process may be better described as reading a human situation in terms of special supernatural belief than as reading a supernatural situation in terms of a human one.

Hence when I discuss Sir Ghost as a figure and as an actor and say that he stands for morality, whereas ghost stands for malice, I am making a valid distinction. I am not saying that Sir Ghost is a dead relation, and that a ghost is a dead non-relative in more elaborate terms than is necessary, as I would be if the ghostly plane were merely the human plane reflected, and no more than that. Of course when I make any such statement I am discussing the real fact, which is the organisation of sentiments in the peculiar Manus way, in terms of the Manus convention.

An oracular system allows such a measure of apparently free play of the oracles' personal attitudes and views that the subsequent detailed account of the religion which I give, may easily lead to a view that the system escapes special convention and merely reflects social attitudes conventionalised outside the religion in social and in economic organisation, in education and in such matters of other than religious convention. An oracular system lets in so many attitudes not especially of the religious convention that this danger of error must be specifically marked with a signal. The fact that one of the Manus religious conventions is essentially an Old Testament convention also makes it none the less a convention. Puritanism need not be supported by the convention that the wages of sin are death; and it is not in another part of New Guinea than Manus. We must not gloss over the fact of convention from a sense of undue familiarity.

In cases of serious illness in Manus the oracles may make as many as three different diagnoses: sin and Sir Ghostly correction, or ghostly malice, or, more usually, both of these in one sitting. There is a premium upon an oracle's ability to make many diagnoses. It will be evident that long continued illness with new oracular sittings every day or every few days strains to the utmost the oracles' abilities in collecting evidence of sin, and in thinking up reasons for ghostly malice; for even ghostly malice must be motivated, as interpreted by the oracles.

Adultery by a married woman is so infrequent as to give hardly any grist to the oracular mill. Adultery by a married man is a little more frequent in affairs with unmarried girls or with widows. Technical adultery, adultery from the point of view of betrothal being as binding as consummated marriage, is more common than adultery in consummated marriage. Nevertheless there is little constant grist for the oracles from contemporary adulteries. In a village of one hundred and twenty-three persons of an age beyond puberty, and with few old persons (correlated with a general very low expectation of life), only one adulterous sin, and that a technical adultery, occurred in a period of six months. One other was suspected, but unproven, and the suspicion was relinquished quickly after a long examination that showed evidence in favour of innocence.

In consequence, during my stay the oracles depended largely on old sins, several years old often. Imaginary complications flowed from old actual sins; ghostly malice was often interpreted as flowing from deaths that followed old sins. My detailed discussion will reveal what may appear to be plenty of sin. It should be remembered, however, that this is a long history of sin which actually contrasts with a prevalent sinlessness over a six monthly period, for example. Even with the free use of old sins in the form of new complications from them, the gross sins are not nearly sufficient to provide the oracles with the continuous running fire of new and different diagnoses that they are expected to provide, of each case, and often for many days for one case. They cannot possibly keep up with the frequent malarial fever in terms of diagnoses based on gross acts of sin.

The religion is adapted to the facts in several ways: a sense of guilt is established over the most trifling offences against the code of sexual manners; a very high, very puritanical standard of ideal conduct is set up, so that the oracles, matching the actual with the ideal, have reasonable room within which discrepancy may be fairly frequent. Thus obscenity between husband and wife may be the diagnosis of the cause of subsequent illness in the house; or a woman once seeing a man exposed by accident in a fall from a house; or a visitor in a house seeing the woman of the house accidentally exposed in her sleep. And even though obscene jesting between a man and his father's sister's daughter, or her mother, the man's father's sister, is enjoined by custom, this jesting may be held by the oracle to have gone a shade too far for a Sir Ghost's approval. The line drawn in this case is exceedingly arbitrary, and due only to the oracle's lack of a real sin for diagnosis. But neither the oracle nor the people generally conceive it so.

Sir Ghost is also believed to punish other offences besides those against the code of sex manners. These are, notably, not paying debts in time, or not making the funerary feasts quickly enough for the dead. As everyone in the community is engaged in a network of economic obligations involving everyone else, and as these obligations are often made suddenly and become unexpectedly due, by death or divorce, as well as expectedly due, by birth, ear-piercing, first menstruation, betrothal and marriage, nearly everyone is always engaged in a violent effort to keep up with events; nearly everyone has credits out and debts out also. The oracles are relentless in finding people behindhand and in spurring them on by a diagnosis that illness in the house is due to debts or obligations not fulfilled in time. What "in time" means is explained, by the fact that all major economic exchanges are arranged for by date many days in advance. If one man is a day late in contributing his sago, for instance, and his baby is ill on the night of the day when it should have been contributed, this slight delay is diagnosed as the cause. His Sir Ghost is inflicting punishment for economic slackness.

Important economic events foreshadowed or being planned usually lead to clustered explanations of several contemporary illnesses, all centred about kinship relations and economic relations between some of the many persons involved.

Again, Sir Ghost punishes any disobedience shown towards the head of the household by the head's younger brothers or sisters, or by economic dependents adopted by the head, thus entrenching the right of the senior capitalist to his dependent's free service for him.

Again, Sir Ghost may punish his ward for not keeping their mutual house in the best of repair.

Again, Sir Ghost may punish a house where, in the opinion of the oracle, his ward is concentrating too much of its economic resources towards the public validation of an event in the life of one of its members to the temporary detriment of the public validation of an event in the life of another of its members.

Again, Sir Ghost may punish his ward for diverting a pig from a possible economic exchange and eating it instead, that is, for not making the best public showing in the great exchanges of property.

The possibility of offences of these last two types causing illness in the family often causes a man before he acts to summon a medium to find out what his Sir Ghost's ruling is. A man who asks the oracular representative of more or less public opinion to decide these matters for him does not leave the oracle room for such diagnosis if subsequent illness occurs in his house. Actually other oracles may intervene in such a case, and they need not respect a different oracle's former finding.

In fact, despite the very real onerousness of the moral code, it is kept very well on the whole by a people very thoroughly intimidated by Sir Ghost. The oracles are often still at a loss for a charge of sin. Nevertheless sin has to be found, if possible, that it may be expiated and the illness cured thereby.

Whenever there is no fault to be laid at the door of a house or no further fault to explain the continuance of an illness, the oracle removes the blame from the mortal plane purely; as, *e.g.*, the Sir Ghost of the house has lately wedded a new wife, the ghost of a dead woman of Y's house. The Sir Ghost is angry because there has been no recognition on the mortal plane of this new ghostly marriage of his. The mortals of his house should have made gift exchange with the mortals of Y's house in recognition of the marriage on the other plane. Let this recognition be made and illness within his house will cease.

This type of explanation is not preferred by the oracles. It makes the Sir Ghost less reasonable and more arbitrary than he is in his rôle of enforcing the social conscience as to purely mortal affairs. I have given but one example of the type. It takes variant forms; for example, upon adultery on the other plane, *kano* should be paid on this plane, the wards acting for their respective Sir Ghosts.

Expiation for a minor sex offence (but not felt as minor by the native) follows the pattern of payment, from the kin of the party whose Sir Ghost has left them well, to expiate the wrath of the other party's Sir Ghost who has visited them with illness.

Expiation for overdue debts or obligations is made by paying them quickly and immediately—thus curing the illness.

Expiation for disobedience to the head of the household by the younger members is made by payment from them to the Sir Ghost of the head (paying the head).

Expiation for a defective house, or for allocation of wealth to validate an event in the life of one of the family members, rather than an event in the life of another member, is made by remedying these defects. It may be noted that a man with a limited possession of wealth, due to make a ceremonially required feast for his son's ear-piercing and for his daughter's betrothal at the same time, is in an unenviable position. If he puts his wealth into one child's affair, and illness follows, the oracle may attribute it to his Sir Ghost's anger at his not having put it into the other child's affair. Or if he acts in the other way the oracle may still give the same kind of diagnosis. The situation is checkmated by the oracle unless the Sir Ghost is consulted through an oracle before action is taken. It is impossible to make expiation for "eating a pig," or the like consumption of wealth, instead of using it in public exchange to validate *rites de passage*, except in renewed hard work to make up the deficit oracularly alleged.

Theft from another man's betel nut or coconut palms is punished by illness due to black magic placed on the palms by a magician hired for the purpose by the tree owners—not by illness due to Sir Ghost. Nevertheless it will be apparent that Sir Ghost punishes a wide range of sin. Since government prohibition of the forcible capturing of a foreign woman or women of another village as prostitutes, any such illicit action has been added as a sin to the Manus code. The last illicit action in this direction led to a man's death in prison. His imprisonment was brought about by the Government, but his death was caused by a ghostly agent, angry at his action. This ghostly action constitutes a precedent, outlined in full at the time by the oracles, for regarding prostitute capture as a sin; and it is now so regarded.

I have covered the catalogue of the main types of sin, the traditional code. I may mention also a foreboding that sometimes attacks diviner or medium. The Sir Ghost that controls the itch in the back, the ghostly control that speaks through the medium's mouth, these must not be given offence by immoral conduct on the part of their mortal channels of communication. If they are offended, then they may communicate deliberate lies from the other plane. So, for the immorality of the oracle, his or her patient may die. And though there be no independent oracular investigation of the oracle under whose advice a patient died, there is always some suspicion. This is a contributory reason why a diviner or medium should give up the art after patent lack of success. "Let him who is without sin cast the first stone." The oracle does not always feel fitted for it in the face of public suspicion following a failure to cure a patient.

This is true even although there is a conventional oracles' alibi. If a death occurs it may be assumed that the sins uncovered by the oracles before death, having been all expiated, were not responsible for the death. Ghostly malice or an outstanding sin not detected in time were responsible, and they may be mooted afterwards by the oracles, or oracle, in a posthumous investigation. Many possible causes of death were removed, but unfortunately there was one too many. This alibi is usually offered and accepted apparently in the heat of the moment, but not always accepted subsequently.

If, as is likely to occur, ghostly malice is given as a reason for a death, this use of the idea may appear as a hypothesis of despair. There is no further use in correcting sin; the sick person is close to death, and the oracle may hasten to offer an alibi for the failure of the sin correction curing technique. Although I found one clear case of a use of this technique, the use of the idea of ghostly malice (in contrast to the use of the idea of sin) is not restricted to the alibi and the hypothesis of despair.

An oracle may exploit the idea of ghostly malice as completely as, or more completely than, the idea of Sir Ghostly correction of sin for all manner of personal reasons, or because facts of sin do not appear obvious or applicable in a given case of illness. But generally speaking an oracle exploiting ghostly malice somewhat exclusively, and disregarding Sir Ghostly correction of sin, may be understood to imply one of two things.

It may be: "This patient is not in serious danger. He doesn't like X— on such a score. I don't like X— either. The Sir Ghost of X— is acting as a malicious ghost in making him ill on such a score," the same score as that which is a cause of dislike between the mortals in many cases. Or again it may be: "This patient will probably not live, will not confess sin anyway. She is an immoral person, but if she will not confess, her blood will not be on my head. I'll go ahead and deal with what I can do without any real knowledge of her sins, and leave confession to her and to her confessors" (cross-cousins with whom obscenity may be used).

Oracles do not explicitly phrase such statements. Ostensibly they are guided by the advice they get from the other plane. At a risk of error I have characterised their practice. I do so with considerable knowledge however. Let me give some facts first, before returning to my inference above.

Expiation is regarded as curative, is made readily and quickly for sin, but not for ghostly malice. Payment is said to be made by the sick person's Sir Ghost to the malicious ghost (not in fact by human beings at all), in some cases where the malice of a ghost is diagnosed. In other cases another more supernatural pressure is employed than that of mortal payment, and yet different from that of ghostly payment. The medium uses her control, the ghosts of native constabulary, and spirit dogs of ferocious nature to intimidate the malicious ghost, and make it return the sick person's soul stuff.

The Manus believe well enough in the validity of supernatural pressure used by the mediums on malicious ghosts. They pay expiation for sin, but use supernatural pressure only on ghostly malice. They do not pay up except on what they regard as just grounds.[14] Payment to wipe off sin is just, payment to keep a ghost from malice, if it were done, would be simply bribery, or tribute.

I must add that, although, in an overwhelming majority of cases of diagnoses of ghostly malice, payment by the kin of the sick person to the ward of the Sir Ghost who was acting as malicious ghost (to the sick person) was not often done, in one case it was done.[15] A woman fell ill, the diagnosis

[14] A close analogy of this situation is found elsewhere in Melanesia in connection with sorcery, not ghosts, but presenting the same separation of malicious supernaturalism and a juster supernaturalism. Cf. "Sorcerers of Dobu," pp. 154–171.

[15] See p. 207.

was made, but no payment was made; she remained ill and the same diagnosis, implicating the same malicious ghostly quarter, was remade, and still no payment was made, although she was in danger of death. Then her blood brother fell into a very serious condition also. The same diagnosis was made. This was too much. A payment was made. The same diagnosis had been given by three different oracles in succession. But this case was not one of clear ghostly malice. It was not clear Sir Ghostly correction of sin either. It was the malice of the ghost of the sick person's sister's husband, who was held to have died for the sick person's sister's sins. Thus the only case of payment of a malicious ghost (actually of the mortal ward) that I knew of, was a case in which the points of malice and of sin were not separate and distinct, as more often is the case.

This case stands in exception to the general rule that diagnoses of ghostly malice do not lead to payments made by mortals, but rather to use of supernatural pressure alone. If such diagnoses led regularly, as they do not, to payments, bribes or tributes which would be in contrast to just expiations, the oracles would hardly practice their craft in Manus without securing gratuitous financial benefits for their kin and friends, or escape accusation of collusion. I never heard a hint of such accusation, although I heard much critical and unfriendly accusation on various other points directed against the oracles. The Manus premium on justice is strong enough to rule out any such malpractice.[16]

The facts being such, the Manus believe further that soul stuff paid for by mortals is a thing more satisfactorily bargained for, than soul stuff left to a Sir Ghost to pay for, or for oracles to collect by supernatural pressure (use of controls, ghosts of native constabulary, spirit dogs to overawe the malicious ghost). The Manus believe in the use of supernatural pressure, but not with the same intensity with which they believe in what seems to their moral and practical natures

[16] In strong contrast to Manus and Dobuan use of an idea of justice in their supernatural systems stands a use such as that of the Omaha of North America. Cf. my "Omaha Secret Societies," *Columbia University Contributions to Anthropology*, Vol. XIV, passim.

a moral and a practical course—expiating sin and paying generously for what they want. A Manus man in dead earnest is quite willing to pay. An oracle equally in earnest will find something that must be paid for, mortal sin, not ghostly malice. From my very keen appreciation of this situation I have made my statements of oracular carelessness or hopelessness in diagnosis of ghostly malice, although an oracle would not admit anything other than the guidance of inspiration from the other plane.

I except from the field of my inference the malice of the ghost of a dead husband at his widow's remarriage. Here the oracles usually attribute malice quickly and in dead earnest, although no payment by mortals is made. But in all other cases a deep oracular earnestness towards securing a sick person's cure leads generally to diagnoses on the lines which the Manus without shadow of doubt consider most important, sins and their expiation in the form of ponderable payments of wealth. In contrast, when an oracle lacks hope of recovery, or feels the illness is too slight to be taken serious, or, more rarely, when an oracle lacks concern for a particular case which is neither hopeless illness nor yet trivial illness, the oracle is likely to turn to diagnoses of ghostly malice and the use of supernatural pressure alone to end it.

7

A Sir Ghost enforcing morality or a ghost inflicting malice can punish a man not only by causing illness in his house, but also as an alternative by spoiling his fishing, the Manus mainstay of life.

There are two terms in Manus for soul or soul stuff, *mwelolo* and *molua*. *Mwelolo* is a term not normally used with any possessive pronoun or form. *Molua* is used with the suffixed endings that indicate the closest possession, such as are used typically for parts of the body. *Mwelolo* is used very generally, *molua* comparatively very seldom. *Mwelolo* is used exclusively when reference is made to divisibility. Thus "one piece of soul stuff here, in possession of ghost X, one piece of soul stuff there with ghost Y" demands *mwelolo* as the proper term; or "a little soul stuff." Again *mwelolo* is used generally when divisibility is not overt in the reference. *Molua* is never used in idioms or phrases indicating divisibility. The closeness of possession, the non-divisibility of *molua* seems to indicate a slightly different view of the soul. But the Manus native is not conscious that there is any difference in concept or of the grammatical differences he observes in the use of the terms. If asked, he says that *molua* is *mwelolo*, and *mwelolo*, *molua*.

One further difference of grammatical usage occurs. *Molua* is used for the "soul" of inanimate things that by convention are endowed with "souls," as generally as *mwelolo* is used for soul stuff of persons, or even more so. For while *mwelolo* is not exclusively personal, *molua* being allowed on less frequent occasion, *mwelolo* is not allowed for souls of inanimate things.

The inanimate soul is practically confined to fishing gear of all types, fish baskets, nets, traps and the like. Only in one other instance did I find *molua* used in a non-human reference. In a song sung at a peace making ceremony after war occur the words:

> "Whosoever may break this peace
> May the soul of peace strike him down,
> Strike him down, and take him east."
>
> *Amo se ku uti morai*
> *Molua morai ki te i,*
> *Ki te i, ki lolo yap.*

The *molua* of peace is believed to be a really efficient agent in hurting wanton peace breakers after the ceremony is made. Apart from this, *molua* is exclusively human or confined to fishing gear.[17]

A Sir Ghost or a ghost may abstract the *molua* from pieces of fishing gear in the same manner as *mwelolo* from a person. The main difference is that many ghosts do not have different pieces of *molua* from the one fishing gear corpus at the same time, as they often do have separate pieces of human soul

[17] One common way of wearing dogs' teeth is called the *molua* of dogs' teeth. This is no more than terminology however.

stuff. The medium in recovering fish gear *molua* does not recover several pieces, and "pile one on top of another." What this means in practice is that fishing gear is not "sick" because its owner has offended ghost X about a matter, A, ghost Y about a matter, B, ghost Z about a matter, C, all at the same time, each ghost taking a piece of soul stuff. Fishing gear is "sick" on only one count at a time.

This suggests that the urgency of human illness, because of the greater danger in it, has provoked a custom of turning over many stones at once, in a more desperate effort to cure it than is customary in the more sedate behaviour over "sick" fishing gear. (Sick fishing gear is of course gear that is temporarily meeting with no luck in catching fish—empty traps and the like.) And this urgency may be the provoking cause of the idea of divisibility of soul stuff. This speculation is certainly suggested by the contrast; whether it be true or not cannot be determined.

A man whose fish basket or fish trap has been sick for some days will summon oracular assistance in the usual manner. The oracles respond as for human sickness, although with but one diagnosis of sin, instead of with two or three or four simultaneous diagnoses. A seance is held by night often but not necessarily in a house in which the sick gear lies. Typically divination of sin occurred beforehand. Reparation of sin was made beforehand. In the seance the offended Sir Ghost details elaborately why he was offended. It is pointed out to him that reparation has been made. Will he now restore the *molua* to the fish trap in return?

The method of restoration of *molua* to fishing gear differs from the method of restoration of *mwelolo* to a person. In the latter case the procedure is as follows: in front of the medium as she conducts her seance, a shallow wooden bowl of water is always placed. At the close of the seance, the medium's control has collected several pieces of soul stuff from Sir Ghosts or ghosts who have been appeased by expiation prior to the seance. The control, and sometimes the Sir Ghost of the house also, or sometimes some other ghost, but always the control, is asked to "rub" the soul stuff, and place it in the water, that is "rub" it into the water. After this request is made the medium waits solemnly a while to give time for this proceeding on the other plane. She then bathes the sick person with the water, so restoring the missing soul stuff to the sick person. Alternatively the sick person may drink the water. One patient in one seance I saw declined the customary water cure, and insisted on having his soul stuff put on betel nut which he subsequently chewed. He was a slight eccentric, declining to observe custom. But the medium obliged him. After all the ghosts can work in many ways.

But no water cure is used for fishing gear. The medium merely requests her control to obtain possession of the *molua* from the Sir Ghost who abstracted it from the fishing gear, and then to put it back in its place in that gear.

As further provinces of the Sir Ghost, it is believed that he can help a man look out for fish and even drive a school of fish towards his ward, if they are fairly near anyway. It is also believed that Sir Ghost can sometimes influence the winds. These two provinces are by no means strongholds of Sir Ghost however. He cannot drive fish near his ward if the nearest fish are far off; and often enough a Sir Ghost speaking to his ward in a seance will say, "When you and I drifted helplessly before the gale off our route last month."

Sir Ghost is not restricted to taking the soul of his ward's fishing gear in order to secure a similar effect, if his ward owns divinatory bones for fishing. His ward will say, "Is there a turtle to the east of me now?" Then if the only turtle near is to the west Sir Ghost can make the itch in his helpless votaries' back answer "yes" to that false mortal suspicion. Ill luck dogs the owner of divinatory fishing bones if he is immoral. His possession of an oracle is only one more hole in his armour. This is recognised explicitly in native theory.

CHAPTER III

MAGIC AND THE *TANDRITANITANI* CULT

1. Manus Use of Magic

Manus magic is greatly influenced in its function by the religious forms, and is of minor importance aside from the religious system. The magic has entirely different forms of its own, but I wish to emphasise my deep assurance that the important fact about Manus magic is that when a deeply moral and religious people, who use little white magic, use black magic, they use it so that it functions with no offence to morality or to religion; and they secure this by some assimilation of the otherwise incompatible forms, in strong contrast to the custom of other cultures where black magic functions dominantly without having to be fitted in with different and locally stronger religious forms.

One of the most remarkable characteristics of Manus society is the very unimportant, and relatively small part, that white magic plays, smaller far than black magic, although black magic itself is often lightly regarded. Manus mythology consists chiefly of tales told against *tchinal*, making out *tchinal* to be mischievous land ogres of vile habits, and often representing the *tchinal* as the butts of practical jokes. Manus mythology is largely one long continued joke on the black magic of the land dwellers. Now these *tchinal* are none other than the magical familiars of the land dwellers of the Great Admiralty, the Usiai, and are regarded with the utmost seriousness by the Usiai, but only scraps and tatters of the Usiai systems of magic have entered into Manus tradition.

It is true that on occasion, in cases of serious illness, the Manus make use of *tchinal* derived exorcism of *tchinal* derived black magic. This use is generally secondary to the use of the customs of the Sir Ghost and ghost cult in order of trial, an order that is also an order of faith. The extraordinary thing, considering the legends, is that there is any place at all for the *tchinal* derived magic. It is only in the extremity of despair that such magic is used, after the proper Manus methods have obviously not succeeded. All Manus men, when in good spirits, or even in much less than good spirits, deride the *tchinal* and the *tchinal* observances.

I do not develop this point completely in subsequent discussion, but I provide the additional material for a full appreciation of it, part of the material necessary having been collected by Father Meier before me. Father Meier has published many Manus legends about *tchinal*. The reader who wishes to gain a full appreciation of my point should refer to Father Meier's collection of legends.[1] He should refer moreover to Dr. Mead's discussion of how the Manus adults use the idea of *tchinal* to try to intimidate children from playing near the land, or from doing almost anything the adults do not desire; and then how the slightly older children use the same technique on the slightly younger children—all without much effect.[2] It will be seen what a joke the *tchinal* become. Then to complete the picture I give in the course of the next chapter two discussions of the use of *tchinal* derived magic. I must issue a warning that all the magic which I discuss is not of *tchinal* derivation; some is of Matankor,[3] not of Usiai origin. But Man of Lorengau's exorcism and Pope's exorcism over Alupwai, to be described in full, are Usiai magic. Man of Lorengau was a man of Usiai blood on his mother's side, but Manus by residence and by blood on his paternal side. Pope was a moron and a cataleptic subject, with no social power except through somewhat aberrant channels. He seized on socially unstressed roles, where he was allowed to assert himself most. My account of these two exorcisms gives the Manus use of the *tchinal* magic in a case of illness that had almost become a case of despair.

[1] P. J. Meier, "Mythen und Sagen der Admiralitätinsulaner," *Anthropos*, Vol. 4, 1909, pp. 354–371. *Tchinal* is translated as *teufel*.

[2] Margaret Mead, "Growing Up in New Guinea," pp. 107–108.

[3] The Matankor are islanders, such as the islanders of Pitilu, Pak, Lou, Baluan, Hus, Andra of the Admiralty Archipelago—land dwellers, but not of the Great Admiralty Island. The Usiai are the land dwellers of the Great Admiralty Island. The Manus are, in contrast to both classes, lagoon dwellers with no land.

The Manus attitude to the *tchinal* derived magic is predominantly a joking attitude. I may illustrate this joking attitude again in connection with another form of magic. The Usiai believe that in trees there are tree spirits, called *ngidrai*. The Manus talk in terms of the same belief but very rarely. *Ngidrai* to the Manus means legend, and *ngidraien* means long ago. But the Manus know that *ngidrai* means tree spirit to the Usiai. During my stay a Manus man had purchased a tree from an Usiai for a canoe. He had felled the tree and partly hollowed it out. A large party of Manus men set out, I with them, to drag the tree down the steep hillside to the water. Each man put an ovalum shell on the penis, as at a dance, and the whole affair of bringing the tree down was the most jovial affair that I saw in Manus. As the tree came near the sea one man, dancing along, beat it with leaves and said, "Get out of this canoe, *ngidrai*. Sir Ghost of mine look after this canoe. Make it fast." There was no more ritual than this one man's one exclamation. For the rest everyone joked, danced about, hung back on the ropes to keep the tree from damaging those who guided it in front on the steep places, and all rushed forward together in a fine frenzy of pulling on the more level places.

It was the first time I heard about the tree spirits. I asked solemnly about the tree spirit, *ngidrai*, assuming belief in it. This occurred in the twilight some hours after the tree had been launched and paddled and pushed to the village. Immediately one man went away to tell others the joke. In a few minutes about fifteen men were about me quizzically teasing. "So you believe in tree spirits!" The face of everyone wore a broad grin. I replied that I had been told about them in New Guinea (*i.e.*, in Dobu and in the Trobriands magic is used to exorcise them from a canoe). I had also known them in New Zealand, my home (Maori belief), where people took them seriously. No one ceased grinning at these remarks, however. One man said the belief was Usiai. Then another man said very solemnly, "But if we call on Sir Ghost that is most real and true." Immediately everyone became sober.

I promised to have the right attitude to the *ngidrai* in future. I noticed that the case is as with the *tchinal*. On very rare occasion a Manus man will mention a tree spirit without joking. It happened two or three times only, and the mention was made casually and privately.

I have recounted the above event in detail because it is fairly typical of much else. The Manus are under temptation to borrow magical beliefs which they themselves do not own, not only from the Usiai, but also from some of the Matankor tribes. They do actually borrow them, and even use them seriously on rare occasion. But for the most part the Manus are satirical about these beliefs, and when serious profess a jealous adherence to the Sir Ghost cult.[4] They are not receptive to free diffusion of culture. Their Sir Ghost is a jealous Sir Ghost, or more exactly, their own cult has its strong roots and makes unrooted concepts look silly and humorous in consequence.

Most of the magic used by the Manus is imported from the Usiai or from the Matankor tribes. This statement can be made absolutely, as every charm has its list of the names of the former owners and of their villages and tribes. Of any spell used in a Manus village it can be learned how long it has been in the possession of a man of the Manus tribe. Of amulets the same cannot be learned. No spell that I saw used by a Manus man had a Manus history of more than two or three generations. The earlier history was Usiai or Matankor. The Manus frequently say of a Manus magician's magic, "That Usiai—or that Matankor—magic is worthless. He can't do anything with it. It might (being black magic) damage infants in arms, but not grown persons."

There is, however, some magic that is probably truly Manus, or old in Manus usage. It is possible that the Manus are always losing their magic, and in each generation a few men go back to Usiai or Matankor tribes to purchase some new magic. The fact that no Manus magic of spells has an old Manus history may mean no more than that. In such cases the usage of magic may be old, but the permanent

[4] See below, Chapter IV.

unreceptive attitude of the majority of a Manus community who are not magicians may effect a repeated loss and a repeated repurchase down the generations. The prominent magicians in the village where I was resident were an adopted Matankor man, an Usiai Manus half-blood (the only type called "half-caste" by the Manus, there being no white-native half-castes of half Admiralty Island blood), the village head man, who had married an Usiai woman, and who had strong Usiai connections, thereby, the cataleptic moron discussed above, and two or three more normal Manus. The use of magic goes with the abrogation of Manus purism on the whole, and such abrogation was probably always present to some slight degree. The present situation in Manus does not date since white rule, but from before white rule, in the particular case under discussion.

Nevertheless a balance has been struck. There are strong claims put forward by the magicians for their magic. There is an equally strong ridicule of magic which is more general. In practice some types of magic have gained a stronger foothold than other types. We have to distinguish between the less accepted and the more accepted types. We have commented upon ridicule of the Usiai *tchinal*, which are familiars of black magic, and of Usiai *ngidrai*, which are the objects of one form of Usiai white magic. I am not sure that the *tchinal* are the familiars of black magic only amongst the Usiai; but I am sure that only in this form the *tchinal* came to my notice amongst the Manus, a form that is congruent with the malicious character given to them in the Manus legends. These legends give no indication that their *tchinal* subjects are actually functioning in magical harness amongst the Usiai, and also to a lesser degree, amongst the Manus. The understanding of the *tchinal* legends such as those, amongst other types of legend, which Father Meier collected depends upon a knowledge of the culture which can now be provided.

I shall consider first the black magic used in Manus, as it is relevant in some ways to the Manus religion and morality, whereas the white magic used in Manus is slighter, and comparatively irrelevant to any other aspect of the social structure. The Manus religion is concerned intimately with sickness and death, and black magic has the same field of reference. The Manus religion is concerned intimately with the maintenance of public and private morals, and black magic is a weapon that can be used either agreeably with that maintenance, or without agreement with it. The Manus use of Usiai and Matankor derived black magic therefore creates a delicate situation. It is a situation that has been met by the use of some unusual conventions regulating the use of black magic, although others are more familiar.

One type of black magic is that employed to place upon private property in palms, coconut palms, and betel-nut palms and sago palms. This black magic is a conditional curse. It does not hurt anyone but a thief who may scale another man's curse-protected palm. I have given a fairly thorough description of how this form of magic operates in Dobuan culture in my book on Dobu. It is a widespread Oceanic form, but its functioning takes different aspects in different cultures. This fact has not been illustrated before, so I shall take the opportunity to cast Manus custom into relief against the custom of Dobu. In Dobu this type of spell is termed *tabu*, in Manus, *sorosor*. In Samoa the same form is called *tapui*. In Oceania very generally the *tabu-sorosor-tapui* is used to punish theft from privately owned palm trees; many different spells go to make up an entire system. It is only the entire system, or any one spell of it referred to without specific reference, that is termed *tabu*, *sorosor* or *tapui*, or whatever the local term may be. Within the system each particular spell has its individual name. Each particular and individually named spell has its own individual result, which is one of the local diseases and deformities. Thus one spell causes elephantiasis, another yaws and so on. The owner of a disease spell can only protect his trees from potential thieves who do not own the spell for the same disease. For with each spell goes its own individual exorcism. The spell owner places his disease spell on his own trees, and must exorcise it before plucking the fruit of his own trees; or at least, even where this is not done, it is considered that possession of magic to cause a particular disease gives its owner immunity to that particular disease, but to none other. Therefore the system only gives protection to trees to the extent that different persons own separate and different disease inducers. I can keep a yaws owner off my trees if I am an elephantiasis owner, but I cannot do the like to another elephantiasis owner. Therefore this system works best where the local grop is not much larger than the range of diseases, as in Dobu, where every family line owns a spell of the system, but yet a different spell.

With the Manus the system is in operation, but not as in Dobu. In Dobu each family line owns its particular *tabu* or disease creator. In Manus there are too many family lines in a village for such individual ownership. Moreover the Manus, as sea dwellers, possess palms occasionally by conquest, but never with any appearance of having had old or secure status in such ownership. Similarly, just as a little shore line was wrested from the Usiai, so also the *sorosor* used by the Manus are of Usiai origin, although these are paid for, not obtained by force of arms. Again there are not many forms of *sorosor* used in Manus. The possibilities of the range of disease are not realised in the *sorosor*. Four or five persons in a large village own *sorosor*, and other men may hire a magician's services, if they wish to, as they usually do. The Manus are very honest on the whole, and their training in honesty protects private property very efficiently. The use of the *sorosor* is a manner of overlay that really is but a finishing touch. In Dobu everyone knows the different families' specialties. They are all different, with very rare exception, and so constitute protection. In Manus only the few magician's specialties are known; these are not always different, and so do not provide protection for the magicians as between themselves; the Manus custom of getting spells from the Usiai, and from any Usiai of any tribe, prevents the possibility of a non-overlapping tradition, for accident enters in too often. The great majority of the members of a Manus village own no spell. Knowledge of what disease is on another man's trees is not reckoned with an eye to possible stealing, as it is in Dobu, owing to a different convention in Manus which will be discussed shortly.

If now we take a purely conjectural place, give it as few forms of disease spells as Manus, as large a local group as Manus, as generally diffused an ownership of disease spells as Dobu, and a Dobuan interest in the possibility of stealing following knowledge of overlapping possession of the same disease by different people, the system would not work. In Dobu, and in Manus, in its different ways, it does work.

The forms that were known in Manus were *souru*, which makes a woman barren, *rutchurutch*, which produces lameness, *tchetche*, which produces a fever, *nam*, which produces stunted physique, *bwokil*, which produces elephantiasis, and *palit a romot*, which produces vomiting. In Manus, as in Samoa, but not as in Dobu, the different forms of *sorosor* when put on trees are marked with different kinds of warning signs. I have not all the data on this point, as I did not wander extensively enough in the water-logged swamp land plantations lined with mangroves, but got through the swamps always up the streams, which are used as roadways to the Usiai country. The *nam* is marked by a coconut stuck on top of an erect stick, with coconut fronds tied beneath it so that the loose ends encircle the coconut in a bush of fronds. The *tchetche* has a *tchetche* leaf impaled on an upright stick planted by the tree. I do not know the forms for the other *sorosor* spells. My informants were all vague.

The great majority of the Manus do not know or recognise the differences in these warning signs. There are *sorosor* that have no definite form. These are said to "strike down" a thief—in any fashion apparently. I saw the *nam* used in exorcism to cure a woman who was suffering from retained afterbirth. She and her husband had stolen from another man's tree, which had been protected with the *nam*, and her husband had confessed to the theft under inquisition by a diviner. Here a *sorosor*, theoretically intended to produce illness of a type X, was held accountable actually for an illness of a type A. The facts of stealing are ascertained and any one *sorosor* is given a multiple potentiality of illnesses in infliction, so that the dogma of one kind of *sorosor*, one kind of illness only, remains largely an empty dogma.

In Dobu the matter is arranged wholly otherwise. If a person gets gangosa, only the magician who owns the *tabu* to inflict gangosa is responsible for its infliction. It is believed dogmatically either that the inflicted victim stole from the gangosa *tabu* owner's trees, or else that the gangosa *tabu* owner worked his evil maliciously on the victim. The dogmatic form of *sorosor-tabu* differentiation makes for a dogmatic belief about stealing, or, if not stealing, for malice. The alternative of malice for stealing allows them to attribute to the owner of the *tabu* the disease a man subsequently contracts, even if he did not steal from the protected tree. In brief the Manus ascertain fact carefully, require confession of theft, and bend, or throw out, dogma to suit, where the Dobuans hold fast to dogma and make their ideas of fact agree, if not in one way, then in another. This difference produces, as one consequence, a possibility of securing a dogmatic formal table in Dobu, specific *tabu* conjoined with specific disease, over a considerable list. On the other hand the Manus think more readily about the elasticity of their practice than about a dogmatic rigidity which in this particular they disdain; though some dogmatic rigidity, affecting mainly the differences in warning signs used, appears even with the Manus.

This Manus elasticity is different from Dobuan custom, but it is not an absolute elasticity. Sometimes a Dobuan-like rigidity is used. Thus as a note on the uses of *bwokil* and *palit a romot* I find recorded that one man always treated *bwokil* (elephantiasis) except when a woman contracted it; in this case he gave his wife power to treat it, as he would have been ashamed otherwise. Three women possessed the *palit a romot*, and if a person had vomiting fits, divination was used to see from which of the three it proceeded. The one selected was called in as exorcist. I did not see anything like this, but the account is probably true. I did see the *nam* used to exorcise an illness not appropriate to it, but appropriate only in an ascertained fact of theft from a *nam* protected tree. The truth would appear to be partly a Dobuan-like pattern in Manus, partly a different elasticity and disregard for magical form in favour of regard for fact of actual theft in Manus. Where there is no fact of theft confessed, but, *e.g.*, elephantiasis, merely, without apparent cause, apparently the Manus make shift as the Dobuans do.

The Manus usage of confession belongs properly to the Manus ghost cult, in which it is used frequently. Confession of thieving results always from an investigation with a seance, or seer's or diviner's oracular judgment. Hence the Manus elasticity in the use of the *sorosor* cult flows from its effective conjunction with the Manus Sir Ghost and ghost cult. The Dobuans have a different form of elasticity in the uses of the *tabu* cult, called *putautaona*, but their form of elasticity is different and designed to promote stealing; it is not a moral sanction against stealing.[5]

The usages of the *sorosor* are not regarded humorously in Manus. Thieving is regarded as a most damnable sin, and an element in a magical cult that is in agreement with this attitude is welcomed and well-integrated into the Manus social forms, even although it uses the otherwise comical Usiai *tchinal*. Not only are the *sorosor* forms adapted to the religious custom of confession of sin, but the *tchinal*, the familiars of the spells, may be, and are, called up in seances by the mediums, and in so far treated as if they were ghosts or Sir Ghosts. A *sorosor* spell's familiars cannot be dealt with exclusively by a medium however. They are controlled effectively by the spell's owner alone, although a medium may hold a dialogue with them, as if they were ghosts. To the magician his familiars are his absolutely to control. To the medium they become almost personalities in their own right, although not nearly as much personalities as ghosts are. However the medium is content with dialogue, while the magician controls action.

We come now to another and a different form of black

[5] Cf. "Sorcerers of Dobu," pp. 133–149. This particular point is a good illustration of what is a very general difference.

magic, literally the *palit am mbwaro*, magic of pregnancy. This is the form of black magic that is in the most frequent operation in Manus. It is not regarded humourously, but it is not taken very seriously either as black magic goes. Excluding ills resulting from the sin of theft from palm trees, partly excluding the ills of child bearing mothers, and excluding the ills of unweaned infants, all ills are given spiritualistic diagnosis, not magical. The Manus very neatly allocate the provinces of spiritualism and magic, both systems being given and retained, each in its proper province; and black magic, in many parts of New Guinea a thoroughly strong disintegrative force, is circumscribed away from its commoner role in the area as the parent of too frequent murder, and constant treachery and lack of social cooperation. For deaths of unweaned infants do not bring about feud and vendetta between their parents and the sorcerers in Manus, even though black magic is held responsible. In a very real sense the black magic is held responsible, rather than the sorcerer. The conventions that bring this about are peculiar and will be discussed shortly. Meanwhile as the *sorosor* are responsible for illnesses that follow ascertained theft, so the *palit am mbwaro* are responsible for the illnesses of unweaned infants, and for some of the ills of pregnant women and of nursing mothers. While the ills of unweaned infants (or at least the first illness of every unweaned infant), are ascribed to *palit am mbwaro*, the ills of women in child birth are not nearly so exclusively attributed to *palit am mbwaro*. Any woman's ailment related to child bearing is so attributed at first, but if exorcism of the pregnancy magic does not produce a cure, the whole Sir Ghost and ghost cult comes into operation. This is the case only rarely in the ills of young infants. Such ills are regarded as the prime province and the exclusive province of *palit am mbwaro*.

Below I present in tabular form the causes of death, as related by the mothers of thirty-one cases of infant mortality. I had to go into past history for the facts here.

The cases in this table are all cases of infants that died young, unselected by any bias except that their mothers were free-spoken and garrulous.

TABLE OF INFANT DEATHS

Infant	Mother	Cause of Death
Kisapwi, Kandra (one other)	Ngakaru	Magic of Songan, the infants' mother's mother's brother, angry at his niece over her refusing him betel nut.
Posanau (as a baby)		The infant's father's Sir Ghost angry at obscenity by Ngakaru.
Four infants (died near birth)	Indalo	Magic of Korotan who had financed Indalo's marriage, but who got no proper return from Indalo's husband's kin for his outlay to them.
A miscarriage named Poliap	Ngamuke	Magic of husband's father, Malan, who was angry at not getting return of his outlay to his son's wife's kin.
Talimatun (very small)	Ngamuke	Killed by husband's Sir Ghost because the mother had been accused of adultery, she said scandalously.
Selan		Magic of first husband's father, because she had run away from her first husband and married another, the father of this infant.
Pondros (near birth)	Kampon	Magic of Korotan because Korotan did not exorcise his magic from the infant properly.
Neku (near birth)		Magic of Korotan, because he did not exorcise it in time. Korotan is financial backer of her co-wife, and handicapped by those who have to repay him having to repay Kampon's financial backers also.
Miscarriage	Ngaten	Magic of Kawe, the mother's grandfather, because as a child she had spoiled his fish trap. The same thing had killed an infant of hers by a previous husband. But after the miscarriage she confessed her sin, and her next child lived.
Popoli, Pondraken (both near birth)	Komatol	Magic of the infants' father's sister's husband, Talipoendrilei, over dissatisfaction with economic exchanges.

TABLE OF INFANT DEATHS—(*Continued*)

Infant	Mother	Cause of Death
X (still at breast)	Patali	The mother discovered her husband seducing another woman. He turned her out for discovering him, she pregnant at the time. When the child was born she kept it, she having remarried. Her former husband's Sir Ghost killed the child because her former husband, its father, should have had the child.
Two still-births, four infants (at breast)	Patulam	Magic of Talikapona, father of a man Patulam's husband killed with a spear.
Popiliu (by another husband)		Magic of Talipaule. Patulam demanded pay for a pig that she had given b and b given Talipalue. Talipalue angry at having to pay before he was ready to pay.
Two infants (by yet another husband)		Magic of Songan because his son had made advances (economic) towards securing her in marriage, but she did not marry him. Songan exorcised the next two infants and they lived.
Piwen (near birth)	Tchomoleo	Magic of unknown origin.
Four infants	Ngamean	Magic of Lapanke of Taui.

Of the thirty-one cases, nineteen could not be named by the mothers that bore them, so brief an impression had they made; and of the twelve named one was a miscarriage.

Of the thirty-one only three were said to have died from the ghosts, the remaining twenty-eight, including all miscarriages, still births, and near births, from magic.

Manus practice corroborates the magician's boast that his magic "afflicts the infants of all," and agrees with the fact that a new-born infant's exorcism by a magician (at odds with the family) when it first cries too much, or seems to, or is ailing, is so regular as to seem almost like a *rite de passage* of the first month of an infant's life. The accounts of infants' deaths agree very well with the practice of such exorcism and the magician's account of his magic as we shall see in the case of Korotan recorded in Chapter IV.

The following are the relationships of the infants' mothers to the various magicians blamed:

Magician	Relationship to Mother
Songan	Mother's brother.
Korotan	Financial backer.
Malan	Father-in-law.
Malan	Former father-in-law.
Korotan	Financial backer and titular father of her co-wife. Her co-wife was the first wife of Poiyo. Poiyo's getting a second wife interfered with the economic exchanges for the first wife; burdened Poiyo's kin with a double burden, and made them less able to pay back the financial backer of the first wife, *i.e.*, Korotan. So Korotan's magic killed the infants of the second wife.
Kawe	Grandfather.
Talipoendrilei	Husband's sister's husband.
Talipalue	None (quarrel over blood feud).
Talikapona	None (quarrel over economics through several intermediaries in linked chain of debt).
Songan	Would be but balked father-in-law, marriage contract broken.

The frequency in which there is relationship is noteworthy. Sorcery and relationship quarrels are closely linked.

It is perhaps peculiar that a form of magic called magic of pregnancy should be actually a magic that affects infants much more exclusively than the mothers. The point here is probably that the mothers, as adults, have opportunities to sin, and so become objects for the Sir Ghost cult to operate on. Adults are also better objects for ghostly malice, just as they might be better objects for sorcerer's malice. It is held, however, that sorcerers in Manus do not habitually use malice, but only just indignation. It is held that this sorcerer's indignation does not damage the adults against whom it is directed, but only the unweaned infants born to those adults or the child-bearing mother.

The Manus regard the death of infants with considerable equanimity, so that the ascription of the ills of infants in arms to black magic disposes of sorcery with the minimum of unpleasantness compatible with its retention. Over and above this, the diagnosis of magic on such occasions is a safety valve for the spiritualistic system, for the infantile sickness and death rate is so high that if on the death of every infant confession of immorality or commercial laxity were necessary the code would become impossible in its severity. The oracles would be forced to rely more on the living's neglect of economic validations of marriages, births, etc., on the spirit plane. As matters stand, the oracles prefer to hunt out more vital mortal sin. But if infants' ills were not disposed of by black magic, diagnosis would tend to lead away from sin hunting.

2. KINSHIP AND THE TANDRITANITANI CULT

Tandritanitani is not magic as magic is generally conceived, for it is a power invested in one relationship line for possible use upon another relationship line. To understand the way in which it functions in Manus it is necessary to discuss the relevant kinship material.

Descent in Manus is patrilineal, but adoption into the mother's gens is not infrequent. The house sites of members of the same gens are in theory adjoining, and in practice prevailingly so, but a man often moves his house out of his father's place for temporary or long stay in his mother's place, father's mother's place or wife's place. Whenever there has been a death in a house, the house is bodily removed elsewhere. Residence, patrilocal in theory, is even more shifting than descent.

Despite this general mobility, a Manus village is divided into permanent gentile territories. Each territory includes a geographically defined lagoon area, and as far as local topography permits, a small uninhabited island in each lagoon area. House sites are always on the sea area, never by any possibility on the island. The small, uninhabited islands are visited ceremonially, and the ghosts that inhabit them invoked on occasion. Some of them are not visited otherwise, except by women looking for straying pigs, or on some infrequent mission. Others are regular resorts, the rear of one as a men's latrine, another as a children's playground, with long lianas used as swings hanging from the trees above the sea. A small minority of the gentile territories have also within their borders a built-up platform of coral rubble taken from the reef, and more or less stabilised by a tree or two growing on the built-up rubble. As fast as the tides wash down the edges of the platform they are built up again. These platforms are flat, and are used for the ceremonials of exchanges of wealth when many persons are involved, and when the exchange is on a very great scale. The platforms are called *arakeu*.

The ghosts that inhabit the islands are used differently from the ghosts that live in the houses with the house dwellers. Ghosts of the islands are further back in ancestral lines; ghosts of the houses are those resulting from more recent deaths. Ghosts of the islands are not credited with independent powers, but are supposed to obey incantation absolutely, although only the incantations of those in a certain relationship to them. Ghosts of the houses are credited with extensive independent powers, and do not obey anyone. They eventually get thrown out of the houses when they can be replaced by new ghosts from new deaths. Ghosts of the islands subserve the interests of a matrilineal group. Ghosts of the houses serve the interests of a patrilineal group. The extended discussion of Manus ghost cult that will be given in this work will be an essay on a particularly intricate development of social organisation, as well as of religion.

The house sites immediately adjoining an *arakeu* are a part of the especial privileges of ranking families called *lapan* in distinction from lower-caste families called *lau*. The other privileges of *lapan* are of the same nature as the privilege of building close to the *arakeu*. They are of a formal nature purely. Actual power in the community is dependent on wealth. A wealthy *lau* who has advanced valuables to a poor *lapan* can fling public abuse at the *lapan* if due repayment is defaulted, and can do this with impunity.

Through the fear caused by a death, or by a number of deaths within a territory, the entire territory is sometimes abandoned, the gens moving *en bloc* to take up a new territory close to the same village, or to a different village altogether, or to found a new village of their own elsewhere. Sometimes a gens splits, part moving, part remaining. Sometimes again an entire village of several gentes may move all together. A solitary man in moving his house does not take up a new site anywhere in the territory of the gens into which he moves. He takes up an ancestral site or an ancestral site of his wife's.

Patrilocal marriage prevails. Any other arrangement is due to a panic at the patrilocal site because it is haunted, or else to circumstances such as the husband being *lau* and his wife *lapan*, so that the wife's house site is the more honourable. First marriages are arranged for young couples by contracts between their respective parents or economic guardians. Infant betrothal is common, but marriage is delayed till several years past puberty. Divorce and remarriage are common within a greatly prevailing monogamous pattern. Only two or three men in every fifty sustain polygamous marriage, and then with not more than two wives. Usually a polygamous marriage is not sustained long, even in these special cases.

The ideal pattern of first marriage, always arranged by contract between the elders concerned, is definite, and based on kinship. Later marriages, following the break-up of the first marriage (which is more usual than its continued stability, although stability is not infrequent) are based on the free choice of the parties directly concerned, a choice only limited by the idea of what constitutes incest, and very largely by the local concept of the primary purpose of marriage—that is, for prospective economic advancement.

The relationships between cross-cousins are essential to an understanding of the arranged marriages. The children of a set of brothers, as distinguished from the children of a set of sisters, are called *lom-kamal.* The latter are called *lom-pein.* A child of a brother is *lom-kamal* to a child of a sister, a child of a sister is *lom-pein* to a child of a brother. We shall term *lom-kamal* child-of-brother in translation, and *lom-pein* child-of-sister.[6]

Children-of-brother is a close group, knit together by patrilineal inheritance of adjoining house sites, and by a common inheritance of all the privileges and functions of a common gens. The group own the special type of fishing apparatus that is the especial privilege of their gens, they practice the special taboo on a species of fish or other food that is a mark of their gens. It is most important to note, however, that they own a separate territory within the one village. Children-of-sister is a completely scattered group, since their mothers have married in any number of divergent directions, and they are of different gentes and different villages. Their inheritances and their territories are completely apart.

Children-of-sister, in relation to children-of-brother, are those who are disinherited from the unilateral descent group that is in power in Manus, the patrilineal descent group. Although children-of-sister are cut off from the gens inheritance, the inheritance of property, which keeps within the gens, and the inheritance of solidarity based on neighbouring residence, all of which children-of-brother have, they are nevertheless endowed, by virtue of relationship, with the exercise of a special magico-religious cult which gives them a certain kind of superior power, magically warranted, over children-of-brother. The exercise of this cult privilege is called *tandritanitani.*

One form of the *tandritanitani* power is the cursing of children-of-brother by the especial magical power of children-

[6] We shall consider the phrase as one word, as it is in intent, in making the possessive form child-of-brother's, rather than child's-of-brother, and similarly for the correlative term; but for the plural form we shall use children-of-brother, and children-of-sister.

of-sister. Children-of-sister, male or female, can curse the wives of children-of-brother with barrenness, still-births, and premature deaths of infants born to them. This curse is very rarely used in point of fact. It is used by the disinherited against the fertility of the gens from which they are disinherited. I have record of several instances of the above use of the curse and no record of any other form in concrete case.

Also termed *tandritanitani* is the power of female children-of-sister to endow female children-of-brother with fertility by magic, magically to control the sex of infants born to female children-of-brother and to space out births for them to prevent over-great fertility. This blessing power is used in frequent ceremonials. It should be clearly distinguished from the cursing power of *tandritanitani*. What is common to the two forms is a magical power over children-of-brother exercised by children-of-sister. The term *tandritanitani* probably refers to "the making come on top of" that is a ceremonial feature in all the incantations in both forms. "Making come on top of" means making a ghostly influence possess, or exert influence on a person. The blessing power is not one belonging specially to cross cousins as such, but is a prerogative of an unbroken female descent line of which the female children-of-sister represent one generation. The *tandritanitani* blessing is a part of the ritual of life crises. This ritual is compact and clear in form. It consists essentially in segregation, with ritual precaution against special dangers, before or after the life crisis, followed by ceremonial release from segregation with invocation of the ghosts.

The actual incantation and the release from segregation are effected always by a person's father's mother, father's sister, father's sister's daughter and father's sister's daughter's daughter, or by as many of these women as are available. This uterine descent line is composed of members who are all called *patieyen*, regardless of generation, by the person whom they release from segregation after life crises, such as ear-piercing, first menstruation, before marriage, after first child bearing, after the death of a husband in the case of a woman, and after ear-piercing in the case of a man.

Each generation in the one male line has a different set of *patieyen*, descending from the woman married into the male line two generations above. The father's set of *patieyen* are called by the children *pin papu*, or "father women." The *pin papu*, women descending in the uterine line from the woman married into the male line three generations above, watch over a person's corpse, wash the decaying flesh from the bones and are the principal mourners, even today, when burial is practiced by Government decree.

The line of *patieyen*, who release a person from periods of segregation, always do so by calling the names of the male ghosts of the person's male line for several generations ascendant, and then the names of the female ghosts of their own uterine line for several generations ascendant, in the manner we have discussed. These powers of the *patieyen* are extended in some degree to the father's sister's son. He, instead of the line of *patieyen*, welcomes his mother's brother's son when the latter secures his first homicide in war. In the blessing *Tandritanitani*, the ghosts are invoked into food which is eaten by the person being released from segregation, or with which he or she is slapped upon the back by the senior *patieyen* of the line of descent. The ghosts are invoked to bestow working, or trading, or fighting, or child-bearing prowess as the case may be.

The religious forms connected with life crises are thus semi-magical in their nature. The ghosts are invoked into more or less automatically bestowing benefits and release from danger—danger of ear lobes breaking at ear piercing, danger of death at child-bearing and at becoming a widow, *i.e.*, fear of the deceased's ghost taking the widow. This automatism in the process is extended into downright magic in attempts to space out child-bearing, to determine sex of infants and to curse with barrenness. Of the curse it is said, "The words go on the air and do their work." The ethnologist said: "But one of the male ghosts so invoked is the Sir Ghost of the person to be injured." "In this connection, no!"

The more open parts of the invocations are admonitory—*e.g.*,

"Let his mouth not err
his speech be straight and true,
I wish to empower him for war,
but Government has come,
War is over.
I do now empower him for trade."

The above is a part of an invocation spoken by the father's father over a boy, and was followed by the senior *patieyen* in similar style. Only in blessing a boy for war, or releasing a male from mourning, does the male line take part and invoke its own ancestry in the ghosts. Otherwise the senior *patieyen* invokes both the ghosts of the male line of the person charmed, and the ghosts of the female line, or *patandrusun* of the *patieyen* themselves.[7]

The economic side of the validation of life crises by exchanges of wealth is a comparatively detached study. Neither the individual in whose name the exchange is made, nor the group of *patieyen* are the principals in the economics. The ritual segregation lasts a fixed number of days by traditional precedent. The ritual release from segregation with its due date of performance acts as the trigger event for starting the economic exchange. It is this tradition of a fixed number of days in segregation that a man offends against when he is late or overdue with his accumulation of wealth for an exchange, so causing perhaps a Sir Ghostly visitation of illness within his house according to the oracles.

Thus the blessing *tandritanitani* differs from the cursing *tandritanitani* in that it is not, like the cursing, specially confined to the relations between cross-cousins. It is not directed, like the cursing, towards the gens; that is, the female descent line does not bless the gens with fertility in blessing a woman of the gens. For the woman of the gens must marry out of it. A wife of a man of a gens is not blessed by those who have the power of cursing her. She is blessed by her own father's mother, father's sister and father's sister's daughter, this last being her female child-of-sister, whereas

[7] Dr. Mead has published two of these *Tandritanitani* invocations in Chapters X and XI of "Growing up in New Guinea."

she may be cursed by her husband's male or female child-of-sister.

There is no belief in non-supernaturally produced deformities, still-births or premature deaths of infants. All such disasters are supernaturally caused. There is no belief in non-supernaturally produced barrenness in a woman proved to be capable of child-bearing and not yet old. The Manus understand that some women and that some men are sterile, despite magic. They will point out clearly that a man has produced no child out of four or five women, and that these women have all produced children by earlier or later marriages, or by both; and they will point out a similar condition in a woman. They take a certain proportion of cases of irremediable sterility as given. These cases, if they are women, have been blessed with the magic of fertility by the female descent line that includes female child-of-sister, and nothing has come of it. The Manus are quite ready to point out such exception to the power of the magic, for most of these cases in a village have been blessed, and not cursed. An unprecedented onset of barrenness in a woman of child-bearing age is in another category.

An onset of barrenness, still-births, miscarriages, and premature deaths of infants in a woman married into a gens may be attributed to the curse of a male or of a female child-of-sister of the gens. In the cases of male use of the curse that I know, the curse was directed by male child-of-sister against one household of the gens only, but, in the cases of female use of the curse, the curse was directed by a female child-of-sister against all the households of the gens. However, disaster of the order covered by the curse is only attributed to the magic of child-of-sister, and to the magic of a specific child-of-sister, when it is definitely known that the curse has been pronounced and not removed by the person who laid it on. There is never a general suspicion. When the only given fact is a trouble in child-bearing, or a premature death of an infant, or an infant in severe illness, there is no suspicion of a child-of-sister's having used the curse in secret. A child-of-sister acts with complete publicity, or not at all. This is an absolute convention, and is relied upon completely. In cases when, as usually happens, there is child-bearing or infant trouble and no precedent curse from a child-of-sister, the influence of the *palit am mbwaro*, pregnancy black magic, described above, is suspected. The magic power of *tandritanitani* is acquired merely by birth or by adoption from infancy into a certain relationship, and everyone possesses it in relation to someone else. The truer magic of the magician is usually his by purchase, but if by inheritance, by no especial relationship path.

We may now further consider the matter of the supernatural production of pregnancy. Manus men do not know that unmarried girls past puberty menstruate monthly. Everyone knows that there is one menstruation at adolescence and this first menstruation is an occasion of ceremony. The ceremony, if the girl is betrothed, is a part of the complex of marriage ceremonies. First menstruation is believed to be due to the hymen breaking. Dr. Mead informs me that even the women do not know enough of their own bodies to discover otherwise. As it is understood, first menstruation is believed to come as a matter of course, that is, naturally. The men think that a girl's first sexual intercourse produces her next menstruation. They conclude that sexual intercourse causes menstruation. They understand a statement that unmarried girls in other places than Manus menstruate monthly between first menstruation and marriage as evidence that Manus unmarried girls are the only chaste girls in existence. They are ready enough to believe it—but only on those terms. When one urges upon them that Manus girls menstruate also they take the statement as an insult upon the chastity of their girls. There is no possible common meeting ground for argument, as most Manus girls do remain chaste for most of the time between first menstruation and marriage, several years later. Dr. Mead informs me that the women do not know the men's misconception. The secret is not consciously kept as a sex barrier. The sex barrier exists in the prevailing puritanical conventions and produces a correlate that is, so to speak, below cultural consciousness.

The Manus associate pregnancy correctly with cessation of menstruation. The Manus men believe that sexual intercourse produces menstruation, first menstruation only being excepted. The foetus is the result of a fusion of semen and blood. But this fusion results from the *tandritanitani* of female child-of-sister, or, more exactly, of the female descent line of female child-of-sister upon female child-of-brother. Otherwise, by male belief, intercourse between the latter and her husband produces menstruation, not cessation of menstruation.

The misconception among the men, as opposed to the women, may play some part in the men's endorsement of the *tandritanitani* usages, which are used by the matrilineal line upon the patrilineal line. But this is an imponderable influence. The cult could dispense with the men's ignorance, perhaps, as the women believe in it without benefit of an equivalent ignorance.

We have been considering cross-cousins, children-of-sister in relation to children-of-brother as a preliminary to discussing the form of arranged marriage in Manus (and in most of the Admiralty Island societies of the islands other than the Great Admiralty Island). A child-of-sister, male or female, who has a son, has the right to demand of a male child-of-brother, who has a daughter, that daughter in marriage to his or to her son. This is the obligatory form of first marriage.

There is a certain logical fitness here, and the Manus realise it fully. A child-of-sister approaches a male child-of-brother, seeking contract of marriage between his or her son and the latter's daughter. The household of this male child-of-brother, he or she being child-of-sister, can curse with barrenness and deaths of infants, in case ill-will arises. At the same time a child-of-sister is vitally interested in the fertility of the household of a male child-of-brother, in the interests of the marriage of his or her son to a daughter of that household. The marriage "road," as the Manus term it, is the road of the *tandritanitani* curse also, as opposed to that of the *tandritanitani* blessing. We may summarise the facts already given, and provide a basis for the understanding of further facts, in the following diagram. Only one marriage is represented in the diagram, descent lines being represented and spouses of persons in such lines omitted.

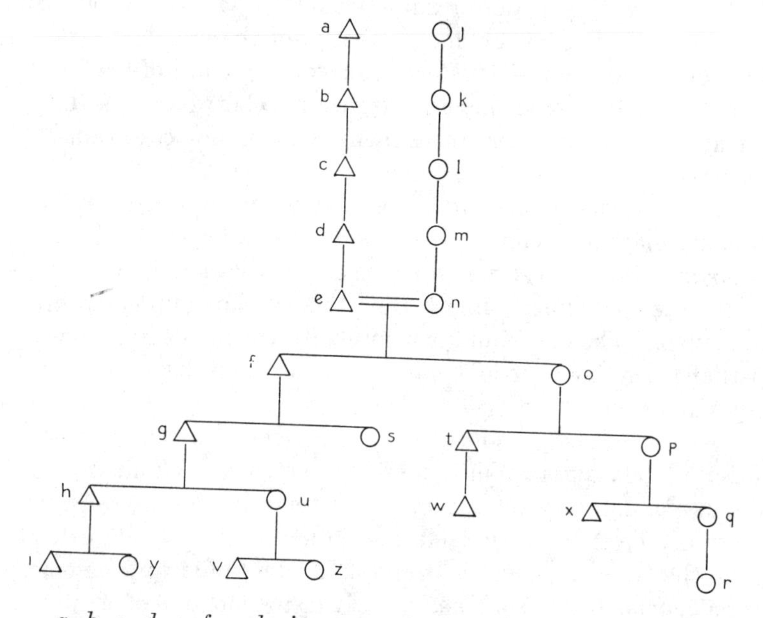

a, *b*, *c*, *d*, *e*, *f*, *g*, *h*, *i* represents an unbroken male descent line; *j*, *k*, *l*, *m*, *n*, *o*, *p*, *q*, *r*, an unbroken female descent line. Let us assume that *e* and his wife, *n*, are still living, with the four generations represented below them; *g* and *s* are children-of-brother, *t* and *p* are children-of-sister.

1. *t* and *p* have the power of exercising the *tandritanitani* curse upon *g*'s wife;

t or *p* can demand *u* from *g* in marriage-contract to *w* or to *x*.

2. *n*, *o*, *p*, *q*, *r* are the group that gather to exercise the *tandritanitani* blessing upon *s*, the two living senior women of the line performing the incantation; this group of women not only bless *s* with fertility, control the sex of her offspring and space out births, but when *s* and *g* were young and unmarried they gave them *tandritanitani* blessings for other

objects—mainly to relieve them from the believed supernatural dangers of crisis periods, or *rites de passage*.

3. In all *tandritanitani*, cursing form or blessing form, the cursers or blessers call upon the ghosts *d*, *c*, *b*, *a* and separately upon the ghosts *m*, *l*, *k*, *j*. These ghosts are the ghosts of the islands, previously mentioned. In due time the women *n*, *o*, *p*, *q*, *r* join the ghosts *m*, *l*, *k*, *j* to displace them in similar invocation in the mouths of the descendants of the line; similarly the men *e*, *f*, *g*, *h*, *i* will join *d*, *c*, *b*, *a*. Meanwhile *n* and *e* being still alive, the ghosts of the islands *d*, *c*, *b*, *a* and *m*, *l*, *k*, *j* are conceived as absolutely under control of the female line to use upon *g* and *s*, children-of-brother to *t* and *p*, in blessing, and absolutely under control of *t* and *p* to use upon *g*'s household in curse. As for *g*, he and his sister *s* are believed to have no reciprocal power and no power even with the ghosts of *g*'s own male line to avoid or palliate a curse, or to produce a blessing. The ghosts are retained absolutely by the female line, and, in one use, by *t*, a son of the female line.

4. All *tandritanitani*, as done within the limits of the persons figured in the diagram, is done over *g* and over *s*. The children of *g* and *s* have *tandritanitani* done over them in blessing, each by his or her own father's mother and the female descent line proceeding from her. But in cursing, *v* or *z* can curse the children of *h*, and so on in each generation. In such cursing *v* and *z* would use against *i* and *y* a set of ghosts that are not figured in the diagram. Again *x* and *q* can curse the household of *w*. In such cursing the male set of ghosts used would ascend from *o*'s husband (unfigured) but the female set of ghosts used is figured, *o*, *n*, *m*, *l*, *k*, *j*, and, if *p* is dead, then *p* preceding *o*. This dual set of ghosts is used upon one generation only, to bless or to curse that generation, by the performers of *tandritanitani*.

5. The male line of descent of the diagram represents a family line in a gens. The female line of descent represents a matrilineal line. Each female line of descent practices a taboo on eating or touching some particular object. This taboo is called the *patandrusun*. Just as a woman of a gens

observes a gentile taboo, so a man of a *patandrusun*-observing line observes a *patandrusun* taboo. So when *t* has *tandritanitani* power in cursing *g*'s household he has it as a man of the *patandrusun*. We may justly style *t* as a man of the female line, and *s* as a woman of the male line, in exactly the same sense as *t* might be a man of a matrilineal clan, and as *s* actually is a woman of a patrilineal gens.

The men who share in the supernatural power of the female descent group are the men who, in a matrilineal society, would belong to the matrilineal clan. They are the sons of the women of the line. Men cannot bequeath the power as women do. Of the powers we have discussed, men's power is confined to cursing and to demanding a wife for a man of their line from males of the male line. It is not as wide a power as the women wield. It will now be clearly envisaged how the *tandritanitani* cult is the formal expression of women's power in a patrilineal society. Sons cannot be had without women, not only in natural function, but in supernatural function also. And a whole regiment of women are necessary for the performance of the supernatural function.

Between a man and the entire female descent line of women proceeding from his father's mother there is a reciprocal joking relationship. In all normal social intercourse a man jests a little with the old woman, his father's mother. With his father's sister and with his father's sister's daughter (this latter being his female child-of-sister who can curse his household) he behaves uproariously. He twits his father's sister on her conjugal relations, he threatens to strip her daughter naked in her presence, he handles the breasts and even on occasion, if these persons are not conspicuously older than he, may mock-handle the pubes of the father's sister and of the father's sister's daughter. He tells lies to these women, whatever their age relatively to his age, and he plays practical jokes upon them. He always makes obscene references when he meets them, if there is no quarrel at the moment between him and them.

Between the man's sister and the same group of women there is no such joking relationship. It is an across-sex relationship for women. I heard of one case of obscene joking between a female child-of-brother and a female child-of-sister. I never saw a like case, and I saw the joking relationship in full swing in the other relationship every day.

Male child-of-brother and male child-of-sister joke reciprocally and almost continuously whenever they meet socially, even at internment of corpses, provided the corpse is not from one of their own families. Only tragic happenings disturb their joking attitudes.

Whenever the curse has been used upon male child-of-brother and his wife by female or male child-of-sister, the joking relationship ends forever. Its absence in such cases is very conspicuous, and the more so that such event is rare.

Man and Wife

We may now go a little deeper into a point of social theory In Manus we have patrilineal lines entrenched in the inheritance of material goods and of neighbourhood solidarity, with their rights protected also by a cult of the ghosts of the houses of which we have given no details as yet. A matrilineal line is entrenched in the inheritance of a special power over the collateral patrilineal line, a power which is secured by these women's exclusive control of the ghosts of the islands. The interests of the matrilineal line and of the patrilineal line are united by one of the two forms of marriage. In one form a man marries his mother's mother's brother's son's daughter. By the other form a man marries his father's mother's brother's son's daughter. This is formally not a union between the lines, but it is a marriage secured in contract between members of the lines. The privileged members of the lines spend a great deal of their time together in jesting and in hilarity. Here we have an almost ideal presentation of social balances. But a balance, such as this between patriliny and matriliny in Manus, does not necessarily balance all the relations between the sexes, including the marriage relations.

The first point to be noted of the relationship between the male line and the female line in connection with marriage is that one line uses its relationship to the other to promote a marriage, but the actual parties to the marriage are outside this kinship category. The son of a male child-of-sister may marry the daughter of a male child-of-brother. The former party to the marriage is neither in the female nor in the male line, although the latter is in the male line, as a daughter of a man of the male line. The son of a female child-of-sister may marry the daughter of a male child-of-brother. Here the marrying parties are in the respective lines, but in a special manner. It will have been noted that no special functions between male child-of-sister and female child-of-brother have been discussed. There are none of importance. Cursing and the making of marriage "road" or contract is done by male and female child-of-sister upon male child-of-brother, blessing is done by the female line upon women of the male line. A male child-of-sister has little contact with a female child-of-brother. He does not bless her, curse her, or jest with her. As between cross-cousins, there is an absence of special function between a male out of a female in relation to a female out of a male.

The point to be noted is that when a son of a female child-of-sister marries a daughter of a male child-of-brother these persons, although in female line and in male line respectively, are in a relation to each other that would produce an absence of the special functions between the lines, were they in the previous generation. They are in the category of relationship between a male out of a female and a female out of a male.

Thus a married couple are never in the same relation to each other as their respective parents on one side are to each other. Here function agrees with the logic of relationship. A man is never allowed to play with his wife's breasts. That privilege is exclusively held by his wife's relatives who are male children-of-sister to her, *i.e.*, her father's sister's sons. Thus play and joking are regimented strictly into one relationship, at least in their pronounced form, and the relationship between man and wife is marked by an equally conspicuous disrespect, even by semi-avoidance. This disrespect is of an entirely serious and disagreeable nature.

The disrespect aspect of the relationship between man and wife is one reinforced by shame. Obscenity between cross-cousins who are privileged by relationship to joke obscenely is not felt as being very shameful, nor is it complicated by any avoidances. Occasionally, however, just this culturally enjoined obscenity is held to be the cause of a ghost-sent sickness. A reproachful social conscience sometimes recoils on what the society allows—but not sufficiently strongly to check the custom appreciably. Obscenity between cross-cousins is all on the surface moreover, words and gestures merely. Sexual intercourse is felt to be a more damning obscenity. Man and wife are in a relationship that can only be referred to openly by the joking relatives, who specialise in obscene reference. The intimate relationship in marriage is not accorded any particular dignity. A person is trained in infancy to be deeply ashamed of the functions of evacuation, and at puberty to be equally ashamed of an added function of evacuation.

An adolescent boy in a canoe passing through the village of his betrothed must be completely covered over. He may not see his betrothed or she him till the marriage day, and then only for a brief instant. He goes to her secretly in the dark of the marriage night, and rarely thereafter feels quite at ease in looking at her by daylight. A married pair do not eat together until after two or three children have been born to them. The detailed account of the religion that will be given will show clearly the great social pressure that is brought to bear to make sex relations difficult.

In practice a man is at ease with his cross-cousins, with his brothers and sisters, and with his father and mother. He cleaves to his kin, and, when he gives his kin his fishing-catch as well as much of his time, his wife often makes angry charges of incest against him. Wifely charges of incest, wifely running away from the husband to the brother, husbandly beating of the wife, are as much functions of the man-wife relationship as obscene joking of a humourous order is between male child-of-brother and the opposed female descent line, including male child-of-sister, or the blessing by the female descent line upon male and female of the collateral male descent line, or the contracting of their children's marriages by male or female child-of-sister with male child-of-brother. Unseemly relationships between man and wife are the rule, whereas the one possible unseemly act between male and female child-of-sister and male child-of-brother, the curse, is hardly ever used by the Manus. Some men keep implements for wife-beating in the house rafters, others rely on occasional weapons. This is not deprecated, nor is the wife's running away frequently to her brother's household, an inviolable sanctuary which the husband cannot enter in such case. Wifely charges of incest against the husband are deprecated, but none the less very frequently used.

The reason for deprecating a wifely charge of incest is that it is an onslaught against a husband's right to cleave first and foremost to his kin, and that the insults are couched in terms that are shocking to the prevailing puritanism. On the other hand, the prevailing disrespect and avoidance between man and wife agree well with the same puritanism, and accord with the feeling that a sexual relationship is essentially indelicate, and no foundation for respect.

The Promoting of Marriages

We might be done with the form of Manus marriage now, if the Manus were as fundamentalist as the folk of some primitive societies. We might leave the point secure in knowing that a lad is married off to his mother's mother's brother's son's daughter. Indeed among the several societies of the Admiralty Islands that insist on this form of obligatory marriage I found one, that of the island of Pak, where the genealogy of one family showed three such marriages. I had no time in Pak to take more genealogies, but a chance sample showed the obligatory form of marriage actually realised. No Manus genealogy of one family would show the same feature, since the Manus cling to the ideal form but interpret it with elasticity, so that the actual range within which marriage may take place is extended.

In Manus the initiator of a marriage contract usually

claims more than one mother. The more mothers he has, then the more gentes he has to which he is a child-of-sister, that is, son of a woman of the gentes concerned. In consequence he has the more gentes which, in theory, he can curse with *tandritanitani*, and of which, in practice, he can demand a daughter of a child-of-brother in marriage for his son. Actually he does not act so towards an entire gens, as if the gens were a blanket classification. He may speak often of being child-of-sister to a gens, but the blanket classification is a manner of speech only. In practice he can only exercise his special power and rights over a household, the patrilineal household from which his mother departed to bear him, in her marriage into the household of another gens, his gens. The claim to more than one mother must be based on early adoption, adoption before puberty. A man has then a mother by blood, and a mother by adoption. So he has right of demand over children-of-brother in two gentes, to one of which he is child-of-sister by blood, to another, child-of-sister by early adoption. Such early adoption is regarded as giving as valid a relationship status as blood, and a use of both of these forms of status at once is fully allowed.

The very great prevalence of early adoption in Manus makes the use of a dual claim of kinship very common. Deaths and divorces make for many adoptions. Taking the proportion of children adopted to the proportion of children not adopted in a Manus village, it comes out at approximately a quarter of the children below puberty adopted, three quarters not adopted. This includes adoption following death of a parent, divorce between parents, and adoption not due to a broken marriage. But if the proportion of children adopted to children not adopted is taken among a group of children who are all at the age of puberty, or close to it, three quarters have been adopted, one quarter not. Death and divorce have had time to operate on the marriages that produced these children. Adoption after puberty is not held to be such adoption as gives a full relationship claim, and so may be discounted for the point in hand. Approximately three quarters of a Manus population can claim a dual set of relatives, and do claim such. A majority of this three quarters, rather than a minority, can claim more than one adoption before puberty, and so claim more than a dual set of children-of-brother.

It must not be supposed, however, that a man with two mothers, to take a conservative estimate, can only claim that he is child-of-sister to the households of two different children-of-brother, of two different gentes. Each woman whom he claims as mother, in her own time, was as likely to have been adopted as he. So a mother, by blood or adoption, usually has brothers by blood as well as brothers by adoption, and these brothers in turn usually have children by adoption, as well as children by blood. The mothers and the mothers' brothers may be dead, but the child-of-sister can claim his mothers' brothers' male children as children-of-brother, whether they be his adoptive mother's adoptive brother's adoptive sons, or his adoptive mother's blood brother's adoptive sons, or his adoptive mother's adoptive brother's blood sons, and similarly an equal set proceeding in the same way from his blood mother. A man is child-of-sister to his mother's brother's sons, or mother's brothers' sons rather, in the extended range that is made possible by the insertion of "blood" or "adoptive" between son and mother, between mother and brothers, and between brothers and sons.

The mere fact of the dual allowance of blood ties and adoptive ties in Manus makes possible a wide range within which two households may make a marriage-contract between the son of the child-of-sister household and the daughter of the child-of-brother household. It must also be remembered that either the father or the mother of the son for whom a wife is to be found may act as child-of-sister, so doubling the above range, which we have considered as one man's only.

The Manus enjoy the comparative liberty this wide range affords in the making of marriage-contract. They enjoy choice. A child-of-sister seeking a contract, and being granted it, commits himself to a long series of exchanges of economic valuables with child-of-brother, to validate first the betrothal, and later the marriage of his or her son to the

PLATE III

A FAMILY ATTENDING A FEAST

latter's daughter. Child-of-sister has to make initial advances on credit, trusting to his reimbursement much later. The economic position of Manus households varies greatly. Consequently the advance of valuables on credit is more safely made to some households than to others. Hence the choice afforded by an extended range of kinship is enjoyed. The Manus are very keen commercialists. In matters of business it is safe to say that they hardly ever act foolishly. It is also safe to say that the manifest care for their economic interest which they display in making choice among the possibilities of a marriage contract has much to do with their use of a wide range of choice. They make the legal or customary form as elastic as possible.

The relationship between a child-of-sister and a child-of-brother in regard to the making of a marriage contract, the Manus term in their own language a "road." There are many roads radiating out from any one child-of-sister that find a child-of-brother at their end, as we have seen. To most of these roads a Manus man or woman pays little or no attention except for the making of a marriage-contract. That is, a person has one set or two sets of relatives on either side whom he or she is accustomed to meet often, and, as cross-cousins, to jest with and accompany often. But an economic choice may go far afield. Hence the making of a marriage contract is termed "making a road." A child-of-sister may make a road in the same sense as we may figuratively use the term "blazing a trail," in this case through a relationship tangle. The term in the Manus usage has still further implication. It not only indicates a person's possibly going somewhat far afield to make an economic choice conform to a legal or customary form. It also means that one person may act for another. One person may "make a road" for another person as a favour as frequently as marriages may be arranged in one's own right. Or a child may be used to "make a road" if the child is adopted, and has a blood kinship that affords a desired road, without the child understanding the matter at all. One brother who has a different adoptive set of kin will "make a road" for another. Two persons with any relationship in which one is ready to help the other may act similarly.

The actual freedom in marriage contracts is not formalised in Manus theory. According to all Manus statement, as according also to all statement of the members of the neighbouring and different cultures of Lou, Baluan and Pak islands, the obligatory first marriage is the marriage of a lad to his father's or to his mother's mother's brother's son's daughter. In discussing the relationship between a child-of-sister and a male child-of-brother the Manus always reiterate "the son of child-of-sister will marry the daughter of child-of-brother" or usually more concretely, "X is child-of-sister, Y is male child-of-brother, so the son of X will marry the daughter of Y." It is a form of speech used to define a relationship, and a definite and a close relationship, not one extended through a "road" largely of adoptive relationship or through the wider extension of one person "making a road" for another.

The ideal form of the obligatory marriage is preserved in speech. The "making of a road" remains a kinship function, although with extensions of kinship flowing from adoption. In practice, the marriage in a number of cases is between the children of the persons who "make the road," but in an approximately equal number it is not. The ideal form of obligatory marriage is in practice dissociated from a sanction, which, however, in theory remains a sanction. The Manus say, for instance: "X is a poor man; he is child-of-sister to Y who is rich; so X can demand Y's daughter in marriage for his son, and if he is refused, curse Y's household." Such use of the curse remains a theory. Rich men prefer to make alliances with rich men, and poor men respect that freedom. An alliance means economic exchange in which the pride of one house must be met with the pride of the other. Economic equality, approximately, is necessary for such exchange. Society is stratified in terms of economic status, and the democratic implications of adherence to an ideal form of marriage irrespective of the wealth of the households so connected by kinship, are set aside in the promotion of marriage-contracts.

3. MAGIC AND SORCERY

We may now consider the relationship of the *tandritanitani* curses and blessings to the functioning of the religious system and to the other kind of magic in Manus. The sons of the women of the empowered descent line do not use this power as a regular kinship function, as their mothers do.[8] But they, as well as their mothers, can use it in anger.[9] In this case the charm is directed, not towards making the wives of the men of the other line temporarily childless, but towards making the children born to them deformed, or so sickly that they all die. It is also directed towards making the economic affairs of the household it is aimed at come to grief. This charm "goes on the wind" to do its work. The charmer drinks salt water, and spits it out while charming. He also pounds one stone on top of another. The charmer can exorcise this charm at will.

This magic uses the family ghosts in an entirely different manner from that of the Sir Ghost and malicious ghost system. They do not rule, but are ruled, for a special purpose and as a special kinship function. The angry use of this function is directed towards the killing off of infants. It is the only true Manus tradition that approximates to black magic. When we find black magic imported from other cultures into Manus we find the belief that it acts in the same manner—killing off infants. How this use of black magic functions well in relieving a load from the spiritualistic system we have seen. But a possible inspiration of it is assimilation to the only local and purely Manus pattern of black magic, the *tandritanitani*. Or, if (as is the case actually, I was informed) the *tandritanitani* exists also in the cultures where the magic came from, a common use is found for the two different patterns, one a relationship function employing the family ghosts, the other free magic employing familiars and herbs, and used by any sorcerer who owns a *palit am mbwaro*.

[8] Women, spiritually disenfranchised in the Sir Ghost cult, are spiritually enfranchised in the *tandritanitani* cult.

[9] The mothers never do use the power in anger. "The men, as well as their sisters" is a phrasing better adapted to facts of usage, although not to the facts of theory, according to which the entire female descent line possess the power of the curse.

It may be because of an assimilation to the *tandritanitani* that the pregnancy magic (*palit am mbwaro*) is specialised to damaging infants, so much more than child-bearing mothers, although it damages child-bearing mothers themselves also. However that may be I do not insist on the point of assimilation. We must take the fact that the *tandritanitani* and the pregnancy magic have a common field of operation in the ills and deaths of infants as given. The point I wish to make strongly is that if the sorcerer's use of the pregnancy magic did not account for the ills and the deaths of infants, for the most part, this infant toll would probably be unloaded onto one of the two other Manus cults, the Sir Ghost and ghost cult, or onto the *tandritanitani* cult.

We have examined how this probably would affect the Sir Ghost and ghost cult. If the toll were laid upon the *tandritanitani* cult, the female line who exercise that cult would be credited with doing very considerable damage amongst the collateral male line, damage now attributed to various sorcerers. There is some evidence that this situation, hypothetical for Manus, is not hypothetical for Western Samoa, where there is also a *tandritanitani* custom closely related to the Manus form, but as far as we know without the benefit of any cultural side-switch like the sorcerers of the pregnancy magic, who in Manus take away most of what might else be a cause of bad feeling between two relationship lines.[10] We do not know enough, however, about Western Samoa to be certain.

Clearly there must be some convention in Manus to decide exactly which ills of infants are caused by *palit am mbwaro*, and which by *tandritanitani*. In Western Samoa given the infants' ills, the use of the *tandritanitani* by the collateral female line seems to have been assumed without any factual evidence that the *tandritanitani* curse was used by them, other than the fact of the ills in point. In Manus given the ill, a sorcerer's *palit am mbwaro* is assumed. Only if there is factual evidence that the *tandritanitani* curse was employed precedently is the *palit am mbwaro* not assumed. Further

[10] Margaret Mead, "Social Organisation of Manua," Bernice P. Bishop Museum; *Bulletin* 76, pp. 139 et seq., especially p. 143.

the use of the *tandritanitani* curse is always in the open. It is not a curse ever done with concealment.

The curse from pregnancy magic, on the contrary, is never known exactly from a sorcerer's open curse. It comes from an unknown quarter, in theory. Divination is used to determine the identity of the responsible sorcerer. Actually the divination selects a pregnancy magic owner who is generally known to have had a quarrel with the household, or with one member of the household, or with one of the kin of one member of the household in which the infant or the child-bearing mother is ill. The sorcerer comes, exorcises his magic and takes his fee. The procedure is usually on a formal, but not on a greatly unfriendly footing. I saw it often, and there were never any bad manners displayed. There was not even any show of rancour when the magician held responsible for a former infant's death or infants' deaths was summoned to exorcise illness from another infant later come into the same household.

This seemed curious to me after my experience in Dobu, where the parties, the kin of the sick and the divined sorcerer and his kin often come to logger heads and "want to cut one another's throats" as it was summed up to me once. Nevertheless even in Dobu the exorcism is the customary behaviour.

In this connection I would point out one simple fact of a kind often overlooked. We actually have our own forms of sorcery in our own society, not usually sorcery to produce illness and death as generally as sorcery to produce social downfall, if possible, which is a type of sorcery that is often practicable in achieving its ends, at least in part. It consists in a venting of personal feeling in terms that are disguised from their origin, and that so do most damage. Our only check on such sorcery is the law of libel, which can often be circumvented, and which is not nearly as stringent in some civilized countries as it is in England, for example.

Where in primitive Oceania most societies have their cultural forms by which the society steps in and puts an end to it, we in our civilization have no form, when, as often occurs, sorcery can evade the libel laws; and very frequently we can put no end to it. This is a point that should be remembered when we set out to "improve" so-called primitive societies. Primitive sorcery is not always conspicuously more socially dangerous than our own forms, and often less dangerous. I should hesitate to commend Dobuan sorcery above our own as less dangerous, but I do unhesitatingly commend the Manus form as no more dangerous than our own, and superior in that social forms for its constant alleviation exist and work well.

In Manus no one so much as imagines the sorcerer doing underhand work. No one pictures the sorcerer's sitting down apart and conjuring up spells in secret. The idea is simply not known. In fact in Manus no one suppresses any cause of quarrel, as far as one can determine. There is a quarrel nearly every afternoon in some quarter in the village. The Manus are accustomed to fighting out their quarrels in public, but they fight and are done with it—unless the *casus belli* continues. If that happens they quarrel until they give it up. But if a *casus belli* remains open between a magician who owns a *palit am mbwaro* and another person, then the magician performs exorcisms and collects fees for them in the event of child-bearing ills in mothers or troubles of infants, when such troubles fall within the kin-group of the person against whom he has a *casus belli* that has not been repaired previously. This procedure usually constitutes what is regarded as a sufficient reparation.

It is taken absolutely for granted in Manus that the familiars of the *palit am mbwaro* magic are never commanded by their magician owner to execute his indignation upon another person. No magician is represented as a deliberate baby killer, and babies and new mothers are the entire possible field of vengeance by this magic. A person in performing *tandritanitani* is a deliberate killer of babies, and action with *tandritanitani* is very rare indeed. The Manus men are thoroughly sentimental about babies. It is assumed that a magician's familiars act purely in rapport with their owner's anger; and no Manus native would ever forego the general custom of expressing anger freely whenever it is felt, be he magician, or a person angry at a magician. Magic simply does not suppress the free expression of anger, although between a magician and a non-magician such expression may become momentous, in terms of the dogmas of magic. To understand this we must remember the facts of the satire upon the *tchinal* magical familiars, and the expressed scorn of magic that sometimes occurs. The Manus are great lovers of their believed rights, great legalists, sincere lovers of court cases in the white courts now that they have them, and are not under any circumstances to be intimidated out of claims of justice by any magician amongst themselves.

This Manus attitude is in very strong contrast to the attitude that I have found in two other sorcery using peoples whom I know intimately. Both the Dobuans of Papua and the Omaha of the North American Plains are more back biting and maliciously minded peoples amongst themselves than the Manus. I do not say that they are more quarrelsome. But the Manus "let off steam" constantly and dare the damage of their sorcerers without worrying one iota about sorcery. Both in Dobu and in Omaha the injunction is "walk softly, do not raise your voice" (in Omaha "do not point your finger" also). The idea is that the sorcerer must divert attention from any anger he may feel, and not betray his mood. Then he must perform his spells in dead secrecy. Everyone knows this attitude. And being socially repressed, private malice and suspicion simply multiply, largely because an overt decorum is made obligatory, and trust and confidence become less possible thereby. These two peoples do not credit that illness comes from a sorcerer's familiars because in rapport with his mood. The Omaha have the concept, but they apply the concept of deliberate and active malice of the sorcerer much more freely. The Dobuans apply this latter concept exclusively, just as the Manus apply the former concept exclusively to *palit am mbwaro*. Moreover in Dobu and in Omaha there is little satire at magic, nothing in comparison to the Manus satire; and no restriction of the effects of black magic away from adults and into a limited field, such as the Manus field of infants and pregnant women or new nursing mothers only.

In all the Manus attitudes towards magic the influence of the stronger religion cannot be discounted. The man who laughed at the tree spirit and then spoke solemnly of the Sir Ghost in displacement of the idea of the tree spirit represented his people's attitude very well. It is general belief that a man and his Sir Ghost share feelings in common and work in rapport. If an affront is laid upon a man, both the man and his Sir Ghost are outraged together. The man feels certain that the other man's Sir Ghost will act to remedy the matter. But the offended man's Sir Ghost does not strike as a malicious ghost at the offending party. The offender's Sir Ghost punishes the offender who must make reparation to recover.[11]

If the offended man is a magician his familiars execute vengeance or retribution upon the offender's household. This is true magic, playing with vengeance. But the sorcerer takes pity by social obligation upon him and exorcises his familiars from the sick mother or infant. He collects a fee. However, the magician, like the non-magician, leaves the supernatural to take its own course, which is conceived as a just course, and one which goes above the volitional acts of men and without need of them. It will be seen why I am dealing with Manus magic as a sub-division of Manus religion. A line may be drawn, but it is a formal line.

I have dealt with the magic of *sorosor* and the magic of *palit am mbwaro.* I come now to the magic of *kussi mburror.* This *kussi mburror* is the least used form of black magic in Manus, used not more often than the *tandritanitani* curse is used. A large Manus village has a record of not more than five or six cases of the use of *tandritanitani* curse, and about the same number of the use of *kussi mburror* in about three decades. I was fortunate enough to witness one case of a sorcerer's use of *kussi mburror* during my stay. There was no secrecy about it. This sorcerer was blind, economically disabled. He was also the war leader and the chief man in rank in the village. He owed debts that the onset of blindness

[11] In a few cases a man's Sir Ghost strikes down his ward to secure reparation to his ward from offenders against his ward. Reparation is here paid from appeal to pity. This is rare compared with the idea of punishment, and reparation made from fear of punishment.

had disabled him from paying. He had suddenly been dropped from the circle of exchanges but not quickly enough to leave him without debts. His debtors dunned him furiously and with great anger. He, insulted by his own predicament as much as by his debtors, and badly hurt by his great fall from the highest rank to the position of a feeble dependent on his very young son, struck back, answering insult with threat of sorcery and with the following use of it. It was all a most furious quarrel by broad daylight which the entire village witnessed; then the sorcerer followed up his threat and mumbled his spells inside his house so that he was clearly heard in neighbouring houses. There was no attempt at concealment.

The conventions of the *kussi mburror* are distinct. *Kussi mburror* is like *palit am mbwaro* in going on the wind or through space, and is unlike the *sorosor*, which only damages a person who comes into contact with an object, always a palm in Manus, charmed with the spell. But *kussi mburror* is unlike *palit am mbwaro* in that it is believed to damage adults, the adult against whom it is directed in any particular case. It is further unlike *palit am mbwaro*, and like *tandritanitani*, in that the cursing spell must be pronounced. The concept of familiars' rapport with their owner's anger does not apply. It is like *sorosor* in its definite unsecretive use, but unlike *sorosor* in being directed against a specific person identified in advance.

About *kussi mburror* there is conflict of belief. Claims are made for it by the sorcerer that it is effective. The sorcerer's intended victim scouts its efficacy. I saw the intended victim under the curse. He was not greatly intimidated. This sorcery is as nothing compared with the sorcery of Dobu, when men cower at times and behave like whipped dogs, and alternate between cowering and displaying bravado. In Manus the sorcerer pours out his rage while the man under threat goes about calmly saying that the *kussi mburror* does not work, that Usiai derived magic is only good to kill infants (a reference to the *palit am mbwaro*, and an assimilation of the *kussi mburror* to it). Instances are further pointed out where the *kussi mburror* was used before, and nothing came of it, the sorcerer having previously pointed out the opposite type of instance where something had seemed to come of it in a previous case. In all, the satire of the *tchinal* applies here to maintain as complete a social and an individual sanity as one could desire; for the *kussi mburror* like other forms of Manus sorcery is imported (the *tandritanitani* curse excepted, of course).

It must be understood that all sorcery is open in Manus. Ethnological enquiry into Manus sorcery is not as similar to detective work as it is in Dobu or in Omaha, for example. In Manus, *sorosor* is in constant use, as also *palit am mbwaro*, but *kussi mburror* and *tandritanitani* curse in very infrequent use. Sorcery is conducted in a manner that produces no social disintegration. Quarrels occur independently, and are sometimes capped with magic, but more often are not so capped. In any case the quarrel does not arise from any sorcery milieu as such, but usually from a conflict over matters of property or women. Just as the Manus sometimes fought over property or women, so they still use sorcery. Two armed groups sometimes confronted each other. If they were parties within the same village their spears used to be taken from them and the quarrelling parties came to grips with their hands and fists.

Spears are out of fashion now under white rule, so that the preliminary situation does not hold any longer, and even the fist fights have been mostly abandoned for court cases by active Manus preference. If we view Manus sorcery from this angle we shall see that the really serious aspects have been taken out of sorcery; spears are threatened but fists are really used.

I have reports also of cases which show that the quarrelling parties, even within the village, did not always submit to disarmament but hurled spears. However such fighting was regulated so that it did little damage as a rule. I believe it is not regular to fight with spears, just as in the sorcery field it is not regular to use the *kussi mburror*, while the *palit am mbwaro* is in regular operation.

I have shown that in Manus the black magic does not impinge seriously upon the religion, although both alike are most intimately concerned with illnesses and deaths. The white magic does not impinge upon any other social form as obviously as does the black magic. Manus religion is aimed at curing, not only sick persons, however, but also "sick" fishing gear. Here is a field in which magic might possibly dispute. Thus white magic might be used to aid in fishing; and then as commonly happens in a thoroughgoing magical system, a failure in success following the use of white magic might be attributed to someone else's black magic of the kind designed to spoil other persons' fishing. This rather dull but socially malicious game is not played in Manus however. There is no system of white magic for fishing success. There are not even any single charms or single magical practices for such success. The same is true of the making of overseas voyages.

There are some charms to secure success in trade and in exchange. These are not usually verbal, although there are one or two spells known to one or two persons in a large village. More usual is a material charm consisting of pigs' heads or tusks fitted on a frame which is covered with a vegetable substance, painted red. This object covers the lower half of a pole inside the front of the house. It costs much to install and is put up by hired Usiai magicians. Once it is installed however there is nothing more done. It is installed only by richer men who can afford it.

A special object is worn on the back in war. This object is purchased dearly as it has magical potency. It is a human head, carved in wood, with a half circle of frigate bird wing feathers attached and a frigate bird wing bone. Once it is purchased nothing more is done about it. It is made by the north coast Matankor.

Similarly a few persons keep luck-giving pieces of mother-of-pearl shell, or odd shaped stones, without doing more about it. There are a few love charms recently imported by young men who have gone to New Ireland or to New Guinea to work, all derivative from foreign cultures. Some persons and some children wear amulets round the neck or carry them in the betel bag. Thus the white magic used is very confined and such as it is derivative, amulets possibly excepted. Manus culture has no system of sacred observances to procure success in advance other than the non-cursing *tandritanitani* performances. For the rest everyone goes ahead with matter of fact business, and when anything goes wrong in fishing or in health the supernatural is invoked to put matters right.

CHAPTER IV

A DIARY OF RELIGIOUS EVENTS

In the following pages the actual action of religious events within a Manus village over a period of several months is represented. The village is Peri village, so spelled to distinguish it from the Pere clan (or gens),[1] the largest clan in the village. At the back of this study is placed a Who's Who, which is for special reference in connection with this chapter. Immediately following the Who's Who is a glossary of Manus terms, also for reference.

It is important to note that in the diary, names of ghosts and Sir Ghosts and ghostly controls are given lower case initial letters, and are moreover printed in italics in order to distinguish them from the names of living persons.

Part One. November 25th–December 25th

1. *A Woman and the Sorcerer whom her Sister had Rejected*

Towards sundown on November 28th, my third day in the field and in Peri, a loud wailing came from a house. Men, women and children put out in canoes towards the house from all directions. When I arrived, towards the front of the house, Alupwai, the woman of the house, was lying unconscious with her head in her brother's lap. About the pair were huddled a group of women with their calico wraps pulled well over their heads, wailing noisily. At the left of the house front Pope,[2] a man, stood erect, continuously stirring with a long stick a little water in a wooden bowl at his feet and shouting vociferously as he did so. Other men and

[1] The Manus clans are patrilineal, and are styled gens or clan, without distinction in American or English terminology.

[2] Pope later turned out to be a moron subject to occasional catalepsy, who always took a prominent part when anyone was ill, possibly because he never could when other persons were not preoccupied. He always stirred water in bowls and called on his Sir Ghost, whether he and his Sir Ghost were related to the sick person or not—in this case there was no relationship.

women, Alupwai's husband among the men, were squatting crowded about, the women adding to the wailing, the men impassive. The group of women about the patient massaged her head, covered her eyes with the back of their hands, pulled her hands gently and massaged the fingers. Occasionally they shouted to the man, Pope, who was stirring the bowl. The din was terrific, the patient completely crowded about and shut off from air, the excitement very tense.

Suddenly, after the house was very crowded, there was a quick consultation. About eight women picked up the patient, carried her out into a canoe, and crowded over her on the canoe platform while men punted the canoe to the next house but one. They carried her into that house and continued the same procedure, only Paliau,[3] another man, joined Pope, with another wooden bowl. The whole procedure was frenzied, the women's wailing loud and uncoördinated, Pope and Paliau stirring their bowls frenziedly and shouting with all the breath they could muster. Pope's bowl had a little water in it, Paliau's had none. A smaller bowl containing water was placed on the rafters directly above the patient's head. About ten women surrounded the patient, and none, or all of them equally, seemed in charge. The children played about on the outskirts and one or two of them cried. One frightened child clung to Pope's leg. Paliau's fourteen-year daughter ceased crying, turned away to braid calmly a piece of pandanus held with her toes. The wailing and shouting grew louder. The women went on massaging. One woman put her face against the patient's face and rubbed her forehead against the patient's forehead. Judging by the movements of her lips she was talking rapidly to the unconscious patient.

For a long while nothing happened, except that Pope and Paliau became covered with dripping sweat from their exertions. Then someone brought water and poured it over Alupwai's face and abdomen. She was far gone in pregnancy. A long snake-like raised scarification just above her navel,

[3] Paliau, unlike Pope, was related to the sick woman, Alupwai. She was his titular younger brother's wife. Paliau was a rich capitalist and his younger brother, Alupwai's husband, was poor and Paliau's dependent.

done for ornament, was now hideously distended and the reverse of ornamental. Suddenly she moaned, writhed and cried out. The women grasped her legs as well as her hands with intent to still her. A woman took the patient's head from off the patient's brother's extended leg to her lap, then to the floor. Now, about forty-five minutes after the onset of unconsciousness, a child was sent to get a piece of rattan, and with it the patient's belt was cut. Her grass skirt was kept carefully in place, but more loosely. A few minutes later she renewed groaning and writhing, alternating thereafter from periods of pain seizures to periods of unconsciousness. Pope and Paliau laid aside their bowl-stirring and shouting, the women their massaging and wailing. Everyone sat orderly and quietly waiting, convinced that the patient still had life in her. Nothing happened for a while except that more water was brought and poured over the patient's face and abdomen.

Then a long hanging mat was put up behind the patient, and behind the mat several women seated themselves. One of them, Isole [4] by name, was in charge of the immediately subsequent proceedings. Pope and several of the others asked questions at intervals. Sounds of whistling, followed by speech in conversational tone, came from behind the mat to which Pope and the others gave periodical assent by saying "*Ua*," "yes," and some antiphonal speeches which sounded like questions. I gathered subsequently that the whistling was ghostly speech, the conversational tone speeches from behind the mat were the interpretation of the ghostly speeches, and both whistles and interpretation came from Isole, the medium, in response to questions propounded by some of the audience. This procedure is called *tilitili*.

The *tilitili* came to a conclusion after three quarters of an hour or so. Then one man, Patalian,[5] stood up from where

[4] Isole was the most intelligent medium in Peri and one of the most forceful women of the village. She was a member of the family that held the hereditary position of highest rank. Her father's brother's son was the war leader and village head-man, Korotan.

[5] Patalian was an adopted war captive taken captive as a child. He was now a great magician.

he had been sitting chewing betel nut and one or two roots. He spat the mixture twice towards the patient from across the house. Then he approached the woman, stood astride of her, took her arms and spat some of the mixture under each arm pit in turn. Then he chewed more and spat on to her abdomen. He then spat into his hands and rubbed them, one in front, one behind, all over her body, finally wetting her face. As he went through this procedure he used a form of words aloud, evidently a charm.

Alupwai, the patient, was sleeping by now. The crisis was past. I had expected a miscarriage, but there was none. Everyone dispersed except a few who remained to sleep in the house.

As this event occurred when I was yet newly come I did not obtain any understanding of the *tilitili*, or of the seance that was held by Isole, or of Patalian's charm. The event turned out to be but an early prelude of later trouble with Alupwai, in which I understood everything including Patalian's part.

The movements first seen proved to be typical, as I found by their frequent repetition later. Brother tends sister, or sister tends brother closely in illness, husband tends wife or wife, husband more remotely. That is, a husband may do all manner of services for his sick wife, but he does not hold her head in his lap as her brother does, and vice versa. The stirring of a wooden bowl, empty or with a little water in it, beside an unconscious patient is always done by one or by two men who shout out in ceaseless repetition the names of their Sir Ghosts, and who now and again may ask help from the Sir Ghosts as they shout; but the shouting of the name is usually the whole substance of their cry. Women wail, crying "My mother, my mother, my mother, how is this, how is this, how is this?" on a high key with a sobbing break in the last "How is this"; as the key changes from high to low, it takes up again on the low key, then resumes again in high. Or the cry may be "My mother, my mother, my mother, this spear, this spear, this spear." The former cry is customary for illness, the latter for outward bodily injury.[6]

[6] Or for internal injury manifested in haemorrhage.

When the patient is unconscious all is din and without harmony. The unconscious patient is always crowded over and shut out from air. The patient is nearly always taken quickly from one house to another, as the house where the trouble first occurred is believed to be in danger from ghostly quarters. A new house with another Sir Ghost is found for safety. Anything practical, like cutting tight body fastenings, is done only as an after-thought, long after it should have been done. The bowl of water put over the patient's head in the case cited is for the reception of her soul stuff in case the Sir Ghost or ghosts relent at the display of mortal frenzy, which is partly real, partly histrionic and directed towards making the ghosts or Sir Ghosts concerned relent. It is this water that is poured over the patient, but not as a practical measure at the onset of unconsciousness, but rather after a considerable time when the soul stuff may perhaps be in it.

The seance is customary behaviour once the preliminary frenzy is over and order restored, subsequent to the patient showing signs of life, and if it is night; unconsciousness is regarded as always being particularly close to death. The use of the hanging mat to shield the medium is not essential to the seance. It is a common device to prevent a woman from being technically in the presence of some of her male relatives-in-law, and it was used in the above case for that purpose. In the general frenzy before the orderliness of the seance, all such kinship taboos were enforced less stringently. All the women mourners covered their heads and faces with their calico over-garment, a cloth carried for the purpose of hiding from a taboo relative met by accident, but no walls of hanging mats were put up on account of the urgency at the earlier stage.

The use of magic, as by Patalian immediately after the seance, is not usual, as we have said. As a general rule sickness is cured by oracular diagnosis of sin and by expiation alone, not by magic until after many seances and many expiations in cases of long continued illness. The present case is only an apparent exception. Magic is most closely concerned with the ills of infants and with the associated ills, and Alupwai was eight months gone in pregnancy. The trouble was from that fact, and the medium, Isole, had diagnosed that evil magic was upsetting the normal course. Patalian was one of the few possessors of magic in the village, and in addition there were circumstances that would have made it seem unreasonable rather than otherwise if Alupwai's child-bearing had not been embarrassed by Patalian's evil magic. Ndrantche, mother of Alupwai and of Alupwai's younger sister, Lawa, had been seduced by Patalian long years before when she was a widow. Ndrantche had wanted to marry Patalian in a virtuous and proper manner. But Patalian, much younger than Ndrantche, aghast at the demands of virtue and the prospect of marrying a woman of an older generation, had fled the village to escape. Many years after this episode, and but a year or two prior to my arrival in Peri, Patalian had tried to negotiate a marriage with Lawa, who was beautiful and young. Lawa's eldest brother had supported Patalian's overture, so that Patalian had paid over some wealth for Lawa. Ndrantche, Lawa's mother, naturally indignant at the idea that her betrayer and publicly recognised seducer should desire to wed her daughter, secured Lawa's marriage elsewhere. Meanwhile Patalian's advance payments for Lawa had not been all returned or met by exchange, Ndrantche holding that the wealth in question should be confiscated as indemnity for the old wrong. Patalian, himself, thought Ndrantche to blame for her seduction by him, and considered himself cheated both of Lawa and of his advance payments for Lawa.

2. *A Younger Brother Disobeys his Elder Brother*

On the evening of December 11th there was a seance held in Alupwai's house. Alupwai's husband, Tunu, was ill, but not dangerously ill. The normal run of illnesses are not publicly broadcast by loud wailing, as unconsciousness is. Nor are they publicly attended by large numbers of miscellaneous people. Only some relatives and the medium attend. During this month there were probably many other seances held that were not brought to my attention. I went with Paliau,

Tunu's eldest brother, to this seance. Tunu had not been moved from his own house (a sign of a minor illness). The medium's whistles and oracular reports were incomprehensible to me. Paliau was attentive, grave and aloof, but I got from him a whisper or two as to the course of the seance. Paliau had commanded Tunu not to go to the white Court to bear witness that might help Tunu's wife's brother to make a new marriage and upset an old one. Tunu had gone in defiance of orders. Furthermore Tunu had not been helping Paliau in his work as he should have done. For this double offence the ghost of the father of Paliau and Tunu was making Tunu ill.

A man is usually friendly and coöperative with his wife's brother; the relationship is a strong one. But Paliau, as Tunu's eldest brother, was head of the family. He had financed Tunu's marriage, so Tunu owed him obedience and economic service in return. This seance is an example of the working of the mechanism which makes the financing of younger relatives' marriages profitable and the source of authority. Rebellion occurs on occasion, of course, but it is always associated with subsequent illness when it has occurred. This naturally enough acts as a strong deterrent to rebellion.

3. *A Birth*

A child was born to the wife of Bonyalo on December 13th. Bonyalo was a financial dependent of Paliau, and gave the firm impression that he was not fit to be anything else than someone's retainer, although he was a mature man. I did not hear of the birth until afterwards. Birth is a very private matter, all men excluded, and only the mother's female kin present. Bonyalo had nothing to do for the ensuing month. He was not permitted to be in the same house with his wife and their infant. He was not supposed to do any work. Further his taboos did not extend.

4. *A House is Built*

At this time we were living, my wife and I, in a small Government barrack at the east and seawards corner of the village. One night when Paliau, Pokenau and our interpreter were late at work with me, Paliau heard a strange sound on the built-up coral rubble outside. He went out and came back scared saying that *sori* [7] was there outside; *sori* was the recently deceased village constable of that end of the village, known as Pontchal. He was the Sir Ghost of his successor and younger brother, Pokenau. As Sir Ghost to Pokenau he lodged in the house of Pokenau, not far from the barrack on the other side of the coral rubble. As ghostly village constable of Pontchal he kept watch and ward over the Government barrack in Pontchal. Theoretically we lived under his Sir Ghostly protection. Paliau and the interpreter excused themselves hastily in fear of this encounter with *sori* and went off. Pokenau [8] went home also in the opposite direction.

Next day I asked Pokenau for his version of the matter. He said:

"*sori* his stomach muddy (*i.e.*, angry). I, and the two, Paliau and the interpreter, were with you. He was angry at it. Pi Yap (Mrs. Fortune) wanted to sleep, and we talked at length. He was angry at it. He said, 'It's after midnight; you go home, all of you and let Moi-Yap (myself) sleep.' So he came. He called out. Paliau was resting on the chair, the interpreter on the chair, Pi-Yap on the bed. Paliau saw *sori*. He was afraid. The interpreter was afraid. 'Moi-Yap, a ghost called out. We must go home.' They got into their canoe. You took a torch and gave it to them. The two of them looked about with it, turning their heads from side to side. They punted towards their house on the inland side and I lit a lantern. I went over the coral rubble and waded over to my house."

I had asked Pokenau for an account, partly as an exercise in the language, partly because as he had gone home with his lantern, I had distinctly heard him chuckling to himself.

[7] The names of ghosts are deprived of upper case initial letters and are printed in italics in order to distinguish them from the names of mortals.

[8] Pokenau was village constable of the seawards end of Peri village, Pontchal, in succession to *sori*. He was an intelligent man, a woman hater, and something of a sociologist. He was no business man as Paliau was, but rather impractical.

A man is proud of the way in which his Sir Ghost occasionally discomforts other persons, especially if he has any antagonism to such persons. Paliau and Pokenau were already rivals as informants. Pokenau had the ethnologists domiciled in his Sir Ghost's territory, and naturally exulted over his advantage when his rival retired in an extremely nervous state. At the time I thought it strange that a ghostly visitation should so scare one man, and yet make another chuckle. The reason was, of course, that to one man a spirit is a ghost, to another man the same spirit is a Sir Ghost. This distinction made our house location a matter of the first importance to our rival informants.

Some time after Paliau had a fever. I think it was about two weeks after the incident of Paliau's being scared by the ghostly *sori*. His mother, Kamutal,[9] was the medium. The control of Kamutal was *nyandros*, her deceased child. The Sir Ghost of Paliau was *pwanau*.

Selan [10] (an associate of Paliau's) asked *pwanau* through *nyandros* through Kamutal, "Why is Paliau ill? You understand what it is. Perhaps when he went overseas the ghosts of the middle seas struck him."

Kamutal whistled (*nyandros* reporting what *pwanau* had told him, *nyandros*); Kamutal interpreted the whistling of *nyandros:*

"No: a ghost of the village struck him, the constable of Pontchal."

Here Selan asked that *sori* be questioned and report made. An interval elapsed (*nyandros* going to consult *sori*, all mortals were silent the while). Whistling introduced the report, subsequently translated as if *sori* were speaking, although it is understood by all that *nyandros* does the

[9] Kamutal had been the wife of Potek, the pair having adopted Pwanau the elder and Paliau the younger in infancy. Now *potek* was an extinguished ghost and *pwanau* was Paliau's Sir Ghost. Kamutal was remarried.

[10] Selan was Paliau's wife's mother's brother's son, and therefore a joking relative to Paliau, and a close associate, although of another gens or of other gentes. Selan acted as a member of three gentes with which he was connected in various ways. He was a versatile man in business, and he was the only male medium in Peri (although he does not act as medium in this seance, but as a questioner of a medium).

whistling, and Kamutal the translating into mortal speech. By convention these two channels, one ghostly, one human, need not stress the fact that they are channels; or with equal propriety the medium need not constantly intrude herself and her control. She speaks as if *sori* or *pwanau* or whatever ghost is solicited at the moment were speaking. On occasion a medium may speak as if it were her control speaking. Terms of relationship, when used to one of the audience, are those appropriate to the control, that is a generation descendant from the generation of the medium, and two generations descendant from the generation of the average Sir Ghost. But the medium does not normally pause to state, "My control (naming it) says that *sori* says." That is understood.

The report came:

"I struck him as compensation for his intrusion upon my coral rubble territory" (against which the Government barrack, my headquarters, stood). "I died. Let my coral rubble territory rest. I said, 'He can't come up.' I saw him come up. I was very angry. I struck him."

Selan said: "*sori*, restore Paliau to health. He will not go on to your territory again."

Then by request *pwanau* was called upon again, and asked if *sori* had told him anything; *pwanau* replied, "No! but I advise you this. Build a house for Moi-Yap [11] in our own territory. Bring him down here. Let him abandon Pontchal. Then you'll not become ill."

Pokenau knew nothing of this seance. A man cannot keep count of what his Sir Ghost says behind his back through the mouth of a rival's mother, or, more accurately, to the control of a rival's mother.

This development suited my plans admirably. I needed a larger house than the small and cramped Government barrack designed for a night's shelter for a passerby, not for permanent residence. I cite it because it illustrates well the terms in which any important proposal is put in Manus. A man wishing you to make any important change does not phrase it as his desire, but as a ghostly injunction. Do you

[11] Man of the East, *i.e.*, the ethnologist.

want X as a servant boy? The family Sir Ghost of X is consulted and announces that X can be handed over, if accompanied by Y. This is no mortal bargain, and cannot be argued with as such. It is oracular, and must be accepted or rejected entirely.

Further, as we shall see later, house-dwelling complications between two families in one house are phrased as quarrels between two sets of respective Sir Ghosts. A new house is always built because of a spiritual direction from the other plane. My house building was no real exception, although the rivalry was between two informants. Neither of them scrupled for a moment to come on the other's territory by day. Night intrusion was viewed more seriously. Later, when the house in Paliau's territory was completed, I could work by night with either one in his own territory.

At the conclusion of the seance that made a new house for me a vital necessity to Paliau also, Paliau was bathed with water from the bowl put in front of the medium for the reception of his soul stuff (taken by *sori* at the prior encounter of Paliau with *sori*). There was no expiatory payment from Paliau to *sori's* ward, Pokenau. But *pwanau* was instructed to make expiatory payment to *sori* on that plane, in order to make all well. In other words Paliau's illness was not serious. It will be recalled that I have said that in case of minor illness a medium friendly to the patient may prefer to impute ghostly malice, rather than sin by the patient, and Sir Ghostly correction in consequence. Paliau was a man who was rich, honest, unembarrassed in paying off debts, very hard working and very clever. He could not be caught easily by any medium, and he usually experienced difficulty in obtaining any outside medium to hold a seance for his household. In the above seance the medium was his mother, with his best interests at heart. Moreover the unusual presence of ethnologists in Peri had led him to go by night to a place that he would normally have avoided completely—an abnormal situation.

5. *A Defaulter in a Debt Wins a Magical Victory*

On December 16th Nyakareu bore a child to Poiyo,[12] thereby absenting herself, for some weeks of seclusion to come, also from quarrels in public with Poiyo's other wife, Kampon.

On December 19th Alupwai was safely delivered of a child.

On December 20th Bonyalo's child, seven days after its birth, was treated by a magician. Sooner or later every newborn infant is so treated, but the treatment is not exactly a ceremonial connected with birth, not a *rite de passage* of the ordinary type. So stereotyped is the custom that it appears as if it might be a *rite de passage*. But what actually happens is that every infant has its infant troubles; it may be only too continuous crying which awakens parental anxiety. The trouble is accounted for by the theory that the infant has been affected by black magic. No oracular diagnosis from a seance is made to establish this theory. It is the general stock explanation. The kin of the ailing infant have divination made. The question is put to the diviner whether it is not the black magic of X that is responsible. The magician, X, is always the magician with whom the kin concerned have been on bad terms. For example Patalian had a regular practice in treating all infants born to Ndrantche's daughters, after birth, just as we saw him treating Alupwai just before childbirth.

For Bonyalo's infant the magician was Korotan, head man [13] of Peri. Bonyalo was too much the economic dependant to have independent quarrels, where quarrels are nearly all economic in origin. As Paliau's servitor and henchman he was a part of Paliau's entourage, and his infant was unwell in that capacity, as was fitting. Paliau, over a year before, had fallen out seriously with Korotan. Korotan, although head man of the entire village, former war leader for the entire village, and owner of the largest and best house in Peri, was now blind, and economically backward in consequence.

[12] Poiyo was a man whose left arm was disfigured from a former attack of leprosy. He was remarkable for having two wives.

[13] War leader, and chief man of rank, entitled to build a larger house than anyone else.

He had failed to meet his debts now for some time. Paliau had dunned him for debt, until a final rupture was made by Korotan declaring publicly that he would use his black magic against Paliau. Paliau survived the black magic, but did not speak to Korotan or enter Korotan's house for a year. Now that avoidance was over, public opinion was free with comment that black magic could not kill adults, that is the black magic got from the Matankor or Usiai (with scorn of such alien cultures). But black magic was fully accredited, as it always is, with causing infant troubles. So Bonyalo's infant was now to be cured by Korotan exorcising what he had caused. This matter caused no important re-opening of the breach between Paliau and Korotan. They still did not like each other particularly, but that was on the original grounds of quarrel. Paliau had given up the debt owed him as hopeless. He could not hope to win his case in the white man's courts, the usual last resort, as the judge would certainly acquit Korotan on the ground that, being blind, he was not economically responsible any longer. The belief that Korotan's magic had afflicted Bonyalo's baby was not an important cause of bad feeling. Paliau, like all his people, regarded such an event as entirely regular, as regular as a *rite de passage*, as inevitable and not calling for blame anger or fury. All such feeling was in the past and more or less dormant now.

The mother and infant were in the house of Bonyalo, Bonyalo himself having been evicted for several weeks from the house.[14] A fathom of shell money and ten dogs' teeth were put into a small wooden bowl and placed before Korotan as he entered the house led by the hand by his small daughter. A branch of betel nuts was placed on top of the bowl, and a coconut placed beside it. Korotan seated himself, took some of the betel nut and began to chew it solemnly and silently. Then after a time he recited the customary introductory history of his magic:

"This charm of black magic of green coconut belonged

[14] His brother-in-law took possession, to fend his sister's needs at child bearing time.

to Talipale of the riverside at Ndrombut. It worked upon the infants of all. They fell ill, near to death. The diviner divined it. He exorcised it from the infants of all. They became well. He held fast to it. A daughter, Piwiru, was born to him. She was betrothed to Kiso, the son of Pakob of Tchalalo. Talipale gave oil, he gave pigs, he gave taro, he gave sago, he gave this charm on top of all the gifts. It went as dowry of Piwiru to Kiso, son of Pakob. He worked the charm on the infants of all. They fell ill. He recovered them. He fell ill. 'I wish to die. Popau, my son, come close to me. I shall give two charms to you.' It was low tide at midday. He dragged his canoe on the mud flats, fastened it to a planted stick. He went to his father Kiso. Kiso, son of Pakob, gave to his son Popau the charm for success in economic exchange, and the charm of black magic against infants and child birth.

"I kidnapped a woman of the dependents of Popau (*i.e.*, by force and for use as a public prostitute). I lost a man, Kele, son of Pwai, in the fight when I captured her.

"His (*i.e.*, Popau's) mother was the woman, and my father was the man (*i.e.*, Popau's mother and Korotan's father were sister and brother to each other). He took stones, laid one on top of the other. He drank sea water. He spat on the stone. He hammered top stone on under stone. The stone broke. I had children born to me. All died. Peace came after war. I took my wooden bowls, my dogs' teeth, my shell money. I went to Popau. He gave me this charm. I work upon all infants with it."

A part of this history requires explanation. "His mother the woman, my father the man" is a conventional way of stating cross-cousinship. Popau, as the child of the sister, had child-of-sister's cursing power over his child-of-brother, Korotan. This cursing power is called *tandritanitani*. The way of its use is described in the above account. The child-of-sister as he hammers top stone on under stone says, "Let his wife bear him children; they will die; let his economic exchanges become worthless." Child-of-sister can do this to child-of-brother, the latter having no reciprocal power.

Korotan's charm that he exorcised over Bonyalo's infant was not *tandritanitani*, but another, a generally applicable charm, gained in economic exchange validating peace with his cross-cousin after war, peace made by his cross-cousin taking off the *tandritanitani* curse that had killed off Korotan's children, as it is understood in Korotan's recital. Korotan, as former war leader and present head man of Peri, carried a typical atmosphere of fights, quarrels and feuds with him wherever he went. His conversation was filled with details of his past preoccupation in this regard. Whenever a quarrel rang through the village, as it did frequently, Korotan had his ear to the floor of his house in order to hear better (close to the water, the best carrier of sound). He took a real delight in his neighbours' quarrels which was matched by no one else in the village. So naturally enough his history of his charm is in character.

Pokenau, who was present as an onlooker, took the green coconut provided, opened it and handed it to Korotan. Korotan rubbed the sides of the coconut between his hands as he intoned the charm aloud. In the course of the recital he spat betel juice three times on three spots round the top of the coconut. He intoned:

"*Ngendral*
Nekup
Ulu
Mat
Pwepwil

you climb on top of this green coconut
green coconut yours, this is.
you are here (*i.e.*, doing this damage)
for a matter of no account
I do but make, not seriously;
let it be finished.

she may eat food,
she may drink water,
she may drink mother's milk,
she may sleep,
she may not wail,
she may not scream,
she may sleep soundly."

The infant was now put in a large wooden bowl. Korotan tipped the charmed green coconut and poured the coconut milk from it over the infant's body.

As Korotan was blind, Pokenau now performed the *tcheritcheri* on the infant for him. He took a betel nut dipped in partly masticated red betel-nut juice (the red is obtained from the betel nut, coral lime and pepper leaf mixture). With this he touched the infant on the forehead, making a minute red spot there; then over the right eye, then over the left eye, then over the Adam's apple, then on the right shoulder point, then on the left shoulder point, then on the mons veneris, then on the right knee cap, then on the left knee cap, then on the small of the back. So the betel nut chewed by Korotan as he intoned his charm was put on the infant's body, together with the coconut milk previously poured on the infant, communicating the strength of the charm to it.

The names *Ngendral, Nekup*, etc., used in Korotan's charm represent supernatural beings, who were never mortal, but who were always supernatural.

Korotan now stood up, and took the infant into his arms. He crooned to it and rocked it until it stopped the vigourous crying that it had set up in response to the above treatment. Then he solemnly passed it between his legs from in front to behind him where it was received by a woman. He then sat down. A pause ensued. Then Korotan took the dogs' teeth and shell money from the wooden bowl that had been placed before him at the opening of the ceremony. As he handled it, testing it by sense of touch, he said:

"*Ngendrul*
Nekup
Ulu
Mat
Pwepwil

your pay
this is your pay.
you come into this wooden bowl.
good pay.

come and you and I will go to our house,
come and guard our (mine and your)
coral rubble territory;
you may abandon this territory.

she may eat taro,
she may drink her mother's milk,
she may drink water,
she may sleep,
she may not wail,
she may not scream,
she may sleep soundly
in the arms of her mother."

Korotan then put the bowl with its valuables in the house rafters (place of supernaturals) and sat beneath it silently a while. He said that it was now prohibited to wash the child for three days. Then without further speech he went. Someone took the bowl with its contents and gave it to an attendant of Korotan's to take to him.

As a note on this magic it may be added that it is recited aloud. It cannot be stolen by another. Its power is dependent on its having been rightfully obtained in marriage exchanges, peace-making exchanges or by more outright payment. After it is handed over it cannot be used by its former owner. It is called *palit am mbwaro*, magic pertaining to infants and childbirth. Korotan had three kinds of black magic, the above, then a *sorosor*, then a *kussi mburror*.

On about the twenty-fifth of December the infant of Poiyo and Nyakareu was exorcised by Talikai.[15] I saw the exorcism. The procedure differed only in minor detail from that described above for Korotan's exorcism over Bonyalo's infant. Talikai spoke the history of the charm, but then muttered his charm instead of saying it aloud. The coconut milk baptism and the *tcheritcheri* procedures were the same. Instead of passing the infant between his legs at the conclusion, after having taken it up and crooned to it, Talikai

[15] Talikai was a member of the family of highest rank in Peri village. Korotan was the village leader, son of the eldest line; Talikai was a son of Korotan's father's younger brother. Isole, the medium, was a daughter of another younger brother. Talikai was Korotan's future successor in the village leadership.

gave it back in an ordinary manner to its father's sister. Talikai believed in appearing more mysterious than Korotan felt to be necessary. I failed to get the history of the charm or the charm itself; nor did I obtain the history of the past quarrel between Poiyo and Talikai.

Somewhere about this time as I learned later Patalian [16] exorcised his black magic from Alupwai's newborn infant. I was not advised of the proceeding at the time, so that I did not witness it.[17]

PART TWO. DECEMBER 26–JANUARY 26

6. *The Troubles of having Two Wives*

Poiyo had but one house, although he had two wives. The two wives would not stay in the same house. Their favourite occupation was to hurl obscenity at each other at half a village distance. Poiyo's own house was broken down and dilapidated. In that house Nyakareu now stayed with her new-born infant and with her brother, Poiyo being temporarily debarred from entering it owing to the birth. Poiyo's other wife, Kampon, was resident in the back of Tchawan's house, by courtesy of Tchawan.[18] Poiyo and Tchawan were

[16] Patalian had been adopted by Pokenau's grandparents. He was reckoned as being brother to Pokenau, the constable of Pontchal. Patalian was a widower, he was near middle age and had had difficulty in finding a wife anywhere. His being a war captive only adopted into Peri had militated against him, for his elders had not given him an inheritance. His magical prowess was an acquisition in a direction that was not cultivated except by a few, since for most persons there were more solid paths to greater social power than that of a magician.

[17] In the above section I have not mentioned the gens affiliations of the various characters. Pontchal was a politically half-independent section of Peri village, but it may be considered now as a gens split off from another gens of the village, namely Peré gens. As the largest gens in the village, Pere gave its name to the village; but to avoid confusion I have written the village name as Peri, and the name of the largest of the several gentes in Peri as Pere. The omitting of gentile affiliations of the characters up till now does not damage the account. The action has had no connection with such affiliations.

[18] Tchawan was Paliau's elder brother by blood. But where Paliau was the adopted child and heir of a rich man of Pere gens, Tchawan was the adopted child, and not the heir, of a man of Matchupal gens. Tchawan was an economic dependent of Paliau and took orders from Paliau. But Tchawan in sheltering Poiyo and Kampon was acting on their common gens membership in Matchupal gens.

both of Matchupal gens; so also was Kampon, Poiyo's marriage to her being against the native code. In the back of Tchawan's house Poiyo normally visited Kampon. Now that Nyakareu was under taboo to him, Poiyo stayed continuously with Kampon for the time being.

The mediums, being women and jealous of women's rights, and being puritan and shocked by obscenity between two women, had indicted Poiyo thoroughly. A child of Kampon was said to have died because Kampon, having no house, had continually moved from house to house, a most irregular procedure. A child of Nyakareu was said to have died because the Sir Ghost of Poiyo had been shocked by the language used between Kampon and Nyakareu. Sickness in Poiyo's own house had been attributed to Poiyo's Sir Ghost, indignant at the dilapidated condition of the house in which he was sheltered. Sickness in Tchawan's household had been attributed to quarrel between the Sir Ghost of Tchawan and the Sir Ghost of Poiyo. One Sir Ghost had stolen the betel nut of the other Sir Ghost. Tchawan's Sir Ghost had become disgruntled and had taken revenge on Tchawan.

This last oracular pronouncement occurred in late December. Poiyo had begun the building of a new house in mid-December, but he did not move out of Tchawan's house too quickly. Between the 28th and 31st of December loud quarrels between Tchawan's wife and Poiyo's wife Kampon rang over the village. Then at the end of the month Poiyo and Kampon moved into an old deserted house, deserted because it was a dangerously haunted spot. The move was said to be consequent upon the quarrels between Tchawan's Sir Ghost and Poiyo's Sir Ghost over betel nut thefts on the ghostly plane.

7. *A Calico Robe is Missing*

On the evening of December 31st, Nane made divination with divining bones to see who had stolen his wife's calico robe. It fell on a Matchupal [19] woman, Loi. Nane [20] shouted

[19] A Peri village gens, referred to above.

[20] Nane was a rich man of Lo gens. His father's older brother's son, Kemwai, had married Isole of the family of highest rank in Peri village.

out public accusation. Loi shouted back that Nane's divining was worthless, and his accusation a lie. Mbosai, the most prominent man of Matchupal, and Nane's wife's close kinsman, joined in, taking Loi's part. A great yelling with great heat and anger ensued. Nane defended his divining power, pointing out his success in turtle fishing, acquired by his divining which had showed him where turtles were to be found. Loi and Mbosai retorted that Nane's divining was uninspired supernaturally, and, in fact, was self-deception.

Mbosai had been a diviner himself once. But after a death in his house he had thrown away his divining bones and given it up. He had not diagnosed the cause of illness correctly or death would not have come of it. He was evidently quite capable of extending his scepticism. Nothing transpired further about the calico robe.

8. *A Girl is Seduced*

In Manus boys and girls are usually betrothed several years before marriage. Each youngster becomes almost a pawn in an economic exchange at betrothal. The kin of the boy on both sides give a great value in dogs' teeth and *tambu* (shell-money) to the kin of the girl. The latter have to repay this by instalments in pigs and in coconut oil. The exchange is repeated in similar terms several years later at the occasion of the marriage, and often yet again years later as we celebrate silver wedding anniversaries. Betrothal is as sacrosanct as marriage. The unmarried adolescent girl is required to remain virgin. The boy, once he became a warrior, used to have access to the prostitute war captive, when there was one in the men's house. Otherwise he was, and nowadays is without exception, required to remain chaste. So the arrangements of the elder generation include the disposal of the younger in betrothal before the children have a will of their own, the quick reinforcement of this disposal by heavy economic commitments, and the protection of it by the enforcement of celibacy.

An overseas canoe from the Manus village of Mok, near Baluan Island, came upon the Manus village by the island of

PLATE IV

PERI VILLAGE

Taui under the cover of darkness. As the crew pulled in they heard the slit gong tattoo for *mbris*, sexual misconduct. They came in and were present at the exposure that followed. They brought the news to Patusi village next day, where I heard the gong call for *mbris*. A girl of Taui betrothed to a lad of Patusi had been seduced by a local Taui lad—it was alleged.

The day after, two canoe loads of Patusi men, with myself and two or three men from Peri village, set out on a day-long voyage to Taui. We encountered a violent storm on the way. We were not more than a quarter of a mile from the shore at the time, but one canoe was submerged and remained under water. The larger canoe, in which I was, came about and stood by. A rope was fastened from my canoe to the submerged canoe. A mast was then taken down, and flung into the water in front of the nose of the submerged canoe. The salvaging canoe was then paddled ahead briskly, drawing the submerged canoe up to the floating mast. It was held on the mast by some of its crew, while others baled it out briskly by see-sawing it over the mast. The load of sago it carried had floated and was salvaged. We then proceeded without further incident. The same storm sank a large overseas canoe of Taui out in the open sea, and the other canoe that was sailing with it was not able to salvage it owing to the violence of the seas.

We arrived at Taui in the late afternoon, and took up our quarters in a Government barrack that stood out a little from the village. The Taui men guessed our mission, and there was no fraternising. Only one man, the village constable of Taui, came over and associated himself with our party. Soon after, at dusk, speeches were made from barrack to village and from village to barrack.

Kukun of Patusi village was the leader of the Patusi group which had financed the betrothal from the boy's side. Pokus of Taui village was the leader of the Taui group which had financed the betrothal from the girl's side. Pokus was away wrecked at sea when we opened proceedings. Talikatin of Taui was the father of the alleged seducer of the girl. He happened to be cousin to Kukun. I noted the speeches as they were made.

Kukun opened:

"Talikatin, on a previous occasion did we lie, or did we tell the truth? We came with many of Patusi, Loitcha and Mbuke villages. On that occasion we fought over just such event as this. Some of us were left dead on the coral rubble. Now we have come.

"Only recently too we made speech over this matter. Not one moon has passed since, and we are come back again.

"The betrothal contract between my sons here and the women of your party, you spoil. Their own father has died, and you remain. You are a man of rank. My sons here are men of rank. If within your party you had refrained from despoiling your women you had not then besmirched my sons. In despoiling your women you blacken my sons.

"When your father was alive he financed your affairs. My sons here have lost their true father. In the time when their father was alive they would have avenged themselves with arms upon you. Now we have white administration we have cast out revenge at arms.

"We have made the speech of our party to the betrothal to its conclusion. Long ago we came. We spent night and day in dispute with only blood in our stomachs. This time my sons here are all men of rank, without their father. Long speech on our part is unseemly. We say only that we are not come to give battle. We do but conduct our enquiry in that manner."

Liankor, head man, and former war leader, of Taui, cried across the water:

"People of my village, they of Patusi and they of Peri have come. They carry indictment against our village. They come to war on the house of Talikatin, but it touches the houses of all of us. Evil is already upon our houses, and on top of it, war is come to bring blood upon the houses of all of us. As for you, native constable of this village, you said I was strong. But you begged me as a favour to refrain from carrying on war while you were native constable. Now in a case like this you strike me into passivity."

Talikatin spoke next from his house, addressing Kukun:

"Cousin, when you arrived I was not on my house platform, but out fishing. They bore word to me. I came. I have often admonished my son saying, 'Do not violate another's rights,' and always he replied to me dutifully. Of old custom it is allowable for youths to sleep in company. And my son made to go where the youths had gathered to sleep. He stepped over a sleeper's body. He thought Ndralina (a youth) rested in the house. He went and took fire to light his cigarette. By the light he saw more clearly. He said, 'But this is a woman.' He stood up and away. He came and sat down resting on the house centre board. The woman stood up. She took the infant girl by her side and gave it to its mother. She returned and asked him, 'Who are you?' He aghast said nothing. He went away without a word and punted home to this house. Ndralina saw him go and beat the slit gong for misconduct.

"You are in the same position as I. I tell what happened to my son. I know it. Yes. Wrathfully from your side you say that my son and I have violated rights. If so, then may my canoe with all my property go adrift, and drift over to you. But it seems that no evil has actually been done, no clear proof of despoiling shown.

"Then too this son of mine comes from your village. The father of those sons with your party was the brother of the woman who bore me this son of mine. Once before you came and made speech. The sons of mine that stay with me speak through me. I do not speak for myself. When you came with complaint against my son, I said, 'I know nothing of it.' His speech I can tell you. His cousins questioned him. He confessed nothing to them. If he should confess that he seduced this woman, I have no property, but I can pay. His speech I convey. If he deceives you, then let the woman said to be seduced tell all from her own mouth. Let us all hear it."

Kukun, speaking again, replied:

"Cousin, when we came before we found you at home. This time, had you not been out fishing when we came, you would have heard all we said. This time true report, not lying report, came to our village, from a third party. Yesterday, my sons wanted to go to the white court at Lorengau to take legal proceedings. But I had to take part in an exchange at Patusi. So we stayed there. Then to-day we came here. Only you were out fishing, or we would be done talking, not going over it again. We'd be on our way home."

The full documentation of all the speeches may be interrupted at this point. The noteworthy point to date is that war might have been engaged in upon this issue in the days before European control. The war leader of Taui admitted that evil was upon the Taui houses, and that war was due on top of them. This expectation of the Sir Ghosts or ghosts bringing evil in the form of sickness or death for sin within a house, is thus but the supernaturalistic obverse of the naturalistic fact of warlike hostility directed from outside from a part of the wider society against the same house. To the extent that it can be said of Sir Ghost "vengeance is mine, I will repay," as also to the extent that it can be said of a king or of a supreme secular authority, just to such an extent can this warlike hostility be reasonably abated. The extent to which the Manus use the concept "Vengeance is mine, I will repay, saith Sir Ghost" in the abatement of warfare cannot be studied now, since warfare is abolished, and has been since 1918. Parkinson, who saw the Manus in their war days, says, however, that in case of fights neutral bystanders usually disarmed the opposing parties. The concept that Sir Ghost effected all due punishment and secured expiatory pay to offended parties undoubtedly worked in the interest of the maintenance of neutral bodies of persons, and in effecting some deference to them. It still influences the Manus temper in dispute. They have a great regard for orderliness, and arbitration by formal speeches in their own affairs, and they stand alone in the Mandated Territory of New Guinea in their respect for the courts of the Australian Administration and for their almost inordinate love of using them. Meanwhile, the point demonstrated is that Sir Ghost, like the District Officer of the present Australian Administration, represents the law. The spirit of submission to a higher power expressed religiously represents also the spirit of submission to the just claims of persons who are on the outer circles of the society, considering a society as a series of widening circles of kin, clan, local group, and outside local groups.

Pokenau, native constable of Pontchal (of Peri village), now spoke for Patusi and for Kukun:

"You there, our speech is finished, quarrel and orating alike. Talikatin has made speech. His speech may be true, or it may not be true.

"It's finished, and the native constable of your village (of Taui) is here with us. He says he will not talk. He is angry with you. He says the whole lot of you constitute yourselves as nothing else than 'bosses,' the whole lot of you. And he will not talk. And this woman of yours. She appears from where to testify? You talk to her. We want to hear. You talk."

Liankor, head man of Taui, replied to the visitors:

"You there. So. Let this speech go to you. You men of the coast line are there, you of Patusi are there, one white man is there. You have come, you remain there. For this side Talikatin has spoken to a finish on behalf of his son.

"And if the father of the woman were here he would speak. He is not here. Speech may rest. But you call for speech. Once before this kind of thing touched us. We made expiatory payment and you carried it off. And now this touches us again. So. If the owner of the (impugned) house were here he might give mouth and speak. You might hear.

"The native constable says he does not understand it. So. You make speeches too as well as we. The native constable is angry that you are not listening to him exclusively.

"This daughter of ours slept beside the fireplace. The boys slept, and the wife of Pokus slept. (Pokus is the father of the girl alleged to have been seduced by the son of Talikatin. He was away on a canoe voyage at the time, and is still away.)

"So; and the youth came. He came and climbed into the house. He went along the centre-board. This daughter of ours says that he put his cigarette to the fire, but saw nothing by it. He came from the wall. He saw her by the light of the fire red glowing. His hand reached out and touched her body. She turned over, and said, 'Who are you?' 'I am the child of Talikatin.' She stood up. She took the girl infant to its mother. They both stood up to see (the intruder). He had punted away in his canoe. The noise went to the house next door. Ndralina punted out. He saw. He asked, 'You, what were you doing groping in the dark about our house?' So the drum-beat for misconduct he struck, and speech was made concerning the matter. This is the talk that was made then. You have come there. I repeat the talk that was made. They instructed me in what had happened. I pass it on.

"He stood on the verandah. He took away the mat and house door barricade. He touched her body. She said, 'Who are you?' He said, 'I am the son of Talikatin.' 'What are you doing here?' He punted away."

From the barrack where we visitors were the native constable of Taui spoke heatedly.

"Talk of all. Yes. I am angry. You make out that this is a minor affair of sexual misconduct. I do not understand that. The men of Mok told the men of Patusi what happened. Their canoe comes to us. My speech is not strong (against them). You all talk the little thing of no importance, but your talk is the little thing of no importance. Talikatin, the talk of your son, like that which you make, is lies. From south side to north side, all people talk of this as a complete and seriously true seduction. Confess it now. The woman seduced did not talk like the male seducer. The woman did not confess to a touch of his hand on her body merely. The report of the real truth, real seduction, went to those of Patusi. You confess it now. This is not a hand caress. Real seduction. Now talk the truth. Let them all hear. All women and all men, come confess it. This was seduction. They all call for truth in speech.

"If rape, talk now. If a touch of the hand, talk. I say even if only a touch of the hand in greeting how could that have proceeded but to seduction? So the talk has flown to all places. I have heard it. And once before this occurred."

The head man of Taui replied:

"My grandfather Maninime said, 'Our backsides do not talk, our hands do talk. If two engage in illicit amours they do not talk. They lie about it.' She thought first, 'He seduced me. I shall lie about it.' If I had said all my mind before, I had said this from a true mouth."

The native constable of Taui said:

"Talikatin can pay. I am here to see that they may take away expiatory payment for this. This is true speech. They forbore to take the matter to the white courts. All they want is the correct expiatory payment."

At this point the constable of Taui had his speech interrupted by the death beat from a slit drum at the end of the village. The attention of everyone went towards this solemnly announced disaster. The father of the seduced girl was back from his overseas voyage, Son-of-Nyapo, otherwise called Pokus. He and his party had put out with two large overseas canoes. One canoe had been lost entirely. No life had been lost, the crew of the overturned canoe having been rescued by the other canoe, which outlived the storm. The returning crews were being wailed over by all their kin.

The Patusi party remained sullenly apart, although news of the nature of the interruption had been privately conveyed to them. I left the party and set out to investigate the disturbance. I found the crew in one house with the mourning relatives. But just two houses away was a situation of which the visitors had not been appraised. Here a girl lay unconscious with her head laid open, and with a subdued wailing going on that was inaudible at the far end of the village where I had been with the visiting party. I was told that it was the guilty girl. Her father had been away, but her brother had not. And, just after the first speech from the visitors, her brother had taken up a wooden head-rest and struck fiercely at her, with intent to kill. He was disarmed before he brought his raised arm down a second time. The girl had a severe open scalp wound and she had been already over an hour unconscious. She "came to" later, and I returned to my party bearing the news.

There was no further communication between Taui men and the visitors that night. We slept apart in the barrack. Next morning there was a sullen silence. At nine thirty my party made ready to go. Several of the men spoke wildly amongst themselves of seizing the girl and taking her off, but as they were avoidance relatives of the girl, as kin of her contracted future husband, it was mere talk. The canoe was punted half way out of the village when Talikatin, unable to endure this sullen, threatening departure, called out:

"Cross-cousin. So. The speech we made last night. We slept after day break, so we said no more this morning. And you want to sail to your village. I stay here. If I stayed in my place I would be with you in that canoe. (Talikatin is living in his wife's place in Taui, not in his own place, Patusi.) If I do not pay, perhaps evil (*i.e.*, supernaturally wrought evil) will come upon me. You return. I shall pay."

The canoe moved over to near Talikatin's house. Talikatin approached in his canoe saying, "So; all the women here say he has seduced her. So. You stay! I shall pay. You may not go yet. Let us rest awhile."

Talikatin and all the Patuṣi party crowded into the barrack. Kukun stood up to speak, some tears in his eyes and running down his cheeks as he spoke:

"We do not want expiatory payment. We want to take the woman and marry her off immediately. If we take payment *pakob* (Kukun's Sir Ghost) may send evil upon us.

"Once before when we carried off payment for this thing *pakob* sent loss, not upon one of these sons, but upon me. This time let it not go to court, but let us take the woman to ourselves, and sail to our village."

(Kukun lost a pig through death just after he had obtained expiatory payment for a similar offence from Talikatin before. The Manus do not greatly like expiatory payment; in this case Kukun attributed the loss of the pig to his taking expiatory payment, when he should have insisted on removing the seduced girl from temptation—an idea that he is sure of now.)

Pokenau, the native constable of Pontchal, had come

along as a comparative outsider, partly to help me, partly in the hope of acquiring a share of the expiatory payment in a general division of it between the party.[21] He spoke up quickly setting aside this latter hope:

"Talikatin wishes to make expiatory payment for his son; but we want to carry off the woman. We do not want to go to court over it. But if we do not carry off the woman we shall go to Lorengau (*i.e.*, to white Administration). So we'll have a native constable sent to bring away the woman to us."

Talikatin, perceiving that Kukun had cried over the matter and weakened somewhat, quickly took advantage of the situation. At first Talikatin had broken down that morning with fear of supernatural disaster, now Kukun was in the same fear. Talikatin recovered visibly, saying:

"Cross-cousin, the talk we have made before. The woman was in the house. The youth, my son, came. He took fire. She asked who it was. He sat down on the house centre-board. He was too astonished to speak. If he had taken her, if he had admitted it, yes, I would pay. (At this point everyone left the barrack in disgust, leaving only Talikatin, Kukun and myself inside. All of Kukun's party went out as a mark of their disgust at Talikatin taking to subterfuge again. Talikatin and Kukun did not look at each other. Both hung their heads and looked down and aside. But Talikatin went on.)

"And this woman you shall take. Good. He did not hold her. He went to ask for fire only. All of Taui tell lies. My son may speak from his mouth, 'Yes, it's true; I seduced her,' and I'll pay. And the woman may then stay and marry my son. But all of Taui tell lies to a man. I shall not pay."

From outside Pokenau replied:

"You, you say that if you pay expiatory payment the woman may remain and marry your son. Eh! this expiatory payment you would pay for the despoiling done by your son. And if you would pay further a bride-price, all right. But

[21] Pokenau however was cross-cousin to the youth of Patusi village who was betrothed to the sinning girl of Taui village.

expiatory payment is not bride-price. If you cannot (pay the further bride-price) you pay for the spoilation done by your son, and we'll take the woman."

(Talikatin had argued that if he paid anything it would not be for offence, but to betroth the girl to his son, so pressing home an advantage that he had seen in Kukun's weakness.)

At this point the brother of the girl came in a canoe to the barrack. Standing in his canoe below he spoke in an almost inaudible voice:

"Constable of Pontchal, Constable of Patusi, Kukun, White Man, you have come. I went to Pak where my sister's husband just died. I came home by way of Lorengau. I heard the tidings on my way. I arrived here just after your party. Had they not held me fast I had killed her, I had struck her dead. Had she died I had killed myself by now. I have no speech to make. You may take the woman, you may take her."

Then Son-of-Nyapo, or Pokus, climbed the barrack verandah and gave a pretentious speech about nothing in particular. He said:

"For this woman you have paid the bride-price.[22] All got it. I got it. Some time ago spoilation (of the woman) was within my house. Speech concerning it we made. I did not talk much about it. I did not talk. So. You gave a bride-price, and the bride-price you gave was great. I did not stay in your village. I went by canoe. I stopped by the way in your village. Talk concerning this affair came to me there touching my house. So. Now here you talk. I wished to make *ekou* (return exchange in part repayment of bride-price). I was sailing the deep sea, and evil came upon my house. This was not my doing. So. If only when I came to my house my canoe had still been mine. I tried to run before the storm. I sank at sea. Fishes might have eaten me, stones battered me. But I came. So. I heard the talk. I shut my mouth. I do not talk. I. So. May I die. The girl's brother is here. The two may go to

[22] The wealth handed over by Kukun and his party to the speaker to validate the betrothal.

Loitcha village (from where the speaker had adopted them and financed marriage of one, the betrothal of the other). I shall remain here. So! The bride-price was large. I went on my voyage to trade for the return payment. I wish to work at it. When I left my house for that purpose evil came upon it. They came. They said, 'A woman of yours.' So. You say you do not want expiatory payment lest later you will have evil visitation. This speech you make. And today do you say that we should make expiatory payment in response to your speech? Not one has said so. Talk of the woman, talk of the bride-price you gave, you bought the woman therewith. And spoilation comes upon it. Speech concerning it you took to yourselves. So. Let me hear it. This woman did not drift to me. She is really mine, close to me (*i.e.*, closely adopted). Speech concerning it came into my house. So. I shut my mouth. I do not talk."

This last remark was oratorical device. But it became reality, for the speaker's cross-cousin (jesting relative) said vigourously in pidgin, instead of in the Manus speech:

"You finish along talk-talk; you talk long fellow, close up sun he go down,"[23] whereat Pokus finished, out of breath. He had made the point that he was engaged in work to return the value of the bride-price for the girl concerned.

The Patusi party punted out and set sail for home in high spirits, cross-cousin jesting going on vigourously in the canoe, and everyone laughing at it. The tension was broken, and everyone pleased at the fact. The financier of the girl concerned had promised to put her into another village, from which she would soon be brought to her Patusi bridegroom. That financier was busy in working to make return payments for the bride-price. The girl had been suitably chastised. The father of the girl's seducer had not paid anything, but he had paid for a similar offence less than a month before, with the result that Kukun's pig had died; and if Kukun was afraid to risk further danger from the supernatural by accepting more payment it was best so.

There was still resentment against the girl's seducer.

[23] You be done with talking or the sun will set (it was actually early morning).

Pokenau was angry at not getting his expected share of the expiatory payment and said privately to me that Kukun's talk about danger from his Sir Ghost was nonsense. Later on he hoped to see the son of Talikatin lodged in the Lorengau gaol. It was the general feeling that the seducer should be gaoled by white Administration. A canoe from Mok bound towards Taui passed near by, and shouted for news. Everyone shouted out, "Calaboosh [24] for him; expiatory payment not taken."

After the canoe got home to Patusi a seance was held to obtain Sir Ghostly advice as to future action. The Sir Ghost of Kukun, *pakob*, sanctioned proceeding to the white court with an action against the son of Talikatin.

About a week later the brother of the guilty girl killed a pig and sent it to Patusi. Pokenau received a share of spoil after all. Nothing was done with the court case at the time, as the District Officer was away visiting an outlying island. Whether the son of Talikatin was imprisoned later on I did not hear. Probably the pig salved the case.

I am sure that Kukun was convinced in his fear of Sir Ghostly displeasure if he accepted expiatory payment from Talikatin. It was not just a cover for the more drastic course of securing gaol for the seducer. It was actually felt by all, except Pokenau, who was actuated by mercenary motives, that Kukun's Sir Ghost had shown his displeasure at the customary action of receipt of expiatory payment on the former occasion. The coming of the white Administration has made an alternative possible, and just as the mediums may diagnose ill luck as caused by a man's using wealth to validate his daughter's marriage instead of his son's betrothal, so they may now diagnose ill luck as caused by the use of native justice instead of the use of Administration's justice—or vice versa in both cases. Wherever there are alternatives a man inevitably has gone wrong, if ill luck follows immediately after his taking one course—unless he has had the foresight to consult a medium before acting. It is interesting to note how culture contact is a blessing to the oracles, harassed for

[24] Pidgin word for gaol.

explanations of ill luck, by providing as it does alternative courses of action. And reciprocally the needs of the oracles help to give the new institutions a real native status, as no new religious institutions could expect to do.

The speeches cited above give a fair idea of the Manus formality in speech-making even at a time when considerable hostility was evident. The speeches did not by any means come pat after one another. They were divided by long periods of tension and silence between speech from the barrack and counter-speech from somewhere in the village. None of the protagonists were in view of one another. The village people kept their houses, the visitors, their barrack. An air of sullen hostility hung over the entire affair, the brother of the girl alone being submissive in his speech the morning after, and he being entirely broken in spirit. Pokus, or Son-of-Nyapo, the financier of the girl and of her brother, was fat, unintelligent, incurably pretentious and somewhat unconcerned. He seemed concerned with the girl as an investment only, and probably was only so concerned. Kukun of Patusi was genuinely hurt, as was also his young financial ward, the future bridegroom of the girl. The son of Talikatin was not seen by any of the visiting party, myself included. I alone saw the offending girl. The whole impulse of the visiting party at departure was to seize the girl's person, take her away and marry her off to her contracted groom immediately, as her guardians had proved themselves insufficient in imposing conventional restraint upon her. This impulse was freely expressed.

Such action would be most irregular, for the girl's financier had not yet made the conventional first repayment of the bride-price. Further the girl's financier should send her to be married with a large gift of wealth to accompany her, a considerable time after repayment of the bride-price. The normal course of economic validation takes a long while, the girl being under guardianship the while. It is taboo for her to see her future groom or any of his elder male relatives, and it is taboo for these males to approach her, until all the conventional course of economic validation is completed, and the marriage day properly ushered in. This taboo in a time of stress, such as that narrated above, functions in keeping the girl's person inviolate from the offended party of the kin of the groom. The disciplinary measures in correction of the girl are restricted by the operation of the taboo to the girl's own relatives.

This purely mortal situation is mirrored in the Manus religion. There is no conspicuous or visible taboo that holds between a man's Sir Ghost (dead relative) and the people of other households; but in regulation of the invisible it is a fact that a man's Sir Ghost is regarded as the correct ghost to inflict disciplinary measures upon his ward or upon any member of his ward's household. Correction of sin or of offence is not done by a man's Sir Ghost upon those of distantly related households who have offended against his ward, of such relationship for example as that between households connected by betrothal between their respective children. Here an invisible taboo holds as the counterpart of the visible taboo that we have discussed. But the invisible taboo is broken, as the visible taboo is not, in analogy, when the man's Sir Ghost acts as a malicious ghost to people of other houses. However, the invisible taboo holds firm for matters of discipline; it is only broken in matters of malice and hence under a different category.

The purely mortal taboo between a girl and her bridegroom with his elder male relatives is not just a pre-marital arrangement however. After the marriage day it is broken by the new relationship of wife and husband as far as those two are concerned. However the former taboo on meeting between them is not broken at a stroke. It infects their new relationship with a great feeling of extreme distance for many years. And the taboo between the wife and her husband's elder male kin continues unbroken by the marriage.

As we shall see later, sexual misconduct is believed to be a prime cause of Sir Ghostly retribution, if kept secret. The above case gives a conception of the publicity that follows detection. This publicity and public settlement of offence is believed to avert the otherwise inevitable retribution that would follow. Hence secrecy is difficult to attain in Manus. Any third party is an informer of entire villages.

9. *To Pay or Not to Pay; a Medium's Self-Interest*

About January 13th, Mwe, the child of Nane,[25] and a child of Ngamasue [26] were ill. I heard the report after the seances had been held. Nane was preparing at this time to give a great gift of wealth to his wife's kin. His wife had borne him many children, and Nane was preparing a gift in honour of the fact. All men do not give this gift; it is reckoned a great achievement. The man and his kin give dogs' teeth and shell money to his wife's kin, which the latter repay later in pigs and in oil. The ceremonial resembles that of marriage and is in fact a second marriage, a kind of silver wedding. It is not obligatory. A man need not lose his wife after she has borne him five or six children if he is unable to finance the *metcha*, as it is called. But only men of no economic prestige, or men who have not been married long to one woman, do not give it.

One member of Nane's wife's kin was away working for the white man. It was held that this absentee's Sir Ghost had made Nane's child, Mwe, ill, because the gifts of the *metcha* were to be made in his absence. Here again we find the medium using the results of culture contact to explain illness. And we have a departure from the general tendency that a man's own Sir Ghost punishes his ward or ward's family for the ward's or the ward's family's sin or error. The absentee's Sir Ghost was a dead brother of Nane's wife, mother's brother to Mwe.

* * *

The child of Ngamasue fell ill, it was said, because Ngamasue had intended to give wealth in his possession to his wife's kin, to whom he owed the gift, rather than to his son's

[25] Nane we have already cited as a rich man of Lo gens, of a younger line than Kemwai, the husband of Isole.

[26] Ngamasue is a man of Kalo gens, a gens relative of Alupwai, the woman ill in child bearing of our earlier account. The adopted son of Ngamasue, Ndroi by name, is betrothed to the daughter of Kemwai and Isole, Lawian by name (to be distinguished from Lawa of Kalo gens, Alupwai's sister, whom Patalian had failed to secure in marriage).

future bride's kin to validate his son's betrothal, which was also long outstanding.

Both courses of action were justly due from Ngamasue, but the medium was the mother of the future bride of Ngamasue's son (Isole, mother of Lawian).

10. *A Man Addresses His Sir Ghost during the Monthly Fishing; a Stranger Dies in the Village*

The new moon had been seen on the evening of January 12th. From that date four days were counted. On the fifth day the run of shoaling fish coming in to spawn was expected.

In daily fishing a Manus man makes no special appeal to his Sir Ghost, unless he has caught little or nothing over several days. But in the times of the spawning of great shoals of fish in the lagoons special appeal is made. The times of spawning are predicted. Every lunar month the Manus watch for the first appearance of the new moon, and then count four days before going out to watch for the shoals. They also watch for the full moon and count four days as it begins to wane. On the fifth day they expect a large catch again. This prediction is almost invariably correct, although on occasion the large shoals come some twelve or even twenty-four hours behind expectation. The tides are then sufficiently high to bring the fish inshore over the reef. The different species of fish expected to spawn in the lagoon in each lunar month are also accurately predicted.

As the new moon had been seen on the evening of the twelfth, at three o'clock in the morning of the seventeenth following I went out with Pokenau and his cousin in a solitary canoe to watch for the expected shoals, and rouse the village if they were sighted before dawn. We were very solemn in our going. Pokenau kept a sharp lookout for the omen bird or the omen fish of his clan, in order to send the canoe in the direction bird or fish was going if sighted. Neither bird flew nor fish jumped, however. So we stopped, and Pokenau made divination with his divining bones whether to go north or south.

The choice came for south. As he paddled Pokenau called on his Sir Ghost, *poendrilei* (fish-hawk) by name.

"My father,[27] fish-hawk, run! Drive the fish flying inshore! I call upon thee. I entreat thee. If a brother of thine builds a house or cuts a canoe it is thine. If I build a house, is it not thine? If I cut a canoe, is it not thine? If it is not, then do not hear my request. If another than I is thy brother, then do not hear my request. Drive the fish flying inshore! Let my speech to thee who art a ghost be readily heard. If these fish in question were thy brothers' and thy fathers', then let them remain in the depths of the sea. But I am thy brother. Do thou then drive the fish into the lagoons that all of us mortals may strike them, and that all of us may praise thee.

"Fish-hawk, if this white man had been here while thou wert yet mortal he would have accompanied thee. If then the fish had not run inshore, their date not yet, but had remained in the sea under such circumstances, how would thou have felt about it?

"But after thou died, this white man came down here. He is of thy house. He is of thy place. He stays with us two, with thee the ghost, with me the mortal. And he wishes to see our fishing. He is out of a far-off place. He does not know much. He came down here this moon. He stays. He wishes to see these fish. Today is their due date.

"This white man wants to see a goodly sight. He will praise thee as a ghost of rank. He will go to his own country and there talk to all men and all women. He will say, 'There is good fishing in Manus. I went with them fishing. I went with Pokenau, native constable of Pontchal. His Sir Ghost is good and strong. I lived in his place. I slept in his house. I dwelt by his coral platform. When I went fishing with him he called upon his brother of the ghostly plane. His Sir Ghost sent fish. The Manus captured them.'

"Fish-hawk, drive the fish to the shoreward shallows. Fish-hawk! Fish-hawk!"

[27] Pokenau's Sir Ghost was his dead older brother, called father by custom, more usually known as *sori*.

Pokenau addressed the air in this manner, with many variations, until the fish shoals were sighted in the late afternoon, and several thousand fish taken in the nets. In one pause I asked him, "Can Sir Ghost make the fish many?" He scorned such notion of miracle or magic. "No ghost can make many. None can make one fish into two fish. Sir Ghost can drive fish inshore. But if Sir Ghost is angry with me he can hide the fish by driving them out to sea into deep water instead."

* * *

On an evening two days after my first witness of the fish-spawning in the lagoon a long speech rang out over the waters of a quiet village. It was subdued in tone and pleading, no speech such as is used between mortals. It was Nyapo calling upon his Sir Ghost, *tchangau* by name, his father's ghost.

"Hearken, *tchangau,* hear me. Go to Loitcha village. Go there to the ghosts of Loitcha, to all the ghosts of rank. Ask there the ghostly father, the ghostly brother of this man, my guest, who lies here stricken. Ask there concerning him. If a ghost of rank strikes him let them offer expiatory payment to him to redeem their mortal kinsman. If the ghost who strikes him is of the inland bushmen, if the offended ghost is of Patusi village, let them offer expiatory payment to him to redeem this man.

"He has lain ill a long time. He lay ill three moons in Loitcha. Now after that he has come here. He felt his skin bad. He said then, 'I stay at Loitcha. But no one does anything for me. I shall die. If I stay in my own place I shall but die there. My wife died in my place.'

"So saying he has come here. He has come down to the house of a friend and of a relative-in-law. He rests with the Sir Ghost here and with the mortals here. He is thy guest, *tchangau*, and mine, thine as Sir Ghost, mine as mortal. I call upon thee.

"Do thou expiate destruction wrought by him. Find it. Pay for it. So. This man may then walk again. He who does not know safe places for his walking, sago-palm spikes run into him. He goes over the place of the sea urchin; spikes of sea urchin run into him.

"From of old if a ghost strikes a man, and one holds seance, or one calls upon Sir Ghost, thou hearest it, thou discoverest the cause of it. Such is the custom of you who are ghosts. Thou sayest to me that I may have food to eat, then have I food to eat. Thou sayest to me that I may drink water, then drink I water.

"Go thou with the great amongst ghosts. Expiate this man to them. Send him health. This man of the north may say that he came to thee and to me who are of the north, but who dwell now in the south. This man is with us two. Guard him. Recover him. Restore him. I make this request of thee. Go to his ghostly brothers and to his ghostly fathers that they may pay for what wrong he did, and redeem him from the angered ghosts. Give him his life.

"If one comes to the pass of not eating food, of not drinking water, and thou sayest that he shall die, eh! he dies. If one abandons food, abandons water, and thou sayest that he shall not die, eh! he must needs return to us mortals.

"I who address thee am bad and of no account. All the ghosts will not listen to my entreaty. But thou art good and great. Thou speakest and all the ghosts cannot but hear thee. Send him health, I entreat thee."

The following day Nyapo's guest died. The appeal, which had sounded so hollowly over the village, had been a last resort.

11. *A Too Tardy House Building*

On January 21st just as Ngamel[28] was preparing to go to a ceremony at another village, his small son Pakob fell into a fit of unconsciousness from a malarial attack. There was general assembly, crying and stirring of bowls. I brought Pakob back to consciousness with spirits of ammonia. This relieved the tension. Ngamel's action was credited with the recovery, not the spirits of ammonia, of course. Ngamel had immediately made divination to see if the trouble was not

[28] Ngamel was a rich man of Pere gens and a quiet man. He owned the house neighbouring to mine.

that his Sir Ghost was angry at his having taken out hoarded tobacco to give away at the ceremony he was setting out for, instead of keeping it to pay for communal work towards building a house for his titular son, a project he had also in mind. The answer to his divination had been affirmative, so he had hastily locked up the tobacco again.

On January 23rd the child fainted again, and the performance was repeated. The divination this time was that Ngamel had not made sufficient speed towards that house building. That evening a seance was held, Isole being the medium. The seance followed the lines of the divination that had preceded it earlier in the day.

"Go ask *nyame* (Ngamel's Sir Ghost) why he strikes this child."

"He strikes Pakob (the child) because you, Ngamel, and Pwiseu with you are slow in building a house for Manuai."

(Manuai was the son of Pwiseu,[29] brother of Ngamel. He had just returned from working for the white man. He had brought home two pigs as part of his wages. It was felt that a bachelor's house should be built for him, as he was too old to stay in his father's house. Prudery entered into this consideration, but the general euphemism was that some return should be made for his two pigs by his fathers, Pwiseu, and Ngamel.)

Ngamel replied:

"So; *nyame*, restore my son to health and I can make it. Already today the posts were cut. Tomorrow I shall set up the marking sticks" (used to chart out the positions where the posts will be placed later).

nyame said:

"So. All the constabulary, and all the assistant constabulary and all the common people may buy rice from the traders, and you two may build a house and pay for the rice for all (feast to validate house building). And this coral rubble territory the house of the white man has gone by it (a new house of mine being built near Ngamel's house); it has

[29] Pwiseu was elder adopted brother of Ngamel, so called because he was said to go about visiting other persons' houses often like a "pussy," of which his name is a corruption.

gone to all the whites. One (coral rubble) up at Pontchal (the barrack) has gone also to all the whites. One (coral rubble territory) in Peri belongs to Korotan. And this new house let it go in the sea between the two coral rubble territories."

The fact that Ngamel had already attended to post cutting did not relieve him from the weight of the system. If a man is not working his child may fall ill because he is idle. If he is working his child may fall ill because he is not working at unprecedented speed. There is no real loop hole for a man harassed by ghosts or by Sir Ghosts. But he strains every effort towards speed in work after such a seance as the above.

12. *A Sinner Betrays His Sins* [30]

This seance of the evening of January 23rd was not the centre of public interest for that day however. In the afternoon following the child's faint in the morning, and preceding the seance, a great and an unusual scandal had been made public.

It began in a fishing canoe out by the reef, where two young men, Noan and Tcholai, were fishing and talking as they fished. Noan talked too much. He was the worthless and somewhat feeble-minded son of a worthless and equally low grade father, Pope.[31] His family was poverty stricken and lazy. Noan had been handed over to the Government, which offered to feed and to educate all the children that parents or foster parents would relinquish and allow to go far away to boarding school and white tutelage in place of native tutelage. From Peri two or three orphans and Noan, who alone was not an orphan, were handed over, boys who were not wanted because fatherless, or because their talents were not prized, or both. Noan was expelled from the school after several years of amazing tolerance. After a few years as a servant to various white men he was black-listed as an incorrigible and a stupid thief, and debarred from all possibility of further service for whites. He came back to his own place, which had

[30] A genealogy of actors in this section is given on p. 153.

[31] Who will be remembered as the inveterate bowl stirrer who stirred a bowl over Alupwai; the cataleptic moron.

only allowed him to depart in the first place because no one wanted him about (and I may add, such is the quality of a boy that the Government may expect to recruit for boarding school far more often than not. These natives do not believe in giving up control of their good material in the coming generation).

In the fishing canoe by the reef Noan made extraordinary statements to Tcholai. "I slept in the house of Kemwai and Isole when their granddaughters from Mok were there. When all were asleep I rolled over and had intercourse with Pwentchiam, then with Pwentchiam's two sisters. Another time when I slept in the house of Kemwai and Isole I had intercourse with their daughter, Lawian. Again I once had intercourse with Salikon, Paliau's daughter."

All these girls were nubile and betrothed except Salikon, who was betrothed, but not yet nubile. Tcholai was aghast with horror and with fear. Here was sin of an enormity sufficient to cause the ghosts to wipe out several houses. Isole was Tcholai's own father's sister, Lawian, her daughter, his own cross-cousin. The Sir Ghosts of Isole's house were also the Sir Ghosts of Tcholai's house, for Isole lived in her own place. Her husband lived with her under the protection of the matrilocal Sir Ghosts, not vice versa, as is the commoner custom. The brothers, *talipolalau,* were divided as Sir Ghosts between Isole, and her brothers, Talikai, and Korotan, Tcholai's father. Lawian was betrothed to a family of the gens of Kalo.[32] The defilement of this betrothal, and of the betrothals of Isole's granddaughters, would not go unpunished by the *talipolalau,* if kept secret and unexpiated; and Tcholai was in the range of possible supernatural punishment himself, as one of the wards of the *talipolalau.* Moreover if he kept a secret such as Noan's, even apart from his own relationship to the endangered group, he or his kin would be liable to punishment for his merely keeping a guilty secret.[33]

Tcholai, recognising that Noan was imbecile to give such an impossible confidence to him, came home, beat a slit gong

[32] To Ndroi, son of Ngamasue.

[33] A genealogy of the principal parts here follows on p. 153 and may be consulted at any point desired.

with the tattoo for sexual misconduct and for war, and announced the facts to the entire village. The village immediately seethed like a disturbed hornets' nest. The drums of Kalo gens and of Paliau's house responded with the tattoo for sexual misconduct and for war. The houses of Isole's granddaughters and of their fiancés were in a far away village forty miles overseas, they being maternal granddaughters; the house of Paliau's daughter's fiancé was in another village. So Kalo gens were the only contracted relatives-in-law concerned who were present.

Angry speeches rang out over the water from the leading men in Kalo gens. So a son of Kalo was betrothed to a wanton, Lawian. Lawian had sinned not only grossly, but worse still, with an incest relative. Noan's father, Pope, was of Lo gens, by his having passed voluntarily out of his own gens by blood; Lawian's father, Kemwai, was of Lo gens.

Back from Kemwai went promise of expiation to Kalo, promise that did not soothe Kalo appreciably, for the Manus hate the offence in all cases of sexual misconduct far more than they appreciate the expiatory payment.

From the quarter of the village where Pope and Noan lived there was dead silence. It was realised by all that not only the *talipolalau*, Sir Ghosts of Lawian's mother, Isole, by right of blood and of Lawian's father, Kemwai, by adoption (he being a matrilocal resident), were likely to strike at their wards, but any of the Sir Ghosts of the gens of Lo were likely to strike at their wards. Lawian's father was of Lo gens, Pope's mother had been of Lo gens before she died, and Pope had been adopted into that gens. His father's gens relatives had had none of Pope, so he had coöperated in fishing and in commercial communalities in his lazy and comparatively ineffectual way with Lo. Any marriage in which the wife is the dominant and effectual person is likely to lead to matrilocal residence and matrilocal dependence on the part of a child of the marriage. So Pope, the son of a matrilocal father, was with Lo, of Lo and reckoned as being of nothing else than Lo, despite his other paternal descent, which in practice was reckoned by no one. His betrothal and first marriage and so on had been financed by Lo long ago.

Kemwai was a matrilocal resident man, himself, of his wife's place by residence, not like Pope, of his mother's, by residence and adoption and economic dependence. Kemwai was dominated somewhat by his wife, Isole. She had rank (*lapan*), while he was a commoner (*lau*). She had brains, but he had only solidity and integrity. Kemwai lived under the care of the Sir Ghosts of Isole and her kin, the *talipolalau*, of Pere gens. But his children were not in any sense adopted or financed by Kemwai's wife's kin, but rather by Kemwai's kin. Kemwai worked in all economic affairs with his own gens of Lo, and with his own gens for his own children, and for all other children of Lo. He was far more independent and rich than Pope's father had been, and independent in the greatest matter of all that determines kinship in Manus, the economic validation of kinship duties.

Since Pope was of Lo gens by all the kinship that counts, and Kemwai equally with Lo, but in spiritual matters connected with Isole's *talipolalau*, for Noan's sins, for Kemwai's daughter's and granddaughters' sins, the Sir Ghosts of Lo gens and the *talipolalau* were the responsible agents of punishment, for sin redoubled in seriousness, if that were possible, because incestuous.

Within the houses of Kemwai and Pope outraged parents confronted a sullen daughter and a sullen son respectively. In customary manner the parent raged because the care and love for a child had been requited by ingratitude and contempt; because of the public shame brought upon the house, the terrible danger of sudden death that hung over the house and the need of confession to avert it.

Noan's talk to Tcholai as reported by Tcholai was not taken as confession unless confirmed by the principals concerned, in response to the tumult of anger from Kalo, from Paliau, and from their parents.

Neither Noan nor Lawian would confess to sin, despite the general assurance that sickness or death would descend upon themselves or on their nearest kin if they were concealing sin, despite their fathers' expressed lack of belief in their sullen denials, despite the fact that they were being wrung for confession separately and apart, so that the one did not know what stand the other was making. Kemwai and Pope spoke telling the denials.

Lawian left her father's house and went to sleep in the house of her titular brother, Nane.[34] Noan left his father's house for that of the father of a young friend.

No one believed the denials. They are customary when there is nothing to be gained from confession but public shame. This shame is great and compelling in Manus, where excretion and sex alike are regarded as disgraceful. Even the offal of the pig pens is cleaned out by the house wife in the complete darkness before dawn. It is most deeply disgraceful to be caught at such an occupation by anyone whomsoever. It is as deeply disgraceful for a man to urinate in the sight of another man. The men of Peri, without exception, do not know that women menstruate between puberty and marriage. The young women, without realising that all their men are so ignorant, faithfully conceal the facts from them.

It is into such an air of shamed prudery that a confession of sin must be launched. Confession will make all but the penitents' close friends talk of the penitents' sin as if it were the copulation of dogs. The girl penitent, whenever for months after she has to appear in a public place, will slink through the village with all the aspect and air of a cowed dog. The boy penitent will avoid all public meetings as much as is possible.

Hence it was natural and not unexpected that Noan and Lawian should meet accusation with sullen denial. Such denial, for the time being, was not accepted as final—time and the Sir Ghosts would determine the truth.

The magnitude of the charges prevented clear cut speeches in quarrel, such as those I have cited in the Taui village episode. Kemwai, for instance, stormed at by Kalo gens,

[34] Kemwai, Lawian's father, was the son of an elder brother, where Nane was the son of a younger brother. Thus to Nane Kemwai was terminologically a father (elder "brother" being termed "father"), while to Kemwai's child Nane was terminologically a brother (father's younger "brother" being termed "brother").

stormed at Lawian. He got denial of the charge from her. He spoke to Kalo, trying to soothe them with it. It had the contrary effect. The next minute Kemwai was storming at Pope as angry with Pope's son, Noan, as Kalo were with Kemwai's daughter, Lawian, just as if Lawian's denial had not been solemnly announced by him. Kalo turned Kemwai's inconsistency back upon him. The usual clarity of thrust and parry in speech was not observed. Lo was not a gens united against an accusing Kalo gens, but one divided by charge of incest, and anger mounted high.

That night Noan, fleeing from home, slept in the house of Pwiseu, father of his young age-mate, Manuai. Awakening before dawn, Noan arose and stirred up the fire. He saw by its gleam that the grass skirt of Pwiseu's wife had fallen off her and that she lay exposed on the women's side of the house. Pwiseu, roused by Noan's return to his sleeping place, got up also and went to the fire to warm himself, and to see incidentally what Noan had been doing. He saw his wife lying naked, roused her and told her to cover herself.

The incident preyed on Pwiseu's mind. All his wife's relatives, male and female, were his present guests. His wife had to cook food for them. He could not beat her immediately. By early afternoon all the cooking was done and half the village assembled in Pwiseu's house to take part in a ceremony.

Pwiseu opened and immediately prevented the proceedings from going smoothly through by publicly denouncing his wife, stating the facts as he saw them and alleging her infidelity with Noan with great show of anger. His wife, crying, gathered together her property to take away with her, protested her utter innocence and counter-alleged that Pwiseu had slept last night with her sister. Her counter charge was without righteous indignation, or anger or continued vehemence, however, and fell weakly, as she took herself out of the house. Then the ceremony proceeded.

Noan was subjected to further cross-examination by Pope, his father, and by Kemwai and Nane, the men of Lo. He admitted to one of his cross-cousins that he had seen Pwiseu's wife as she lay naked the night before. Further he admitted that he had seduced Pwentchiam of Mok, but said that he had not seduced Pwentchiam's two sisters. So Thursday passed. On Friday morning Pope took propitiatory payment, *kano*, to Kemwai, to expiate the offence between Noan and Pwentchiam in Kemwai's house, and another propitiatory payment to Pwiseu's house to expiate Noan's having seen Pwiseu's wife naked. Standing in his canoe before Kemwai's housefront Pope addressed the *talipolalau*, calling on them by name and saying, "Here is your payment, you ghostly ones, to expiate the evil done under your roof." The payment, a cedar wood box with its lock and keys and a European axe, he had first placed on the house platform. Kemwai did not appear. But after Pope had gone away Kemwai, as the mortal ward of the *talipolalau*, took the offering made to them unto himself. So also *kano* was offered at Pwiseu's house to Pwiseu's ancestors, and finally collected by Pwiseu. In this manner the *talipolalau*, Pwiseu's Sir Ghost and Pope's Sir Ghost were all appeased and warranted not to cause sickness in their own respective houses, or death in one of the others' houses on account of Noan and Pwentchiam, or on account of Noan having seen Pwiseu's wife naked. The village accepted this latter affair as a matter of accidental exposure only, not of infidelity by Pwiseu's wife, an event very unlikely with the public attention focussed so intensely upon Noan at the time, and with so many visitors sleeping in Pwiseu's house. Moreover Noan in committing his sin in Kemwai's house had rolled over several times, as if accidentally and in his sleep, in order to escape detection. Sleep rolling showed guilty intent. But in Pwiseu's house he had risen up and gone openly to the fire. The small children about the village by this time were calling Noan "sleep roller" whenever they met him.

Kano was paid for the sin in Pwiseu's house nevertheless; and this is the custom, not an exception. The sight of an accidental exposure is a heinous offence in the eyes of the spirits, and is as likely to cause sickness or possibly death as anything done with intent; anything, that is, short of incest. The charge against Noan and Lawian still remained as a possibility pregnant with the greatest disaster. The spirits are not always or even usually expected to grade the punishment to the offence. In consequence the mortals concerned do not grade the offences as we might grade them. But it was impossible not to think of incest as a far more dangerous situation than the more usual run—despite for example a lack of such differentiation between Noan's adventures with Pwentchiam on the one hand and with Pwiseu's wife on the other.

The next day, Saturday, was marked by an important marriage ceremonial in which great stores of wealth were invested, a dance at forenoon over the wealth, and canoe races between several villages in the afternoon. The dates for all these had been fixed long in advance and they proceeded as a matter of course. As soon as the canoe races were over Kalo beat the sexual misconduct tattoo on their drums; Tcholai took it up and the tattoo came from the drum in his father's house. There were more speeches against Noan and Lawian, renewed attempts at the extortion of confession. But nothing came of it. Gizikup, head man of the neighbouring village of Mbunai, said, "All right; if they are hiding it, illness will come up from their concealing; then, unless they wish their own kin to die, confession will be made. Let the talk die for the present."

With foreboding the kins concerned waited for illness or possibly sudden death. A whirlwind felled a house in the next door village, Patusi, but the event aroused no interest except some remarks about the house having not been built strongly. One remark only from past history told how Korotan's house had once been broken by a whirlwind owing to Korotan not having paid a large debt. That whirlwind had evidently been a ghostly visitation. But damage to another village of none too serious a nature was not of much concern to Peri village with a threat of imminent calamity hanging over it. So January 26th went out in tension.

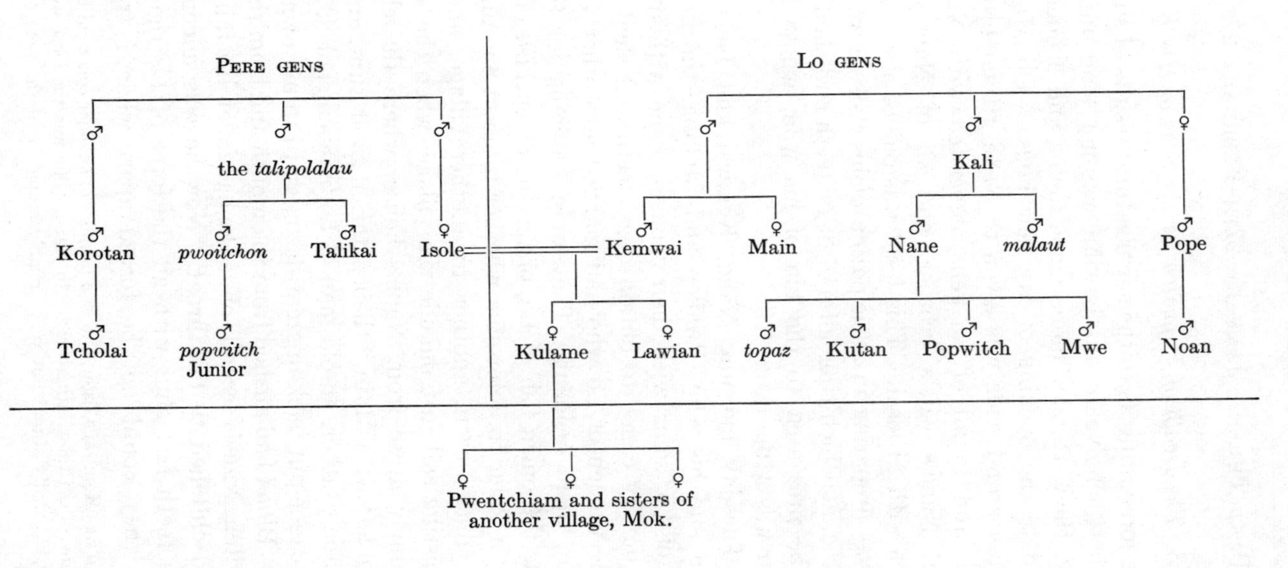
PERE GENS
LO GENS
the talipolalau
Kali
Korotan
pwoitchon
Talikai
Isole
Kemwai
Main
Nane
malaut
Pope
Tcholai
popwitch Junior
Kulame
Lawian
topaz
Kutan
Popwitch
Mwe
Noan
Pwentchiam and sisters of another village, Mok.

PART THREE. JANUARY 27TH–FEBRUARY 27TH

13. *The Death of Popwitch for the Sins of His Kin*

The foreboding as to the supernatural results of suspected incest between Noan and Lawian was not long unfulfilled. Sunday, the 27th, saw more canoe racing and a house feast to validate the opening of my new house. On Monday a feast on a grand scale was given to Nane, titular brother of Lawian, and to all of Lo gens associated with Nane, by Mbosai, Nane's wife's brother, and all of Nane's wife's relatives with Mbosai. This feast was one of a series which Nane was preparing in anticipation of his "silver wedding," his *metcha*, at which time gifts of dogs' teeth and shell money would be presented to the kin of his wife, whose leading financier was Mbosai.

On Tuesday morning Nane, Kemwai and Isole, Pope, Kalowin and his wife, Pwailep and Molung, the men and women of Lo, some with their spouses, some without, were setting out by canoe to obtain dogs' teeth and shell money from the women of Lo who had married into other villages, and were there resident. They were watching for the fish that was the omen fish of Lo, or for the omen bird of Lo to appear, in order to determine whether to go in one direction to one village, or in another to another village, and they were hoisting sail just outside the village, when the wailing for calamity arose from Nane's house, where the children had been left with Main,[35] their paternal great aunt, and with Kali, Nane's father, an old man of Lo, now enfeebled.

The canoe put back in great haste, and I in my own canoe with it. Blood had gushed from the mouth and from the nose of Popwitch, Nane's second son, as he had fallen in a faint with his hand clutched to his throat. Now he was unconscious with his teeth fast shut with all the force of his rigid jaw, so that they could not be forced apart when I tried to

[35] Main was Kemwai's sister, and as a member of an elder collateral line than that of Nane, was titular father's sister to Nane. She was the loose woman of the village, decidedly stupid but very amiably stupid, as if she were always a little drunk.

introduce half a teaspoonful of spirits of ammonia into his mouth, inhalation having proved ineffective. It was conceived that a ghost had cut Popwitch in the neck with an axe, not naturally as mortals cut, but invisibly as ghosts may do. He did not recover consciousness before his death, just before dawn next day. In the interval, and immediately thereafter, I saw the Manus religious system in full operation, and, I think, missed nothing as I would have missed points in my earlier inexperience, had the affair come earlier in my stay.

Popwitch was hastily lifted up from amongst the wailing crowd of women and the bowl stirring, shouting men, and taken away from Nane's house, now malignant. The general intention of the canoe punters was to make for the house of Ngandaliu,[36] a man of Lo. This house was separated from Nane's by almost the entire length of the houses of Pere gens and then by a space of open water. Some one shouted out that the Sir Ghosts of Pere gens should not be offended, and the canoe which had set out in front of the Pere gens houses was hastily reversed, and punted in the same direction, but now behind the houses in question. Then there was a cry that the ghosts of the open sea space should not be dared. The open sea spaces between houses within a village and between different villages are believed to be haunted by malignant anonymous ghosts, long ago Sir Ghosts to someone, but now cast out. They are not greatly feared, except when panic rules, as it did at such times as this. The canoe was punted behind two houses of Pere gens and put in at the third at the insistence of its owner, supported by the panic which prevented the original intention of going about seventy yards to the house of Ngandaliu. The owner of the house which received the unconscious Popwitch and the terror-stricken crowd was Pwiseu. Pwiseu was secure knowing that expiation had been made by Pope for Noan's offence in his house. Nane and Pwiseu now took up the bowl stirring,[37]

[36] Ngandaliu had been adopted by Kali, father of Nane. He was elder brother of Selan, who had been adopted differently into the Matchupal gens.

[37] Pope was not in evidence, owing to shame as father of the lad who had committed incest in Lo, and therefore father of the person responsible for the calamity.

shouting the while to their Sir Ghosts. Over Popwitch's body crowded women crying, and using the "I am struck with a spear" wail as if the trouble were a wound and not a sickness (a reference to the ghostly cutting of the boy's neck).

Out from the house of din, sweat, close sluggish air about the crowded wailers, and less even about Popwitch, Tcholai and another man slipped away and sought out Noan where he kept apart. "Confess now, come tell it all, or you do murder," they said. Noan, obstinate, sullen and cowed, denied any seduction of Lawian. Off, leaving Noan curled up in his father's house, went the pair to Lawian, who like Noan had hung apart, afraid to go near where Popwitch lay. "Noan has already confessed to having seduced you. It is all out," they said. "Come confess quickly and save Popwitch from death. We have come quickly to let you have some credit in the confession also."

"Yes. It is true," she said. "He had connection with me in the house of his father, Pope."

Tcholai and his companion confessor,[38] triumphant, literally beaming with triumph, rushed, the one to his father's house, the other to my house, on the verandah of which a big gong was kept. The tattoo that signals a confession secured was broadcast from both houses. The house of Talikai (Lawian's mother's brother) took it up, as well as the houses of Kalo. The criers paused for a moment over the prostrate body of Popwitch, then renewed their crying with new vigour and fresh hope. The men of Kalo came up in their canoes with a burst of anger, cursed Lawian for a wanton and threatened to raid the house and the pig pen of Pope, all the time beating on the smaller gongs with them in their canoe the tattoo for confession secured. Kemwai stepped from crying over Popwitch to the front verandah of the house and answered them, saying, "Sickness and close danger of death is at the doors of Lo. Pope is of us of Lo, Noan is his son. Is

[38] Tcholai was cross-cousin to Lo gens, his father's sister Isole having married into Lo. He was doing the duty of a cross-cousin in trying to secure confession from the son. His companion was an assistant village constable who was acting as a representative of white law, as Tcholai was acting as a representative of native law.

it not enough that I have to recognise incest in Lo? Does it appear seemly to you of Kalo to intrude on a house of sickness? You have given no moiety of the wealth due from you to validate our agreed betrothal contract between your son and my daughter, Lawian. What rights have you to act overzealously or to talk of raiding our property?"

Yielding to this statement, the men of Kalo did no violence. No expiatory payment was made by Kemwai to Kalo, as the latter had not yet paid the betrothal contract validation, or a preliminary bride price.

Expiatory payment was made hastily to the Sir Ghosts of Kemwai's house by Pope. Popwitch, however, gave no sign of recovery. The wailing, bowl stirring and frantic entreaty continued till nightfall.

Amid the confused wailing and entreaty two acts of divination were performed. They were not performed conspicuously or noticeably. The majority of the wailers in the house did not notice them, far less know the results secured. But a few persons were made conversant with them, and two payments of expiation were made inconspicuously in two different quarters outside the house. The great stress of public interest was over the unconscious form of Popwitch and was entirely unattracted by these moves.

At nightfall, according to custom, the crying was stopped, the fires in the house damped so that no light showed and a seance began. Now in the seance the course of divination and of expiatory payment during the confusion of the day was made clear to everyone present. In order to avoid repetition I shall discuss the divination and expiatory payment as it was made public in the seance, not discussing it also as it was done precedently and unnoticed in the general disregard.

The medium was Pikaro, a widow and a sister of Korotan. Pikaro's dead male child, her present control, was *kukan* by name.

Kemwai: "*kukan,* who struck this child?" (the medium's constant whistles, etc., are omitted in account).

Medium (translating for *kukan*): "I don't know whose

feud it is. I am like all you mortals in that. I'm with you in that. Let all the ghosts make speeches. You want to hear. So do I."

Pwiseu: "Yes, you don't know. Let *nyame* talk. Let me hear from him." (*nyame* is the speaker's Sir Ghost.)

A wait followed while *kukan* went to see *nyame*, not as long a wait as usual, for that night the case was urgent, and *kukan*, *nyame* and Pikaro rose to the occasion.

Medium (reporting from *kukan* from *nyame*): "The *talipolalau*, all of them, are striking this lad. They exact revenge for Noan defiling Lawian. They strike for that reason."

Pwiseu: "Yes, *nyame*, you bring here all your grandfathers (*i.e.*, the *talipolalau*). Let them all come. That sex offence has been confessed and paid for.[39] Let them all bring back the soul stuff. Let them bring it into this house. Let them send it back to the lad here."

Medium (for *kukan* for *nyame*): "Yes, for myself. I don't know any further. Those who struck this person struck him in deadly feud. And I, I shall do some work on his behalf. They may, of course, say that he shall die. Then he must needs die. They may say that he shall return. Then he must needs return."

Kemwai: "Where is *tchemilo; tchemilo* is making war upon us. He does not speak." (The said *tchemilo* is the dead male child and present control of Isole, the medium, mother of Lawian and wife of Kemwai. The medium, Pikaro, is fastening the Sir Ghostly blame upon the *talipolalau*, Isole's ancestors and Isole's and Kemwai's Sir Ghosts, on the one plane, and on Kemwai's and Isole's daughter's sin with Kemwai's gentile and titular grandson [40] on the other plane. Kemwai wants to stop more of this.)

Isole now takes over the prominent role of medium and holds it for the rest of the seance.

[39] Although no expiation was paid to Kalo gens on the heels of Lawian's confession, expiation was then made by Pope to the *talipolalau* who, as Sir Ghosts of Isole and of Kemwai, were thought to be striking the son of Kemwai's younger brother.

[40] Noan.

Isole: "*tchemilo*, come, make your appearance."

Isole (after a pause, and whistling, *tchemilo* speaking): "I'm here, and yes, I am striking this person. But it was my opinion that ghostly action against him should have been deferred until after my brother (Nane, Popwitch's father) had completed his silver wedding payment of gifts; and I said so to my grandfathers (the *talipolalau*) when we discussed the question. I was overruled, so for the meantime I am at your service to help you. I'll do some work on your behalf here."

Pwiseu: "Yes, *tchemilo*, you go and bring those responsible here; and let *nyame* stop here in the house to stand guard over us mortals."

(Pwiseu told *nyame* shortly before to go and canvass the *talipolalau*. Now he has become nervous at his own idea of telling the guardian Sir Ghost of his house to go on an errand, so leaving the house unprotected, as he now perceives, somewhat late.)

Medium (for *tchemilo*): "Yes, in this house there are mortals in great need of guard. Let *nyame* stand sentinel. I'll do the errand. What little we (the *talipolalau*) have of the soul stuff (of Popwitch) I'll bring back. But some of the soul stuff is in the hands of *popwitch* (not the mortal lad lying ill, but a ghost of the same name). To do an errand towards getting that back some have already gone shorewards to Patusi,[41] the neighbouring village."

In response to *tchemilo's* reference to the ghostly *popwitch*, which must be carefully distinguished from the dying child Popwitch, Talikai, Isole's brother, comes into the seance.

The original mortal, who is now the ghost *popwitch* senior, was killed suddenly and mysteriously. A bullet was subsequently discovered in his head by the natives, but the theory was that the ghosts used rifles. As a ghost *popwitch* became greatly feared. The mysterious circumstances surrounding his death invested him with a believed maliciousness, and as a ghost many subsequent illnesses and deaths

[41] Here the medium refers to the results of one of the two acts of divination that occurred during the afternoon.

were attributed to him. So great became the fear of him that all the people of the two villages of Peri and Patusi refused to touch a certain species of fish named *pwitch* in fear of the ghost named *popwitch* (*po* being merely a common prefix to the names of males).

The spirit, *popwitch,* was the Sir Ghost of Talilona of Patusi. Talilona's daughter, Ile, died and became, in my way of writing, *ile.* Talikai's brother, Pwoitchon, died and became *pwoitchon.* A marriage was announced between *pwoitchon,* male ghost of Talikai's family, and *ile,* female ghost of Talilona's family. The marriage exchanges of property to celebrate the marriage of *pwoitchon* and *ile* were made between Talikai and Talilona. At a later stage a medium announced that a son had been born to *pwoitchon* and *ile.* Exchanges of property to celebrate childbirth were made between Talikai and Talilona. This son had been named by his ghostly parents *popwitch.* I shall call him *popwitch* junior to distinguish him from *popwitch* senior; *popwitch* junior belonged to the house of Talikai, the child born to Talikai's brother as the issue of his ghostly marriage. Talikai on hearing *tchemilo's* reference to *popwitch,* his *popwitch* junior, says:

"Yes, *popwitch,* you're fighting this person to give punishment, to secure expiatory payment for that fish taboo to the house of Taliposala (*i.e., pwitch* fish).

"Kali [42] fastened it to the under surface of his canoe, took it to the market at Ndiwandro. He exchanged it for betel nut. This betel nut was used as a gift to Mbosai,[43] and the odour of fish from its body came to your house. You came up, and inhaled it. You struck this lad; but expiatory payment has been made for it.[44] Let the lad recover.

"Kali took it to market. There is sickness on account of it. This water to hold the soul stuff we for our part have already put out, and that soul stuff you have, you two may

[42] Nane's father, it will be remembered.

[43] Nane's wife's brother.

[44] Following the divination that first uncovered this delinquency of Kali, and that had been done without much public notice during the afternoon.

PLATE V

VISITING LANDSMEN

The man who is standing is wearing bones of the dead made-up into a back ornament

give together with that of *tchemilo*. Let him return it to the body. His mouth may unfasten."

Talikai's last reference is to the rigidly set jaws of Popwitch. Kali is the father of Nane, grandfather of Popwitch; he bartered the dangerous fish, *pwitch*, for betel nut with which to repay Mbosai when Mbosai and his group feasted Nane and his group. Mbosai's sister, living now in Mbosai's house with him, is widow of Talilona, original ward of *popwitch* senior. Hence it is given out that *popwitch* senior detected Kali's covert action—the smell of the fish came into his house; ghosts are supposed to be supernaturally sensitive to odours; *popwitch* junior and *popwitch* senior are conceived as working together, the former having seized Popwitch's soul stuff in Peri and taken it to the latter in Patusi.

Talikai referred to the *pwitch* fish as "that fish which is taboo to the house of Taliposala." Taliposala was the oldest man of Kalo gens and the *pwitch* fish was taboo to that gens. It could not be eaten by them. This was an old prohibition, one thoroughly traditional, and an instance of the Manus variant of totemism. In Manus villages other than Peri and Patusi the *pwitch* fish was generally eaten, except by Kalo gens people settled afield. What was originally a gentile taboo had become a general taboo in Peri and in Patusi, but only since the mysterious death of *popwitch* senior and the ensuing havoc that resulted amongst surviving mortals (possibly some epidemic).

It will be noted that a bare reference to *popwitch* by *tchemilo* set Talikai talking at length and explaining the whole matter. The medium gave a cue, then held her peace. This particular has a reason. The medium does not initiate every new move in the seance. She may bring up a new point if she knows one, that is truly a sin or an infraction of a taboo by someone of the house or of the gens wherein there is sickness. But the men do not leave everything to the mediums (who are all women—with extraordinary exception only), nor do they leave some possibilities alone during the day, before night comes and the medium may work.

Some one of the diviners had got knowledge of Kali's

act, despite Kali's concealment in tying the fish beneath his canoe. In view of this divination Nane, son of Kali, had already made expiatory payment of dogs' teeth to *popwitch* junior, dogs' teeth appropriated by the human ward of that spirit, Talikai. This had happened that afternoon. Now in the seance the ghosts so propitiated are asked for the soul stuff so purchased. (Talilona was dead, and *popwitch* junior was now the only link with *popwitch* senior.)

After Talikai's speech, Pwiseu said: "*nyame*, if they will not give up the soul stuff they have, you pay them."

Medium (for *tchemilo* for *nyame*): "Yes, suppose they all refuse to give it up, I, I have no dogs' teeth, I have no shell money, I have no pigs, I have no pots of oil (this is ceremonial depreciation as used also by mortals, and does not mean what it says) but if I must pay, I can pay all right. Though they may all deceive me and trick me there."

Kemwai: "Yes, *tchemilo*, go and bring all your grandfathers, and bring all the white women. (*tchemilo's* grandfathers, the *talipolalau*, on the ghostly plane married the ghosts of white women.) Let all of them be thrown out." (This is vexation at the *talipolalau*. Popwitch is showing no recovery from his unconscious fit, and Kemwai is threatening the *talipolalau*.)

Medium (for *tchemilo*): "Yes, I can bring my grandfathers and get all of them thrown out. And I'll get the soul stuff into the water and to the sick one's body. I'll get to work.

"A male ghost has seduced a female ghost. The (ghost) child of Nane has committed adultery with the (ghost) wife of *malaut; malaut's* belly is muddy (*i.e.*, angry). He waited for all of the mortals. They all set off by canoe. He spied on the mortals going off by canoe. All the ghosts gone (*i.e.*, the guardian ghosts of the mortals always accompany them—so when the men and women of Lo set out on a canoe voyage the guardian ghosts of their houses went with them) he struck Popwitch. (Popwitch had been left at home with his great aunt and his grandfather. So Popwitch had been left without the Sir Ghosts of his family, except his grandfather's Sir Ghost, *malaut*, who was angry.)

"He wished Popwitch to die. He took the soul stuff. He wished to embark with it to Mbunai village. But the Sir Ghosts of Paliau, *masati*[45] and *pwanau*, seized that soul stuff from him. It rests with them in the house" (*i.e.*, Paliau's house).

The charge of sin here laid is that *topaz*, dead son of Nane, has committed adultery with the ghostly wife of *malaut*, dead brother of Nane.[46] Kali, alone of the men of Lo, stayed at home, as he was very old. Kali had as his Sir Ghost his dead son, *malaut*. Hence suspicion falls on *malaut*. The ghost offending *malaut*, *topaz*, is the especial guardian ghost of Kutan, Nane's eldest son, not yet come to adolescence. In order to expiate this sin, Nane had sent Kutan as messenger round to his relatives-in-law. They had given bead work and Nane had made expiatory payment to *malaut* with it. Kali, Nane's father, as mortal ward of *malaut*, had collected the bead work. All this had occurred earlier in the day.

It will appear at a later stage that someone saw some blood on Paliau's floor. This fact, combined with the way in which Popwitch bled at first fainting, was the foundation of the medium's charge that the Sir Ghosts of Paliau's house now had Popwitch's soul stuff.[47] Of course it was not said that anyone mortal first saw that blood on the house floor in question. It came direct from the medium's communication with the ghosts. There will appear later evidence of an old antagonism between Paliau and the medium, Isole. It is noteworthy how the expiatory payments keep within a group of relatives, and how a personal factor brings in charges against Paliau's Sir Ghosts.

The medium left the seance hanging at this point. The last payment had been made to *malaut*, and it was assumed that *malaut* would get back that soul stuff. Meanwhile Popwitch's protracted unconsciousness looked as if there were little chance of recovery for him. If Popwitch did not recover

[45] In English called *master tim*, ghost of a former employer of Paliau.

[46] This is the other sin that was first uncovered by divination during the afternoon.

[47] Here the medium, Isole, announces news that had not been obtained by the diviners before her earlier in the day. This news is her sole original addition.

it could be quickly assumed that *malaut* had been unable to prevail over the Sir Ghosts of Paliau's house, to recover the soul stuff from them. No payment was made to Paliau's Sir Ghosts, just as no payment had been made to the Sir Ghosts of Kalo on account of Lawian's sin.

With the seance ending at this point, it could be quickly said in the event of Popwitch's death that the Sir Ghosts of someone completely unrelated to Lo had been responsible. This was just where the medium wished to leave the matter.

It is the conventional belief that expiatory payment had wiped out all possibility of Noan's sin with Lawian causing Popwitch's death, for example. So also of Kali's infraction of the fish taboo, so also of *topaz's* sin with *malaut's* wife. The medium left one loophole. The soul stuff had been seized by Paliau's Sir Ghosts. These Sir Ghosts had not cause of quarrel with any of the gens of Lo, for the accusation that Noan had seduced Salikon, Paliau's daughter, had been dropped before this. Salikon had not menstruated yet; she was but a child and no one could think of any occasion upon which the alleged seduction could have taken place, whereas Noan's opportunities with the other girls concerned, who were related to him, had been many, as is usual within the group where sexual intercourse is incestuous. Neither the medium nor any of the Peri folk had this prior accusation definitely in mind. As became clear later a report of blood on Paliau's house floor originated the idea, and was solely responsible for it, in conjunction only with the medium's appreciation of the case being probably hopeless and her desire to put the case beyond the possibility of certain cure by expiatory payment. It was assumed that Paliau's Sir Ghosts had no legitimate business in seizing Popwitch's soul stuff from Kali's Sir Ghost, *malaut*, but only a malicious reason. The medium, Isole, gave no account of Paliau's Sir Ghosts' reason, nothing which would make expiatory payment in order. What she intended became clear at a later stage, as we shall see in due time. It was the hypothesis of despair, in fact, to which we have referred in our general statement of the Manus religion.

Popwitch was still alive and breathing a little more easily. I had managed to thrust some spirits of ammonia in a spoon between his tightly clenched teeth, so that he recovered partial consciousness for a brief while; but I knew of nothing more that could be done. Exhausted by the day's frenzy, and by the ominous conclusion of the seance, everyone slept. About an hour before dawn wailing cries broke out and wakened me immediately. I found Nane with the head of Popwitch's corpse in his lap crying over it, the mother crying stretched out beside it and embracing it, and the keening being done by Nane's sisters and father's sisters.

Suddenly Nane rose and went quickly and determinedly from the house where the corpse lay. He paddled quickly to his own house. Main, his father's sister and I followed him there, sensing importance from his demeanour. Main undoubtedly guessed what he was about. I was thinking that he looked potentially suicidal. In his own house Nane seized an axe. He did not hack at the skull and skull bowl of his Sir Ghost, but he attacked the house front just near the skull bowl and broke it up, until Main seized the axe as he paused a moment with it poised in backward swing. His action was in fury at the ghostly plane, and at his Sir Ghost, but he did not attack his Sir Ghost directly through his skull as some men in excess of rage do under similar circumstances.

We may pass over here the mourning rites held over the corpse of Popwitch in the house of Kemwai, selecting for discussion only the incidents of an especial religious nature. On the day of the fatal fit, word had been carried to an Usiai seer, with payment and a request for the exercise of the seer's powers on the case. Some of these seers merely stare into vacancy and, without any convulsive evidences of possession, act as oracles that are believed to be possessed. Others of the Usiai seers practice through alleged dreams that are taken as oracular. These dreams, when produced, resemble the results of the Manus seance, however, and represent possibly what a sound sleeping seer thinks of on waking up in the morning, rather than being real dreams. News of Popwitch's death was carried to the seer before he could communicate his results of the day after. He took advantage of the news to say that he would dream further for two or three nights, since now there was no immediate urgency about diagnosis. Nothing in the way of expiation could now be done to recover the patient.

The burial occurred on the fourth day after death. Here again our selection of material forbids our lingering long. We may note only that at the foot of the grave a magician made an exorcism. He tied a croton shoot to a short stake, and spat betel juice upon it from betel he chewed while he repeated a charm which ordered *popwitch* (*popwitch*, the third, the ghost of the recently dead) not to damage the health of his surviving kin. The magician was called Man of Lorengau, a character that we shall see more of later. I may note that this magic is theoretically a compelling power over the ghost exorcised. Actually since every ghost is so laid, the Manus religion would not exist if it were believed that the magic actually did lay the ghost finally. In practice every ghost is believed subsequently to act in a manner incompatible with the theory, claimed by the magician, that his magic is all powerful and acts compulsively on the supernatural. The dogma of complete control of the supernatural by man through magic, and the dogma of almost complete control of man by the supernatural cannot be held together logically. But the Manus retain the two dogmas agreeably in different connections. What is done over a grave is one matter. What is done when sickness follows subsequently amongst the kin of the man that was laid in a grave is another matter; just as the illness of an infant in arms is one matter in which the magical dogma is credited, and the illness of an adult is another matter in which the logical antithesis is credited. Actually the incompatibility makes for a differential cultural emphasis in Manus, as also in Dobu. In Manus a far greater emphasis is attributed to the religious dogma, in Dobu a far greater emphasis is attributed to the magical dogma.

On the day after the burial, news of the Usiai seer's dreaming oracular charges was brought. A Manus messenger brought it from the Usiai territory committed to memory. It ran:

"In sleep he went; he saw a coconut palm, a betel nut palm, a towering tree; the ghosts gave him to understand it was a tree belonging to Man of Lorengau.

"In sleep he went; he saw a pig belonging to a 'silver wedding' (*metcha*) payment, the prime gift of the payment. It went to the territory of the white men where it fetched a hundred shillings. Nothing went towards the *metcha*. The brothers say, 'O the pig belonging to your *metcha* gift; the due date of the *metcha* is past and the gift overdue, but nothing comes of it'; vision of this came upon me.

"In sleep he went; shell money, food, betel nut, pepper leaf; they make preliminary *kurra* [48] feasts; you do not return their *kurra* feasts with the *metcha* [49] gifts quickly; the ghosts rage at it.

"In sleep he went; he saw within the house of Nane an act of sexual misconduct; one has died for it already; and if you do not confess it another may shortly die for it also."

So ran the Usiai-derived oracle. The first charge was that one of Nane's kin had stolen from a palm belonging to Man of Lorengau, and the black magic which protected the palm had caused the death of Nane's child. The charge was ignored. Popwitch was dead now, and there was no call for confession. The charge was probably unfounded, or founded on an association of ideas only. The corpse of Popwitch had been buried in a coconut plantation belonging to Man of Lorengau. The latter had no heir. He wished to make Nane's heir his heir also, and had chosen this way of publishing the fact.

The second charge was derived from fact. Nane had sold a pig to a trader for five pounds. The oracle said that the pig should have been used to raise native wealth, dogs' teeth and shell money, which kind of wealth Nane was collecting to give to his wife's relatives. Then that gift could have been made by the due date, which had been deferred.

The third charge was that the future recipients of the

[48] Feasts made to those collecting dogs' teeth and shell money and bead belts by the affinal relatives of the collectors, who will ultimately be presented with the dogs' teeth and shell money collected.

[49] Dogs' teeth and shell money and bead belts.

metcha gifts of shell money and dogs' teeth from Nane had made the counter feasts that precede *metcha*, gifts to Nane, but Nane was not responding quickly enough. This charge, with the one before it, are of the pattern that if a man is working hard at something he is not being quick enough about it, or a part of his investment has gone in another direction. These charges are infallibly safe, and might catch anyone justly at any time.

The fourth charge was the most serious. It alleged sexual misconduct in Nane's own house, undetected as yet, unconfessed, and liable to lead to another death.

Nane, in practice, did not make any great account of this oracle. Nothing could be done now. He had not heard much of the seance before Popwitch's death. "I was crying over him and I did not hear it." But he knew the theories advanced in it. He pointed out to me that the Usiai seer got different results from Isole, and that there were so many different theories now that he had no opinion on any point. I read from my notes the part of Isole's seance that said that *malaut*, Sir Ghost of Kali, the old man, had taken Popwitch's soul stuff because his ghostly wife had been seduced by the ghost of Nane's dead son, *topaz*. Nane immediately said, "A lie of hers," then recovered himself quickly on second thoughts of policy, and said, "I know nothing in this matter. I was not concerned with the seance, but with my son." His first "A lie of hers" expressed very evidently what he thought, but what he also evidently considered it impolitic to think aloud.

Nane explained further that the sexual misconduct within his house referred to by the Usiai seer was not really sexual misconduct. There had been some obscene jesting between joking relatives in his house. The seer had magnified that beyond due proportion. The obscenity used between male cross-cousins, or between a man and a woman he calls father's sister,[50] is perfectly regular and usual in Manus. It is even felt to be obligatory behaviour. Now and again a medium with no finesse of resource diagnoses this obscenity as an

[50] More exactly *patieyen*.

offence to a Sir Ghost, but the obscenity is obligatory kinship behaviour and continues, unchecked by the mediums, as such. In this case Nane explained that Songan and Kamutal had playfully poked at each other's pubic parts in his house. Kamutal was Songan's true father's sister's daughter, his cross-cousin in fact, but by term of address his titular father's sister. The pair acted in a perfectly regular and culturally sanctioned manner in this obscenity. Kamutal moreover was past child bearing and Songan was very old indeed, one of the two oldest men in the village. Nane thus disposed of that count in the Usiai oracle, not with complete scepticism, but with a more than semi-sceptical carelessness of it, and reduction of it to very minor proportions.

That night, being the fifth night after the death, Isole held a public seance in a house crowded with mourners, there to sleep all night for many nights to come. She called up *tchemilo*. The latter said:

"Yes; the talk within this house comes from where? Sexual misconduct comes from where? As to who struck Popwitch dead, the ghost responsible will not confess it on this plane, as you perhaps conceal sexual misconduct on that plane."

Pokenau: "You, confess it! Let us hear it."

Medium (for *tchemilo*): "No. I decline. I cannot inform you. It must be kept hidden. You mortals cannot but arrive at your own conslusion. We ghosts cannot but arrive at our own conclusion. And we on both planes probably agree in our respective conclusions. But let there be no more speech on the subject."

This deliberate reticence of the medium, Isole, was for a purpose as we shall see later.

The medium continued translating *tchemilo's* whistling: "No matter. Give out the food. He has eaten his fill of it. You mortals may take the food."

The food referred to was bowls of taro that had been put out on the house floor every night for the last four nights as an offering to the ghost of the recently deceased Popwitch, now *popwitch*, the third ghost of that name. The food was now inspected. Supposed traces of *popwitch's* having eaten from it were pointed out. The food was distributed to *sori* (received by Pokenau),[51] to *yonku* (received by that Sir Ghost's ward, the constable of Tchalolo),[52] and to the *talipolalau* (received by one ward of those Sir Ghosts, Talikai).[53]

Isole told her husband Kemwai to utter an exorcism and an injunction to *popwitch* the third. Kemwai took a handful of the taro and said over it:

"So. I speak sacred words on to this food to my grandson *popwitch* here. I have no war record. I cannot make speeches. I enjoin *popwitch:*

If sickness arises, you restore the damage done amongst us;
you hear our entreaty readily;
you restore us to health;
when we call on you to show us where turtle are, where dugong are, where fish are, you hear our request readily;
so all will praise you."

Kemwai laid the taro aside for *popwitch's* later consumption, and said, "That speech is done with." Then turning towards Isole he asked for *tchemilo*, and on *tchemilo's* appearance asked that the latter convey to the *talipolalau* the fact that he wished them to pay attention to his words. He then said:

"So! you *talipolalau!* man and wife the two of us came to live in Pere gens territory (Kemwai and Isole had lived patrilocally at first for a short time in Lo gens territory, Kemwai's own place, with Kemwai's own Sir Ghosts, others than the *talipolalau*). We two came here to my wife's place. We had three children born to us here. Betel nut that I planted have come to bearing also within the days of our stay; and coconuts that I planted have grown and come to bearing. I have become an old man. So. A house of large proportions, like this one, my father built for himself in his place and mine, that I left for your place so long ago.

[51] Sister's son of the father of the dead child.

[52] Gens father of the dead child, Tchalolo village being entirely of Lo gens.

[53] Brother of Isole and with Kemwai of Lo a word of the *talipolalau.*

This house here of yours, you *talipolalau*, may remain as the storing place of your goods, may remain here in place close to the house of Talikai. This child who is dead like an unloosed canoe he unfastens me. I must leave your territory, and go to the place of my fathers."

Isole whistles, then translates for *tchemilo* for the *talipolalau:* "So: you go away. One of us instead of a pot of oil, one of us instead of a turtle, one of us instead of a pig, one of us instead of a canoe towards the gifts for your departure, we will accompany you to the place of your fathers. We will not stay here any longer."

It may be noted that this is a conflict of interest between Kemwai and his wife, Isole. Isole had made their marriage matrilocal. The pair had lived under the Sir Ghosts of Isole's paternal line. Now Kemwai wishes to bid those Sir Ghosts farewell by building a new house in his own place, on the grounds that the Sir Ghosts in question have not protected his grandson, Popwitch, from death. It is customary for a man to move his house after a death in it.[54] He seeks a new site with a new Sir Ghost. The ghosts are conceived generally as owning each his own locality and house site. By taking a new site, a man takes a new Sir Ghost, that being the whole object of moving a house. Kemwai now wishes to remove to his patrilineal site and to his patrilineal Sir Ghost's protection.

Isole, using her position as medium, counters Kemwai as much as is possible. When a wife stays away from a husband for a holiday with her kin, her kin send her back to her husband with gifts to him. These gifts are called *tauiai*. Isole reports the *talipolalau* to the effect that they will give themselves to Kemwai as *tauiai*. They will not give him departing gifts of oil, turtle, pig and canoe, but they will give themselves instead. They will leave Pere gens territory and go with Kemwai wherever he goes.

This is entirely contrary to the general belief that a ghost must stay as guardian in his own territory, in the gens terri-

[54] The death in point had not been in Kemwai's house but in Nane's. But Kemwai and Nane were always close together in their affairs, although not actually in their house sites, as the sites were placed before the death of Popwitch.

tory of his gens and in the site within that territory that was the site of his fathers before him. But in Manus an intelligent oracle does not act in traditional terms necessarily. The oracle brings new intelligence on ghostly affairs, and is free to make it as new and as modern in innovation as she thinks advisable. Isole wished to circumvent Kemwai's project of taking her away from her own place, close to her brothers in their and her father's place. Isole was the real master in her marriage. She wished to make her own will law. So she calmly spoke as oracle a pronouncement that stripped Kemwai's project of its major aim.

Nane spoke through the medium to *popwitch* the third: "*popwitch*, my house we wish to break up and go to a new site."

Medium (for *tchemilo* for *popwitch*): "Yes. The house in which I was struck down, blood of mine stays in it. Go elsewhere lest blood of your dead enter into you and cause death by stomach swelling. Yes! but delay your house moving until you get your *metcha* over lest you do not meet fairly the preliminary *kurra* feasts that your relatives-in-law have given you in anticipation of your *metcha* gifts to come to them. Get a magician to exorcise the blood."

Nane: "Yes. I shall give to them. And afterwards I shall get one to exorcise the blood, and then break up the house."

Nane and his family and everyone else were avoiding Nane's house in which Popwitch fell stricken in his faint. The house stood empty, and stood so until it was broken up and set up again elsewhere, some three weeks later. Kemwai was still in Isole's house three months later when I left. He still said that he intended to move. But I think Isole will have had her way rather, and will have blocked the project. Houses are moved for reasons connected with ghosts; when the wife of the house is a medium and a clever medium she has a good chance of making marriage matrilocal in defiance of the common custom of patrilocal marriage which rules in Manus. When a husband's divining results and a wife's medium's results begin to clash the struggle is carried on decorously in terms of the supernatural. But the Manus are quick to impute natural human motives. Kemwai, Isole's husband, was less intelligent than the average however.

The seance concluded with this discussion of house moving plans. Everyone settled down to sleep in Isole's house, a great proportion of the village being there. When everyone was thought to be already asleep, Nane, Kemwai and Isole held a brief and intendedly secret seance, Isole as medium.

Isole called up *tchemilo* and instructed him to get into touch with *pwanau*, Paliau's house spirit. The latter was reported to say:

"When I was yet mortal I was just planning to give a *metcha* (the type of gift exchange Nane was planning to give Mbosai just when Popwitch died), but I was cut off before I gave it. My sons had to take it up. Now Nane was about to secure the honour of giving a *metcha;* and I was unable to do so."

In brief Isole's seance attributed Popwitch's death to *pwanau* being jealously malicious and envious of the honour he had failed to secure himself, but which Popwitch's father was about to secure.

Some one of Paliau's kin thought to be asleep nearby overheard the drift of the covert seance, and roused the others of Paliau's kin who were there. The five of them rose immediately and walked out of the house furious with Isole, Kemwai and Nane for attempting to hold their seance in secret, and certain that if they stayed in the house a moment longer any one of them might be stricken by *tchemilo* at any moment as a counter stroke for their spirit, *pwanau*, having stricken maliciously a member of the house of *tchemilo*. If Isole, Kemwai and Nane had succeeded in keeping their secret they would have allowed the members of the house of *pwanau* to sleep on for several nights in their house in the hope of squaring the score.[55] Both parties believed in great danger for *pwanau's* relatives under the circumstances if

[55] When a man's Sir Ghost is said to have maliciously killed (as ghost) a member of another kin group, that man and his kin are in danger if they approach the houses of the kin of the dead—danger of ghostly reprisals.

they came near the house of *tchemilo*. Hence secrecy by the one party was not relished by the other.

In what followed Isole and her party blandly denied that any such seance had ever been held. But Paliau and his party as stoutly swore that it had been held and overheard. It appeared that *tchemilo* had said even more at the suspect seance. He had said, "Let each party of kin keep their dead in their own houses, and let there be no more shame; this line of houses on the north side of Peri is a good safe line, and has not a bad past history in its record of sicknesses; but the line of houses on the south side of Peri is dangerous and has a bad past history."

Kemwai's house, where the corpse now lay while this seance went on, was on the north side. Nane's house was on the south, not far from Paliau's, which latter was not far from Pwiseu's. Pwiseu heard this account of Kemwai's and Isole's and *tchemilo's* gratitude for his having offered Nane and them his house to shelter Popwitch when the lad was stricken down, and not disbelieving the report of it was indignant.

Paliau was too indignant and furious to speak of the charge against *pwanau* beyond saying that Isole lied foully and *tchemilo* was in league with her in lying.

Next morning, Monday, Paliau with his kin and with the full support of all the south side of Peri came in canoes midway over the sea towards Kemwai's house. Paliau sitting in his canoe publicly charged Isole the medium with having held a secret seance the night before and with saying that *pwanau* killed Popwitch. He charged her with making lying statements, her and *tchemilo* with her, that her seance contained nothing but lies, that she had also maligned all the houses on the south side of Peri.

Kemwai, Nane and Isole allowed a third party, Pokenau, to lead off in reply, as he had news to tell in connection with charges of lying against mediums. Paliau's and his kins' reaction had been whispered about privately the night before, and, in the house of Pokenau, a visitor from Mbunai village named Man of Lorengau had held a seance over the matter.

Man of Lorengau was one of the rare men who used his Sir Ghost as a control also, claimed full power to do so and held seances himself. His seance of the previous night had been interesting, Pokenau was full of it and he replied to Paliau first. (I may add that Man of Lorengau's Sir Ghost and control was a ghostly white man.)

"I, I talk. Yes. The speech here is that they held no seance. Their control ghost did not talk. Speech concerning it. I have spoken. The white man understands it. It's all down on his paper. The talk here is all of Man of Lorengau and of his white Sir Ghost. The latter talked and said, 'All you ghosts who are native police (ghosts of men who were native police appointed by white Administration and who are now conceived as native police among the ghosts) you ghostly police talk to all mortals. Tell them that each seance must be conducted in private to the family concerned. If there is sickness in a family let that family hold their own seance to themselves. Their own Sir Ghost may talk. If he says that the man shall die, he dies, if that he shall survive, he survives. Each family keeps to itself. And if a seance is at Patusi only those of Patusi, and if at Loitcha only those of Loitcha, Mbunai for Mbunai and Pomatchau for Pomatchau, and Tchalalo for Tchalalo.'

"The talk of all the ghosts that they talked it came here. I speak it. Yes. This. Some ghost talked to the white Sir Ghost of Man of Lorengau. He in turn talked to the policeman (ghostly) of Pontchal and to the policeman (ghostly) of Tchalalo.

"In the seance last night the white Sir Ghost of Man of Lorengau told what he had already advised the native police (ghostly ones) to perform in this connection.

(The speaker's Sir Ghost, *sori*, was the ghostly native policeman, or constable, of Pontchal.)

"I asked Man of Lorengau to call up the policeman (ghostly) of Pontchal. I said:

"'*sori*, you speak. All you ghosts speak. Tonight you give the power of great mediumship to my wife that she may hold her own seances. Give the power of divination to me, the man, that I may divine for myself. Let me watch for these powers now, and if my present request becomes realised tomorrow I shall announce it. But if not, the word of you ghosts has not truth in it, but is the production of us mortals only.'"

To interrupt my account of Pokenau's speech for the moment, the gist of it so far is that Man of Lorengau in a seance had arrived at the intelligent and innovating idea (derived from his Sir Ghost in his belief) that there would be no charges of lies against mediums if all seances were held in private instead of in public, and also if such privacy were enforced and respected; and that a ghostly movement to this end was afoot mediated by the ghostly native constabulary.

Pokenau, present at the seance, had entered a possible objection. His family, a type of many, was without its own medium and diviner. Divination and seance private to his family was impossible under these circumstances. He put the proposition to his Sir Ghost that either he and his wife be granted power immediately, as an evidence of earnestness on the other plane in the reported project, or else the report of the project was really unfounded.

Man of Lorengau, a fine linguist who spoke about seven of the languages of the Admiralties, pidgin English and good German, who, although a man, used his Sir Ghost as a medium uses her control (as well as using the regular divination), who had a white man's ghost as his Sir Ghost, was the very type of man to attempt to produce cultural changes. He used his Sir Ghost as a control to hold seances with; why could not everyone? Then with real privacy in seances there would be no bickering such as was arising between Paliau and Isole, and such as had arisen often before.

Pokenau on the contrary was the staunch conservative, a real fundamentalist in religion, as far as fundamentalism is possible within the Manus system.

To continue with Pokenau's speech to Paliau, quarrelling publicly with Isole:

"'Then *sori* came. He said, "Yes, tonight I have little to say on my own account; but I have to report the ultimatum of all the mediums' controls of all the children." They say: "You mortals say that divination results in lies, that seances lead to lies. You say that they do not bear the truth. The foreheads of all of us controls are bowed in shame thereat. Let there be this talk and we decline to work except under this condition: that each seance be held in private to the family of the medium only. Let all such families as have no member a medium at present produce one." I carry the word of all of us who are ghosts many and united. Not that I speak for us adult ghosts primarily, but I carry the word of all the children who act as intermediaries between mortals and ghosts.'" (Close of report of *sori's* speech.)

"I speak, and I have spoken to a finish. Now you say that you overheard a seance which said that *pwanau* struck down Popwitch. I don't know anything about that. I can not talk to that point."

Isole had been wise in allowing Pokenau to reply to Paliau first. Man of Lorengau's seance had mooted a genuine innovation. But it might also appear as a reaction, and an emotional reaction, to charges of lying made against an oracle. Man of Lorengau, as one oracle, had raised a barrier against such charges, in defence of another oracle, Isole. The defence was simply that the oracles would let illnesses and deaths in non-oracular families go unmet and unprovided for, if charges of lies were made against oracles. So Isole used Man of Lorengau's seance in any case, whatever its origin. Judging from Man of Lorengau's general versatility, it might have easily been an idea which seemed practicable to him. In fact I gathered from him that such was the case. Let everyone be an oracle was his real attitude. Isole had this idea put by a conservative to a group infinitely more conservative than Man of Lorengau himself, knowing well enough that it would appear as a strong defence of the established oracles, rather than what Man of Lorengau probably intended. Isole was a very clever woman as oracle and as defender of her own interest.

Paliau did not reply to this extraordinary bombshell from Pokenau, sponsored and encouraged by Isole. He was taken aback very clearly. As he told me afterwards the whole development was new to him, and previously unheard of.

Isole pressed her advantage, speaking herself: "The talk from your side we for our part do not understand. That from Man of Lorengau's seance, Pokenau has told you. But the control, *tchemilo*, made no speech whatever of the kind that you name. Only a word or two he uttered to the effect that it may be this, or it may be that, or it may be something else again. Perhaps the Sir Ghosts of my house, perhaps the ghosts of the middle seas climbed into the house of Nane and struck down the child so recently dead. It is seemly for a ghost to talk above the body of one dead, where it is unseemly for a mortal to quarrel above it. For our part, we who are old and who belong to this side of the village, and to the place in it that is most honourable, know nothing of the speech that you bring up yourself alone.

"If indeed you are jealous of the *metcha* that we are preparing that is true enough.[56] But we know nothing of such jealousy from the Sir Ghost of your house. This speech you make, *tchemilo* did not utter. It belongs to you only. You just talk, that's all. We know nothing of it.

"But one thing is true. Yes. The ghosts said that we should go, that all we mortals should embark to a new place. But as matters stand now some stayed, and some went. You have seen it."

This last statement of Isole's was a direct hit at Paliau. Some time before when *pwanau* was still alive and Paliau his heir presumptive, Pwanau was preparing to make a *metcha*. Talikai, Isole's brother was planning to help Pwanau in this effort. But Pwanau died. Paliau took over the affair and completed the *metcha* for which his predecessor and adoptive father had begun preparations. Talikai withdrew and gave no help to Paliau. At the time Paliau had his house side by side with Talikai's and Isole's houses on the north side of Peri village. Shortly afterwards Paliau fell ill. A male medium from Mbuke, a far off island, made the seance

[56] Isole was associated with her husband and her "brother-in-law" in the latter's (Nane's) *metcha* making.

for the illness. He said that Paliau was ill because *pwanau* was indignant at his continuing to live side by side with Talikai and Isole, after Talikai had withdrawn from the economic obligation he had assumed while Pwanau was yet alive. It was *pwanau's* opinion that Talikai should have honoured his heir as if his heir were himself (as is the usual custom). On his recovery Paliau dismantled his house and set it up in *pwanau's* adoptive father's old house site on the south side of Peri village.

Isole had stoutly opposed Paliau in this removal. In the seance that initiated it *pwanau* had said that the entire north side of the village was dangerous and tainted with possibilities of evil. Everyone should remove from it. This, and Paliau's defection had made Isole furious. She had said that the results of the seance in question were nothing other than lies. Now she points out that Paliau ran away to the south side, while she and her brother stayed. And here the next death took place on the south side, not on the north side, a fact in support of her charge that the seance over Paliau's illness had been lies. Isole used a *tu quoque* argument here with effect.

Paliau said no more. He and his party drew off and went to their houses. His party did not act on the assumption that Isole's secret seance contained nothing but lies. They believed firmly that they would be in great danger if they were to go near the house of Isole. The Sir Ghost of Paliau had acted maliciously and from envy against Nane's group. Because *pwanau* had been cut off just as he was nearly ready to give a *metcha*, he objected to seeing Nane's group ready to attain an honour that he had just missed. This being so, the Sir Ghosts of the houses of that group would be likely to retaliate with malice for malice, to even the score by killing a member of Paliau's group.

The two groups were not divided according to gentile allegiance. Nane and Kemwai were of Lo gens, and Isole of Pere gens was with her husband, Kemwai of Lo, although Paliau was of Pere gens, Isole's and Talikai's Sir Ghosts, the *talipolalau*, and Isole's control, *tchemilo*, were against Paliau, although the *talipolalau* were ghosts of Pere gens men (but *tchemilo* was of Lo, taking his father's gens). Isole's house, a Pere house, was dangerous to Paliau's group.

What is known as a "middle space" arose. The Manus idiom a "middle space arises," means that two groups or parties practice a temporary reciprocal avoidance, each party avoiding members and houses of the other party. The "middle space" may be due to a quarrel over commerce, or, as in the present instance, it may be due to allegation of the Sir Ghosts of one party having killed a member of the other party. In this latter case, it is sustained by anger in the injured party, and by fear in the wards of the alleged offending (ghostly) party of supernatural retaliation from the Sir Ghosts of the injured party. The idea of malice on the one hand, retaliation on the other, is shifted cleanly into the supernatural sphere, which it is believed is entirely out of the control of mortals. The "middle space" commonly is bridged again after an avoidance of two or three months duration. Fear of retaliatory measures is dissipated by the expiration of that time.

That the secret seance which Isole held and attempted to keep secret, but which she later denied, was actually held was substantiated by an event that occurred shortly after. Naturally Isole would deny it; for its secrecy was an attempt to avoid a "middle space" arising for the protection of Paliau's group from ghostly retaliation. Paliau's group, had they not discovered the secret, would have continued to sleep in the house of Kemwai and Isole, as half the village did for three weeks or so after the death, in customary expression of sympathy and of mourning.

Talikai, Isole's brother, had two wives. He was not successful with the two. He had tried to keep them both in one house, his own. One had run away to another house, and Talikai, from pride, would not go to her there. So he was left with one wife for all practicable purposes, and she was considerably estranged from him because she had a co-wife. The wife that was living with Talikai, Lomot by name, was of the same gens as Pwanau had been. Before Pwanau had been adopted by Potek of Pere gens, of Peri village, he had been of a gens of Patusi village into which he was born. Now as a ghost *pwanau* was Sir Ghost to the kin of his adoption who survived him. Lomot was kin to *pwanau* by the other tie of blood. She had been associated with Paliau's party in detecting the secret seance by Isole, and in walking out of the house of mourning. Thus *pwanau's* kin by adoption, who were several, and *pwanau's* kin by blood, who was one present, had walked out in a common fear of retaliation from the Sir Ghosts of Isole's house. Lomot, unrelated to Paliau otherwise, was with Paliau's party, although she was married into the other party. She kept her husband's house, however, only avoiding her sister-in-law's, Isole's, house, when the "middle space" arose.

After the opening of the "middle space" Lomot told Paliau's wife that on the day of Popwitch's fatal fit she had seen blood on Paliau's threshold. She had wondered at it and told the circumstance to Isole. Paliau came into possession of this fact through Lomot. Now he had the origin of Isole's move in her seance attributing the death of Popwitch to his Sir Ghost, *pwanau.* It is interesting to note how the dual reckoning of kinship by blood as well as by adoption brings about solidarity between persons who are not usually in such solidarity.

Some days after, Talikai learned that Paliau knew of the fact of this communication between Lomot and Isole, preceding the latter's seance on the evening of Popwitch's fit. Paliau said that it was fish blood inadvertently not cleaned up, clearing himself and neglecting to protect Lomot.

Talikai at a public ceremony charged his wife, Lomot, with having betrayed a contributory piece of evidence to Paliau's charges of lies against his sister. Lomot, in great fear, swore upon her mourning costume, containing relics of her family dead, that she had not betrayed any such evidence. She had, however, and Talikai knew it. For a week thereafter sounds of Talikai storming at his wife, and even beating her, rang out periodically over the village.

Paliau was more convinced than the women and younger

men of his group that the charge against *pwanau* in Isole's "secret" seance was a lie of Isole's in conspiracy with her control, *tchemilo.* In about a week's time he dared the risk by going publicly into Isole's house, saying that if Isole had told the truth, he risked death from her Sir Ghosts. He did so only by day, however, and only two or three times in the course of a month. The rest of his party ran no such risk. After two months' time the avoidance broke down completely. But Paliau's daring before that time had elapsed was everywhere regarded as a substantial backing of, and testing of his charges against Isole; he emerged unscathed, and satisfied himself very well.

The continuity in Isole's two seances should be noted. The public seance before Popwitch's death ended in an unexplained seizure of Popwitch's soul stuff by the Sir Ghosts of Paliau. Being unexplained in terms of a ghost enforcing a legal right, no expiation could be made, and none was made. After Popwitch's death the secret seance continued from the point at which the public seance preceding death had left off. It explained Paliau's Sir Ghosts' action in terms of malice. A loophole had been made in the public seance through which an indictment of a stranger ghost could later be made, exculpating the kin of the dead from any sin against their Sir Ghosts, exculpating Isole's daughter, Lawian, for example, from her sin with Noan.

Tcholai, who had obtained first news of that sin from Noan, and who had later extorted confession from Lawian on a pretense, carefully avoided going near his father's sister, Isole, in the ensuing month. He did not expect any quick forgiveness from her. Lawian her head shaven (as if a married woman), remained in seclusion at home for several weeks, then emerged, but in company with her own kinsmen of Lo only, Noan excluded. A rigid avoidance ruled between Noan and Lawian. And the two of them kept conspicuously absent from all general public gatherings for a long period. Small children jeered at them, and adults having to pass them, made wide circuit. Over the heads of both of them hung a suspicion that maybe they were responsible for Popwitch's death after all.

It may be well to note that Popwitch at the time of his death was a boy ungrown, and probably about ten years of age, as yet not contracted in marriage. He was one of five children of a family that was *lau*, common, not *lapan*, of rank. His social importance when he was alive had been negligible. No commercial transactions had been made in his name, nor had he taken part in any communal work, being yet so young. In his death he caused the religious system of his people to be exercised over him to its full limits. It is only for infants in arms that the less considered and more private operations of magic are used alone. A child out of arms in dying becomes one of the autocracy of ghosts, and such is the power of that autocracy, so strong its hold upon mortals, that a certain democracy rules the cultural manners at the decease of children and adults alike. Nevertheless Nane's was a wealthy household. A child or an adult of a wealthy house dies with more attention paid in Manus than an adult or a child of a poor household.

14. *The Illness of Alupwai and of Her Brother, Sali* [57]

The excitement over the death of Popwitch was barely over, and its ramifications, the attitudes set up in the village by it, were still new when another focus of interest arose. Alupwai's child had been delivered with apparent success, but by now Alupwai had entered upon a wasting fever. On the 12th of February she fainted several times, and, as long as she was conscious, did nothing but writhe in pain. Her abdomen was somewhat swollen, a condition that became steadily aggravated later.

That night Kamutal, titular mother of Paliau, was the medium, Alupwai being the wife of Paliau's younger brother, Tunu. The medium said first that *sori* and *sori's* wife were angry because the white man and the white woman had left *sori's* territory and gone to live in their new house built by Paliau in Paliau's territory (so passing out of *sori's* guard—Pokenau's Sir Ghost's, to *pwanau's* guard—Paliau's Sir Ghost's). In revenge *sori* and his wife were striking down Paliau's brother's wife, Alupwai.

[57] A genealogy of persons involved is given, p. 193.

It may be noted that *sori's* wife was the ghost of a woman who had died of some after-birth trouble. Now Alupwai had similar trouble. The medium never states a fact of this nature in a seance, but everyone knows such a fact and reckons it in account. Ghosts are credited with wishing to widespread whatever fatal misfortune they themselves had suffered as their last mortal experience.

The medium said next that *nouna*, the ghost of Alupwai's and Tunu's dead son, had married *kasalo*, the ghost of the dead daughter of the brother of the wife of Nane. This marriage had been arranged as a betrothal on the mortal plane, but consummated on the other plane. News of its consummation on that other plane had been announced by a medium four years ago. Therefore Tunu and Alupwai were relatives-in-law to Nane's wife. At the recent ceremonial over the corpse of Popwitch, son of Nane's wife and of Nane, all the relatives-in-law of that couple had laid wealth ceremonially on Popwitch's corpse. But Tunu and Alupwai had failed to do so. Therefore the ghost of the son of Alupwai, *nouna*, angry at this outrageous neglect of his marriage to *kasalo*, was striking his mother.[58]

The medium said finally that the ghost *ndrake* was striking Alupwai. As mortal Ndrake had married Nyakareu. After his death the widow went to the house of her titular father, Ngamel. From that house Tunu assisted her in getting away and marrying Poiyo, despite the more conservative general feeling that she should have waited longer before remarrying. There is always such a general feeling about all widows at all times shared by all who are not immediately and personally interested in a particular widow, and even this personal interest is a single particular interest without a change of general attitude. The ghost of the widow's former husband, *ndrake*, was now punishing Tunu for his rash daring by striking down his wife. It is interesting that Tunu's offence to *ndrake* was now seven or eight years old.

Next day Alupwai again alternated between faints and

[58] A genealogy summing up most of the following oracular counts will follow on page 193.

spells of conscious agony. Patalian's [59] magic was summoned in, as this was a case connected with childbirth, and one relevant to Patalian's grievance against Alupwai's kindred. The magic soothed Alupwai not at all, and everyone remarked on the fact that it obviously had no effect. That night another seance was held with another medium.

In all this account I omit further mention of the public wailing and crying that began whenever the patient lost consciousness, and only ended whenever the patient recovered consciousness, just as I omit also mention of the medium's whistles and waits for ghostly intercommunication on the other plane in description of seances. Such phenomena are regular and therefore monotonous in print.

The medium for this evening's seance was a man, Selan, the only male medium of Peri village. Selan using his Sir Ghost as control, with the regular female medium's method otherwise, blamed *sori* and *sori's* wife again, and on the same count as that of the previous evening's seance.

In the second place the medium said that the ghost, *kialo,* was striking Alupwai. As mortal, Kialo had been Alupwai's sister's husband. Kialo had died, killed by the Sir Ghost of his titular father for sins committed, not by himself, but by his wife, Lawa,[60] Alupwai's sister. As ghost, *kialo* was taking his revenge for his death, which had been retribution for his former wife's sin, by striking his former wife's sister, Alupwai.

No more than the above was said in this count of the seance, but in the minds of the medium and of his listeners the statement aroused more old history. Just before the death of Kialo, the latter's wife and his mother respectively had had a grand quarrel. The wife began it by asking Kialo's mother which one of them was really Kialo's wife. The question was aroused by the wife considering that her husband had been giving too great a share of his fishing catch to his

[59] Who will be recalled as the magician who had been frustrated in his advances towards marrying Alupwai's sister, Lawa, and who had performed exorcism over Alupwai previously.

[60] It was in her widowhood, after the death of Kialo, that Patalian had made overtures towards marrying Lawa.

mother, and too small a share of it to her as his wife, the two women being of different house residence, as is the usual custom. The question may sound innocent enough. But it is really a regular form of abuse in Manus, and by Manus idiom it conveys a definite suggestion of incest. The question is rhetorically abusive. Actual incest is not usually suspected in most of the cases in which the abuse form is used. It is called *sobalabalate*. Manus women do not use *sobalabalate* freely upon their mothers-in-law and upon their sisters-in-law. These relationships are respect relationships in common and in correct behaviour. Anyone acting incorrectly and using *sobalabalate* brings down the wrath of the Sir Ghost of the house. After Kialo's wife had used *sobalabalate* upon her mother-in-law, it was Kialo that died by a reversal of fate, struck down by his Sir Ghost. Naturally he was now enraged at his mishap and was bringing retribution to his widow through the person of his widow's sister in an act of delayed justice, still not as perfect retribution as it might be, of course, especially considering that his widow had given further offence by happy remarriage.

Furthermore there had been another item contributory to Kialo's death. Selan, the medium, had previously had an intrigue with Kampon, then a girl. Neither of them had confession wrung out by the incidence of subsequent illnesses until Kampon was obviously perceived to be pregnant, although unmarried. Still Kampon would not confess. She swore that it must have been a love charm which had been wafted on the wind to her which had made her pregnant. Love charms are not a part of the Manus tradition, but work boys bring back tales of such power and actual possession of the charms from their contacts with members of tribes of New Ireland, New Britain and New Guinea whom they meet in the white capital or on the gold fields or elsewhere. Kampon's story was a product of Manus lack of familiarity with the exact scope of love charms, which is very accurately defined by the peoples that have magic as their main tradition, and amongst whom no such story as Kampon's would be likely to be conceived. Later on, however, some stress of illness in his kin forced a confession out of Selan. He did not confess publicly in person, but confessed in private to Paliau,[61] asking for a few hours' delay in its publication. In the interval he started on a sixty mile trip, and he did not come back until months after. Paliau beat a sexual misconduct tattoo on a drum and announced the confession. The kin of Kampon, due to make expiation of sin to Selan's kin (not vice versa—because the illness that wrung the confession was in Selan's kin and payment had to be made to that kin's Sir Ghosts accordingly to relieve their anger), brought Kampon, dressed up as a bride as expiation. All the wealth given was on Kampon's person as wedding finery. (It is customary to dress the bride's person with gifts to her groom's relatives on the marriage day.) This is a form of expiation that is always open to the woman's kin group in such case, if they wish it. They may give their seduced girl in marriage to her seducer. More often the seduced girl is betrothed elsewhere and the arrangement so made previously is not upset.

Selan's elder brother, informed in advance of the turn expiation was taking, had barred up his house and fled to the bush, in order to evade receipt of it.[62] So when the expiation arrived it, or rather she, was not accepted. Naturally the affronted offerers of one form of expiation did not offer a second form. So *kano* was not paid at all except in intention. Selan's kin held that his confession was a sufficient averting of Sir Ghostly wrath, without the undesired expiation.

Kampon bore a girl child that died. Later she had an incestuous intrigue with Poiyo, of her own gens. This intrigue was confessed subsequently by Poiyo while his brother, Komaiyon, lay seriously ill. Expiation was made by Kampon being brought, dressed in bridal finery again, this time to

[61] It will be recalled that Selan was Paliau's wife's mother's brother's son, and therefore *pauaro*, a joking relative to Paliau. Confession of sex sin and obscene joking liberties go together in kin function. The above relationship is a duplicate of that between cross-cousins; often it is a weak duplicate, but between Selan and Paliau such was not the case.

[62] To evade taking Kampon and keeping her in his house as Selan's wife pending Selan's return.

Poiyo. Poiyo took her although he already had one wife, Nyakareu or Ponyama by name. Despite confession and expiation by Poiyo and Kampon's kin respectively, Komaiyon died. And it is interesting to note that when I was in Peri, several years after these events, the death of Komaiyon was generally attributed to Poiyo's seduction of Kampon. What actually happened at the death of Komaiyon was presumably something like what happened at the death of Popwitch—a series of different causes named by the oracles. Even one seance contains at least three separate counts attributing the illness to different ghosts. Soul stuff is divisible, seizable by many ghosts at once. It is supposed to be recovered piece by piece as exposure, confession and expiation is made count by count. Theoretically the last count is the cause of death. It is not probable that the last count at Komaiyon's death was Poiyo's sin with Kampon. But that is now the general explanation of Komaiyon's death. So later on Popwitch's death will almost certainly be laid to Noan's sin with Lawian. I speak speculatively, but that is my firm feeling. The Manus undoubtedly think of sexual misconduct as the greatest conceivable sin, far more damning than any other. They also definitely think of past deaths as all due to sexual misconduct—even including the wholesale slaughter wrought by the postwar influenza epidemic. At the time of any particular death a series of counts of debts unpaid, economic affairs not run quickly enough or run in the wrong choice of alternative directions (such as are commonly presented at any one time), or taboos broken, may pile on top of the count of sexual misconduct. On top of all this blame attributed to erring mortals, the final blame may be laid to the malice of a ghost as contrasted to the error of a mortal. All these counts are taken seriously at the time of making, and it would go even harder than it does now with the sinners against the sexual code if the case were otherwise. Immediate rancour against sinners against the sexual code is pressed and pressed hard, but relieved again temporarily by other preoccupations. But after all the worst feeling is over, expended in diffuse channels, the Manus think of many of these channels negligently, but still think very strongly about what they consider the great sin. So much is this the case that the dogma that exposure, confession and expiation clear away the consequences of a sin, that a new sin must be exposed, confessed and expiated to recover a different piece of soul stuff still outstanding (as evident from the continued illness of the patient), remains very much a dogma that controls only the practice of diviners and mediums during illness. It does not control popular non-oracular retrospect long afterwards. Thus Isole, the medium, will swear that Popwitch died because of *pwanau's* malice and envy and will maintain that view until she dies. But Paliau will swear equally stoutly that Isole's account is false, and countercharge that Popwitch died because of Noan's sin with Isole's daughter. Popular opinion will agree with Paliau, because popular opinion is that sexual misconduct is the great sin, and because it is fitting that major results should be attributed to major causes. In actual fact expression of opinion will be rare because all opinion on such matters is invidious, and moreover calculated to irritate the ghosts unnecessarily.

It was just because of too free talk that Kialo died. Nyakareu or Ponyama, Poiyo's first wife, naturally resented Poiyo's intrigue and subsequent marriage to Kampon at the time of Poiyo's brother's, Komaiyon's, death. In the house of Poiyo where *komaiyon* was now Sir Ghost, Ponyama or Nyakareu discussed with Alupwai's sister, Kialo's wife, Lawa, all the details of the scandal that had led to Komaiyon's death. The two women raked up the scandal and talked of it with such obscenity and freedom that *komaiyon's* rage mounted, so that he struck down Kialo, Poiyo's titular son, because the wife of Kialo listened and added to scandal raked up by Poiyo's first wife gratuitously, and long after the affair was confessed.[63]

Accordingly *kialo* was now wreaking vengeance on his wife by striking his wife's sister.

[63] This is reason number two for Kialo's death. Any number of reasons, credited oracularly at the time for X's death or sickness, may be used by the oracles subsequently to explain X's activities as a ghost.

It is, of course, true that a death may occur, and no actual act of sex be found to explain it. Kialo, for instance, died according to the above because of improper talk about sex. The talk arose, in part, from an actual act of sin between Selan and Kampon which was the making of Kampon into an abandoned woman, and a cause of future trouble and death thus remotely. But proximately no one died on account of Selan's sin with Kampon. The Manus do not comment on such a fact. In such a case they think of Selan's sin with Kampon as the beginning of a bad business that culminated in Komaiyon's death and Kialo's death, and they exculpate no one who has acted improperly, remotely or proximately. Selan, the medium, in attributing Alupwai's trouble to *kialo* was in some measure speaking from a conscience still active.

As the third and last count in his seance Selan said that *pwanau*, Paliau's Sir Ghost, was striking down Alupwai. This was because Tunu, Alupwai's husband, as an unmarried man formerly had sinned with Ngalowes. As a result of this sin Pwaliap, brother of Ngalowes, had died. As a ghost, *pwaliap*, angry at dying for a sin not his own, struck down a child of Pwanau, the child dying. This child as a ghost, angry at dying for a sin that Pwanau as head of the house was more responsible for than he, struck down and killed Pwanau. As a ghost *pwanau* was now shifting the responsibility for the sin nearer home by striking down Tunu's wife.

The house in which Tunu had sinned with Ngalowes was the house of Selanbulot of Matchupal gens. Tunu and Luwil were brothers by blood, both being sons of Potek (♂) of Pere gens and Kamutal (♀) of Matchupal gens. Luwil was adopted by his mother's brother, Selanbulot. Tunu, although not similarly adopted, made free use of his mother's brother's house. There he sinned with his mother's brother's daughter, Ngalowes. Potek and Kamutal adopted Pwanau as a child (Pwanau being by blood of Patusi village), also Paliau (who was by blood of Mbuke village).

Now Pwanau succeeded Potek, who had become *potek*. Pwanau later became *pwanau* because of Tunu's sin, Tunu being brother to Pwanau, and a dependant of Pwanau despite the fact that Tunu was a child of Potek by blood and Pwanau by adoption (a fact that was repeated again when Paliau succeeded Pwanau, Tunu the child of Potek and Kamutal by blood being now a dependent of Paliau).

The above case of sin was a very shocking one as it was between cross-cousins who should have been only joking relatives. The shock was so great that a chain of deaths followed, and now Alupwai's illness.

That there were other counts also that were contributory to the deaths of Pwanau's child and of Pwanau, it may be safely surmised. The above account is one outstanding, a trail of deaths resulting from sexual misconduct. I used some pressure but got only one other of the counts for Pwanau's death. Pwanau had grown weary of his principal Sir Ghost. He had installed another as his Sir Ghost and moved from his former Sir Ghost's territory to another territory to complete his Sir Ghostly spring-cleaning and renovation. His despised former Sir Ghost, however, was not extinguished. Pwanau had not thrown out or destroyed the skull *potek* that was the seat of that Sir Ghost. He apparently kept *potek*, but put another in the principal place and degraded the rank of *potek* in his own eyes and ceremonial usage. Accordingly *potek* turned against Pwanau and had a hand in slaying him; this reason was given although it is common practice to degrade an older Sir Ghost and to rely upon a Sir Ghost of more recent acquisition as a new principal Sir Ghost. New Ghosts are more potent, it is believed. Degradation of the old compatible with his retention is the usual custom. Pwanau thus did nothing irregular. He died very shortly after he did a regular thing, but an action that a man does not usually perform more than two or three times in a lifetime. The coincidence was noted and diagnosis of death made accordingly. The sons of Pwanau took *potek's* skull, broke it into dust and threw the bone-dust into a bonfire.

Selan, the medium, was not reckoning this latter count in saying that *pwanau* was striking down Alupwai, but on the former count of the trail of deaths resulting from Tunu's sexual misconduct. Thus seances long after an event may emphasise one of the counts of former seances to the neglect of other counts.

Selan ended his seance by saying that the causes of illness due to the ghosts were now all known and remedied. Any residue of cause was not the work of ghosts but of mortals, *i.e.*, of magic. It was understood that the next step should be counter magic of a curative or exorcising kind.

The ethnologist in a Manus village would find it comparatively easy to detect expiatory payments which were being made if they were made only after a seance, for the seance is orderly and more or less public. But usually an unobtrusive act of divination takes place somewhere amongst a frenzied crowd of wailers and shouters over a seriously sick person. Someone slips out from the crowd and unobtrusively punts expiatory payment off in a canoe from one house to another. Meanwhile all the pitch of public attention is fixed on the sick person, never on a diviner. The expiatory payment is made so in comparative obscurity, and few know about it until at night the medium elaborates the divination and asks the ghost, already propitiated by payment, to restore the soul stuff to the patient. Even then there is possibility of error. It cannot be assumed that every count in a seance follows a propitiatory payment made. In many cases no propitiatory payment is made. In these cases a man's Sir Ghost is said to have made propitiatory payment to another man's Sir Ghost on the ghostly plane.

The mortals certainly take the making of propitiatory payment into their own hands when the issue is deadly serious. Thus over Popwitch all the three major counts of the seance followed payment made by mortals. On the contrary when Paliau was ill as narrated previously and *sori* was blamed, jealous at my leaving a house in Pokenau's and *sori's* territory for a new house in Paliau's and *pwanau's* territory, then Paliau did not make any payment; payment was made by *pwanau* to *sori* I was told by Paliau's wife. Pokenau subsequently said he had been ignorant of the entire matter until I told him of it. Paliau had not been dangerously ill or the payment had likely been made by mortal hands.

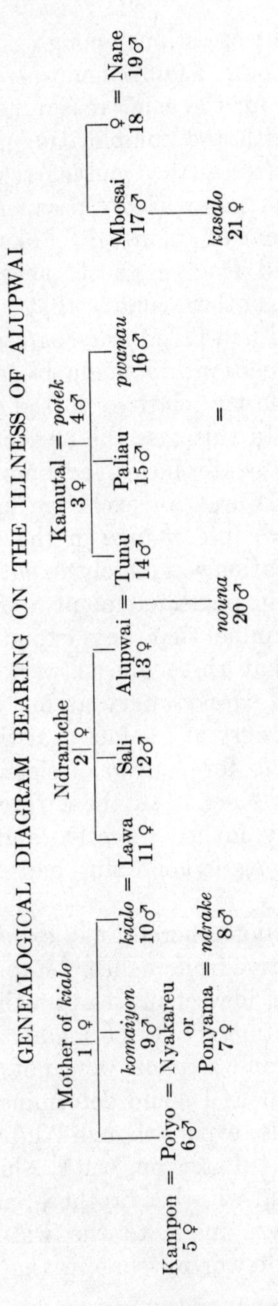
GENEALOGICAL DIAGRAM BEARING ON THE ILLNESS OF ALUPWAI
Mother of *kialo* 1 ♀
Ndrantche 2 ♀
Kamutal 3 ♀ = *potek* 4 ♂
Kampon 5 ♀ = Poiyo 6 ♂
komaiyon 9 ♂ = Nyakareu or Ponyama 7 ♀ = *ndrake* 8 ♂
kialo 10 ♂ = Lawa 11 ♀
Sali 12 ♂
Alupwai 13 ♀ = Tunu 14 ♂
Paliau 15 ♂
pwanau 16 ♂
Mbosai 17 ♂
♀ 18 = Nane 19 ♂
nouna 20 ♂
kasalo 21 ♀

Alupwai's case was serious enough. As she was Paliau's sister-in-law one count against her was *sori's* activity in the same manner and for the same reason as he had been active against Paliau (with the complicating fact that *sori's* wife had died from after-birth trouble, relevant to Alupwai's present case). Yet no expiatory payment was made to *sori*, received on the mortal plane by Pokenau (whatever *sori* may have received from a ghost) according to Pokenau's statement. For another count, that according to which Tunu and Alupwai had failed to recognise relationship in law to Nane's wife, relationship made by a marriage between their respective ghostly relatives on the ghostly plane, Tunu made expiation. In this case the neglect of the relationship had led to neglect to enter into an economic exchange between relatives-in-law. It was an exchange in which no one lost wealth, a reciprocal interchange in the end. So Tunu lost nothing. His expiation was merely an entry into the exchange system at a certain neglected point. On the other counts I could not determine that any expiation was made. It will be recalled that three ghosts were concerned, *ndrake, kialo* and *pwanau*, *ndrake* angry at his widow's remarriage, *kialo* and *pwanau* angry at the fact that they had died for the sins of others, *kialo* for Alupwai's sister's sin, *pwanau* for Alupwai's husband's sin. All these three counts embodied the idea of ghostly malice directly, and long bygone sins indirectly. The long bygone sins had been expiated long before.

The Manus do not generally pay expiation to ghosts that are conceived as active from malice. Expiation is made freely for mortal sin. An idea of justice prevails in the determination of when expiation should be made. Thus the wards of *sori, ndrake, kialo* and *pwanau* were not recipients of expiatory payment as far as I could determine, in the first stages of Alupwai's trouble, even although Alupwai was thought to be close to death. Later on, with Alupwai still in close danger of death, and with her brother, Sali, also in danger of death, expiation was made to the wards of *kialo* and of *pwanau*.[64] It is noteworthy that in the Popwitch case the

[64] However expiation was made to *pwanau* on a new and a more serious ground that was only disclosed subsequently.

counts were of immediate sin rather than of immediate ghostly malice, with the exception of the last count in that case (against *pwanau*), and expiation was made readily and quickly on the mortal plane, with the exception of payment to the ward of *pwanau*, which was not made. But no expiation was made to Lawian's contracted groom's kin of Kalo as the latter had not "paid for" Lawian, *i.e.*, entered upon the exchange that would seal the contract of marriage. In the Alupwai case on the contrary, as far as we have gone, all the trend is towards immediate ghostly malice resulting from deaths for old sins long before expiated, but expiated ineffectually as far as the prevention of death in consequence of such sin went. And this trend has not resulted in present expiation. Thus an idea of rough justice prevails in the making of expiatory payment by mortals, nominally to ghosts, actually to the wards of Sir Ghosts, but need not prevail absolutely under the stress of calamity piled upon calamity. When the case is comparatively unjust, the expiatory payment is said to be made between one ghost and another only.

Early in Alupwai's case we meet with the dominant hypotheses of ghostly malice, not of Sir Ghostly correction. Only one count in six of the first two seances stresses Sir Ghostly correction (that of the non-recognition of a relationship due to a marriage of a Sir Ghost, *nouna*, dead son of Tunu and Alupwai). All the other counts are of *sori*, *ndrake*, *sori* again, *kialo* and *pwanau*. Of these ghosts *sori*, *ndrake* and *kialo* were not related to Tunu and Alupwai in the manner of Sir Ghost. The last ghost, *pwanau*, as Sir Ghost of Tunu's brother, Paliau, might be conceived as Sir Ghost to Tunu by a usual enough extension; but in this case that ghost was acting in a malicious manner that is not according to the correct Sir Ghostly behaviour, but rather according to general ghostly behaviour. Similarly *potek's* Sir Ghostly behaviour in killing his ward Pwanau was decidedly malicious. I have said that this is not typical Sir Ghostly behaviour.

When, however, we envisage the ideas of sin and the performance of expiations that occurred over Popwitch, and compare the ideas of malice and the lack of expiations over

Alupwai, we have a difference that demands an explanation. To begin with Noan's sin with Lawian was known before Popwitch fell ill, and stirred a consciousness of sin and of disaster in everyone connected with the affair; a feeling which functioned when Popwitch fell ill. Moreover there was a great effort made to save Popwitch. Isole was the dominant medium, closely interested in her husband's gens, and since Popwitch's father, Nane, was due to give a *metcha* shortly, any precedent ill luck was felt as more than an individual calamity. It concerned everyone due to take a part in the *metcha*, most of the village in short.

Alupwai, on the other hand, was not connected with any economic affair of prominent general interest at the time. The factors entering into the movement of the oracular diagnoses over her were undoubtedly several, but I think that I can judge of them. The fact that Alupwai was not a centre of economic interest tended to a comparative disregard of her, and ghostly malice as a diagnosis is often connected with a comparative oracular disregard of the patient, because usually nothing is done about it in the way of expiation. It may be a hypothesis of despair or of disregard because usually nothing ponderable is done (although rarely a payment is made).

Tunu, Alupwai's husband, was an economic dependent of Paliau; and Paliau's mother, Kamutal, and Paliau's friend and joking (and confessing) relative, Selan, acted as mediums. The comparatively distant relationship of the mediums to Alupwai was another factor leading to disregard. Thus Selan was concerned with the developments from his own sin with Kampon, the way in which he made Kampon a loose woman and the results that followed. The conscience of the oracles was not the conscience of the gens kindred of the woman as much as it was the conscience of her affinal kindred. The developments because Kampon had been made a loose woman included a sin of Alupwai's own sister, Lawa, it is true. Here there is a fusion between sins of Selan and of Lawa, on either side of Alupwai, on her affinal side and on her kindred side. But for the rest the oracles were concerned

A LADEN CANOE RETURNING FROM A TRADING EXPEDITION

with Tunu's sin with Ngalowes, Tunu's indiscretion in helping the widow of *ndrake* to remarry, *sori's* anger at Paliau because Paliau had built a house for me to get me out of *sori's* territory in which I had previously lived. The mark of the unilateral kin egocentricity of the oracles, of Selan and of Kamutal, is clear upon these earlier oracular decisions over Alupwai. As far as she was concerned her misadventure came apparently from affinal sources. It had to do with Paliau and his brothers decidedly more than with Alupwai and her brothers and sisters.

This fact will be thrown into very nice relief later when Alupwai's brother, Sali, falls ill before Alupwai recovers. Even before that, when Alupwai's kin take up her case the aspect changes. It will be made even more evident than it is already that Alupwai's case opens with ghostly malice rather than with Sir Ghostly correction, primarily because Alupwai is a married woman. The ideal working of the Sir Ghost system is not a matter for married women. Such women have left their own Sir Ghosts and gone to live patrilocally amongst strange ghosts, and ghosts that are malicious to them. That is the great fact to be remembered in Alupwai's case. Neither of the mediums stressed Tunu's Sir Ghost importantly. Alupwai had no Sir Ghost.

Alupwai's case opened (in her first attack before her child was born) with an idea of mortal malice in Patalian's magic, before proceeding later to ghostly malice, just as the case of Popwitch opened with pre-known mortal sin before proceeding to further ghostly sin—and further mortal sin not ostensibly pre-known. This particular fact might appear to have some influence upon the oracles. Actually, however, it is the point of difference in status between a male, such as Popwitch, and a married woman, such as Alupwai, viewed from one limited angle only. Popwitch was under definite Sir Ghostly auspice, Alupwai in her husband's house was in no spiritual home at all, or at least not in one that might be expected to be other than maliciously spiritual to her.

There was one complicating circumstance particular to Alupwai's case, but not sufficiently particular perhaps to make her case atypical for a patrilocally resident married woman. Alupwai had sinned before and refused to confess, even after the man involved had confessed as he lay dying. Alupwai's refusal to admit the sin had been thought contributory to the man's death. No one had believed her denial. Paliau now was not greatly urgent about saving Alupwai, nor were the above mediums. They acted, but they acted appropriately to their knowledge of Alupwai's character. There was not much use to look for sin. Alupwai was believed to be dying anyway—and just after child bearing which might have everything to do with it (although such a fact is thought of in terms of magic). That Selan thought as much was evident from his closing his seance by saying that magic was the trouble that remained undealt with. The ghostly effects had all been dealt with; there remained uncompromisingly some mortal effects (*i.e.*, effects of black magic). Alupwai's was certainly a most serious case.

The day following Selan's diagnosis Alupwai's own kin of Kalo took up her cause seriously, incurring the comparatively heavy expense of an Usiai seer (and later of a magician) and not depending on Paliau, who had not effected anything much with the two mediums he had employed. The seer was brought into Peri village by Sali (Alupwai's brother) and Luwil,[65] and taken to the house in which Alupwai lay.

The seer called first for betel nut and chewed it while he sat with two unopened coconuts in front of him. He then called for sago. A package of raw sago was handed to him. He took a piece of it about the size of an orange in his hand, and pressed it talking softly and undramatically the while in his own language (a charm of some kind). Everyone kept still in the house, all requests being made in whispers. He then handed over the sago to a woman to make into a dish of sago boiled in coconut milk, a liquid food for pregnant women, new mothers and babies. While the dish was preparing the Usiai called for a coconut shell container and a bivalve shell to use as a pounder and scraper. He scraped and pounded a root in the coconut shell container, poured some coconut

[65] Another younger " brother " of Paliau, and Paliau's economic dependent.

juice into it, and spat a betel nut and lime mixture that he had chewed into it. When the dish was ready the Usiai poured his medico-magical mixture into it, and gave it to Sali. Sali fed Alupwai with it. The Usiai gave her a betel nut to chew and spat betel nut juice over her abdomen (swollen greatly now).

Someone (Tuni I think) now put six dogs' teeth into a small wooden bowl and put it in front of the Usiai. He looked at the proffered fee, then looked away (dissatisfied). Sali added two shillings, dropping them into the bowl. The Usiai began his seer's vision. He began staring hard at Alupwai. He did not close his eyes or feign convulsion. He simply stared hard, earnestly and with a great air of intense fixation and of importance. He made a suggestion now and again. Tunu answered him. The general point was that the Usiai saw various vague hints similar to leading questions, Tuñu filling them in. Thus the Usiai would say, "A tree and a man climbing it by a wide river." Tunu would say, "Yes, by the Metawarri River," supplying information from a sense of guilt (stealing in this case), and from the conviction that the seer was finding out his guilt, and he might as well own up quickly. The seer was sensitive to Tunu's reactions and probed here and there much as a dentist probes for a live nerve in an exposed cavity. It was understood that the seer was possessed though he performed no violent antics.

The final results of the seer were as follows:

"A coconut palm; a man climbs it, it is by a river mouth; the man's war charm (hung on his back) slips off as he climbs; he is unaware of it; he goes away and leaves it lost there.

"The ghost of Alupwai's father (*talipoitchalon* of Kalo gens); he looks angry; he is angry because Kalo got no expiatory payment for Lawian's sin from her kinsmen (of Lo gens).

"A sago swamp; it is land that belongs to another; a snake supernatural being eats the food leavings of Alupwai there.

"A house; taro is being cut up there."

The last scene of taro being cut up is a symbolic prophesy of death. The other two symbols to the same effect that are in common use in Usiai seers' diagnoses are a canoe full of sago sinking, and a pig being killed. It is said of these symbols that the spirit of a man may be seen in taro, in sago or in pig as a portent of death. The term used for spirit here is *molua*, not *mwelolo*, which means soul stuff rather.

If on the other hand the seer sees dogs' teeth or shell money, that portends recovery. The spirit of the man is seen in dogs' teeth or in shell money in this case.

It is interesting to note that the symbolism is derived from the marriage exchanges. The man's kin group give dogs' teeth and shell money, the woman's kin group, pig, sago and taro. In a seer's vision the gifts of the woman's kin portend death, the gifts of the man's kin portend life. This may or may not be derived from the fact that the gifts of the one group are the destructible, ultimately consumed valuables, the gifts of the other, the indestructible, unconsumed valuables.

My knowledge of the sequence of events directly flowing from the Usiai seer's diagnoses is unfortunately not as good as it might have been, had I known what to expect. In this case I missed seeing some developments that I heard about afterwards, and the hearsay evidence subsequent to events was not as detailed or as reliable as that which I obtained in a later similar episode from personal witness, and from some knowledge of what to expect, derived from the case now under discussion.

Regarding the first count I gathered an impression that Tunu had stolen from a coconut palm belonging to someone, and protected by black magic put on it by Man of Lorengau.[66] Tunu had apparently confessed sufficiently to lead to Man of Lorengau being summoned in to exorcise the effects of the black magic that were in Alupwai. The confession of theft was not announced by a crier with loud public drumming, as confession of sexual sin always is, and I found by later experience that this was so always. I was not informed who was

[66] But see below a qualification.

the owner of the palm stolen from. I did not see Man of Lorengau at work at his exorcism, but I was told that it had been done when, days afterwards, Man of Lorengau was summoned to exorcise again.

Regarding the second count I do not know whether or not Lawian's kinsmen of Lo, Kemwai, Nane and Isole, paid belated, long denied expiatory payment to Lawian's future groom's kin of Kalo. If they did, I was not informed of it then or thereafter. But from my knowledge of a later Usiai seer's diagnoses and the results, I suspect that they did.

What I was told at the time were the grumblings and the opposition on both counts. Tunu said to me, "If it were true I should have been hurt myself, not my wife, for my stealing from another man's palm. My wife is ill. So it is a lie." But I think Tunu had confessed and paid magician's fees to an exorcist all the same. Only he did succeed in hiding his confession from me by his statement, taking advantage of the conventional lack of public drumming and crying out of confession in such cases. I believed him at the time. I believed that he represented the facts from the inside, whereas outsiders saying "Tunu stole" were possibly misled. Of course I was wrong. There was one speculative conversation that took place on my verandah that interested me. One man said, "I wonder if they found that lost war charm" (lost from Tunu's back as he climbed the palm stealing, according to the seer's vision). The other said "No; it was seen by the seer in vision only." On the second count someone whom I thought disinterested [67] remarked explosively, "A lie of the seer's; Alupwai has married away from Kalo and from the houses of Kalo's Sir Ghosts. She should not be one to bear the brunt of Kalo's Sir Ghosts' anger, even if they are angry because Kalo did not receive expiation for Lawian's sin with

[67] This was Poli of Kalo gens. He was disinterested. He was of Lopwer gens by blood, but actually he functioned as a member of Kalo amongst whom he lived. He had been adopted completely by Songan of Kalo. So Alupwai's own gens kinsman repudiated the idea that a Sir Ghost of her own gens was afflicting her, despite the fact that if this Usiai seer's idea were acted upon, Kemwai and others of Lo would make expiatory payment to Kalo gens, and Poli would get a share of it.

Noan." (Alupwai lived in a house of Tunu's Sir Ghosts of Pere gens, not of Kalo gens.)

At the time that I heard these rumblings and discontents with the Usiai seer's results, I credited them as being likely renunciations of action that might have been taken on the seer's results. I was later to find that discontent and action usually went together, just as amongst ourselves a person disgruntled with the medical profession's methods does not act upon his aversion. He seeks whatever can be done for him, and avows skepticism all the while. A fear of calamity rides him, and drives him to action.

The third count was taken up, that a snake-like supernatural being, had eaten Alupwai's food leavings. These snake-like supernaturals are *tchinal*.[68] They live on the land in the bush, in trees or in caves. They are not primarily believed in by the Manus. The inland Usiai peoples practice a *tchinal* cult in detail. Usiai men go out on solitary expeditions under rigorous taboos in the hope of entering into communication with a *tchinal*, and securing magical power therefrom. The Manus do not go on such quests, and they generally treat the *tchinal* as a joke. But the Manus are sometimes a little afraid of land trespass in Usiai country, owing to possible reprisals by *tchinal*. Moreover the *tchinal* are the familiars of the *sorosor* charms, or conditional curses placed upon palms to punish thieves and trespassers. In this aspect the Manus have considerable regard for the *tchinal;* it is only the general idea of *tchinal* that they deride, not particular usage except such particular usages of the Usiai people as they themselves have not adopted.

The charge in the seer's vision was that Alupwai had been affected by a *tchinal* of a sago swamp. Moreover it had occurred in a sago patch owned by another, according to the seer. Tunu owned up that he and Alupwai had trespassed without permission on a sago patch owned by Pwiseu of Peri. Accordingly the *tchinal* was duly represented as a just punisher of sin.

It was generally understood that the *tchinal* was now

[68] See p. 60.

lodged within Alupwai's swollen stomach. This was understood, although the seer's vision had mentioned only that the *tchinal* had eaten Alupwai's food leavings in the sago swamp. The seer had concluded his vision by saying that he had not the power to cast out *tchinal*, or *tchinal's* influence himself.

I believe that a magician was brought to do the exorcism, but I missed seeing his performance. However, I saw an exorcism of a *tchinal* later on.

It is possible that the magician whom Pwiseu had hired to protect his sago palms was Man of Lorengau. It was he who performed an exorcism later, when I saw the procedure and discovered that he had been called in earlier without my knowledge. Since there had been no public crying of confession of theft, as occurs of confession of sexual sin, I was misled at the time of the seer's enquiry. Whether the coconut palm theft, as well as the trespass on the sago palm patch, led both to one exorcism by the one and the same magician, Man of Lorengau, I am not certain. I am not certain whether or not two different magicians were called in on the two different counts. Or again Tunu may have confessed to sago patch trespass on Pwiseu's sago patch, but not to the coconut palm theft. I am in the dark, except that I know certainly that Tunu did admit to trespass on Pwiseu's property. This confession was made specific to me, though the other, if it were a confession, and not merely a seer's charge (unsubstantiated) was not.

The day after the Usiai visionary came to Peri to diagnose Alupwai's case, Sali, Alupwai's brother fell unconscious in a fit at about eleven o'clock at night. I revived him somewhat with spirits of ammonia. At last he "came to" sufficiently to recognise me and to make a wild rush at me. It took about eight men to hold him and to put him down again; whereat he lost consciousness again.

There was some talk about Nyameros, the mad woman in the house. It was generally recognised that she was mad because she would do anything almost that she was told to do—even if it was strenuous work without compensation. She had just confessed that a ghost had been pulling up her skirts and exposing her. She had come in a fright from the women's half of the house to the men's to tell of it. And just at that moment Sali had fallen down in his fit.

I could do nothing except to hold a wet cloth on Sali's forehead and clear space for the air to get to him—things I was allowed to do by now, if I did not choose to efface myself. They allowed me to try my air and cold water methods, for a time. Then there was some divining. I gathered that the result was as follows:

Sali and Luwil had gone together by canoe to embark the Usiai visionary and bring him to Peri. They went by way of Patusi village. In the sea between Peri and Patusi, *kialo* aided by *pakob* had struck Sali for the same reasons that we have seen motivated *kialo* in his attack upon Alupwai. There was however also a new one, of the same general pattern as those already raised by Selan as medium over Alupwai. Sapisapi, brother of Pokenau, had committed a sex offence with Isongo, sister of Kialo. In consequence Sapisapi died; then *sapisapi* as ghost, angry that Isongo had not died instead of himself, struck down and killed Isongo's brother, Kialo. This is now the third reason we have heard for Kialo's death, for it is still the same Kialo. It will be recalled that Lawa, Kialo's wife had charged incest insultingly (*sobalabalate*) between Kialo and his mother over a matter of the division of fish. Lawa had also resurrected scandal with Nyakareu, Poiyo's wife, about a sin of Poiyo's other wife (incest with Poiyo before marriage), a sin for which Poiyo's brother, Komaiyon had died. Kialo, titular son of Poiyo, and husband of Lawa, had died for these sins committed by Lawa. Now it appears that he died for his sister's, Isongo's, sin also. Enraged at his death, *kialo* was striking down Alupwai and Sali, Lawa's sister and brother. Alupwai and Sali were not related to Sapisapi, Isongo's partner in sin however, so why the diviners over Sali brought up that matter remains illogical. Kialo died for his own sister's fault there, and in so far Lawa might be exonerated for her sins. However the diviners evidently thought otherwise. They were not ostensibly trying to clear Lawa and thereby cure her kin. They were ostensibly accounting for Sali's illness, but evidently doing so in terms less invidious to Sali's kinswoman, Lawa, than had been done previously, and in terms more invidious to the character of *kialo.* In this they, as closer kin themselves to Sali, Alupwai and Lawa than the mediums Selan and Kamutal, were awarding less semblance of justice to *kialo.* It will be recalled that Selan and Kamutal were close to Paliau, Alupwai's husband's elder brother. The diviners over Sali were of a collateral patrilineal line to the lineage that included Lawa, Alupwai and Sali. Hence flowed the difference in point of view.

The point has been made to me that my readers may think that this comparatively late in the day mooting of the sexual sin of Kialo's sister, Isongo, in explanation of Kialo's death may seem to discount my previous insistence that deaths of long standing are always attributed to sexual sin. I was unaware of this possibility, but I may explain that the death of Kialo was comparatively recent. The great majority of the ghosts credited with activity in this account are those from comparatively recent deaths. The deaths from the influenza epidemic of 1918, in contrast, yield ghosts that were almost all not credited with any activity during my stay in Peri in 1929–30. All those deaths were said by nearly everyone to have been due to sexual sins, and to the grossest sins of illicit sexual intercourse. I say "nearly everyone," because the feeling in Matchupal gens of Peri village differed considerably from the feeling of most of the rest of the village. By some accident the influenza epidemic killed off most of Matchupal gens, and touched the several other gentes of the village lightly. In Matchupal gens I heard the deaths that other gentes referred to as caused by gross sexual sins put down to *sobalabalate,* (wifely charges of incest against the husband which are not credited as indicating actual acts of incest), and breaches of the Matchupal gens taboo on the handling of red sago. Thus where non-related persons give brutal and blunt accounts of deaths, those related to the dead may give less brutal and less blunt account, but usually one that has at least some reference to some breach of the proper puritanical code in a matter related to sex.

In regard to more recent deaths there is a like division in the type of explanation preferred by the non-related, as opposed to the related groups. Thus Isole, mother of Lawian, attributed the death of Popwitch to the malice of *pwanau* over Nane's *metcha.* Paliau, ward of *pwanau,* and the Kalo gens into which Lawian was betrothed, as befitted angry and affronted persons, attributed the same death to Lawian's sin with Noan. Those not interested agreed on the whole with the affronted group rather than with the defensive group. In any case no one said much after the event, because scandal-mongering is dangerous. It stirs up ghostly wrath.

The same manner of division occurs similarly over Alupwai and Sali. Mediums such as Kamutal and Selan, very distantly related to Alupwai, recalled Alupwai's sister's sins of impure language as the cause of the death of Alupwai's sister's husband, Kialo. Diviners over Sali, closely related to Sali, recalled that Kialo died for his sister, Isongo's, gross act of sexual sin. Kamutal might have done that also, as she was not related either to Isongo, Kialo, or Sapisapi, Isongo's partner in sin. But Alupwai, her patient in hand, was not related to Sapisapi at all and was not related to Isongo except as sister-in-law, and sisters-in-law are not expected to suffer, the one for the other's sin. They are too remotely related. A sister is expected to suffer for a sister's sin in contrast. Kamutal, unrelated closely to either party, and Selan, although he was related to Sapisapi as gens brother, therefore followed the regular rules, where the diviners over Sali were partisan in apparently not blaming Lawa at all. Such partisanships must often be reckoned with.

Even when an oracle is non-partisan, however, and is using a theory of a death that is not a comparatively recent death, it need not be the popular theory that all past deaths were due to sexual sin. That popular theory is only more or less present in the oracular statements which are the subject of my main discussion.

Oracles who are non-partisan, and even many oracles who are somewhat partisan, follow the rules on the whole. One such rule is that a sister may die for a sister's or a brother's sin, for example, but not for a sister-in-law's sin. Where the diviners over Sali recalled the sin of Sali's sister's dead husband's sister, and attributed Sali's illness to the wrath of the ghost of his dead brother-in-law who died for that sin they were making out Sali's illness to be unmotivated apparently. For in terms of Manus rules a man should not be stricken for his sister's sister-in-law's sin, although it is quite right for example that he should be stricken for his sister's sin. The diviners were simply acting thoroughly as partisans.

Thus it was only through strong partisanship and through a departure from the proper oracular rules that the popular theory of death for a gross illicit sex act was brought up by some oracles in connection with the death of Kialo at all, in so far as the death of Kialo was relevant to the illnesses of Alupwai and her brother, Sali. It was brought up by some oracles who were more interested in not agreeing with other oracles (Kamutal and Selan) than in following the rules, although they all agreed in fixing the responsibility for the illnesses on the ghost, *kialo.*

The next day Sali lay with a serious fever. In the morning Kalo gens gave two small children of Kalo as expiatory payment to *kialo*, on the basis of the divination of the night before, and on the basis of the general oracular agreement that *kialo*, whatever the grounds, was responsible for Sali's illness, as also for Alupwai's. In this light the divination of the night before over Sali may be regarded, since the diviners were of Kalo gens, as a grudging admission by Alupwai's and Sali's kin that the earlier oracular judgments by Kamutal and Selan had some basis; for this was the first expiation to *kialo*, although Alupwai's illness had been attributed by others to that ghost. Now, with calamity redoubled, Kalo acted, although previously they had been unwilling to take the course of paying expiation to an affinally related ghost, a ghost of another gens, a ghost of a former husband of a woman of Kalo. The two children who were yielded up by Kalo gens in expiation to *kialo* were received by the mortal ward of *kialo*. This ward has no particular significance in the sequence I am describing except as ward of *kialo*. He was an unobtrusive man who was always called the son of Paliau (actually he was a titular son-in-law of Paliau's).[69] Formerly he had been adopted by Kialo. However the fact that the son-in-law of Paliau, (also called more rarely by his name Pomaleu) ultimately received expiatory payment from Kalo is noteworthy, considering that the medius (Kamutal and Selan) who stressed *kialo* as the responsible ghost had Paliau's interest at heart. For Paliau's son-in-law was virtually another limb of Paliau in all economic affairs, a dependent and a helper. The stress of Paliau's oracles upon ghostly malice appears now in this further light.

As we have seen Poli of Kalo gens repudiated the idea that Alupwai should have been stricken by a Sir Ghost of her own Kalo father, on the grounds that she was married away from Kalo. She was denied her own kin's Sir Ghost's attentions by one of her kinsmen, although granted such attention by an Usiai seer. Thus there seems to be some support on both sides for a woman being denied Sir Ghostly correction unless she has sinned grossly and sexually. For Selan and Kamutal did not give Alupwai much more benefit of her husband's Sir Ghost than Poli, as a diviner, would have given her of her own gens' and family's Sir Ghosts.

I do not intend to convey for an instant that Kamutal and Selan in making *kialo* responsible for Alupwai's illness were consciously trying to benefit a member of their own group. The Manus quite sincerely are not avaricious for expiatory payments. On the whole they dislike receiving expiation. In this case Kamutal and Selan probably did not expect that Kalo would make expiatory payment to the ward of *kialo*. Malice of ghosts is woman's lot and due to no special wrong that can be righted by expiation. Kalo undoubtedly would not have paid the ward of *kialo* if Sali had not fallen ill and so redoubled the intensity of the situation. All I intend to convey is the complete enough manner in which a woman is delivered over to the malice of ghosts of a wide kin group of her husband.

The case of Sali's illness opens with *kialo* still active, as if

[69] Very rarely he was called by his name Pomele.

Sali were as deprived of his own gens' Sir Ghosts as Alupwai. This is interesting as an oracular continuation in the manner already begun in another connection. It is continuity essentially. The interesting point is the way in which the pattern changes once *kialo* is disposed of. This change will appear shortly, but not until after considerable trouble with *kialo*.

In the evening Itong, a gens "mother" [70] of Sali and Alupwai, held a seance; her control was named *polum*. The seance is concentrated upon Sali, for whom, much more than for Alupwai, the expiatory payment of the day had been made by Kalo to the ward of *kialo*. The following is my record of the seance; *polum* is called up and asked the reason for the illness. He says through the medium:

"Yes, you wait a while with this man; *pakob* and *kialo*, the two of them struck him. You wait and I'll go and bring them. We'll make speeches then."

After a due space of time *pakob* through *polum* through the medium says:

"I, I did not strike him. I was resting in my house when *kialo* saw Sali and Luwil as the two were going out to solicit Tchapo (the Usiai visionary), as they were going to Lokale River. He came to me punting his canoe. He said, 'Come, the two of us will lift up (*i.e.*, take up) my war, my feud; and you, if you want to make war you say so to me at any time and I can lift up your war in return.' I went with him. He whom we wished to strike had gone inland hidden now up river. The Usiai had not come out yet, nor the Manus. We waited, *kialo* said, 'We shall wait for him and strike him.' But I was unwilling; *popwitch* [71] called me; he said, 'You two come, I want to embark in your canoe.' And *kialo* said, 'No! you stay there and we shall punt our own canoe by our two selves.' But *popwitch* said, 'I want to embark; you come here. I want to go to see my Usiai friend.' Well, he embarked. We three went; *kialo* took an axe suddenly to hit Sali and Luwil. But *popwitch* was unwilling. He struck aside *kialo's* axe and seized it. Only the axe haft or the flat

[70] Itong was mother of Bonyalo, the dependent of Paliau. As a member of Kalo gens she had titular relationship to Sali and Alupwai of Kalo gens.

[71] Ghost of Patusi village; not Nane's recently dead son, but *popwitch* senior.

side of the blade hit Sali. If *popwitch* had not interfered Sali would have died at once at the river; *popwitch* seized the axe. Sali did not die. The two got back home. Sali's soul stuff is still with the one that struck him. You stay here and I'll go to see him. I'll ask him for it. If he brings the soul stuff I'll come back with him. Let him come, bring the soul stuff and tell his story of why he struck the person here."

After a decorous pause to give the ghosts time, *kialo* spoke through *polum*, through the medium:

"I, I was angry at his sister (*i.e.*, Sali's sister, *kialo's* former wife on earth). She talked too much about me. When I brought fish in I divided it, part to my mother, part to her, and she said 'This kind of fashion is that of a man who has two wives' (*i.e.*, charged incest). Myakareu (Poiyo's wife) and she maligned Kampon (Poiyo's other wife). They said that Kumaion had seduced her. (*kumaion* was dead and this was not an official account of his death, but plain unoracular scandal and *kumaion* as a ghost punished this unoracular scandal concerning him by killing Kialo.) One thing went with another so that I died from it. I stay with the ghosts. I am sorry for myself that I while yet a youth left behind my two children and my house, and died irrevocably. For the scandalous talk of women I died and now bemoan myself. I said, 'The sin was not mine; the scandalous chatter of Sali's sister consumed me. I died. I am with the ghosts here.' She (Sali's sister) went with all her kinsmen (of Kalo). I am still clutching at all of them. I struck Ngamasue [72] (before). All his ghosts (Sir Ghosts) and all the mortals were potent. So he returned (to life). I struck Tuwain.[73] You mortals and your (family) ghosts were potent. He returned (to life). I struck Alupwai. You mortals and your ghosts were potent. She returned. I struck Tunu, [74] You mortals and your ghosts were potent. He returned. Now after all that, I am striking Sali [75] also, and you are potent. He rests halfway at present between you mortals and us ghosts."

[72] Ngamasue was of Kalo of a collateral line to the line of Alupwai.

[73] Tuwain was Alupwai's elder brother.

[74] Tunu was Alupwai's husband.

[75] Sali was Alupwai's younger brother. Note that Lawa, the offender, is one of the few persons of Kalo not stricken, although she is the sinner.

The tug of war for a person's soul stuff is the concept used in the above; for scandalous chatter and scandalous charge of incest *kialo* died and the list of his revenges upon the kin of his wife is large. Four men, Sali, the fourth, and one woman comprise his list, and he has only inflicted illness. He has secured no death in revenge as yet, but he seems to hope for one. In his statement above he is quite non-commital about the present case.

Korotan, who was adoptive father of Sali, now addressed *kialo*:

"*kialo*! So! That which you say is the body of a fish (*i.e.*, is absolutely true). Yet all of your fathers, all of Matchupal gens were about to die. They took all their men and put out to sea. They sailed to Lou. There was not a rich man to call to them and to hold them to him. I, and I alone, took them to me, collected them again and brought them back, children and men. I made the funerary feasts for them, and financed them throughout.

"And you are the only one of them to behave like this, and to strike down a son of mine. So. You strike down my son. You send back this son of mine in place of a canoe, a sail and axe that you might have given me (but did not) to repay my outlay on the funerary feasts of your fathers. You owe it me."

kialo replies through the control through the medium:

"Yes; what you say is well and to the point altogether. You made the funerary feasts for my fathers and later for me also. But the speech I have is just this. Only the talk of Sali's sister consumed me. I stay with ghosts. She stays with all of Kalo gens there. I struck all of Kalo, many of them altogether. You solicited them back and they came back (to life). Later this one also you solicit. But this one has already come amongst us (*i.e.*, his soul stuff is with the ghosts). He may return to you, or he may stay here. I'll go and try to find the soul stuff. I have given it to the Usiai (ghosts). So."

Korotan did not relish this non-committal reply from *kialo*. He tried a new pressure.

"Yes!—Now, *kialo*, this son is not a son of Kalo. He is a son of mine. (As a matter of fact Sali was a son of Kalo. Korotan had him by a tenuous adoption only.) The name of my gens kinsman is his name. You send him back. So. But if not, listen. My mother was not of your house or of your house platform. (*i.e.*, Korotan's mother was the sister of *kialo's* father;[76] Korotan is therefore cross-cousin to *kialo*, and of the woman's line. He can therefore curse *kialo* with the *tandritanitani*). And if I wish to fasten you I can fasten you. I shall take two stones, one on top of the other. I shall hammer. Your strength will be finished then there. You will not be able to strike a man again.[77]

"And if I come to cry for my son here, his brothers will build no house to shelter you. You will have no mortal ward. You will become a little what not (*i.e.*, nothing much)."

At this point *salopati*, father of that *pakob* who was associated with *kialo* in the ghosts' canoe at the hitting of Sali with an axe by *kialo*, spoke through the control and the medium:

"For me I have little to say. But I am angry at *pakob*. I said that when I died here all of Patusi and Peri had their buttocks cold on account of me (*i.e.*, were all afraid of me). The ghosts all said that I should break up Patusi. But I was unwilling. I sent peace to all Patusi. They all made my funerary feast. Of my two widows one went and remarried into Pomatchau. By myself I struck her down for it, and she died."

(Here *salopati* speaks still, but includes *pakob* in his speech, addressing *pakob* directly, but so that all the mortals hear it—through *polum*, through the medium of course.)

"And you (*pakob*) don't listen to the talk of all (the ghosts). Don't lift up their battles. And this new house that the mortals are building out seawards let your eyes be red over

[76] When a woman leaves her father's house she is said to go to another house and house platform (*i.e.*, her husband's) to replenish that platform (*i.e.*, bear heirs to that house). Hence Korotan says to *kialo*, "My mother was *not* of your house platform," that is, she had left it.

[77] Note the idea that a man can *tandritanitanu* a ghostly cross-cousin.

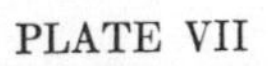

PLATE VII

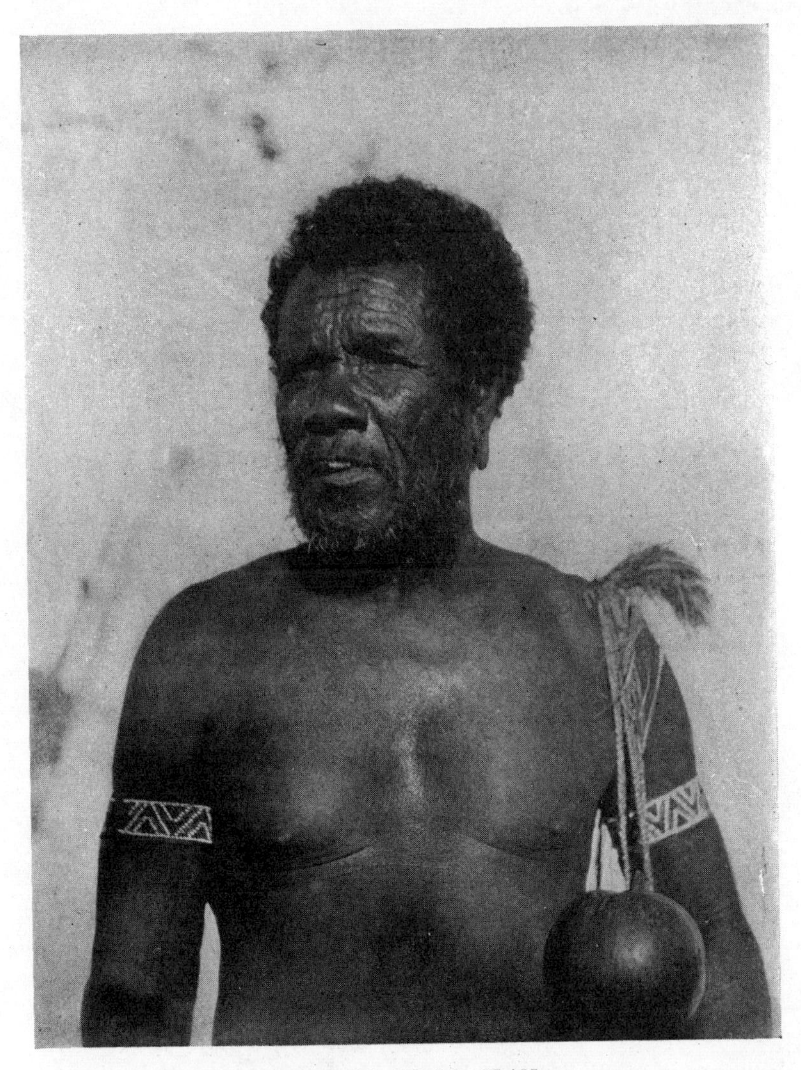

KEMWAI OF LO CLAN

it (with watching over its safety). You rest. You guard your house and all your dependents. And tomorrow or the day after your new house will stand up."

To this exhortation *pakob* replied through *polum* through the medium:

"Yes; previously I did not rest my axe. I struck down Patusi and Peri also. Some of them that they solicited back (to life) returned. Now this time that they move my house out seawards I have cast away my axe. I do but rest in my house. At the time I struck men down, my brothers and children (surviving me) found that they could not rest inshore, lest their ghost (Sir Ghost) strike them down, so they moved to the other side out seawards. I by myself am not a match for all the ghosts. If they all object to you and all strike you, I would solicit for you from them in vain. You stay. I shall find *kialo* and the two of us shall solicit the soul stuff that he sold to the Usiai near Taui Island."

In the fighting days the Manus were not cannibals, but the Usiai were. If the Manus captured the corpse of a slain enemy they held it for ransom, or else sold it at a large price to the Usiai in the market. Correspondingly we find the Manus ghosts trading soul stuff to the Usiai ghosts, a trade that Government has not put down, as it has the old, more fleshly custom.

A request was made for *popwitch* to be heard, since *popwitch* had snatched *kialo's* axe as the latter struck at Sali. In due time *popwitch's* advice was communicated:

"If this man dies, the funerary feast for me, his father-in-law, will be spoiled. (A brother of Sali is married to a younger sister of *popwitch,* a marriage on the mortal plane. So Sali and his brother are due to help to give a funerary feast for *popwitch* shortly.) His soul stuff I held fast. It rests with me. One piece was not taken by the Usiai. And the soul stuff that *pakob* struck I took. It rests with me also. But this morning *popenau* [78] was not in the village. If he had been in the village I would have already given him the soul stuff in my possession to return to you. But he was not here. I'll go to get him so that he'll return it to you."

[78] Identified immediately below.

It must be noted that the said *popenau* is the Sir Ghost of Sali's "brother."[79] Sali's "brother" had been out fishing that morning; *popenau* naturally had gone out with him. So the above speaker, *popwitch*, had missed *popenau* when he had sought for him.

At this point Korotan suggested that Sali might have been stealing from his coconut or betel nut palms, on which he had placed a charm of black magic, a *sorosor*, to punish thieves. He suggested that someone make divination to see if this was so. Sali's "brother," 'Poli, made divination, the result being affirmative.

The medium immediately called up her control to interview the spirits of Korotan's *sorosor*. These spirits never had been mortal. They were magical familiars purely. But they were named and could communicate through a medium. One of them called *Popeu* answered for all of them:

"Yes; we were guarding the coconut palms of our father (Korotan is their father by term of address only). You (Korotan) said to us that we were to do so. You said, 'I send you to look after our coconuts here, and if any person comes to steal you take an axe and hit him with it so that he'll die forever.' So. It stayed in our ears, when we saw Sali begin to climb the palm we struck him. We took an axe and cut him with it. Now you talk differently. Let the fire blaze up. I want to see him. Let him eat food again."

At this point the night's seance concluded. The dating of events was:

12th February—First seance over Alupwai.
13th February—Patalian's magic exorcism and second seance over Alupwai.
14th February—Usiai seer's vision.
15th February—Sali falls unconscious late at night; preliminary divining.
16th February—First expiatory payment to *kialo* and above seance over Sali.

Both Alupwai and Sali were in serious danger of death,

[79] A gens brother, Poli of Kalo.

but Sali was temporarily, for some days now, in the more serious state, as judged by the Manus standard of frequency and length of fits of unconsciousness. Alupwai was in great agony, but kept conscious more in a worn delibitated state, whereas Sali was fighting fiercely against a sudden and swiftly moving attack of cerebral malaria.

Next day there was renewed confused wailing, shouting and din from the house where Sali lay. Most of the day he lay unconscious, but towards late afternoon he rallied and recovered consciousness. I was fortunate enough to see Korotan take expiatory payment to the house of Tuwain [80] and Tuwain's Sir Ghost, *talipoitchalon* or *papi*. As I have mentioned before, the expiatory payment is usually made before the seance, on the basis of divination alone. It is paid quickly and is over before an ethnologist can be informed of it and put out in his canoe to see it. I was lucky to chance upon Korotan as he made it. He punted to Tuwain's house and laid out expiation of one trade chest with lock and keys, and one rusty, but good axe-head on the front platform of the house. Then standing erect in his canoe outside the house (the people of which did not appear), he addressed the Sir Ghost of the house:

"*papi! E!* expiation to you this. Let my man come. Send him back (to life) to my outrigger platform (*i.e.*, put back his soul stuff on my canoe). Let me take it to him that he may recover. Come and take your expiatory payment here, take it off to the ghosts.

"And if you were not bought off, but went through with your badness, where would you find a ward amongst the mortals then? You would try in vain to strike down a man easily then. If you strike down this man for ever so that he dies, where will you find a house to rest in then? You'll just scorch in the sun and be wetted in the rains.

"You are of no rank. You come from your father that carried you, your mother that carried you. You are of no rank. But your mother took you to the coral rubble territory

[80] Alupwai's elder brother, and Sali's. The reason for this payment is made public in the seance that follows in the evening.

of a man of rank (by a subsequent marriage). So you ate your food from a wooden bowl (poorer families and families of no rank eat from plastered basketry). Take the word of a man of rank to yourself now. Send Sali to return to me.

"And expiatory payment is yours here. Come and get it. You bore two sons and one helps the other. If the younger (Sali) stays with mortals the two of them can work together, the two can build a house together; and you can stay there, you can shelter there. It will be well. But if you strike down the younger so that he dies:

(Korotan here raises his voice to a great thundering shout of rage for the next phrase.)

"Then you will be made to understand!!! This man dies and you rest in no house. You will but wander about the edges of the islands (used for excretory purposes).

"You send this man back into the canoe of mine and of *salaiau* (Korotan's Sir Ghost); we two may take it to the man. He may recover. And come and take your expiatory payment here (with strong disdain in Korotan's tone)."

Later on, after Korotan's departure, Tuwain, as ward of *papi* or *talipoitchalon*, took the payment to himself. It is because expiatory payment is often offered in Korotan's style that the mortals who acquire it do not always appreciate it highly. They may have their Sir Ghosts, with whom they are identified considerably, dragged into great contempt as the price of it. But they can do nothing about it.

Shortly after Korotan's payment, Sali, at the instance of his cross cousins who were pressing him to reveal any secret sin he had committed, confessed that he had seduced an Usiai woman that he had met in the bush, the wife of a Government appointed native medical assistant of a certain village. Drums were beaten and Sali's cross-cousins looked triumphant. The confession quickly was noised about the village. But there was no pattern of expiation to the Usiai; and I am fairly certain that the Usiai were not informed of the matter, certainly not openly.

The older wiseacres shook their heads and said that this was no confession of sin that would be of any value in recovering Sali his health. Seduction of a foreign woman was not a sin at all.

That night Isole was the medium. In the seance she concluded the affair with *papi-talipoitchalon*. The first ghost to give evidence was *nyapokaleu*,[81] sister of *papi-talipoitchalon*.[82]

"I, when I was yet mortal, you wronged Tuwain. I took compassion on him. I said he was the eldest. My brother bore him. The features of my brother rest with him there, completely reproduced; and you shall not wrong him.

"Then I died. I watched you. You went together, took sides against him and quarrelled against him. A "middle space" arose between you and him (*i.e.*, an avoidance). I said that you should not quarrel against him. I was angry. I spoke to my brother of it. The two of us struck down Sali."

talipoitchalon next gave evidence: "Yes, I was angry that you did nothing but quarrel with him. Women and men you all quarreled against him. And when my sister spoke to me about it I heard her speech. We acted together, we struck Sali. And I said, 'Yes. This one (offended against) was my first born. The image of my body and of my face complete is his. He built this house that is mine. I shelter in it. Then you quarrelled at him. It stuck fast to him. I was angry. I strike this man to the ground.'"

The gist of this affair concerned Patalian's desire to marry into Kalo. Ndrantche opposed Patalian's marrying her daughter, reasonably enough considering that Patalian had seduced her (or she, him) long before and had run away to escape the furore that ensued. Ndrantche was the mother of a majority Kalo gens, and the widow of *talipoitchalon-papi*. Tuwain, the eldest son of *talipoitchalon-papi*, had taken Patalian's side and encouraged the idea of the projected marriage. All the rest of Kalo sided with Ndrantche against Tuwain. Tuwain as eldest son of *talipoitchalon-papi* was the ranking

[81] Also named *nyalel*, the mother of Talikai, Nyakareu (wife of Poiyo) and Pwoikaton, and the second wife of the father of the above three, father also of Kotortan, war leader.

[82] Who was paid expiation by Korotan, Isole's "brother", earlier in the day—the pay being received by Tuwain, ward of *papi-talipoitchalon*.

member of the group. He was the head of the gens. By Manus custom the eldest son has authority over his younger brothers and over all his sisters. Thus there had been a flouting of authority in the setting aside of Tuwain's will, which had taken place. The ghostly father and father's sister of Tuwain and of Sali were now striking Sali as a member of the rebellious group concerned.

Expiatory payment had been made to *talipoitchalon-papi* and received by Tuwain on Sali's behalf, so that ghost was asked by the medium to restore Sali's soul stuff and to place it in the bowl of water in front of her, water with which she subsequently bathed Sali.

It turned out however that *talipoitchalon-papi* had distributed the soul stuff to some gens brothers of his (all ghosts). These ghostly brothers were in different and far away villages, for Kalo gens had been widely dispersed some two generations ago; *tchabornan* of Tchalalo village had some of the soul stuff, *mwenal* of Mbunai had some, and *ponyape* of Pomatchau village had some. Moreover *talipoitchalon-papi's* sister's husband, *potoan* of Peri, had some of it.

Again, *kialo* and *pakob* still had some of Sali's soul stuff also in their possession, despite the previous measures of the former seance of the night before, and all Korotan's threats against *kialo*.

Isole's control *tchemilo* said that he was not equal alone to collecting all this from the "close" possessors. So *tchemilo* summoned two of the native constabulary (ghosts of native police). They went with him. Then *tchemilo* and the policeman of Pontchal, *sori*, and the policeman of Tchalalo, *yonku*, went together to use the authority of the native police backed by white Administration [83] to collect.

This use of native police ghosts in difficult cases is obviously a comparatively recent introduction. One or two of the mediums have controls that have large and fierce ghostly dogs to help them to collect outstanding soul stuff. This latter is the older traditional form; it is not of recent introduction.

[83] Ghostly white Administration only, mortal white Administration not being conversant with this.

With the aid of the police, *tchemilo* recovered the soul stuff and put it in the water of the bowl. Ndrantche bathed Sali with the water. Divination was made at several stages by Poli to determine whether or not the several pieces of soul stuff had been brought in before this bathing was done.

It was noteworthy that Sali's confession of his sex affair was passed over entirely. It did not come up in the seance at all. An affair with a foreign woman was of no interest to Manus ghosts. They only punished infractions of the code within the Manus circle.

At the end of the above seance the medium Isole put forward a new inspiration concerning Alupwai's case. Speaking through her, *tchemilo* said: "*sori* has taken Alupwai's soul stuff because *pwanau* killed *popwitch* [84] of *sori's* mother's gens; he took a piece of Alupwai's soul stuff and put it aboard a boat of the white men; he also gave a piece to the native constable (ghostly) of Tchalalo, who put it in the wooden bowl of *pomat*, the wooden bowl called by the name '*Ngausaie*.' He said, 'This person's soul stuff may just remain in the wooden bowl, and she may die forever.'"

It was agreed that *tchemilo* should be instructed to recover this soul stuff. He did so and put it into water, with which Ndrantche bathed Alupwai.

The foster mother of *sori* was of Lo gens, to which Popwitch, son of Nane, belonged; *sori* was getting revenge upon *pwanau* by striking *pwanau's* ward's younger brother's wife. The wooden bowl called "*Ngausaie*" was a ghostly piece of furniture belonging to a ghost, without mortal counterpart.

This concluded the seventeenth of February. Next day Sali recovered considerably and in a few days he was well again although his attack might have been very easily fatal. He passed from the religious scene with his recovery after the seventeenth. But Alupwai's condition grew steadily worse.

On the eighteenth, Alupwai, who had been free from faints for three days and nights, went into several faints again, and into states of increased agony while she lay conscious. In one

[84] The recent death of Popwitch is referred to here.

of her conscious periods while her cross-cousins urged her to confess any secret sin, she suddenly decided to confess. Her endurance had been remarkable. She might easily have died before this, so serious was her state. But she had not confessed for over five days of great suffering, despite the general firm belief in confession as a cure. The strength of Puritanism in Manus is of this nature.

Now Alupwai confessed to a grave sin, committed long ago and for many years secret to her. When Pwanau was alive many of the village were sleeping in mourning in a house that had recently held a corpse. Pwanau amongst them and Alupwai also. In the night a child had fallen through the loose flooring of the house into the sea. Startled by the noise of the fall Pwanau rushed from the men's half of the house down into the sea, while Alupwai rushed from the woman's half of the house down into the sea. When many miscellaneous people sleep in a house of death the men all sleep segregated in the front half of the house, the women segregated in the back half. The child had fallen somewhere about the middle of the house, Pwanau thought it his child, Alupwai her's. So Pwanau, naked and without pubic covering encountered Alupwai, also naked, beneath the house, both having rushed to save life. Alupwai seized hold of Pwanau's penis for a moment before they climbed back separately, Alupwai with the child.

Between clenched teeth in an agony of physical pain Alupwai confessed the substance of the above. Instantly there was horror and excitement. Men rushed to beat drums and to cry out the story to the village. The horror was genuine enough, for this had surely been a cause of the death of Pwanau, hitherto unrevealed. If it had been confessed while Pwanau lay ill and expiation had been made then, Pwanau probably would not have died.

Selan reached a drum first and called out the news, calling on *sori* and on *topwal,* the latter his own Sir Ghost.

"*sori! topwal!* So! You ghosts of rank and you mortals of rank! Concerning an evil we have just caught, this drum beat that I have made. Speech concerning it I now make.

You may hear it. And *sori* and *topwal* send this person who has become evil to good. All men may praise you for it.

"You there, you ghosts of rank, you mortals of rank, this drum signal concerns the house of death, that was Katoli's house. All were sleeping there when the little child of Tunu fell. Alupwai went out of the half of all the women, the *ketut* (back half of the house). She had no skirt on. Pwanau rushed out of the half of all the men, the *palakeu* (front half of the house—each half has its own exit). He had on no G-string. The two wished to catch the child. Alupwai caught the child and put it into Pwanau's arms. She caught hold of his penis. The ghosts saw it and struck down Pwanau for it; *pwanau* was with the ghosts. He fought his fate. He now wishes to catch Alupwai for it.

"And a further count of sin she confesses. Long ago Pwaliap confessed sin with her. But Alupwai on her part refused to confess. She concealed it. Now later, as she is about to die, she confesses this sin also."

It will be remembered that Pwaliap was a link in a chain that we mentioned earlier in this study. Pwaliap died because Tunu, cross-cousin of Ngalowes and Pwaliap, committed sin with Ngalowes, Pwaliap's sister. Tunu confessed as Pwaliap lay dying, but confession and expiation duly made did not save Pwaliap. Pwaliap (as *pwaliap*) in revenge for death for another's sin killed a child of Pwanau (Tunu's elder brother); for the same reason the ghost of the child killed Pwanau; then *pwanau* made Tunu's wife, Alupwai, ill.

Now appears an addition to the facts of Pwaliap's death. Like all deaths Pwaliap's was from several reasons. It appears that Pwaliap had committed a sin on his own account with Alupwai, and had confessed it, although Alupwai had refused to confess to it. He had been conceived from one angle to have died for his own sin, and from another angle for his sister's, Ngalowes', sin.

Alupwai's confession of what Pwaliap, her partner in sin, had long ago confessed was not news. Her denial had not been greatly believed in the face of the man's confession. It was a relief, of course, that she had now experienced a change of heart. But it was not felt to be very important. Alupwai's kin paid no expiatory payment to the heirs and wards of *pwaliap*. As a matter of fact *pwaliap* had no ward. He was no longer anyone's Sir Ghost. Furthermore when Pwaliap was dying, and confessed on his death bed, Alupwai's kin had paid expiation on the spot despite Alupwai's sullen refusal to confess. That matter had been settled, although it had not led to a recovery for Pwaliap.

It was for these reasons that the oracles had not urged Alupwai to confess her sin with Pwaliap earlier in Alupwai's present trouble. All that could be obtained by such procedure now was a too long delayed change of heart in Alupwai. The matter had been dealt with in all other respects. The ghost *pwaliap* had not been diagnosed as the present cause of Alupwai's trouble because he was now no one's Sir Ghost. He was a ghost removed from the social structure. That was why an oracle had used instead the alternative of *pwanau* dying ultimately for Tunu's sin with Pwaliap's sister, Ngalowes, proximately through *pwaliap*, through a ghost of a child of *pwanau*. Of this chain only *pwanau* was a Sir Ghost of the contemporary social structure.

In contrast to a mild reception of Alupwai's confession of sin already confessed by Pwaliap, Alupwai's confession of her sin with Pwanau was received with great excitement and energy. Selan, in concluding account of the confession, concluded with a renewal of his opening request to the ghosts to restore Alupwai to health.

The confession had been forced from Alupwai by Nyamilo making divination. He had said, as a result of his divining, that Alupwai was concealing secret sin. If she confessed it she would not die today, but if she did not confess it she would die today or tomorrow. This was the kind of pressure that was employed and that had been employed earlier without success; the confession came after an accumulation of such pressure. Nyamilo was unrelated to Alupwai, and was son-in-law to Pope. He acted merely as a member of the village.

As a result of the confession the Kalo kin of Alupwai

immediately gathered together property to pay to *pwanau*, and to *pwanau's* ward, Paliau. The payment was not made directly to *pwanau* and Paliau, but to *topwal* and *topwal's* ward, Selan. Selan and *topwal* were but intermediaries in receiving this payment. Selan had been the medium that had said that *pwanau* was striking down Alupwai, because Tunu sinned with Ngalowes and Pwaliap died for it; *pwaliap* killed Pwanau's child; that child killed Pwanau; *pwanau* now struck Alupwai as Tunu's wife, Tunu having caused the beginning of the chain. Now a more immediate motive was ascribed to *pwanau*, Alupwai's confession revealing it. But Selan as the oracle who had been close to the present truth, was in charge of the case. He transmitted the payment to Paliau. It is noteworthy that there was no bearding of *pwanau* or harsh language to him offered by Kalo as they made this payment. They chose to make it through an intermediary because they were well frightened of *pwanau*. Kalo gens were thoroughly shamed and frightened. The village believed that one of their number had caused Pwanau's death, and had caused it because of deliberate refusal to confess in time to save life.[85] Kalo were ashamed to face *pwanau's* heir and ward, Paliau. That was why they chose an intermediary to hand on their payment—in strong contrast to Korotan offering expiatory payment to *talipoitchalonpapi*.

Next day at dawn Paliau offered up the payment to *pwanau* and to other Sir Ghosts, relatives of *pwanau*, and divided up the payment among the wards of these Sir Ghosts. The payment was considerable.

The wealth was spread out on the coral rubble just outside my house at about six a.m. I woke up and saw the procedure. Paliau said briefly; "I give this expiatory payment to *pwanau*; this canoe goes to the white man, *master tim* (Sir Ghost of Paliau's five year old son, Popoli).

"This other canoe goes to *nyame* (Sir Ghost of Pwiseu).

"This third canoe goes to *pwanau* (Sir Ghost of Paliau).

"This calico wrap goes to *powaseu* (Sir Ghost of Ngamel).

[85] Alupwai, by refusing to confess in time to save Pwanau.

"This fish spear goes to *ngamel* (Sir Ghost of Mbosai).

"This other fish spear goes to *sori* (Sir Ghost of Pokenau).

"This wooden chest with lock and key goes to *tcholai* (Sir Ghost of Luwil).

"This calico wrap goes to *salaiau* (Sir Ghost of Korotan).

"You distribute it, and, Pwiseu, you make a speech!"

Pwiseu said: "*pwanau! E!* expiatory payment to you this. You struck them down. That was well. But they did not flee from their place. They all remained here. Later on you struck them down (again) and this time they fled to a house of Pontchal (Alupwai had been moved from Tunu's house to Ngandaliu's house of Pontchal gens). You restore the soul stuff that you have! Send it to *topwal* who will send it to *poketa!* (*topwal* is Sir Ghost and control of Selan, the medium, and *poketa* is Sir Ghost of Ngandaliu in whose house Alupwai lies—Selan is Ngandaliu's brother and their Sir Ghosts are related similarly). The real person, the real soul stuff is in your possession. Send this person to health. E! expiation has come and has gone to all the ghosts who are great. All may grant your request. You made war. Expiation has come to you. You give it to all who have allied themselves with your war! You expel this person (from the ghostly plane) that she may return (to the mortal plane)! All shall praise you for it. But if this person whom you strike dies all shall not praise you, but the evil will be yours."

The wealth was now distributed to the wards of the Sir Ghosts enumerated by Paliau previously, and the small private gathering broke up. Kalo were naturally not in evidence. Their expiation was very considerable for so poor a group as they. They had stripped themselves of necessities.

On the night of the day of Alupwai's confession there was certainly a seance in which *pwanau* was asked formally to put Alupwai's soul stuff in the water for Alupwai's subsequent bathing, after he had spoken his mind about his attack on her. For the normal course is confession or divination or both revealing a sin, then expiatory payment is made, then a seance asking for soul stuff back that night. Owing to indisposition I did not attend the seance in point. The system is so clear, however, that I missed a formality only. Due to the non-direct way in which expiation was paid it did not reach Paliau till the morning after the seance I missed, the morning of February 19th. For the remainder of February nothing was done with the supernatural for Alupwai. She remained steadily ill, her abdomen as swollen as ever, taking hardly any food. She became extremely emaciated and weak and did nothing but lie in the one place day and night, never rising. She was in great pain all the time, but as I remember the case her pain was unrelieved by unconsciousness other than sleep. She had a more or less continuous fever. Her kin had asked me for money with which to buy light foods for her, but they had spent the money on the Usiai seer as part of the seer's fees. I sent rice, sugar and tea to her often. We shall have occasion to take up the case of Alupwai and of Kalo again when new developments occurred in late February and in March. Meanwhile we may turn to two or three other events of February.

15. *Charge of Incest*

The infant of Ilan and Topaz [86] fell ill. It was at this time about three months old. The treatment followed was not magical. I did not see the divination, but I attended the seance. Itong [87] was the medium, *pokamitch* Itong's control.

pokamitch through the medium: "So, no ghost of another house struck down this girl infant, but the Sir Ghost of her father's house, of this house struck her. He was angry at the talk of *sobalabalate* that Ilan made, and sorry for her husband. (*I.e.* Topaz had been spending his evenings with his sister and mother, not with Ilan, his wife. Much of his fishing catch had gone to his women kin, not to Ilan. Ilan had said, 'So your mother is my co-wife,' charging incest insultingly—although the grievance felt was lack of loyalty and lack of fish really.) She was sorry for her husband with his sister and with his mother. He said that the kind of talk indulged in

[86] Topaz was a young man of Matchupal gens, related through his mother to Kalaat gens. Ilan, wife of Topaz, was a young woman of Kamatatchau gens.

[87] Itong was an old widow of Kalo gens, the mother of that Bonyalo who was a stupid, unassertive retainer of Paliau.

by Ilan was evil; *pokalang* (Sir Ghost of Topaz) was angry. He said: 'Talk of this kind is taboo to a house of ours of Matchupal gens. One taboo is *sobalabalate*, sex jealousy and vile obscenity; and another taboo is the red sago prohibited to us of Matchupal gens. We long ago were many men and many women. Many of us said that we were a gens that was dying out completely. Our dying out came from sin of which the talk you like to make is an example. I was angry at it. I struck down this girl infant. I think you can see by this, you can be made to understand.'"

The mother of Topaz: "Yes. You strike the girl infant for that. And you appeared through the seance and you confessed. You send the soul stuff back that the child may recover!"

pokamitch through the medium: "Yes, you stay a while. I'll get the soul stuff."

After a wait *pokamitch* had placed the soul stuff in the water, and "rubbed" the soul stuff. ("Rubbing," as rubbing in the hands, is always done by the control to the soul stuff after the control has placed the soul stuff in the water.) Itong poured the water over the infant. Next day it was better.

Red sago is a traditionally prohibited article of food for all of Matchupal gens and for that gens only. The association of the gens taboo with the taboo on bad language, such as *sobalabalate*, is loose. For the taboo on bad language is not a gens taboo. It is general.

Matchupal gens had been afflicted with a disproportionate share of the Peri deaths from the 1918 influenza epidemic. Although as a gens it numbered less than a quarter of the village population it had ten deaths out of twenty-two in all in Peri from that epidemic. It was a ghostly visitation for an abnormal accumulation of wickedness.

It will be noted that when the infant fell ill resource was made not to magic, but to the seance. The general rule that the ills of infants are caused by magic and must be cured by exorcism of such magic is not an absolute and binding rule. We have seen that the very first indisposition of an infant after birth is always treated by exorcism of black magic. So regular is this custom that an exorcism of such magic from a newborn child is as regular as baptism in a Christian community. But when the exorcism has been done once, if the child falls ill again the diviner who divines the cause of the trouble may not know of any cause of quarrel between the kin of the infant and a magician other than the magician who has already done an exorcism once, or of a new cause of quarrel with the former exorcist. Since black magic is not suspected except as a sequel of quarrel, the diviner may not know where to turn to find a sorcerer and exorcist, since such men are a very small minority in a large village, one man in ten as sorcerer and exorcist being an approximate estimate. On the other hand a cause of offence to the Sir Ghosts may lie right to hand as in the case of the illness of the infant of Ilan and Topaz above.

However, despite the fact that some of the ills of infants in arms are attributed to Sir Ghosts, the deaths of such infants are with a steady regularity, attributed to black magic. A dead infant leads to diagnosis of black magic, just as a dead adult with a swollen abdomen leads to diagnosis of trespass in a place where an ancestor was killed in war—unless there is some other clear explanation such as post-child-birth complications in a woman.

16. *Pokenau Fails to Meet an Obligation*

As preface to the following seance we may take some preliminary note of the house in which it was held. I obtained notes on the ghostly conditions of quite a number of houses, but not until after I had come to know this house of Pokenau's well.

As one entered the front door of Pokenau's house on the right hand was to be seen the large wooden bowl which held the skull of *sori*. It was hung close to the rafters with pendant ovalum shells falling in strings below it, the mark of a *lapan*, or man of rank. The skull and the shells were blackened from years of exposure to the drifting smoke of the house fires, sifting from the interior of the house to the outer air by way of the stored pots and the skull bowls close against the roof thatch. This blackness of a skull is considered admirable. Pokenau's father's sister, Isau, lived in Pokenau's house. She was lazy, allegedly, and did not do her fair share of the housework. In particular she did not get firewood, much to Pokenau's resentment; *sori* resented his skull not being blackened, and said so in a seance held over Isau when she fell ill for her sins against Pokenau and *sori*. A man's Sir Ghost keeps the women resident in the house in order with regard to work, as well as with regard to *sobalabalate* and the use of bad language in rebellion.

On the left hand of the front part of the house hung a smaller bowl, plain, without pendant shells. It held the head of *gizikau*, Pokenau's grandfather and foster father. Pokenau's actual father, Tano, was killed and his corpse burnt in his house destruction by a German trader, while his son was yet early at the breast. The infant, Pokenau, was suckled by several women, for the mother that bore him died but a few months after her husband, Tano, came violently by his death. So the grandparents, Gizikau and his wife brought up Pokenau; Gizikau lived to a ripe old age as the three or four worn-down teeth left in his skull bore witness. Pokenau's closest solidarity had been with his elder brother, Sori, for although he did not discover in his youth that Gizikau had not been his true father, there had been great discrepancy of age between them, and less of the playfulness between father and son than was usual. In Gizikau's youth, a white man's ghost had been taken by him as his Sir Ghost. Gizikau and Nyakam were younger and elder brother respectively. Nyakam had as his Sir Ghost their father, *salaiau*. After the death of Nyakam, *salaiau's* skull was thrown out and burnt and Gizikau kept the skull of *nyakam*, and had *nyakam* as his Sir Ghost. Later when his son, Tano, was killed, Gizikau threw out the skull of *nyakam* and reverted to the ghost of the white man that had been the Sir Ghost of his youth for his Sir Ghost again.

The head of *gizikau* now hung in Pokenau's house. Sori had had a house of his own, and had taken their father, *tano*, as Sir Ghost. A coconut had represented *tano's* skull, lost in the manner of *tano's* death. After Sori's death, but a few years before my arrival in Peri, *tano* had been no one's Sir Ghost. Pokenau took *sori's* skull and *sori* as his Sir Ghost, and alloted *gizikau* as Sir Ghost to his six-year-old son, Matawai. That was why *sori's* skull bowl was large and adorned with shells, while *gizikau's* skull bowl was small and plain.

The white man Sir Ghost of *gizikau*, and *salaiau*, *nyakam* and *tano* were all thrust out of house, home, and guardianship of the present generation. They haunted the open places of the seas between the villages unhappy because of lack of shelter and care, such as *gizikau* and *sori* still possessed. They were due to haunt the open seas for a while before becoming crabs, sea snakes and the small vermin of the sea. Perhaps some of them had already suffered their sea change. Pokenau neither knew nor cared.

The skull of *gizikau* was in the bowl in the customary two pieces, the lower jaw disjointed, but the lower jaw of *sori* (together with the finger and toe bones of *sori*) was locked up in concealment somewhere by *tano's* sister, Isau, lest marauders steal it, break it and burn it. Only the upper skull of *sori* was in the large bowl. The more recent the death, the more evil is attributed to the ghost by outsiders, who would only too gladly damage the ghost's power by spoilation of the skull. Pokenau and his father's sister, Isau, depending as they did on *sori* for protection, naturally took precautions against spoilation of the skull, by locking away part and keeping watch over the other more exposed part.

On occasion Pokenau would put a large bunch of aromatic herbs into *sori's* bowl and a little left over into *gizikau's* bowl. This was a private any day performance.

During most of January and half of February a titular sister of Pokenau, a Pontchal woman, had been in Pokenau's house. She had left her husband in order to bear her child in a brother's or titular brother's house, as custom required, and to keep the taboos incumbent upon a new mother for several weeks after the birth in a brother's house. She could not be released from her taboos until her brother and his brothers and sisters real or titular, had collected and worked a great quantity of sago to make the gift that had to go with her to her husband and her husband's relatives. A date for the giving of the gift and the returning of the woman to her husband had been arranged.

In the interval of the mother's stay, the newborn infant seemed to be sufficiently sickly once to cause anxiety and the need for doing something. I did not hear of the customary exorcism of black magic from this infant. The mother was from many miles overseas and Pokenau was not very closely knit to her in any real interest, other than that of acceptance of a gift giving obligation in her name, a gift due to bring in bead work later as a return. Moreover Pokenau was impractical, very strongly wedded to *sori* and to the entire ghost cult, which struck a chord of fundamentalism in him, paralleled in very few, if in any, of his compatriots. Further he was always impecunious. He cared far more for religion and for argument than for business, in a culture that put business first, second, third, fourth and fifth and everything else a poor following. He had a very quick mind, but he refused to bend it more than casually into business. He had a special and very strong opinion of the inferiority of women and thoroughly enjoyed elaborating their social disadvantages, even though these disadvantages were more formal than real. He despised the uses of magic largely because he never could afford the relatively large fees, but also partly because he had a really keen feeling of attachment to *sori* that made the ghost cult seem far more real to him. Sori as a man had been universally liked. He had been remarkable for the characteristic of being modest and shy before his social inferiors, or before younger men. He did not bully and hector and maintain his economic prestige by being short and sharp to his dependents and debtors, and urgent in dunning them for services and for debts. The successful and typical Manus man of importance generally has the manner of a rough foreman supervising his labouring gang. Sori lacked this manner entirely, threw away his inherited place of ascendancy by his respect for personalities and died leaving a legacy of debts only. Everyone had liked him, and Pokenau his younger brother had apparently worshipped him. Certainly Pokenau did so now. Pokenau, himself, although like Sori in lacking the business qualities, lacked Sori's more placid good fellowship. He attempted leadership too much for a people that only recognised economic success as real leadership. And he was contra suggestible and obstinate.

These characteristics were such that Pokenau could not be depended upon to act in a general normal way in many respects. I do not think that he had any exorcism of black magic made over the new born infant in his house. Instead he called upon *sori*, terming *sori* by his other name, *frigate-bird*: [88]

"*frigate-bird*, you talk to your two wives and to *gizikau* who are striking this child. This child belongs to another place. It would be better if your feud were to lead to me being struck down. I am adult and I understand. Strike me or my wife or my own son of my own house. But to strike down the child you are striking is as careless as the striking down of a fish that swims towards you, as towards a stone that he would shelter beneath.

"This child is ill like this. Your father (*i.e.*, *gizikau*) and your two wives strike him like this. I am ashamed.

"You tell your father and your two wives that they must send the soul stuff to him, that his body fever may cool again and his wailing cease. So all will praise you, say you are good and one of rank. The office of police constable before all the whites is yours. You guard all of your house. No ghost of another place has penetrated into your house. Send this child health that he may go with his mother to the place into which she has married with no shame upon our house."

This prayer of Pokenau's was provoked by divination which resulted in a declaration that *gizikau* and the two wives of *sori* (ghostly wives) were doing the damage. The diviner had said, "Is *gizikau* striking down this child because Patalian

[88] I have previously termed *frigate bird, fish hawk* in the context where Pokenau and I went out watching for the run of the fish shoals.

has not moved his trade chest of his possessions into Pokenau's house?" The back of the diviner had itched on the left side affirmatively. The diviner had said, "Are *sori's* two wives striking down this child because they are angry at *sori's* way of dividing fish between them?" Again the itch had been affirmative. This divining and Pokenau's prayer occurred during the day. By day also Patalian moved his trade chest into Pokenau's house. By night Pikaro, as medium, got communications from *gizikau* and from *sori's* two wives, saying for themselves what had only been a mortal's and a diviner's suspicion before the divining process confirmed the suspicion, and the medium got a ghostly echo of the words of the diviner's suspicion.

The seance was uneventful. It broke no new ground. Patalian was a widower who moved from house to house.[89] At the time he had been sleeping in Pokenau's house, but he had left his chest of possessions in the house of his immediately prior residence. Naturally enough *gizikau* was displeased and he showed his displeasure. The displeasure of the two wives of *sori* was with *sori*.

Pikaro, the medium, was Pokenau's father's cross-cousin, so she charged Pokenau no medium's fee. The entire affair cost Pokenau nothing.

The due date for the returning of the mother and child to her husband came and passed. Pokenau was not ready with his sago. Moreover he had no overseas going canoe, but had to hire one in order to take the woman and infant and the sago gift overseas. He had not yet hired a canoe, when the husband came from far overseas to enquire why the arranged date had been broken. The husband could not take his wife back himself. The woman had to wait on the sago and both on Pokenau. But naturally his business fault rankled somewhat in Pokenau; and also in Pokenau's Sir Ghosts. Pepi, the small child of Pokenau, fell ill. The divination went directly to the obvious point.

The seance was conducted by Pikaro, she using her con-

[89] It will be recalled that Patalian had been adopted as a child into the family of Pokenau by Gizikau, Pokenau's grandfather. He was Pokenau's brother.

trol *kukan*. The customary preliminaries opened the seance. (I often omit mention of the preliminaries and constant elements, but I repeat them again here in order to ensure their being fully kept in mind.)

Pokenau: "Where is *kukan?*"

Pikaro whistles several times solemnly; then says: "*kukan* is here; he asks your purpose."

Pokenau: "Who has struck down my son and why?"

Pikaro whistles, then says: "I don't know. I'll go and enquire." A silent wait ensues. A pig comes swirling in the water under the house. Someone descends and chases it off quietly.

Pikaro whistles a long time; then says: "*gizikau* strikes him. He says, "You, how's that? You are to take the sago for Nyalin's [90] post-child-birth-taboos-releasing-feast to Mok, and you, you have not taken the sago. Her husband sailed here. He sailed here to get her. And you, how's that? You wished to do something else?'" (This last is satirical: Pokenau had nothing else of importance to do.)

Pokenau replies: "Yes, if we had been obedient we would have taken the sago quickly and we were not obedient. We did not take the sago quickly. Her husband came. He came to bring her. Yes! Patalian (a clan brother helping Pokenau to make the taboos releasing feast for their sister, Nyalin) borrowed a canoe. He took sago. He has sailed. And I have no canoe. I must wait. If I have a canoe later, I shall set sail."

gizikau (mollified) through *kukan* through the medium, whistling, then speaking: "I strike your child over this matter and I say now that tomorrow he will be better."

Pokenau: "*sori*, where?"

kukan through medium in the usual manner: "*sori* is up on the built up coral rubble."

Pokenau: "Let him come. I wish to hear his speech."

kukan brings him, saying through the medium: "*sori* is in the house."

[90] Nyalin was the titular sister of Pôkenau who was come to Pokenau's house (to bear her child) from her husband's village, Mok.

Pokenau: "My child, how is it he is ill?"

sori through *kukan* through the medium: "You have been walking about. I have been walking about with you. You ask all the women." (*sori's* two spirit wives and *gizikau's* spirit wife.) "As for me, I don't know. You wait. I'll ask the women who struck the child."

sori, talking with ghosts, but also to mortals at the same time, reported by *kukan* and translated into the Manus speech by Pikaro item by item of speech and reply from and to *sori*: "'Who struck this child? You, out with it. If not, I'll beat you!'"

They two, afraid, say: "'Your father and mother struck him, not we two!'"

He goes to *gizikau* and his wife. The two say: "'Our talk we have talked already. We fought in regard to the child bearing feast. The talk of it we made before. We are not saying anything more.'"

sori: "'Yes. Just once again let you two strike this child so that he's ill and I can beat you two. You'll go out on the coral rubble outside. The rain will wash you, the sun will scorch. . . ."

Pokenau, intervening with soothing intent: "Yes, you look after me well and all your women folk look after the children and women. You look after me. And you all make war this time. Good. You all reveal it now in this seance. I can understand your motive. I'll borrow a canoe. I'll go out to Mok in it. You restore the child to health."

sori says: "Yes, come, water for the spirit. Give the spirit to *kukan*." *kukan* put the soul stuff into water and rubbed it. Pikaro and everyone waited, Pikaro with the bowl of water before her. Then she poured it over Pepi.

Next day Pepi was considerably better. Pokenau bestirred himself with unwonted pressure, borrowed a canoe and got away the day after.

It will be noted that illness, disease and malarial fever in Manus stir up a response of "We have done these things which we ought not to have done, and we have left undone those things which we ought to have done, so there is sickness in the house," and also a response of "You'll go out on the coral rubble outside. The rain will wash you. The sun will scorch you. And you'll be miserable for a long while before you become a crab or a jelly-fish." The religion of the Manus people combines the attitudes that are characteristic of the submissive believer in the goodness of God and the proneness to sin of man on the one hand, and of the denouncer of God's cruelty, viciousness or impotence on the other, as we know these attitudes. The Manus do not necessarily impute cruelty, any more than our own people. A Sir Ghost is thrown out usually more for impotence in protection rather than for direct cruelty. He is not normally thought to kill his own. There is no room in the Manus system for men to curse God and abjure religion because idiot children have been born to them, or because a favourite child has been smitten with a cruel disease or for any great personal calamity.

A Manus man thus combines within himself attitudes that divide men into believers and non-believers in our own culture; and down the generations a religious system is transmitted that is a subtle enough synthesis to allow for a natural enough recoil, to be swayed by that recoil, even to provide social forms for it, but, because swayed by it, to be never broken by it. Rebellion becomes but a momentary flash in the pan, or a wound that is quickly healed because it is expected and provided for in a tradition that does not blink facts.

It is true that a diviner here and there may lay aside his divining, or a medium her making of seances; but nevertheless these defections are not blows at the system. Divining and the holding of seances continues as strongly as ever, new and fresh oracles displace the old. The retired oracles believe in a purely personal inadequacy, with some doubt sometimes as to the adequacy of the new oracles also. But even these skeptical ones do not disbelieve in the essentials, and they would do nothing in the face of calamity, nor would they be willing to originate, if they could, another system. They believe firmly in their Sir Ghosts and in ghosts even when they doubt the validity of oracular communication with the other plane, as they sometimes do to a certain extent.

Skepticism like rebellion is provided for within the system of belief. The system of belief is two sided; and its synthesis makes skepticism and rebellion no antagonistic force to religion but an expression of one of its aspects, an expression so familiar that it becomes no personal issue of any special personal importance, or with any great personal elaboration.

It is true that the Manus religion breeds its own divisions between its believers as we have seen between Paliau and Isole just after the death of Popwitch. But such divisions are formal, brief and impermanent. In two months or so they blow over. Although Paliau and his kin did not go casually to Isole's house during that period, Paliau alone with special daring excepted, they all went in force to a ceremony of mourning that followed the death, ten days after, and held in Isole's house. I was perplexed at this sudden release of a taboo that had been set up so rigorously, but I was told that the taboo was still in force, as indeed it proved afterwards. Only the ceremonial event offered a special exception. There were many persons gathered there and their accompanying Sir Ghosts were equally many. The house had ceased for the occasion, but only as long as the occasion lasted, to be a house of Isole's Sir Ghosts indignant at Paliau's *pwanau*. It was temporarily a house of many Sir Ghosts where everyone met ceremonially, mortals on one plane, Sir Ghosts on another.

The system goes forward equipped to nourish belief and faith, rebellion and skepticism, social cohesion and the maintenance of good faith between houses, and divisions between houses. All of these elements are aspects of its synthesis. All are cultural forms, not greatly subject to personal idiosyncrasy, or personal elaboration. The oracles can and do produce new ideas on occasion; but we do not find believers as one class set over against rebellious skeptics as another, or any irregular pattern dominating the behaviour between houses. A man is in rapport with his Sir Ghosts and with his fellows, or out of rapport with his Sir Ghosts and with his fellows, in fairly well determined cultural moulds, most of which in connection with his Sir Ghosts and many of which in connection with his fellows are laid down in the religion.

The seance over the sickness of Pepi at Pokenau's house was not entirely completed before the digression above. Or rather the seance was over as far as Pepi's illness was concerned, but Pokenau continued it by raising some other questions. About eight days previous he had been somewhat ill, but not so seriously ill as to be laid up or to call a seance. Now purely for the sake of curiosity he wanted to know why he had been ill. Or rather he made out that he had been continuously ill ever since, probably as an excuse for his sins which had just been brought home to him.

Pokenau: "Before I was ill and I had no seance. Now that I am ill again (sic) I want to hear about it. My soul stuff has been with the ghosts for eight days now." (Sic, certainly a very little soul stuff, if any. He had been active and about all the time except for one evening eight days, before.)

sori, through control through medium: "I'll make divination on this ghostly plane." Pause while *sori* does it. "You there, you went to cut sago at Ndiwandro, you went there and I left you by the river for a while in order to go and get a torch for myself. Then *man of yang* struck you. You stay there. I'll go and look for the soul stuff."

Long pause while *sori* goes to get it; then control whistles through medium, and medium: "He went to *man of yang*. He got the soul stuff. He went to *pwanau*. He said, 'You, you have struck Pokenau'; *pwanau* said, 'No! I did not strike him but only my cross-cousin (*man of yang*).' *sori* said, "So." He came into this house. He said, '*pwanau* did not strike him; *man of yang* struck him.' I[91] have got the soul stuff. It rests in the house."

Pokenau: "Yes, I want to sleep. Here with the soul stuff."

The medium gave her control time to put the soul stuff into the water and to rub it there. Then she gave Pokenau the water to drink.

[91] The oracular manner changes in this paragraph, as it sometimes does. In the previous passage *sori* is represented in the third person. In this final passage the control is the first person in speech.

Pokenau was as well next day as he had been the day before, that is quite well.

When Man of Yang was alive, he and Pokenau (who were not related) had had a dispute about the ownership of a certain patch of sago palms which both claimed. Now Pokenau had the claim, and *man of yang* was dead. The young son of *man of yang*, Kapeli, was one of my house boys and the most devoted of them. Next day Pokenau said to me laughingly, "*Man of yang* struck me; now never mind his being on another plane, on this plane I'll beat up Kapeli yet."

Later on in the day I told Kapeli of this remark of Pokenau. Kapeli laughed happily and said nothing. "Well, what about it?" I said. "Now don't you understand Pokenau?" retorted Kapeli. I kept silent. "He tells lies," said Kapeli. A small youngster of some seven or eight years standing nearby said solemnly, "No! he was talking true." The small youngster was left alone to meditate on the truth. He was rather young to have summed up the adult worlds yet.[92]

I have interposed another digression. Pokenau raised a third matter in the seance before it concluded.

Pokenau: "No more seance now; but I want some advice."

sori, through control through medium: "About what?"

Pokenau: "Long ago I and Nyamaka could meet."

sori: "Yes, but I can't say anything. Let *kialo* come. Later on you have a seance made and hear what *kialo* has to say. If he says you and Nyamaka may meet, then you may. If he says that a middle space (avoidance) must stay between you, then it must stay."

Pokenau: "*sori*, if Nyamaka and I meet, good! (with much feeling). The bride-price paid for her went to my fathers, the wedding gifts paid for her went to my fathers, the *metcha* (silver wedding) paid for her went to my fathers (*i.e.*, Nyamaka is Pokenau's father's sister). And if she abandons me I go to the bad. I wish we could meet together."

sori: "Yes. Later on have a seance! Bring to it all of Matchupal gens on the mortal plane, all of Matchupal gens

[92] This child was aberrant in being reflective and interested in the culture, Bopau of Dr. Mead's book "Growing Up in New Guinea," p. 116.

on the ghostly plane. If all those mortals come into our (dual) house, and all agree, and *kialo* agrees that the middle space between you and Nyamaka be over, then you two may meet." (Note how a perfect agreement between the mortals of Matchupal and *kialo*, a Sir Ghost of Matchupal is demanded and expected.)

"But if *kialo* says, 'I have died, you and Nyamaka may not meet,' let it be this way. Let me hear only. I cannot advise."

So Pokenau got no further there. His father's sister, Nyamaka, had married a Matchupal man, and borne Kialo her son. Pokenau had had the bad luck to be with Kialo in the mangrove swamp, when Kialo collapsed and died there. For the past two and a half years since that event Nyamaka had assiduously cut her nephew, Pokenau. The avoidance, so long sustained, was irking Pokenau exceedingly. He was careful to respect the avoidance and never approach Nyamaka. But he talked everywhere in the hope that his feelers towards meeting would be accepted by Nyamaka.[93] This Kialo was the same person as Alupwai's sister's former husband, so often mentioned earlier in this work.

17. *A Barter in Soul Stuff is Attempted*

Alupwai still lay ill in the house of Ngandaliu. This house normally sheltered Ngandaliu and his wife in the front half, and Ndroga and his wife, Kamutal, in the rear half. Ndroga left the house to sleep away from it for several nights at least during Alupwai's stay. He fell ill during one of these excursions, when he was in the house of Sanau.[94] I did not obtain the divining results as medium Itong presided. My record reads:

pokamitch (control) through medium: "Last night Ndroga was sleeping in the house of Tunu. The two sons of Tunu

[93] I find in my notes an informant's generalisation—"The ghosts do not enforce avoidances except those following a sexual sin." I record the note as a comment on the use of the talking-at-large informant. I made no general use of any such poor method, but worked inductively myself.

[94] A rich man of Kalaat gens, who was conspicuous for never undertaking oratory on any occasion, because he "could not orate."

struck Ndroga (two dead sons of Tunu and Alupwai are Tunu's Sir Ghosts). The two took his soul stuff. The two sent it to all (the ghosts) of Kalo, to the place of their mother, to *tchuka* and *papi-talipoitchalon*, saying with it, 'This soul stuff you take and keep it. For it you can barter the soul stuff of the mother of us two, which *pwanau* has; [95] let *pwanau* give our mother her soul stuff, then you can give Ndroga his soul stuff; but let *pwanau* not give our mother her soul stuff, then do you not give Ndroga his soul stuff. If our mother dies, then let Ndroga die also. If our mother recovers, then let Ndroga recover also.'"

Sanau: "Yes! *pokamitch*, you summon *molean* (brother and Sir Ghost of Sanau) and *paware* (father and Sir Ghost of Sanau) and his wife, and summon the native constable of Pontchal (*sori*). Then you go and get the soul stuff."

pokamitch after a long wait, through the medium: "*Molean, paware, sori* and I, we went; we asked them to the limit of annoyance; but they were unwilling; *tchuka* and *papi-talipoitchalon* both said, 'This soul stuff we did not strike.' It was the two sons here who struck Ndroga. They sent the soul stuff to us with an injunction, 'Soul stuff, this must stay with you, and if the soul stuff of our mother which *pwanau* has comes, then the soul stuff of Ndroga may go.' The two said just that. The two gave us what we have. It is the concern and the feud of the two of them. It is not our feud nor our concern."

Sanau: "You return and try to buy them!"

After a long wait for this proposed bribing of the Kalo ghosts, *pokamitch* through the medium: "We have come back. You make divination on that mortal plane. See if the soul stuff is returned. If it is all back our seeking it is over. But if you make divination and the soul stuff still remains out there we shall go there again for it."

Sanau: "We have no one here who is a diviner."

pokamitch, through medium: "Long ago did not *polum* give divination power to Pokenau there."

[95] It will be recalled that *pwanau* was one of the ghosts responsible for Alupwai's illness, because he died indirectly for Tunu's sin, a sin of the husband of Alupwai.

Pokenau: "Yes, long ago I had divination power and I divined. But the time when I went fishing with Kalo and they caught a shark my divination (of the whereabouts of fish) gave untrue results."

pokamitch, through medium: "*polum* is here and he will rub your divination bones for you again."

A pause followed while the ghost rubs the divination bones.

Then Pokenau made divination, and said, "Soul stuff is still outstanding."

Sanau: "You go and take your dog and get the soul stuff!"

After a pause *pokamitch* through the medium: "We went. We took the dog that bites ghosts. We took him to the house of *tchuka* and to the house of *papi-talipoitchalon*. He made to bite the two of them. The two were scared. We got the soul stuff. You divine and see for yourselves!"

Pokenau: "The soul stuff is all back. Let it be put into the water."

Ndroga: "No, no water! Never mind water. Let the ghosts put it onto betel nut."

So *pokamitch* rubbed it on a betel nut. The medium gave the betel nut to Ndroga who chewed it. The usual procedure is to bathe the patient with water in which the control has rubbed the soul stuff. Ndroga made a very independent point. He wanted betel nut instead, and he got it.

Ndroga's father and *pwanau's* father were younger and elder brothers respectively. Hence pressure could be brought on *pwanau* through Ndroga. The use of the dog which foiled this design of Tunu's Sir Ghosts, his and Alupwai's dead sons, is the old device that has been largely replaced now by the use of ghostly native police. The dog is purely ghostly, of course. In the above seance it is noteworthy that the ghostly native police was tried first, in the person of *sori* of Pontchal, but without success. Then the dog was tried later with success. Itong was the only medium who clung hard to the old concept of the ghostly dog, always discounting the virtues of the ghostly police. She was well known for her especial reliance on the dog.

The fact that Alupwai had not recovered was attributed to *pwanau*, despite the expiatory payments made some time before. Itong's dog trick having undone the proposed barter of Ndroga's soul stuff for Alupwai's, Ndroga duly recovered quickly, but Alupwai did not. Ndroga however kept away from Tunu's house, for fear of a repetition of this kind of incident.

18. *A Medium is Stricken for Overriding her Control*

On the 23rd February Isole had an indisposition. The wife of Pokenas [96] was the medium, her controls were *pope* [97] and *matanamo*. This medium used a dreamy, languorous voice and manner when inspired, a very marked characteristic and one peculiar to her as compared with the other mediums of Peri.

The controls *pope* and *matanamo* (one eye), ghosts of her dead children, were summoned and they reported.

Medium addressing her controls: "You two summon *tchemilo* (control of Isole). Let him come and hear his mother's speech, his mother who lies ill here."

Controls through the medium: "*tchemilo* is not here; he has put out to the deep sea to guard Kulame (daughter of Isole now on distant overseas voyage). He thinks that he will come quickly. He is out guarding her. The two are together, and will arrive here together. (Kulame is coming from far away towards Peri—*tchemilo* went out to escort her.) But as yet he is still on the deep sea."

Kemwai (husband of Isole): "You two may punt your canoe and pick up the *talipolalau* who are on the coral rubble territory. Let them come here and attend to the sick person here."

kapopoi, wife of one of the *talipolalau* brothers, through the controls through the medium: "Yes! *tchemilo* struck

[96] This was a very intelligent woman of Pere gens who ruled her husband with an iron rule. She was always called "the wife of Pokenas" in public reference, probably as a compensation for the fact that in private Pokenas was known to be the dependent of Nyambula, his wife.

[97] Not to be confused with the living man, Pope. This control was alternatively called *pakob*.

down this mortal. He said, 'Long ago you held a seance over Popwitch, and people said that the seance, mine and yours together, was false. They were skeptical of it and said it was not to the point. Then I and all the controls of all mediums said that the seance held in a house should be done by a member of that house, and that a control should not be asked by a medium to enter the house of anyone else. Each house should attend to itself. So there would be no more shame. All mortals and all ghosts heard this decision, and I said it is good.[98]

"'Then you went to a house of Kalo to make a seance over Sali. We both went. You worked for Sali. I was ashamed to stand out alone. So I worked for him with you. I searched out his soul stuff and when it was finished Sali was well. But I was angry. I struck you for it, and am now striking you for it.'

"So *tchemilo* spoke to my husband. So I have spoken his speech to you. He said, 'Grandfather, this soul stuff here I struck; you take up my speech for me, and take the soul stuff for me also. For I want to go overseas to Mok. This person here, don't let her become very ill. As soon as she falls ill first they will all enquire why. Then reveal what I have to say as I have told it you and let her have the soul stuff back.'

"So here is the soul stuff. I give it back."

Isole here said: "Tomorrow red clay paint should be in the hand, and on the foreheads of all women."

(Tomorrow the *metcha* of Nane, his silver wedding gift payment, was due to begin.)

Nane: "Kemwai, you ask the *talipolalau* about my *metcha* that I hope to complete by the day after tomorrow. Shall I display and give out the dogs' teeth on the coral rubble territory or inside the house?"

Kemwai put the question to the medium.

"So! the mother of this man was of the coral rubble territory; the father was of the coral rubble territory. And

[98] This will be recalled as the innovation suggested by Man of Lorengan after the death of Popwitch above.

your *metcha* and your dogs' teeth let them go tomorrow to the coral rubble territory.

"Tomorrow watch to see if rain falls. If so, the ghosts spoil your *metcha*. But if rain does not fall tomorrow, let the dogs' teeth go to the coral rubble territory, let them be danced over. The news of the wealth you have gathered has flown to all mortals and to all ghosts without exception. Your wealth can go only to the coral rubble territory that all may dance over it."

Nane was tremulous over the great wealth he had amassed and was about to give away. The *metcha* is usually given only by *lapan*, men of rank. The *lapan* always have hereditary rights to house sites near the built up patches of coral rubble, which belong to them. Actually all public events of importance are held on the coral rubble.

But Nane was not *lapan*. All the *lapan* of his gens of Lo had fled Peri in a scare at outbreaks of sickness. So all of Lo that were left in Peri were *lau*, dependents. The situation was anomalous. The dependents were left with no one to depend upon. So they financed their own affairs, very poorly and miserably at first. Now, however, Nane was reaching the pinnacle of economic success with his *metcha*.[99] As a *lau*, not a *lapan*, he had qualms about the use of the coral rubble for the ceremony. He got his reassurance. His father and his mother had not been "of the coral rubble," as the ghosts said that they had been, through the medium. They had not been *lapan*. But Nane had risen to *lapan* heights, in wealth, and the ghosts and mortals were kind.

Isole recovered duly and was up and about at the *metcha* ceremony that took up the next three days. The dating of a sequence used by the presiding medium over Isole's indisposition was February 4th. Paliau's avowal of skepticism of Isole's charges against *pwanau;* and the announcing of Man of Lorengau's seance idea, that the controls were on strike against the mediums going to hold seances in houses

[99] Kemwai, older than Nane, but his close associate in Lo gens had already made his *metcha*. But Kemwai had married Isole, of the aristocracy of Peri, and so made his way far more easily than Nane ever did.

other than their own, since it led to skeptical charges from men like Paliau.

February 17th. Isole's seance in a house of Kalo over Sali. (So she took no heed of the threatened mutiny.)

February 23rd. Isole's illness and the above seance.

I date the above events in order to show the retention of Man of Lorengau's idea. Isole paid no very serious attention to it, at least not later. The plain fact was that the mediums were few, and the houses of sickness many. If Man of Lorengau's idea were carried out, the wife of Pokenas herself would not have been conducting a seance over Isole, in Isole's house as she was. She evidently was of the opinion that *tchemilo* alone was angry at not having had his individual strike respected by Isole. She probably was expressing some professional jealousy at Isole's getting more outside work than she, for each such seance was paid for with a stick of tobacco or with two dogs' teeth. Ostensibly, of course, she was securing a cure of Isole's indisposition.

19. *Disaster at Sea*

The twenty fourth and twenty fifth days of February saw the great economic event of Nane's *metcha* go through with drumming, dancing, pomp and ceremony. The ghosts sent no rain to prevent a man of lower rank, who was wealthy, from giving this event in the open, as it had been half expected they might. But on the afternoon of the twenty fourth, in the middle of the ceremony, a sudden great wind blew with nearly hurricane force for an hour. It stopped the ceremony for its duration. Far out to sea it hit a two-masted canoe under full sail, manned by some men of Kalo clan. It struck from the quarter opposite the canoe's outrigger, forced the outrigger under water and swamped the canoe.

On the night of the twenty fifth a canoe following from Mbuke Island made Peri village. Its crew reported that they followed a day behind the men of Kalo from Mbuke bound for Peri. Instantly consternation reigned in Peri, for the Kalo men had not come in, nor had trace of them been seen by the following canoe. At six in the evening the news came. By ten o'clock six large, deep-sea plying canoes were manned and out to sea, scattering to different quarters to search by night and day till the fate of Kalo was determined.

Next day passed into night again with no word. The day after the village lookout from a high tree top perch signalled distant canoes under sail at one o'clock in the afternoon. They arrived at four in Peri, the men of Kalo worn and battered, but still in their own canoe. Wailing broke out over the men, sisters and mothers embracing brothers and sons and crying freely over them. I obtained the following account of the mishap:

"They went to Mbuke Island where they obtained pots from their friend. They left and set sail for home. The gale struck them suddenly. The outrigger went under. They sank. They stayed in the sea, their canoe lying bottom up and submerged. They unfastened the outrigger boom, placed it beneath the canoe, and, using it as a leverage ground, turned the canoe over upon it. The canoe, rightened, remained still under water. They hoisted sail and drove before the wind with the entire hull submerged. The seas battered the wife of Pondramet. The seas battered all. The legs of the wife of Pondramet went numb and became swollen. Tuwain prayed to his father:

"'My father, of all of us there is not one safe at home. We are all here. Send us to shore and safety.'

"The seas battered Tuwain. He had swallowed much sea. He said to Sali, 'My brother, I am about to lose consciousness. Do not throw me into the sea. If I lose consciousness let me stay fastened on the canoe. If you throw me into the sea we shall not make land. But if you keep me, we shall make land, and our sister shall see us.'

"Tuwain collapsed. Only Sali and the wife of Tuwain remained still strong and active. The canoe was under water, the sail up above water. They drove under sail. It was still so by night.

"Their father was compassionate to them. He drove them to shore. They drove upon Patu.[100] They baled out

[100] An uninhabited and small island not far from Rambutchon Island, about fifty miles east of the course from Mbuke Island to Peri village by the Great Admiralty Island.

the canoe by see-sawing it over a shoaling rock. It floated. They set sail again to Rambutchon. They were hungry. Tuwain said, 'Sali, climb a coconut tree.' Sali threw down nuts. They ate. They tried to cut into a sago palm. They had no axe. They tried to force out sago with sticks. The sticks broke. They slept. Dawn broke. The search parties had sought them in Taui, in Mbunai. They had sought them at Patu. They were not there. They came sailing up to Rambutchon, and they found them."

Those who were in the canoe mishap together with a large number of sympathisers and relatives went into a *mwandrin*. The *mwandrin* is the house where a corpse is laid, and where everyone resorts to sleep, partly because it is the customary way of showing sympathy, partly because a crowd gathered together is felt to be safer than separate families divided in separate houses. Feeling of security obtained from a *mwandrin* is felt to be necessary in time of trouble.

Kalo assuredly were in trouble, what with Alupwai seriously ill most of the month and as yet neither dead nor better, with Sali's serious attack of fever, and now with a narrow escape at sea. They feared the relentless grip of the supernatural world which seemed to be dogging them unceasingly. So they went into a weeks' *mwandrin*, with considerable wailing. Paliau was annoyed at the wailing and said to me, "If they had had a real death there would be some reason in it."

Disaster at sea in believed to be a ghostly or a Sir Ghostly visitation. I was told how Tchawan, Pusen and Pomalat once sank at sea similarly. A sex intrigue had taken place in Tchawan's house between two young relatives while Tchawan was away at sea. Tchawan's Sir Ghost caused the canoe to sink. "Had we all died," said Tchawan, "it would have been for the sin of another." But I did not hear of any divination or seance, or of any sin causing the sinking of Tuwain, Sali and the others. Kalo had already been but recently searched for sin, and for cause of trouble, and searched meticulously. It was just assumed that the ghosts were carrying on the way they had begun with an unusual and even phenomenal relentlessness. Meanwhile it was well that no life had been lost.

This concludes February 27th and the third month of my stay in Manus.

PART FOUR. FEBRUARY 28TH–MARCH 28TH

20. *The Illness of Alupwai Continues*

Over Alupwai spiritism and magic had been applied without avail. As a last resort a Roman Catholic convert, a native from a missioned area some distance away, was called in to apply the possibly healing powers of the new faith. His prayers did little good, but he supported my offer of giving Alupwai chlorodyne, an opium morphine mixture, which would give her some sleep despite her pain. The convert persuaded Alupwai to try the white medicine, and induced a willingness to experiment with it that would have been impossible before. For the Manus faith is not one that allows the supplementing of religion with herbal medicines.

About March 1st, Alupwai recalled that her foot had slipped on a log bridge at the village of Loitcha, half a days' voyage away. Slipping is not a common event, but a curiosity in Manus. In consequence some supernatural influence was now thought to have been operative![101] This influence was a *tchinal*, a familiar of Usiai magic. Alupwai's husband, Tunu, sailed to Loitcha in order to throw a propitiatory offering of food to the *tchinal* and to ask it to remove its bane from Alupwai.

On the fifth of March Alupwai's hostess' generosity and hospitality came to an end. Alupwai had lain in the same house now for over three weeks without any recovery. She had been nursed constantly by Kamutal, Ndroga's wife. Ndroga had slept away often, and as we have seen, fell ill once because he slept in Alupwai's husband's house, the Sir Ghosts of which house took his soul stuff in order to barter it for Alupwai's, as they hoped. I asked if Kamutal was evicting Alupwai now because of the manner in which Alupwai's

[101] See Margaret Mead, "Growing Up in New Guinea," Chapter III, for an account of child training in physical proficiency in Manus.

dead childrens' ghosts had dealt with Ndroga. I was told by outsiders that such was not the case. Mortals put aside such ghostly actions, assuming no responsibility, imputing no blame amongst themselves. In this case the statement was probably correct, for it was now over a week since Ndroga's short indisposition and rapid recovery (although in a more serious case such as Popwitch's death we have seen a very considerable identification of a mortal with his Sir Ghost). Kamutal was evidently influenced by purely natural motives. She stormed, saying that on a previous occasion Alupwai had once malingered, and now she was malingering again. She was not ill at all. This was obviously untrue, but equally obviously a true statement of a hostess' hospitality overstrained. So Alupwai was moved into another house, into the house of Pokenas. Pokenas was away at the morning market at the time, so he found an unexpected guest in his house when he returned. However he was a friend of Kalo gens, although both he and his wife were of other gentes.[102] The Kalo Sir Ghosts were being sedulously avoided, and some of the mortals of other gentes felt the obligation to support and make good that avoidance for Alupwai's sake. Immediately Alupwai was lodged in a new house there was a renewed burst of attempts at cure.

Divination confirmed a suspicion that the Sir Ghosts of of Selan and of Ngandaliu were afflicting Alupwai, and expiatory payment was immediately made to them by Kalo gens. Ngandaliu was the house owner of the house in which Alupwai had lodged, also Selan, Ngandaliu's younger brother. It was by Ngandaliu's courtesy that Ndroga and Kamutal lodged in the back of his house, and Kamutal, in caring for Alupwai, had been acting for Ngandaliu, as Ngandaliu's debtor. Consequently this expiatory payment to Ngandaliu and to Selan was in a sense payment for services rendered to Alupwai, now being made by Alupwai's kin. On one plane it was that, on another plane it was a measure towards recovering Alupwai. The motive on the mortal plane purely

[102] Pokenas' gens was reduced to three individuals only. So he cooperated often with Kalo.

was not made overt. I do not infer it from any native statement, but solely on the responsibility of my own observation. The motive that involved supernaturalism was dramatized in full, overt manner, so that it appeared ostensibly as the entire gist of the matter.

The wife of Pokenas was the medium. Her control reported: "Yes. She stayed in that house of theirs. And the Sir Ghosts of that house, *poketa* and *topwal*, took her soul stuff." (*topwal* was only of that house indirectly, his brother *poketa* directly, being Sir Ghost of Ngandaliu. Note how the new host maligns the house of the former host, even in having expiatory payment paid to that house of the former host. So expiatory payment is made very generally with a touch of malice, and of objection.)

"*topwal* said, 'So. If you had kept quiet about the scandal (that led to my death) I would have done nothing but look after you. But you resurrected that old scandal. I head it. I was angry. I struck Alupwai for it. Long ago I wished to capture a prostitute for the bachelor's house. My father, and my brother were with me as my Sir Ghosts. But I captured that prostitute only in vain. I died for it.[103] And now if you had kept your silence about it there would have been no war from me. But you did not keep your silence.

"'You have sent expiatory payment from mortals, expiatory payment from ghosts (*i.e.*, expiatory payment was made from man to man and parallel with it from Sir Ghost of man to Sir Ghost of man). I respected it. And I gave back the soul stuff to them (*i.e.*, to Kalo gens Sir Ghosts). They took it with them.'"

The control now talking for himself, "Is the soul stuff all back yet or not yet? You make divination on the mortal plane and see!"

Pokenas divines with the bones and says, "Two pieces are outstanding yet. You return and take the native police (ghost—*i.e.*, *sori*) with you to collect!"

Control through medium after a pause: "The native policeman said, 'Yes. It is good that we should collect the

[103] In a European gaol.

soul stuff paid for by expiatory payment, until we have it all. The person (sick patient) left the ghostly plane, was about to return to the mortal plane (*i.e.*, was recovering, coming back to life and health). I forgot about it. I was in my own house and about my own coral rubble territory. Now it transpires like this that the two (ghosts, *poketa* and *topwal*) went on with their feud, and did not send back the soul stuff as they made a beginning shift to do. I am ashamed (of my negligence in going to my own house and not supervising a proper cessation of the feud and return of paid for soul stuff).'

"We went to *topwal*. I (the control) said to *topwal*, 'Brother-in-law, you have not given the soul stuff to me and to my grandfather. Let my two sisters' children and my sister come with me and we'll go.'"

(Note: *topwal* as a ghost married the female ghost of a dead daughter of Pokenas' wife, a sister of the ghost of Pokenas' wife's son, who is the control of Pokenas' wife speaking. The control's sister had two children (ghost born) born to her out of *topwal*. The control is bringing pressure to bear on *topwal* by threatening to take away *topwal's* wife and children, his sister and sister's children, because *topwal* played him false over the soul stuff, he and his grandfather together. The last person is Pokenas' dead father and Sir Ghost, therefore the control's grandfather.)

"*topwal* said, 'Yes. You take my two children and my wife. But I'll go with you all also.' We went. We punted our canoe to the other wife of *topwal* at Patusi. (*topwal* has two ghostly wives, both secured by marriage on the ghostly plane.) *topwal* got the one piece of soul stuff that he had left with her from her. Then we punted our canoe to Matchupal (gens in Peri village). We got one piece from *topwal's* grandmother in Matchupal."

(Note: this last ghost has no house to shelter in, but frequents a village open space only.)

"Now have we got all the soul stuff back. You make divination to see! If the soul stuff is all back we on our side here may rest, but if not we'll go forth again."

Pokenas makes divination with the bones. "The soul

stuff is all recovered. Let *topwal* be urged to come into the house. I want to talk to him."

Pause.

Control through medium: "*topwal* is here."

Pokenas: "*topwal*, you married my daughter (ghost marriage). Now this person (Alupwai) has come to my house. You send the soul stuff of this person to my house instead of a canoe, instead of a sail, instead of shell money, instead of a hundred dogs' teeth as the bride price you should pay for my daughter! Send this person to recovery in my house." (*I.e.*, soul stuff should be sent as a bride price for the acquisition of a ghostly bride, instead of the type of bride price customarily exacted from mortals.)

topwal through control through medium: "Yes! the soul stuff is all given. You sent expiatory payment from out of the mortal plane, and from out of the ghostly plane. It rests with me. The soul stuff is all given."

Pokenas: "Yes, the soul stuff is all given. You rub the soul stuff in the water!"

topwal rubbed it in the water, the father and Sir Ghosts of Pokenas rubbed it in the water, the dead son of Pokenas' wife, *matanamo* (who was not control in the above seance) rubbed it in the water, the other dead son, *pakob* (who was control in the above seance), rubbed it in the water. After a due pause for all this activity on the unseen plane, Pokenas' wife took the water and poured it over Alupwai.

topwal, Sir Ghost of Selan, appeared in this affair more importantly than *poketa*, Sir Ghost of Ngandaliu, although it was understood that Selan and Ngandaliu as brothers were together on the one plane, while *topwal* and *poketa* also as brothers were together on the other plane, and the four of them closely associated in all inter-plane associations. Twelve years before I was in Peri, native wars had been suppressed by white influence. This suppression told hardest upon the young men, as it deprived them of all opportunity of capturing a strange woman and keeping her as a prostitute. The suppression of this privilege was still bemoaned in my time. The suppression had not been carried out without trouble. After Government edict against the custom, a number of young men, Topwal amongst them, captured an Usiai woman and kept her as prostitute. This capture split the village, as the head man of Peri village, Korotan, was related by marriage to the Usiai woman captured.[104] He set Government in action against the captors. About thirteen of them were taken and put into prison, two or three of the capturing party escaping, and two or three innocent men being informed against as guilty, by a personal gloss upon justice as the evidence was supplied by the informers.

Topwal died in prison shortly after. The conscience of the Manus people was hard set against sex offence among themselves, but it had never been set before against the prostitution of captive women taken in war. The ghosts had never before stricken anyone for taking a woman captive and prostituting her. Now, however, Government edict had made the established old custom criminal. And with Topwal's death Manus opinion hastened to make the old custom sinful. Topwal had died for sex offence.

Naturally there was already a feeling in Manus that welcomed Government interference. The Manus women welcomed it as avidly as the men objected to it. In the old days the men had taken their prostitute with them when they went to war, or when they went out fishing, because prostitutes unprotected would be killed by the men's mothers and wives (married men as well as unmarried youths lay with the prostitute). The presence of this feeling amongst the women, obviously aided and abetted by white feeling and armed interference on behalf of the women's point of view, made for a new extension of the Manus conscience, at least as far as Topwal's death was concerned.

As a ghost *topwal* was represented as being wroth with the injustice of his death being atonement for the sin of the many men who had been associated with him in the capture and the prostitution of the captive; *topwal* did not approve of

[104] Or rather it split the village temporarily into two parties, for and against Korotan. It split Pere gens permanently, the members of Pere gens involved in the taking of the Usiai woman forming a new gens, Pontchal, and taking up new territory.

vicarious atonement done upon his once mortal person. He had stricken others of his associates merely as protest against the injustice, amongst them Tunu, Alupwai's husband now, and Tuwain, Alupwai's eldest brother (both had survived). Nowadays he had cooled off, and was not so generally feared as he had been while his death was yet recent. But naturally gossip of the old affair that led to his death revived his anger, if ever he heard it. The medium probably knew that the old talk had been revived by a kinsman of Alupwai's not long before.

My notes on the marriages of *topwal* as a ghost to the daughter of Pokenas (as a ghost) and also to the daughter of a man of Patusi (as a ghost) show that there had been no economic exchanges on the mortal plane between the mortal kin of the ghosts wedded to validate the marriages on the ghostly plane; but for the ghostly issue of the marriage of *topwal* to the dead daughter of Pokenas, there had been an exchange of the wealth conventoinally associated with childbirth between Selan and Ngandaliu on the one hand and Pokenas on the other. Pokenas had given sago to Selan and Ngandaliu, which they had later repaid with bead work.

On this same day of Alupwai's removal to Pokenas' house, March 5th, a fee had been sent to an Usiai seer for a diagnosis of the case obtained by a dream. One divining done in Peri alone was not judged sufficient. Three persons amongst them Pope, father of Noan, went to fee and engage the Usiai dreamer, a woman.

The results of the Usiai dreamer's version did not come until the 7th March two days after. Meanwhile on the sixth Man of Lorengau was induced to come and perform an exorcism of his black magic on Alupwai. Man of Lorengau had been sought before. He was of Mbunai, another village to the north, but he had frequent relations with Peri. As one of the few magicians, he had protected the private property in palms of some of his Peri associates with spells of black magic. The Usiai seer that had visited Alupwai in Ngandaliu's house at an early stage of her trouble had charged

Alupwai from his vision with stealing from a coconut palm that was protected with a spell of black magic placed upon it. By confession from Alupwai it had appeared that she had indeed stolen from a palm protected by a charm. She identified the owner of the palm, so that it was known that Man of Lorengau's spell had been on it. Now Man of Lorengau had already performed an exorcism I believe, in Ngandaliu's house. I did not see it. Alupwai did not recover. Man of Lorengau said that his exorcism had been rendered nugatory by the Christian convert coming in immediately after him and using prayer and holy water upon Alupwai. Since Alupwai continued as ill as ever Man of Lorengau's explanation was credited, and he was asked several times to come again. While Alupwai was in Ngandaliu's house he had declined to come again, maintaining a haughty dislike of the Christian convert and the holy water. Now that Alupwai was in a different house, under new management, and the new management desired him, he came.

Man of Lorengau appeared in Peri dressed up in pompoms of leaves, a wreath of leaves in his hair, a long stem with leaves on the end of it through his nose, and a feather in his hair. Upon being questioned he insisted that all this was just decoration. It turned out to be no more indeed. In the house of Pokenas special ingredients had been gathered with care, star fish, sea anemone and two kinds of sea weed, also the more usual leaves and roots of customary magical usage, *Cordyline terminalis* or *ti* plant as it is known in Polynesia, and ginger. There were also two other more rarely used plants *endros* and *paris* (leaves) (unidentified).

When I arrived Man of Lorengau had already a concoction ready made from the pounded starfish, sea anemone, sea weed and pounded leaves and roots. It had been mixed with chewed betel juice and boiled. Now Man of Lorengau took the hot, red liquid from a woman cook. Alupwai was now little more than a skin flapped skeleton in all her body except at her huge distended abdomen, which was now swollen more than it had been when she was heavy with child not long before. Man of Lorengau had her propped up into a sitting position. He then poured the mixture all over her, over her head and over her body. He then took a bundle of *ti* leaves and dusted her over with them. The *ti* leaves were placed in the thatch. Someone put the bowl that held the now half-stripped leaves and stems which had been partly used up in making the concoction in front of Man of Lorengau. Everyone now settled down to a long wait.

Special food was being cooked by some women in the back of the house, large crabs and *pongapong*, a large fruit with a tough reddish skin, something like breadfruit, but much larger. This food was peculiar to Man of Lorengau's ceremony and had to be eaten by all in the house after the ceremony before they could leave. From time to time Man of Lorengau strolled about and looked over the cooking preparations. Alupwai lay alone and neglected on the floor, not on her bed of old ropes and mats, which was for the time denied to her. She lay and groaned, then objected to the presence of some small children, who were duly chased out. No one was supposed to leave the house during the progress of the ceremony from beginning to end at danger of death if such leave were taken. The small children had come in with me, and as they could not be trusted to observe the taboo against leaving during the progress of a long drawn out affair, they were chased out early. I expect it had to be assumed that the ceremony had not begun when they were sent out. As a matter of fact it had begun, and they had not been particularly noticed until Alupwai objected. For the purpose of expelling the children it had not begun, although for everyone else it had begun; and no one else could leave. An adult man of Mok had once broken this taboo associated with Man of Lorengau's charm, and died for it.

The men present were Tunu, Pokenas, Patalian (a magician himself), two men of Kalo (Tuwain and Ngamasue), and three others as well as the presiding magician. The men lay about chatting inconsequentially, while the women cooked, and Man of Lorengau hung apart, trying to appear supervisory, important and trying not to notice any of the inconsequential gossip. His rôle of having to appear aloof obviously hurt him at this juncture. Pokenas remarked at length on the virtues of his house and of his Sir Ghost, and pointed out that Alupwia had not fainted off once since she had been under his roof. Everyone agreed that such was indeed the case. An old woman from outside shouted out that her pig was missing. Man of Lorengau forsook his dignity and he and Pokenas and Pokenau all spat betel juice on the middle of *Piper methysticum* leaves to make divination of the non-serious type. Man of Lorengau's and Pokenas' juice went down the left side of the mid-ribs, an affirmative. It appeared that what they had divined was whether the old woman would find the pig or not. Pokenau's juice went down the right side of the mid-rib, a negative. Pokenau said promptly that his divination was play and the result was not correct. The outcry over the pig went on outside. Presently it was sighted by someone outside. A woman, newly returned from an overseas voyage to a great economic event abroad came in and told about it. At this stage anyone came in or went out freely. Apparently no one was afraid of dying. The interpretation of the taboo seemed flexible.

Now after about two and a half hours the food was cooked. Everyone sat up fairly straight. The women remained in the back of the house. The atmosphere was reasonably solemn, although Pokenau grinned slily throughout at something best known to himself. I think he did not like Alupwai particularly. Alupwai was bidden to sit up. She pulled herself up with great pain and difficulty by a rope attached overhead to the rafters.[105] Ngamasue, her "brother," kept his eyes fixed on her with the greatest anxiety, but neither he nor another helped her up. No one else paid her any attention, not even Tunu. Man of Lorengau sat down opposite Alupwai. The cooked food was put out in wood bowls along the house centre board. It was taro and sago, the ordinary foods of most ceremonies, as well as large crab of a special species and *pongapong*, the special

[105] Either a rope or a rattan was especially put up to the rafters for Alupwai over all the time of her illness to pull herself up by, and "to grip hard when she was in pain."

foods peculiar to Man of Lorengau's particular ceremonial of exorcsim.

A bowl containing taro, *pongapong* and a large trussed crab was set in front of Man of Lorengau. He chewed betel nut and ginger mixed, took a piece of taro about the size of an egg, worked it over in his hand, spat betel and ginger upon it and delivered a long sing song speech, said at great speed—mechanically with few pauses and few emphases, in the incantation tone of voice. He was reciting the history of his magic:—

"You *tchinal*,[106] *tchinal* belonging to Lowa, *pel*[107] of the *Nam*[108] belonging to *tchinal*. Salikai, Lord[109] of Tulu.[190] And so Salikai, Lord of Tulu went to his garden. It fell night. He slept close to a stone. A *tchinal* came, lifted him up, took him to the house of *Sir tchinal*. He crumbled *ku*. he crumbled *kawe* (aromatic herbs). Salikai smelt and thought he was sleeping in his own house. Close to dawn he looked about. He was sleeping in the house of *Sir tchinal*. He sobbed as he lay. He was sorry for himself. He sobbed to the *tchinal*.

"The *tchinal* said, 'Yes. I am a *tchinal*. I am accustomed to eat human persons. You sob there. You eat taro.'

"The *tchinal* gave him taro to eat. The *tchinal* gave him body ornaments. The *tchinal* said, 'I want some valuables that are in the sea, star fish, sea anemone, seaweed *mot*, seaweed *mbwala*. You go get them and bring them to me.'

"The *tchinal* took Salikai, Lord of Tulu, to see the back of his house. He said, 'Yes. I am a *tchinal*. I am accustomed to eat human persons. In this rear of my house human skulls are collected together like a heap of coconuts. I ate all those so represented here.'

"The two returned. He said to Salikai, Lord of Tulu, 'Yes, it is my custom to eat human persons. But I am giving

[106] Snake like supernatural being, familiar of magic.

[107] Special food.

[108] Special type of magic.

[109] Chief man or man of highest rank of a Northern Great Admiralty inland tribe.

you safe return to your place. What I want is star fish, sea anemone, *mot* and *mbwala*. Bring them to me.'

"Salikai, Lord of Tulu, descended home. He talked to his wife. He took a bag. He bore star fish, sea anemone, *mot* and *mbwala* in it. He went to all the *tchinals*.

"The *tchinal* saw. He said, 'Good!' And he loosed down the Wooden Bowl of the *Nam* to the floor. He gave it with *kawe* and with *ku* (aromatic herbs) to Salikai. (This Wooden Bowl of the *Nam* is the fetish object of the magic power.) Salikai took the spirit (*i.e.*, of the magic power) to himself (with the Wooden Bowl of the Nam). He slept with the *Sir Tchinal* with him (evidently the *Sir Tchinal* was the familiar and was himself the spirit of the Wooden Bowl of the *Nam*, and of the magic power). He knew no harm from it. He became very old. His teeth fell out (with extreme age).

"It (*i.e.*, the magic) went to Wati, Lord of Ndrukul.[110] He took the *pel* of the *Nam*. He gave a woman to Salikai. Salikai wanted to give him betel nut. He declined it. Salikai wanted to give him pulverised coral lime (chewed with betel nut). He declined it. Salikai wanted to give him food. He declined it. He said 'I am desiring the magic.' Salikai loosed down the Wooden Bowl of the *Nam* to the floor. He gave it to Wati, Lord of Ndrukul. He took it to Ndrukul, to look at men. He put it to guarding his house, to guarding his betel nut palms, to guarding his coconut palms. All those who tried to steal from his coconut palms, from his betel nut palms it struck down. They died. He did not own up to it. Thirty days concluded, he bathed. (For thirty days after receipt the new owner of transferred magic must not own up publicly to having the power, even if men die from it meanwhile; nor must he bathe during that time. He must go unwashed for the time so that the magic becomes "securely attached to his skin.")

"By grace my mother's brother struck many down. They died from him. They said of him that he had but to walk abroad and he would die (from revenge wrought on him). He

[110] Northern Great Admiralty inland tribe, truculent warlike, killed a white man recently.

heard of the magic that was on the other side (*i.e.*, on the far north coast of the Great Admiralty, amongst the tribes there), that was possessed by all dependents there, that was possessed by all the lords there. It was nothing but good. My mother's brother took his spear, put it in his canoe, took his wooden bowls, put them in canoe, took his shell money, his dogs' teeth, put them in canoe, and went to Wati, Lord of Ndrukul. He charmed my mother's brother with the *pel* of the *Nam*. He gave the magic to him. Wati said to my mother's brother 'Just wait five days; at the conclusion of that time I shall die. You burn up my house, oversee it, then return to your place!'

"My mother's brother heard this. He made his stay until the five days were over. Wati died. He burnt up Wati's house. My mother's brother came away, bringing the *pel* of the *Nam* and the Wooden Eating Bowl of the *Nam* in his possession. He spoiled all with it. He struck down all with it. They all died. To the place of blood, the place where his brother was killed in war he went, breaking the taboo (against risk of "blood" entry into the body of the intruder). Everyone said he would die. They mixed the oil from the body fat of his brother (they being cannibals) with the food, the taro they offered him. He ate. He did not become ill.

"Then the influenza epidemic (of 1918) came to us. The family line of Talipopangang died out to a man. Nyamwe (an Usiai female seer) made a seer's vision. She saw *talipopangang* (now a ghost) and me in company. (In real life the two had gone about together a great deal, the seer was seeing that in death they would not be divided.) The men of *talipopangang's* line were paddling the two of us by canoe. Then the wife of Talikomuli, not a Manus woman, an Usiai woman she, was sorry for me. She told me saying, 'Nyamwe saw you, you had died.'

"I heard it. I did not go by canoe. I plunged into the jungle. I took the dogs' tracks, the pigs' tracks, the ghosts' tracks, no tracks at all. I went. I went to my mother's brother. He was out fishing. I climbed up the rafters on the beams beside the Wooden Bowl of the *Nam*. I ate a little pongapong and large crab. I ate *musu* (like camphor wood bark). I ate ginger. I ate *ku* and *kawe* (aromatic herbs). My mother's brother came home from fishing to see me.

"I had lifted up the Wooden Bowl of the *Nam*. My mother's brother saw me. He said not a word. I said to him, 'My mother's brother, if you had born a son, if you had born a daughter it might belong there. And you might remain (*i.e.*, alive). You have born no son, no daughter have you born. I want to take it.'

"My mother's brother heard it. He gave the *pel* of the *Nam*, the Wooden Bowl of the *Nam*. He gave it to me.

"I did damage with it in New Ireland (where the speaker went as a workman). I returned to Manus. I spoiled all with it. All said I had but to walk abroad and I should die. But I had a little (power) in my possession. I violated the tabooed places of the ghosts, of blood and war, of the *tchinals*. All said what little (power) has he to act so. I did not reveal it. But after thirty days I bathed in the sea, and revealed it."

At this point, Man of Lorengau having concluded this history, flung the ball of taro he had been holding in his hand against the cross pole of the house front. Everyone present paused, breathed heavily and looked hard at where it had hit.

Man of Lorengau took the bowl of half stripped leaves and rattled off a charm over them;

> "By your grace you spirits of ours,
> you *tchinal*, unloose the creeper tied round the body, and
> away with it, the creeper away.
> You fly off to the south,
> you fly off to the north.
> You ascend out to the deep sea,
> you descend unto the shore.
> You strike people of the other places in all other
> direction.
> Now these people here are with us
> you go away."

Man of Lorengau sighed with heavy relief, pushed the

bowl away and said, "The chattering is over." Everyone laughed, including Man of Lorengau. He distributed the food and everyone ate. Then he took the bundle of *ti* leaves down from the thatch and broomed Alupwai's bed of old ropes and mats carefully, and all about it, "to chase the *tchinals* away," I was told. Then Alupwai was allowed back on her bed.

We have not been able to give a detailed account of a magical performance before this. Now we may pause a moment to consider it. The *tchinal* are regarded by the Manus with more than a grain of humour. In Manus legend they figure as tricksters and ogres of an order that the Manus feel as distinctly childish. Tales of the *tchinal* are used by the adults in an attempt to discipline children. "Don't go there or the *tchinals* will catch you." But the children see through the deception and use the same deception on still younger children to mask wishes and desires that contain no sincere reckoning of *tchinal* dangers whatever.

To the inland peoples, the Usiai, the *tchinal* cult is real and sincere. Usiai seekers for magic power often go out alone into the jungle to live only on wild fruits and water for thirty days. The seeker camps by a hole or a cavern and waits for a snake-like *tchinal* to appear to him and to give him the desired magic power. If the seeker is rewarded he must slay an enemy and lay an offering of a human head beside the hole of the *tchinal.* No water may touch the seeker's body during this time of search. He must shelter from rain and keep out of streams, although he may drink from a cupped hand.

The man who acquires a charm with its fetish object of validation of possession from another must keep his body clear of water in the same way for thirty days. Such handed-down charms are often conceived as originally obtained by ritual search and watch beside a *tchinal's* hole by a magic seeker, although Man of Lorengau's charm claims different origin. For in that charm the first man to obtain it from the *tchinal* was sleeping in his garden. The deliberate seeker must avoid all human habitations and all gardens, and all common jungle tracks during his thirty days' search.

In time of illness the Manus acquire something of the Usiai seriousness in reckoning with the *tchinal* and the magic of which they are the familiars, although at all other times the *tchinal* are rather comical figures.

The idea that the new acquirer of black magic must not reveal his possession of it for thirty days, even although he knows that someone is dying by being affected by it is general in Manus magic. It is the local form of the wider concept that the new possessor of black magic must kill someone with it. Here that vigourous positive idea is softened down to the concept that if the new owner were able to confess his power during the thirty days of concealment of it, he would be able to exorcise the evil it was wreaking. But he cannot confess it just as he cannot bathe during that time or the spiritual force of it will not be "attached fast to his skin."

The concept that the giver of the magic dies five days after giving it away, and that the beggar of magic virtually kills the former owner if his begging is successful is also general. But it is not taken very seriously. For example an old man I knew gave his son his fetish object and charm, and fell ill shortly after. The son promptly gave it back and the old man recovered. The pair indulged in this practice in the same way and with the same results several times. By experimentation they found that sometimes the son could hold the power longer than five days, sometimes not.

All the exorcisms have special foods connected with their ceremonial, but the full style of a special feast is not usually maintained. The average magician in Manus does not keep up with Man of Lorengau who spoke the Usiai language fluently and was more conversant with the Usiai magical customs than any other of his brother magicians.

The reference to the creepers (bush trailing vines) in the charm exorcism itself rings significantly to the student of Melanesian sorcery. A way of "getting" your man is to breathe a spell on to a creeper twined across his path, and then to take the creeper afterwards and smoke it over a fire (see my account of Dobuan sorcery). The Manus man is innocent enough of such special use of the bush creeper, but the Usiai, who are the local Admiralty tribes who "carry" most of the local magic as their special field in contrast to spiritism, may not be so innocent. In any case the Manus magician is not believed to practise secret vendetta, or to use secret, stray trailing vines or some substitute of sea lagoon environment, in the Dobuan manner.

In Man of Lorengau's account the deliberate daring of supernatural dangers done without damage incurred by the owner of magic should be noted. It seems to be a common attitude closely associated with sorcery in many places. I have found it in every field I have been in as yet, in Dobu, in Manus, both of the New Guinea littoral, and among the Omaha of North America.

Man of Lorengau's magic was especially respected. He had acquired it from his mother's brother during the panic of the influenza epidemic of 1918. It had carried him through that time, and as he came into possession of it then, with death occurring all about, he probably thought it potent, although the later explanation of the deaths from the influenza was *mbris,* sex offence, a view that Man of Lorengau probably held with modification, since he liked to advertise the power of his magic.

Next day the 7th March, the results of the Usiai dreamer's vision were brought to Peri. They ran:

1. When Sali of Kalo came home from working for the white man he gave all of his massed earnings to Korotan (who had adopted him and financed his marriage) and to his mother, Ndrantche. He gave nothing to his elder brother, Tuwain. But when Sali wanted shell money to wind round his neck as body ornament he borrowed it from Tuwain. Tuwain's Sir Ghost, *papitalipoitchalon,* was angry at this and was striking down Alupwai, sister of Sali and Tuwain, for it.

2. A widow, a dark-skinned, tall man; the two steal away to the bush. The two have connection there.

3. Tuwain quarrels with the rest of Kalo gens over Patalian's proposal of marriage to Alupwai's sister, Tuwain alone taking Patalian's part. At the conclusion of the quarrel, during which both Tuwain and Alupwai had sworn

that each wanted to die out of the cognisance of the other, Tuwain sent a pig to Alupwai as a peace offering. Alupwai and Tunu sent dogs' teeth to Tuwain in acknowledgement. The Sir Ghost of Tunu was not first consulted as to whether the dogs' teeth should have been sent. He was now expressing his anger at it.

4. A river, the smell of blood of a man killed in war.

5. A betel nut palm; they climb it; as punishment for it two snakes fall on them and strike them (snakes = *tchinal*).

6. A coconut palm—they climb it; the charm on it enters into them.

7. A canoe with sago in it; it sinks.

The above is the form in which I heard the results of the vision, new brought to Peri. Then followed immediately the *tandridrian*, the filling in of the details suggested to the consciences of Alupwai's group by some of the vaguer references of the vision.

The first charge was complete and needed no *tandridrian*.

In the second charge it was recognised that the widow was Ndrantche, Alupwai's mother and that the dark-skinned tall man was Patalian, her seducer. This affair was many years old now. I commented on the fact and was told, "as far as we mortals are concerned it is long over and done with, but it must needs remain in the stomachs (*i.e.*, minds) of the ghosts forever."

The third charge was complete without *tandridrian*.

The fourth diagnosis it was felt at once referred to the grandfather of Alupwai, who was killed by Usiai enemies at Kolognan, where Alupwai had gone, apparently. I could not ascertain certainly whether she had gone there or not. She should not have done so as it was a place dangerous to her from her ancestor's blood.

The fifth charge was of stealing from another's betel nut palm. The two snakes that had stricken the thief were, of course, the familiars of the owner's black magic placed on his property as protection. In *tandridrian*, Alupwai confessed now to stealing from Pokenau's betel nut palm.[111] This

[111] Note how retentively Alupwai has kept her sins secret, confessing only inch by inch when the oracles have approached a truth. She had been set upon for confession of sin for a very long time now.

palm had been protected by a charm put on it by Pope, acting for Pokenau who had paid him to do it.

The sixth charge was of stealing from another's coconut palm. There was no *tandridrian* for this. Neither Alupwai nor any of those closely associated with her could call up any new memory of any such theft. It was generally said that it must have been so long ago that Alupwai's memory was worsted—not that the seer's diagnosis was untrue.

The seventh element in the vision, a canoe with sago sinking at sea, was a prophesy of death for Alupwai (in a standard symbolism).

Action was taken on every point in the series of diagnoses, except that of the coconut palm theft which was not substantiated by the *tandridrian.* Tuwain had a seance held and interviewed his Sir Ghost, *papi-talipoitchalon.* The latter said (through the control, through the medium): Yes, that he had been annoyed at Sali's behavior to Tuwain, and had stricken Alupwai for it; but now that he had succeeded in calling attention to his displeasure it could be considered as all over. He had restored the soul stuff. And Tuwain might freely continue to lend his shell money to Sali whenever Sali wanted it as ornament in future, without fear of any further reprisals from him.

On the second point Ndrantche sent a calico cloth, a trade box, and some bead work to Tuwain, as expiatory payment for her seduction by Patalian long ago having precipitated so much trouble. I was told that if Alupwai recovered, Tuwain would share out the spoil amongst Kalo. If she died he would return it to Ndrantche.

On the third point Tuwain gave Tunu and Alupwai back the dogs' teeth, which they had given before in peace-making exchange—without Tunu's Sir Ghost's consent. Tuwain had meanwhile given those dogs' teeth to Patalian, who had given them to Ngamel in the course of economic exchange. Ngamel gave them back to Patalian who took them to Tunu. The whole matter of settling debt, Tunu to Tuwain (for the pig) then Tuwain to Patalian and Patalian to Ngamel again would be adjusted later on, I was given to understand—with more respect for the Sir Ghosts liable to object, and with their prior consent, which they would naturally give, as in the final issue, ghosts support economic straight dealing as rigidly as they punish crooked dealing.

On the fourth point of Alupwai having gone to a place of dangerous blood (her stomach being greatly swollen), the mother of Pokenas, an aged widow, performed an exorcism for "blood" entered into the patient's stomach. Unfortunately, I did not see this exorcism.

On the fifth point of Alupwai having been damaged by the black magic of Pope placed on Pokenau's betel nut palm, in stealing from that palm, Pope exorcised Alupwai, an exorcism that I saw myself.

The sixth point, theft of coconuts, being without *tandridrian* was passed over, especially as Alupwai had just been exorcised by Man of Lorengau for a former Usiai seer's charge of the same type exactly, which had met with the only *tandridrian* Alupwai possessed for that particular charge.

All this endeavour to cure was made despite the prognosis of death which concluded the seer's vision.

The night of the day on which the seer's report was received saw not only the seance made for Tuwain and his Sir Ghost, *papi-talipoitchalon*, but also a seance made by the wife of Pokenas, as medium, over the black maglc of Pope put on Pokenau's palm, from which Alupwai had stolen. The medium did not get in touch with ghosts, but with the *tchinals* who are the familiars of Pope's magic. When the seer's report charges theft from a palm only the *tandridrian*, or filling in of facts, is not normally done easily or quickly by the guilty parties, kin to the ill person. There may be quick confession, but more often there is divination first on a particular suspicion in the mind of some outsider. This suspicion is likely to be the result of some private detective work in the past, and founded on some private information. Thus suspicion, and divination on a particular charge comes on top of the seer's more general and vaguer charge to elicit confession which thus emerges reluctantly, but does not emerge at all if the suspected person is innocent. Confession of theft thus emerges from a strong resistance to confession, as in the case of confession of sexual offence also.

My notes state that the *tandridrian* to the Usiai seer's charge of theft from a betel nut palm was not made until the night, although the seer's report was received early in the day. Only by night a diviner divined that the stealing in question was from Pokenau's palm, and was done by Alupwai, Tunu, and a third person, Pomalat. His divining confirmed the suspicion, and the charge was admitted by the guilty parties. There had been some private leakage of information, previously hushed up, as in common in these cases. Then immediately after the confession Pokenau stated that Pope's black magic had been placed on his palms, and the wife of Pokenas, as medium, got into communication with the familiars of that black magic, first consulting Pope.

Pope said: "Yes, the *tchinal* familiars of my magic are similar enough to the ghosts (of the dead) that we may embark on a seance to consult them."

The medium summoned up the familiars and her control reported their presence in the house. Pope said (to them):

"*Borukom,*
"*Mwatalai,*
"*Wati,*
"*Palankei,*
"*Komunkei.*

"You of my magic here. Whom you do now strike you may yet recover."

Through the channels the familiars said: "Yes, previously others have made exorcism of their magic (*i.e.*, Patalian and Man of Lorengau). Their magic was as fire, (*i.e.*, hot and potent). They all worked. But they did not hurl away the affliction of this sick one here. Now you say that we should go to work to recover her."

Pope: "Yes, at daybreak tomorrow I shall come and work on her from the mortal plane. Meanwhile you had better sleep in this house.

"And you, *daughter of Pokenas,* you see that all these familiars, *tchinal,* stay with you! You all stay in the house!

"My father and I shall sleep in my house and at dawn I shall come here. You get plenty of ginger, pepper leaf and betel nut! At dawn I'll come and work."

In this speech of Pope's he first addresses the familiars ("you had better sleep in this house"). He then addresses a ghost, the *daughter of Pokenas*, advising her to keep the familiars in Pokenas' house. He finally addresses everyone, supernatural and mortal, warning them to procure the necessities for his magic for the morrow, an address naturally directed at the mortals, but not couched directly so, or separated out distinctly from his prior injunctions.

The ghost, the daughter of Pokenas had been married, as a ghost, to a son of Pope, a ghost. Pope had paid a bride price on the mortal plane to Pokenas for the ghost wife for his ghost son. Pokenas had repaid it with wedding finery, dowry, sent with the bride to Pope's house. This dowry is called *mwelamwel* and must by custom be sent on the bride's person with the bride when she goes to her groom. As the payments were material, substantial and ponderable in this case, the *mwelamwel* being very notably and markedly ponderable, whereas the bride was an insubstantial ghost, a living daughter of Pokenas impersonated her dead sister's person. She "became ghost" for the purpose and shortly after was allowed to resume her mortal, distinct personality. It was from this past history that Pope elected to speak to the *daughter of Pokenas*, his ghostly daughter-in-law, and to entrust her with the charge of his magical familiars for the night in Pokenas' house, while he and his father (*i.e.*, his Sir Ghost) retired to sleep in their own different house.

Dramatically enough just as Pope was about to retire, Alupwai's condition came to its crisis. The day and the evening had been particularly wearing. Alupwai's pain had mounted to a peak again and she had fainted two or three times. There had been much mourning and wailing by the women, stirring of wooden bowls with sticks and shouting on Sir Ghosts by the men. All the divination, confession, expiation and seance following the receipt of the Usiai seer's diagnoses had taken place rapidly and under pressure of excitement. Alupwai's death at any moment would have surprised no one.

She did not die however. Just as the day's proceedings closed, streams of pus burst forth from her navel. She had been suffering from a retained after-birth which had putrefied within her. About half a bucket of pus was collected from the flow from the navel that night. The natives still did not understand that the case could have been prevented by skilful mid-wivery at its inception. They had no knowledge of how to remove a retained after-birth; all they concentrate upon is magic and ghosts, the causes of all misfortune. So next day the exorcism arranged for from Pope proceeded without anyone feeling a hiatus. As far as I could determine no one realised that the pus proceeded from a putrefied, retained after-birth. If the midwife who presided over the birth of Alupwai's infant knew, she had kept her own counsel up to this point, and she continued to do so. If she had talked she would have been generally censured as an indecent, indelicate, scandal-mongering person, who discussed indecencies merely because she was lewd.

Later I talked to Man of Lorengau, one of the most intelligent and most receptive to new ideas of all of them. I said: "I advised you early to have Alupwai taken to the hospital at Lorengau (where Administration provides free medical treatment for all who desire it). Alupwai suffered from retained after-birth. It could have been washed out from her womb early before it putrefied within her. The white doctor would have known what to do. It is a common usage amongst us. Why did you put faith in magic?"

Man of Lorengau was a native assistant to the local Government doctor. In each village in Manus there is at least one native who is supplied with drugs and medicines by Government. He is supposed to use these for the benefit of local village ills. Serious cases he is supposed to have brought to the white centre at Lorengau, if possible. He has authority to order removal to Lorengau, but not complete authority, as no native is guilty of a crime if he refuses white medical treatment. In practice the position of village native assistant (to Government medical service) is highly prized. These village native "doctors" are given a "hat" as uniform, and exemption from taxation. The honour of the "hat" is keenly valued, even more perhaps than the tax exemption. The honour is taken as an honour, without much feeling of obligation in return, however. The local "doctor" bandages his own kin freely if one of them is cut, but feels free to abstain from bandaging anyone else in similar circumstance, unless the wound is severe. He has liquid quinine in stock, but he, like everyone else, puts his faith in divination and manipulation of ghosts to cure malaria. On occasion he empties his quinine stock into the sea, to pretend that his duties have been performed. Antiseptics and bandages alone are used correctly.

Under the circumstances, and, as Man of Lorengau had used magic on Alupwai, I thought it fair to make a point in favour of the white doctoring, to which he owed a nominal allegiance and his exalted position. The native assistants address each other as "Doctor" when they meet, and they with the native police form a real aristocracy in the eyes of their less exalted fellows who have not "the hat."

Man of Lorengau was hurt bitterly by my comment. He did not attempt to question the facts as I had put them. He said very bitterly, "You whites know more than we," and turned away in mortification.

I knew the situation that confronted him. In the first place he could only be convinced of the worth of white doctoring when the case against spiritism and magic was unusually strong, as it was with Alupwai. In his long experience as native medical assistant he probably had known that a retained after-birth could be removed. But more importantly he knew that Manus public opinion would not tolerate any male person, native or white, having anything to do with child-birth. A former local white doctor had attempted to institute a general medical examination for venereal disease, but had been compelled to abandon the project quickly. By Manus ideas all male examination of child-birth, or of post child-birth complications, or examination of females must necessarily be lewd.

Moreover no woman was ever sent to the white hospital in Lorengau, if she had relatives to control her. The white doctors there were male, the native orderlies in the hospital were male, the police attached to the Government post there were male. So even if a woman's trouble were merely a large and a gaping wound in the lower leg which needed stitching she was not taken to the central hospital to have it stitched. I asked that a woman be taken in for such treatment once. But it could not be thought of. There was no objection to stitching as such, for when it became evident that I would have to stitch the wound if it were to be stitched at all, no objection was offered. All the objection was directed against the isolation of a woman in a hospital run by males. I sewed up the wound without anaesthetics.

From this digression we must return to Alupwai on the morning of March 8th, her condition having attained some release overnight. Whether or not Man of Lorengau accepted the white point of view afterwards when Alupwai had progressed gradually but surely towards recovery from the night when the pus came from her navel, no one suspected the truth of the matter at the time, or thought of it independently afterwards, unless it was the midwives at Alupwai's child bearing.

Pope performed his exorcism without any conspicuous style. He was as stupid as Man of Lorengau was intelligent, and was commonly known by name that is about equivalent to our moron. Mwengo, he was called, at least as often as Pope. He came back from the morning market at about ten thirty, and went to Pokenas' house to perform his exorcism over Alupwai. He sat down solemnly and waited for the pay for his exorcising services to be put in front of him before he began business. The people of the house also waited. They were in no hurry. This rather strained wait continued for about an hour and a half. Then the pay was produced. Apparently it was the correct way to do business with Pope, for he began work without further delay (further delay by the magician being a demand for more pay).

He chewed betel nut and ginger, saying:

"*Borukom,*

"*Wati,*

"*Mwatalai,*

"*Kolumat,*

"*Palankei* [112]

belonged to Selan of Lolomondru. He put them as black magic familiars on coconut palms, on betel nut palms.

"I went to him. I had heard of his magic. I begged him, plaguing him for it (*kekesani* means to beg and to annoy by reiterated begging). I might get it for myself. He did not grant my request. He was unwilling (and fed up—*papwen* means both unready and annoyed). I went on begging him and plaguing him by begging. I did this for three days. Then he granted my request. I threw dogs' teeth to ground before him. He transferred the magic to me. I took it to myself.

"I looked (on a level) at children, dogs and pigs. I was not grown although I was full in years. All cried over me on account of it.

"Once I had the magic I became well. I grew taller and well. Had I not had the magic I had died. But with the magic I recovered.

"I have a beard. I have magic. If it seems that I have not a beard then I have not magic.

"E! in five days' time I shall see her (Alupwai). I shall send scattering the body of ghosts which surround her. When I am done, the pus will be done. If she eats sago boiled in coconut milk she shall die."

Pope's account of his stunted growth before he had the magic may or may not be true. It is possible that his magic was the *nam* form, but I could not discover what form of *sorosor* it was, and he being the village idiot probably did not know himself. The *nam* is of course the magic to produce stunted growth in those it afflicts, and perhaps ownership of

[112] Note the familiars' names are in different order from that of the seance of the night before, and the name of one of the five is now different, possibly because Pope is a moron.

the *nam* had been suggested to Pope as a possible cure for his own poor growth at an early stage in his life. As I knew Pope his mind was far more stunted than his body.

Sago boiled in coconut milk is the taboo on food laid on Pope's patients and associated with his magic. It is an unfortunate taboo, as sago served liquid in plenty of coconut milk is a customary Manus food for invalids, and the best invalid food they have. It is also given to suckling infants when they are being weaned gradually.

Pope now spat a circle of masticated betel nut juice on Alupwai's stomach round the navel. He spat also on a bunch of *ti* leaves (*Cordyline terminalis*). He then beat Alupwai's stomach with the *ti* leaves to cast out the magic influence in it. He then bound two or three *ti* leaves together in two sets to make two girdles. One girdle he tied above Alupwai's stomach round her body, one below her stomach similarly—to ward out the influence with "gates." He then rubbed Alupwai's back with more *ti* leaves, muttering a charm under breath as he did so. Then suddenly with an histrionic effort he made as if he hurled something violently away, abandoning Alupwai.

The wife of Pokenas very impressed said, "He's got it and hurled it away." Pope then gingerly tried to squeeze a little pus out of the pus-covered navel. But he quickly decided that it was better not to touch it. He put the small wooden bowl with his pay in it up in the rafters and said that in five days' time Alupwai would be better. He'd come back to see that she was and he would leave his pay in the house till then, when he would collect it over a cured patient.

I got from Pope the underbreath charm he had used. Pope was sly and cunning in his comparatively feeble mind. His face had expressed a low cunning all through the performance. So he angled with me, but finally told me the charm. Like others used in Manus it was simple. It named the familiars already mentioned above. Then:

"You stand up. Climb on to this betel nut, on to this ginger. And come out and go away (*i.e.*, the influence is to come out of Alupwai's body, attracted by the betel nut and ginger spat on to the body, and then to go away). Let her eat food and be well. Let her drink water and be well. Let her remain alive, and be well."

So ended Alupwai's trouble. She recovered slowly but certainly thereafter. Her tenacity and strength had been remarkable. It was an amazing survival. A month later she had not regained normal weight, and was still emaciated, but she went about the ordinary work of a Manus woman. Her recovery was attended with no setback, so that Pope's exorcism was the last call upon magician, diviner or medium that was made for her.

21. *Other Sins in Kalo Gens*

The same day as that of Pope's exorcism, a child, the daughter of Poli, fell ill—another trouble in Kalo gens. The diagnoses were as follows:

1. Poli's dead father's sister, *ingon*, the wife of Ngandaliu as mortal formerly, as ghost the wife of the ghost *pondralis*, was striking down Poli's daughter. The ward of *pondralis* was the owner of a house in which there was a girl under the taboos and ceremonial of first menstruation. This girl, Kiteni was betrothed to the future heir of Paliau. Her kin had given sago and pots to Paliau and his associates the day before, an obligatory gift. The ward of *pondralis* was a gens "brother" of Kiteni. Hence since Poli's father's sister, *ingon* was married to *pondralis*, Poli was an affinity to the ward of *pondralis*. Therefore Poli should have been associated with Kiteni's kin in giving sago and pots to Paliau and Paliau's kin. Poli had not given anything in the ceremony the day before. His father's sister, *ingon*, slighted by this neglect of her marriage as a ghost to the ghost *pondralis*, struck down Poli's daughter immediately.

2. That ghost *popwitch* whom we have found before causing trouble because the fish, *pwitch*, was taken by Kali and sold to the Usiai, had detected Ngamasue of Kalo, brother of Poli, taking a *pwitch* fish also. This offense was the more serious in that the sister of the ghost *popwitch* was the present wife of Poli.

The illness was attributed to these two counts by the diviners. Poli made a quick contribution of sago and pots to Paliau and a payment to the ward of *popwitch*, the ghost. A seance was held and the soul stuff already paid for collected from the two ghosts who had taken it.

22. *The Skulls of Isole's Ancestors*

I learned about this time that the skulls of the *talipolalau*, the Sir Ghosts of Isole and Kemwai and Isole's kin, had been shattered and burned long ago. The *talipolalau* had functioned by Isole's disregard of the convention that mortals can control the ghosts by manipulation of the skulls. We have seen already one case not quite so striking, where Pwanau as a mortal demoted *potek*, formerly his chief Sir Ghost, to a secondary rank, and by one count, was killed by *potek* for it. The ghost does not always submit to the conventional control as readily as the dogma and the practices of skull shattering, skull burning, skull throwing out, or demoting of skull from a principal wooden bowl to a secondary and smaller, wooden bowl, enjoin. Everyone states the dogma of complete control of the ghost through skull manipulation as absolute, of course. Variation of belief is learned by accident only in the course of minute investigation.

23. *The Sins of Ndroso's House*

On the tenth of March a seven- or eight-year-old daughter of Ndroso [113] was the subject of divination and seance. The child had been ill a long time, I was told, but nothing had been done until now her condition seemed dangerous. The divination fell upon the ghosts of the mother and father of Ndroso, each ghost acting for itself on a different cause for offence given by Ndroso.

In the seance the ghostly mother of Ndroso, *nyaputchi*, stated: "I became a ghost. I said, 'What did I die for?' And all the ghosts replied to me, 'Ndroso and his wife used scandalous evil language to each other when they quarreled and the ghosts struck you for it.' I heard it. I knew then

[113] Ndroso was the brother of the wife of Pokenas.

PLATE VIII

ISOLE THE MEDIUM

it was not for my own sin that I died, but for others' sin. I was angry. I struck down this daughter of Ndroso for it."

The ghost, *nyaputchi*, was then asked to return the soul stuff she had taken. I do not think that there had been any expiation paid, as the affair was all in the family.

In the seance also the father of Ndroso, *son-of-bamboo*, or *talibunyo*, stated his separate case: "Long ago I died. Ndroso did not cut sago to make a funerary feast for me. Then later my widow, *nyaputchi*, died and Ndroso's wife died, and Ndroso cut sago and made their funerary feasts. Although I died first no funerary feast was made for me. I was angry. I struck down this daughter of Ndroso, my grand-child. But you have heard now. I shall give you the soul stuff."

I did not see Ndroso make up for this omission, but he was bound to do it, or be blamed for his child's illness. Two comments of a general nature may be made at this point, however. When an important man dies, his mother's brothers and mother's brothers' sons and mother's brothers' sons' sons may come and smash up his house and plunder the household possessions (such as the dead's brothers and heirs have not secreted quickly beforehand. I was given to understand that as a rule the brothers and kins got away as much as they could for themselves before the plunderers came, the plunderers on their part also acting as quickly as possible). This smashing and plundering is a relationship function between cross-cousins, but the rationalisation for it is as follows: "Our paternal aunt or paternal great aunt went to her husband's house, to his Sir Ghosts. She replenished that house with a child, born of her pain, who has died under the Sir Ghosts of that house. Therefore we smash and plunder that house and avenge our paternal aunt (or paternal great aunt) for the wrong done her by the circumstance that she had to bring up a child to Sir Ghosts who by allowing her child to die, have made themselves enemy to her and to us, her kin." The house smashing is directed at the Sir Ghosts of the house primarily. The skull or skulls kept in the house are an object of first attack and go into the sea first.

I did not see this custom during my stay. No local

important man died. Anyway the custom has been prevented lately. Although the custom is traditional, and was normal, the Manus took the first practicable opportunity that presented itself of breaking the tradition. They complained to the Government. The child-of-sister's heirs (who lose by the plunder and the smashing of the house they else inherit) complained about the objectionable habit of their father's child-of-brother [114] (men complaining about their father's mother's brother's sons and sons' sons). So Government helped the plaintiffs and made the tradition illegal. I cite this fact because there was obviously a feeling of blame and resentment. It was evidently a ceremonial attack, not too ceremonious in feeling. And it illustrates the attitude of blame that arises at a death, the attitude of blame that Ndroso would incur, for example, if he did nothing about appeasing his father's ghost with a funerary feast when his daughter was in danger, and if his daughter died subsequently.

As a further general comment it should be added that elsewhere in the Admiralties the failure to make a funerary feast for a dead person is the most important count upon which the ghost of that dead person causes illness or death amongst the survivors. The Matankor peoples of Pitilu, Pak, and Baluan islands, differing as they do amongst themselves, agree in stressing the point that ghosts punish neglected funerary feasts, and laugh at the Manus for supposing that the ghosts punish anything to do with obscenity or with sex. They say "The Manus are our missionaries. Now amongst you white people the Germans are your missionaries" (all the local missions are still German).[115] It is an error, of course, but a fair one. From the local context it does actually appear as if we whites had isolated our tradition of sin and punishment for sin, by making one nation bear it all for us in the Admiralty manner. The point illustrates a real difference between the wholesale diffusion of culture that we know has taken place in Western Europe, and the freedom from any

[114] Children-of-brothers and their male heirs. (Cross-cousins are children of a sister on the one hand, children of a brother [to the sister] on the other hand.)

[115] The Admiralties are now a part of the Mandated Territory of New Guinea, previously a part of German New Guinea.

comparable diffusion that is a commonplace to the student of Melanesia and New Guinea.

The daughter of Ndroso continued to be lastingly ill. Some three or four weeks later another stirring of the supernatural took place, which I shall narrate here out of its proper chronological order, in order to close the affair. There was a new seance with a different medium. From my notes on the seance it would appear that the medium was offered a chance to make a diagnosis that had not been divined by a diviner. For Ndroso asked whether his Sir Ghost was not angry for some reason unknown to him, and through the medium the Sir Ghost replied no, he was not angry. This type of occurrence shows that the medium may be an independent oracle in her own right on points not previously settled by divination.

Ndroso addresses his Sir Ghost, having first asked the medium to have the Sir Ghost directed to be present: "You strike my child. Yes. I do not know in what I have disobeyed or offended you that you strike my child for it. Tell me now in what have I sinned. Let me hear it. Regarding many things you have had but to mention them slightly and I have fulfilled them. But what is in your mind now I do not know or guess. Speak. Let me hear."

Sir Ghost of Ndroso through control through medium: "No. I do not strike anyone. Had I struck one that one had already been stricken unconscious. But I struck no one. Let a person go to summon the two children that are at Patusi village. Let them come and let us hear their speech."

The two children referred to are the ghosts of Ndroso's two dead children. It appeared that in the past the present chief Sir Ghost of Ndroso, his dead brother, had expressed his jealousy of multiple and divided ghostly control of Ndroso's house by causing illness. To placate him Ndroso had cast out the ghosts of his two children. The two, cast out, had gone to Patusi village to stay with the ghost of the elder sister of the wife of Ndroso, the sisters belonging by birth to that village.

The medium in this seance was the wife of Pokenas. Her two controls, *matanamo* (one eye) and *pakob* replied: "You stay here, and we two shall go to bring the two children who are at Patusi. Once the two come up here we shall all hear their speech."

After a pause the two children from Patusi reported through the controls through the medium: "Yes. We two obeyed the word of our grandmother (*i.e.*, mother's elder sister [a ghost]). She said, 'Your mother and I are sisters. When I died she did not come to see me. She did not come to the interment of my bones on the island. She behaved as if she were another, a stranger.' We two heard her lamenting her fate. We struck this child for it."

At this point one count in the seance concluded. I do not know what was done, or if anything could now be done, in reparation. The medium continued; controls speaking through her:

"Now not many ghosts strike at her. But now there is also black magic on her. The smell of ginger and of *ti* plant (*Cordyline terminalis*) is on her. You get a magician to exorcise her! She will recover. This magic is that of him who exorcised her before while she and her mother were staying in Patusi. He did not get his pay for his exorcising. So his black magic has entered into her once again. Bring him. Let him exorcise again. She will recover."

Ndroso: "Yes: this black magic is Tchokal's. He exorcised her at Patusi. True, we did not pay him his fee. His black magic enters into her again."

Unfortunately Tchokal could not be approached to exorcise again. The old unpaid exorcism must have been done over two years before. For Tchokal had since been accused of having committed adultery with her by the dying wife of the native policeman of Patusi. Despite her confession she died. Tchokal had denied the truth of the charge. He had refused to submit and confess. So after the woman's death he was charged with adultery by the native policeman of Patusi before the white court. Tchokal had been imprisoned for two years on the charge. On his release he had left his home village forever. He was without a wife since no one would betroth a daughter to a man believed to have caused a death by refusing to confess. His attitude seemed that of an innocent man, so steadfast had he been in a denial that had hurt him incredibly more than confession ever could have. The wife of Ndroso was sister to the native policeman of Patusi. So Tchokal could not be approached again for an exorcism.[116] Another magician, *faut de mieux* was briefed to undertake an exorcism.

The ghosts commonly detect magical work by "smell" of the herbs used by magicians on the sick person, or violation of a fish taboo by "smell" of the fish. The "smell" in question is of course, metaphysical.

The above case is normal in that it begins in ghost hypotheses and ends, after long obdurate illness, in magical hypotheses; Alupwai's case proceeded in the same way if we except Patalian's early magic over Alupwai at her first attack on the third day of my stay in Peri.

24. *A House Breaking*

The same day that Man of Lorengau performed his exorcism over Alupwai, Nane began to break up his house. No one had been living in it since the day that Popwitch fell down unconscious in it. A magician had exorcised "blood" from it, but I did not see that exorcism or any other exorcism of "blood" later. During the days following Pope's exorcism, Alupwai's setting towards recovery and the events above narrated, Nane worked on his house. With him worked Pope (but not Noan), Lawian, and some others of Lo gens. Lawian, the sinner, was just now beginning to go about the village in the open. But she only went with her kinsmen of Lo gens. After a weeks' work Nane's house was re-erected in a new site, one that had belonged to Lo gens of

[116] Avoidances, apart from regular relationship avoidances, develop from sorcery quarrels, follow public exposure of illicit sex relations, or public exposure of suspicion of such relations, develop between houses when the Sir Ghost of one is though to be acting maliciously towards a mortal of another house, and between the nearby kin of a dead person and another who was alone with the person at the moment of death.

old. Then, shortly after, one evening Man of Lorengau came to the new house bearing the skull of *popwitch*, taken from the now clean skeleton in the grave. There was wailing from Nane and from the women of his house sounding over the village.

25. *Sequel to Disaster at Sea*

To revert back from the middle of March, to about the fifth previous, the wife of Pondramet[117] had been ill as a sequel to her exposure at sea in the canoe mishap to Kalo gens. On the evening of the fifth there was a seance. Pondramet told his own Sir Ghost to stay in the house to protect all present and told the ghost of his mother's brother to seek out the ghost *posaleu*, of Mbuke Island. The medium's control and Pondramet's mother's brother duly went to Mbuke to seek out *posaleu*.

It will be recalled that the canoe disaster occurred on the way home from Mbuke. The ghost, *posaleu*, Sir Ghost of a Mbuke business partner of the canoe crew was ghost of a white man. Several white men had been killed long before in the place called Mblut. One corpse drifted to Lou island. There the Mbuke man found it, buried it, and took the skull and the ghost, which he called *posaleu*, as his own.

The ghostly messengers to *posaleu* came back in due course and reported.

"*posaleu* said, 'I did not strike her.' He asked the women (his two ghostly white wives). They said, 'The wife of Pondramet and the wife of you ward indulged in playful obscenity. We struck them for it.' They gave us the soul stuff however. We bring it back."

It should be noted that female cross-cousins do but very rarely indulge in cross-cousin jesting. I never saw it, and the above instance is the only case that I have in report. It is evidently felt to be somewhat improper. Equivalent jesting between male cross-cousins, or between one male and

[117] The wife of Pondramet was a woman of Kalo gens, Pondramet being a poor man of Matchupal gens. The woman had been taken in war in her youth and held as a prostitute in another village until Korotan, her cross-cousin, won her back.

one female who are cross-cousins is, of course, an everyday affair.

Pondramet: "Leave the soul stuff here. Now go to Rambutchon. Their canoe drifted to Rambutchon. The ghosts of Rambutchon have stricken her."

In due time the messengers came back, this time without a story. They said merely: "That from Mbuke we have brought. That from Rambutchon we have brought also. If later on she falls ill again, you make divination again and we shall search and find her soul stuff again. But for the present the soul stuff is all come. Is it a lie? Or is it true? You make divination and see for yourselves. If she does not rest hereafter then make another seance anew."

On the other plane, controls and a fellow messenger "rubbed" the soul stuff in the water. Then on this plane the medium said, her control from the other plane whistling as usual through her mouth before she translated:

"So: the rubbing is done. Let her drink the water. If it settles down and rests in her stomach the soul stuff is recovered entire and she will recover. But if it goes down and pounds uneasily within her stomach, she will be ill and the soul stuff is not yet recovered."

Two days later the wife of Pondramet was well enough to be up and about and to engage in a violent dispute with another woman. Two weeks later she was ill again. There was renewed convassing of *posaleu* of Mbuke Island, and also of the ghosts (unnamed) of Rambutchon Island. No new facet was brought up. The wife of Pondramet rallied again. She was only down twice in the month that followed the canoe disaster, and then not for long at a time.

26. *Trouble over Widow's Remarriage and Custody of the Children*

The mortal son of that Kialo who had figured as a ghost so conspicuously in the troubles of Alupwai and of Sali, fell ill. He was a child only and in the care of Pokenau's father's sister, the mother of Kialo, the woman who had set up an avoidance between herself and Pokenau since Kialo died in

Pokenau's company. The child was removed to Pwiseu's house. Pikaro was the medium, *kukan* her control, *nyame* the Sir Ghost of Pwiseu.

Pwiseu: "*kukan*, where is *nyame?*"

kukan through medium: "*nyame* is here. He says he will go to search for the soul stuff."

After a long pause *kukan* through medium: "*nyame* went to Loitcha village. He got not one (piece of) soul stuff there. He came to Patusi village. There *talipanditch* had struck this boy; *talipanditch* said, '*kialo* struck Lawa, the wife of my son; *kialo* of Peri struck the wife of Kialo of Patusi. I, as the father of Kialo of Patusi, paid back the debt. I struck the son of *kialo* of Peri.'"

That is, Kialo of Peri as a mortal was the husband of Lawa, Alupwai's sister. After Kialo of Peri died, Lawa married again, this time marrying a man of Patusi also called Kialo. Then *kialo* of Peri as ghost, wroth at his widow's marriage, made her ill. So now the Sir Ghost and father of her new husband makes the son of *kialo* [118] of Peri ill in revenge. The seance continued:

"*talindrian* and *talindramiti*, both of Patusi, received the soul stuff from *talipanditch*. It rested with those two when *nyame* received it from them, and brought it back.

"Then again *nyame* went to Tchalalo village to the native constable of Tchalalo on the ghostly plane. The native constable said, 'What have you to say;' *nyame* replied, 'The son that is in our house, the son of the deceased Kialo, is ill and about to die. Your wife (a ghost) struck him.' The native constable of Tchalalo entered his house and spoke to his wife. She said, 'Yes, I took the soul stuff you mention. I gave it to the house of *talitumanu*. It rests with his wife.' Then *nyame* and the constable of Tchalalo embarked in a canoe and went to the house of *talitumanu* in Matchupal (a gens of Peri) and recovered the soul stuff from the house wife there.

[118] Properly, "son of Kialo," *i.e.*, mortal. The use of the distinction in manner of writing is sometimes liable to lead to confusion rather than distinction, especially here where Kialo of Patusi is living and *kialo* of Peri is dead, and the widow married to her dead husband's namesake.

"Then again *kialo* had stricken his own son also. He had ordered (previously) that his son stay with the old woman Nyamaka (Pokenau's father's sister and *kialo's* mother) rather than with his widow, his son's mother, as a revenge for his widow's remarriage. Then that son went on a canoe trip to Loitcha. And on the way back he wanted to see his mother who was ill then in Patusi, and went to see her. But *kialo* had said that he was forbidden to see her. He struck him for it. The soul stuff was recovered by *nyame; kialo* gave it to him. Then *nyame* said, 'Is that all of it.' *kialo* replied, 'That is everything;' *nyame* said 'You are lying;' *kialo* said, 'It is true upon my honour.'"

Pwiseu: "Yes. If *nyame* says that *kialo* told the truth let us restore the soul stuff to the bereft one (*i.e.*, sick one). But if *kialo* is lying let them all punt back again, and if they exchange accusation of lie for protestation of truth, I may wait the while."

nyame through control through medium: "Pwiseu, *kialo* said it was all right, the truth. The soul stuff he took he sent to Matchupal and you have it now. And if all the ghosts had struck this child mercilessly he had long been dead. The soul stuff is completed. Now the soul stuff goes into the water."

Pwiseu: "Yes, *nyame*, rub the soul stuff in the water first, then let *kialo* rub it in, then let *kukan* (the control)."

Control through medium: "*kialo* is still telling lies. Let the other two rub in the soul stuff alone. I decline to do so."

A long pause, then control through medium: "All right. I'll rub the soul stuff. Only while you ghosts were still being deceitful I could not. But *nyame* says 'Even if *kialo* still lies you rub.' So I rub."

In the above seance we see how the theory that a ghost punishes his widow's remarriage functions in securing the children to the kin of the dead rather than to the kin of the new husband. The widow on remarriage is prevented from custody of the children sometimes, and generally through fears raised by the angry ghost-husband dogma. I never heard of a case of the ghost of a wife striking at a widower for remarrying.

27. *More Trouble over Custody of the Children*

Ndrapol,[119] a middle aged man who lived next to Ngandaliu was ill for five days. On the sixth evening he not recovering, a seance was held. Pikaro was again medium.

Pokenau: "*kukan!* what ghost strikes him."

kukan through medium: "*pwapwai* strikes him."

Pokenau: "So; let *pwapwai* come and talk." (*pwapwai* is the dead brother and Sir Ghost of Ndrapol.)

pwapwai as reported by *kukan* through medium: "I strike him on account of my daughter's leaving him and going with her mother. I strike Ndrapol for it."

Pokenau: "Yes. You strike him for it. Tomorrow they'll go and fetch your daughter to him. Let him recover."

pwapwai as reported by *kukan* through medium: "Yes. You go and recover her, and let her return and I can give Ndrapol health."

Pokenau: "Yes, at dawn she shall return." Then addressing his Sir Ghost, *sori*, the ghostly native constable of Pontchal.

"Policeman you of the ghosts! This man is ill. Now you tell all the ghosts that before they make attacks they must consult you first, you being police officer of the ghosts. Make them all yet tremble before you."

sori as reported by *kukan* through medium: "Yes. Now you were away at Mbunai village when this occurred. I was there with you naturally. We were both absent when this occurred. I know nothing of this attack. When I returned I heard of it. I vilified *pwapwai*, and he said, 'Now look here. I was not striking anyone so that he would die from it. I struck only to draw attention to what I wanted and to make it known. Now you talk. Well, that's all right. Tomorrow if my daughter returns to Ndrapol he shall recover."

Pokenau: "Policeman. Perhaps one other ghost struck him also."

sori reported by *kukan* through medium: "No."

[119] Ndrapol was a poor man of Pontchal gens, and the only man in Peri who had an Usiai wife. His house was the neatest in Peri, possibly because his wife did not engage in public life.

As usual a bowl of water received the soul stuff, which was put back where it belonged into Ndrapol. There had evidently been no divining done before the seance, as is usual in more seriously urgent cases, because reparation had not been made in advance of the seance, and Pokenau did not know of any other ghostly attacks than the one which the medium brought up.

This medium, it so happened, was confronted with a similar case in two successive seances, one over the child of the dead Kialo of Peri, one over Ndrapol. Pwapwai, as mortal, was married to Nyakareu. After his death she remarried, marrying Poiyo. At the time of Ndrapol's indisposition, Kisapwi, daughter of Pwapwai and Nyakareu, was staying with her mother, Nyakareu, instead of with her father's brother, Ndrapol.

The sequel was that Nyakareu was requested to give up Kisapwi to Ndrapol with whom she had been before. Nyakareu refused flatly, saying that, if Ndrapol's Sir Ghost did not like it, that was Ndrapol's bad luck. And to confound the medium, more or less, Ndrapol made a rapid and complete recovery. The medium and others hinted darkly at future trouble and stormed at Nyakareu. But Nyakareu was used to abuse. She was one of the two wives of one man. She told Kisapwi cooly that if she went to stay in Ndrapol's house he would kill her.

At first sight this type of seance result may appear aberrant from the general aspect of the spiritualistic system. It looks as if a Sir Ghost strikes down his ward in order to awaken pity and indemnity for his ward from some other person; wheras usually a Sir Ghost strikes down his ward in order to make his ward indemnify some other person, a precisely reverse proceeding. Actually the case is not such. The ward, as in the case of Ndrapol above, is not necessarily granted the custody of the children merely because he becomes ill. The ward is stricken by his Sir Ghost because he has acted in a morally weak way in letting the custody of the children slip from his hands. Only weak men fail in keeping the custody of the children, because custody depends on the dead father's kin having made economic validation of a child's betrothal. Thus where a man is stricken by his Sir Ghost for not having the custody of his dead brother's children he is stricken actually for economic slackness. The procedure for recovery of the custody is a financial laying out of wealth before the mother's brother makes the financial advance and so secures the children irrevocably. So actually, even in this case, a ward stricken by his Sir Ghost should give wealth to some other persons to assure his recovery, not be given as a present merely the custody of children.

In practice the type of man stricken for this kind of slackness may be unable to take the correct course for the correction of the slackness. In such case he depends for his recovery on chance rather than on the cure warranted by the social system. A wealthy and a strong man would not depend on chance similarly; but such a man would not normally allow himself to be put in a position that gave the oracles opportunity to correct him. Men like Ndrapol are made to appear as horrible examples, exemplars by negative instance of the Manus idiom that assimilates health, strength and riches under the one category and the one term, *pwokean*.

28. *Antagonism between Sisters-in-law*

To the house of Keah [120] had come his young sister to bear her child, sister in brother's house as is the custom. She had come from far away Pomatchau village. Some three weeks after the infant was born it seemed to be ailing, and the wife of Keah was medium in a seance held over it. Keah was a moron, and his wife was a moron; so her services as a medium were not in general demand. But as medium in her own husband's house she saved the fee that would have to be paid to another.

Control through medium to Keah: "My father, I did not strike this child, but *kisolel* struck it." (*kisolel* is Keah's father's sister's ghost.)

Keah: "Why?"

[120] Keah was a poor man of Kametatchau gens, a gens now almost wiped out. His wife had fixed delusions of his permanent infidelities such as Keah could never have accomplished at any time.

Control through medium: "Who knows? I don't know. However you stay and I'll go to Patusi and ask her."

After a pause, control through medium: "Loloan (Keah's younger sister, the new mother) stays here and her infant is close to death; *kisolel* came up by night and said, 'I said mother and child should not come to this village. The two should stay in Pomatchau. But the two came to this village (naturally enough, since *kisolel* had said nothing articulately before in disapproval). I was angry. I worked upon this child. Its body is sick from it. But give me a little water and I'll rub the soul stuff in it. I did not strike the child for any reason. I was just sorry for mother and child, and their having to come so far."

The infant's soul stuff was duly restored in the usual manner. This seance sounds imbecile, and actually was done by a stupid medium. But there is expressed crudely in it the usual Manus antagonism between sisters-in-law, Keah's wife venting the feeling on Keah's sister. The stupidity lies mainly in the crude way in which the feeling is so poorly disguised. The feeling between sisters-in-law would be disguised by a better medium who would give a ghostly father's sister a good reason for attacking the ghost's niece, the medium's sister-in-law. Then the medium could not be so easily charged with expressing personalities only of a mundane character.

The infant recovered, so that charge was not made, as it might have been else, and Keah's sister stayed on in Keah's house till the customary time was up some weeks later, and, her post birth taboos over, she rejoined her husband in Pomatchau village.

29. *In Comment*

Thus the month of March went with a number of minor illnesses here and there dealt out like scatter shot. I rather believe that almost any period, or every period, would present such an appearance, were it investigated with the utmost thoroughness. In previous months an interest in major calamities has rather obliterated our observation of the above type. But I knew that minor illnesses with their seances went on unobserved by me at times, for I had often learned of such events after they were past. But the reader can safely imagine the current of lesser illness and seances which I followed in March as a continuation of a similar current that probably flowed by while public attention was focussed on the death of Popwitch, or on the illnesses of Alupwai and Sali, the canoe wreck of Kalo, and so on.

I have now taken this diary through the events of four months. I stayed two months longer in Manus, but during the last two months I was in and out of Peri village a great deal; now I was on a visit to other places following up an investigation of mental defectiveness in some Peri family lines, now in the inland country of the Usiai to see an important ceremonial occasion, now in one or another of the many islands of the Matankor people, collecting kinship facts, general ethnography and material culture, and bartering for specimens. I always took off from Peri as a base. Hence I kept up with the important events of the next two months, and with occasional minor events also. But naturally the whole shoal of minor events did not fall into my net.

PART FIVE. APRIL AND MAY

30. *A Man in High Fever Cannot Account for it in Sin*

For these two months I have recorded an approximate chronology only. Except for one or two important events we shall neglect the exact dates.

One day I found Pomat [121] of Matchupal in a high fever of at least a hundred and four degrees. He was more than half delirious, but he recognised me and talked incessantly in the following fashion:

"Pwoikaton [122] and his wife raged at each other over shell money. She said to the child, 'You poor child, you are an orphan' (*i.e.*, Pwoikaton is as good as no father at all to you).

[121] Pomat was an economic dependent of Mbosai, financier of Matchupal gensmen generally, but especially close to Pomat.

[122] Pwoikaton, younger brother of Talikai and Nyakareu, half brother of Korotan (Pere gens).

The woman committed a sin in her wicked speech. But I cannot be ill for her sin. I have nothing to do with that house in any way.

(The semi-delirious man was correct here. This recent scandal was running through his head, but he was entirely unrelated to it.)

"Yes, I like quinine. I know it is good. I went to work for the white men. I worked for X. Pwoikaton's wife said, 'You poor child, you are an orphan.' That *pwanau* [123] cannot be killing me. When he was alive he used to come to my house. But I gave a pig towards his funerary feast, although he was not related to me. I gave a pig, and I have not been paid back for it. I lost a pig for *pwanau.*

"My sister has gone to get my soul stuff. It was stolen by a *tchinal* in the shore swamps. If that's no good I'm ill with a white man's trouble, and I'll try quinine. The ghosts have no cause of offence against me. I paid back the debt I contracted when they gave me a share of the sago feast for the marriage of the girl from Mok. I paid back my debt when all the others paid back theirs. Mine was a small share anyway. It was not much. The ghosts cannot have anything against me.

"The seance last night. There was a seance last night. I slept through it. I did not hear it. But they say my sister has gone to get my soul stuff from the *tchinal.*

"Then Nane laughed at us young fellows. He said that our line and generation was soft and degenerate not to have captured a foreign woman as a prostitute. So because he laughed at us we went and captured that Usiai woman. It was not our fault. It was Nane's for laughing at us. If this is not the *tchinal,* then it's a white disease."

Somewhere about this point the fever stricken man vomited and had to cease his flow of semi-delirious talk. He was remarkably silent as a well man. But all the items of the above comment he had repeated over and over, protesting ceaselessly.

The seance the night before, I gathered, had said that

[123] The Sir Ghost of Paliau (Pere gens).

topwal[124] had stricken Pomat, because they had both been in the affair in which the Usiai woman was captured as prostitute, and Topwal had died in prison for it, whereas Pomat had not died for it. Also it had raised the *tchinal* point. The fevered man was going over possibilities, and swearing his freedom from unpaid debt and cause of just offence. This canvassing of possible sins (and of impossible ones, such as Pwoikaton's wife's bad language which could not possibly be linked up with the sufferer) and declaration of duties fulfilled, was very striking, for the man was delirious, without being completely out of his senses, although nearly so. The capture of the prostitute was during the first days of Government suppression of the old custom of warfare, several years before.

31. *A Medium's Technique in an Unusual Situation*

A stranger from a Manus village, forty miles away, consulted Isole as medium. He wanted to know why his fishing results were consistently bad. The medium did not know his affairs at all. An interchange on the following lines took place.

Medium: "Your Sir Ghost is here. He asks what you want to know."

Stranger: "Why is my fishing bad? What have I done wrong?"

Medium: "He says that you know very well. You are concealing it."

Stranger (truculently): "What is it then I have done? I know nothing of it. (Addresses his Sir Ghost directly.) You, come out with it! Speak up and tell me. I want to hear it. I'd like to know."

[124] The Sir Ghost of Selan, *topwal*, was the ghost of the brother of Selan's adoptive father, Tchokar, of Pontchal gens. But Tchokar's wife's mother was of Matchupal gens, and Tchokar had affiliated himself strongly with Pontchal gens, Matchupal gens and Lo gens, Tchokar's own mother being of Lo gens. Selan followed Tchokar in this triple affiliation, especially as his blood brother, Ngandaliu, had been adopted by Kali of Lo gens. Pomat although of Matchupal gens strictly was assistant village constable of Pontchal gens, this latter gens having won political autonomy from the rest of Peri village from the white Administration. Matchupal and Pontchal gentes held adjoining territories and were often not kept sharply distinct.

Medium: "He says that you must speak first; he objects to the appearance of dissembling that you wear."

Stranger (in a veritable fury now): "I will not speak first. Let him speak. He's spoiled my fishing. It's up to him to account for his action, not up to me. I've done nothing that I shouldn't have done. I've paid all my debts. Nevertheless he spoils my fishing. Let him speak."

Medium (firmly): "He says, no! you must speak first."

Stranger: "About what? As if I had anything to conceal. I have not. You (rages at his Sir Ghost, looking above and beyond the medium's head at an invisible presence), you, come out with it. It's for you to speak and explain yourself, not for me to explain you. What have I done? Come on. Say now (the stranger's voice is straining into a yell. At this point the stranger's wife, seated nearby, is unable to endure the tension between her husband and the invisible presence any longer).

Stranger's wife in a low voice: "Is it because we did not pay the wife of Taliraku those pots?"

Medium: "He says that your concealment offended him. But he knew you failed to pay the wife of Taliraku the debt of pots you owed her. He waited for submission from you. Your fishing will not succeed until he has it. But once you have paid those pots, your fishing will come back to normal the day after."

Stranger, still in a temper: "Yes, but I have to buy some pots first. And if I get no fish what can I buy pots with?"

Medium, sternly: "Your fishing will recover the day after you pay your long overdue debt, not before."

32. *Medium's Technique Again*

The aged wife of Maku [125] (also an aged person) fell ill. The seance was made by the medium Pikaro with her control *pokamitch*. Pikaro called up *pokamitch*, who professed ignorance of the affair promptly.

[125] The wife of Maku was functionally of Pontchal gens, her mother's gens. She resided in Matchupal gens in the house of a former husband of that gens. Maku was of another village which he had left.

Ndrapol:[126] "Where is *topwal*?"

Control through medium: "He is down in his house" (Selan's house).

Ndrapol: "Let him come."

topwal[127] through control through medium: "I did not strike her. But lately she went to Patusi village and there the wife (ghostly) of *saliwiti* (a ghost there) struck her. Her soul is at Patusi."

Control through medium: "You all stay here while *topwal* and I go to Patusi to recover her soul stuff."

After a long wait, control through medium: "We went to *pakob* and *pominis*, both cross-cousins through their mothers to this village of Peri; *topwal* said to them, 'You two cross-cousins of the wife of Maku, behind me she is on the point of death.' *pakob* replied, 'Which ghost strikes her?' *topwal* said, 'Your mother, the wife of *saliwiti*.' *pakob* returned, 'Well then, let us go to my mother.' We went to her. 'Why do you strike the wife of Maku?' She said, 'From the fashion of old, the fashion of us ghosts. Some die. Some remain mortal. We who die see the mortal survivors and we strike them down.' *pakob*, 'Well, give me the soul stuff that I may give it to *topwal*.' She gave it; *topwal* received it. *topwal* said (to *pakob*), 'My cross-cousin,[128] you ask your mother if it is all here. If she says it is all there, let us punt home. If part is not delivered yet let us wait in the canoe.' His mother said, 'It's all given you.' We

[126] Ndrapol was of Pontchal gens, and was present as a neighbour. He was poor and fairly old, like Maku and his wife, and therefore friendly.

[127] This *topwal* was the Sir Ghost of a neighbour of Maku, Selan, the ward, living nearby. Maku's own Sir Ghost was old and unimportant, where *topwal* was new, important, and of Pontchal gens.

[128] *pakob* and *pominis* were sons of a Pontchal gens woman married into Patusi, who now as a ghost is the ghostly wife of *saliwiti; topwal* as the son of a Pontchal man is of course cross-cousin to *pakob* and *pominis*, sons of a Pontchal woman. Of course *topwal* cannot be cross-cousin to *pakob* and *pominis* in exactly the same sense that the wife of Maku is cross-cousin to *pakob* and *pominis*, as she is reckoned to be above. The mother of the wife of Maku was of Pontchal; therefore the wife of Maku is cross-cousin to Pontchal in the same sense as *pakob* and *pominis* are. But the wife of Maku has taken to herself her mother's place. Therefore she is thereby Pontchal herself. This is just how elastically kinship in Manus is reckoned.

punted away. The soul stuff we have brought here. It rests in the house."

After all the preceding seances the reader will note the sheer effrontary of the above oracular diagnosis. The medium alleges no sin, but only impersonal malice of the ghosts. It is interesting to note the case as an instance of the latitude that the oracles allow themselves. The seance continued to a second issue.

topwal through control through medium: "That from Patusi village we have settled; but one still from Peri village not yet."

Ndrapol: "Who of Peri village strikes her?"

Medium (for the other plane, as always): "*nyalel*, the mother of Pwoikaton." [129]

Ndrapol: "She strikes her for what reason?"

topwal through control through medium: "I'll go to her." (After a wait) "I went to *pwoitchon*. I said to him, 'Cross-cousin,[130] your sister, the wife of Maku,[131] is near death.' He said, 'Which ghost strikes her?'

"I said, '*nyalel* strikes her. The daughter of *nyalel*, Nyakareu, and the daughter of the wife of Maku, Kampon, became the two wives of the one man, (Poiyo). For their obscenity to each other Nyalel died.' At first she said, 'Let the wife of Maku live and be with the two daughters.' Now she says, 'No matter about the two daughters. I, the

[129] As mortal Nyalel was sister of Papi-Talipoitchalon of Kalo gens. Potoan, former head-man of Peri, by his first wife begat Korotan, now the head-man. Potoan later married Nyalel and by her begat Talikai, Pwoitchon, Pwoikaton and Nyakareu. Talikai is living now and is Korotan's probable successor; *pwoitchon* is now a ghost married to *ile* and a parent of *popwitch* junior. Pwoikaton is living; so also is Nyakareu, now one of the wives of Poiyo.

[130] *topwal's* mother was of Kapet gens, and a sister of *topwal's* mother married Papi-Talipoitchalon, brother of Nyalel, the mother of Pwoitchon. Thus *topwal* is (somewhat metaphorically) a child of Papi-Talipoitchalon, and a cross-cousin of *pwoitchon*.

[131] The wife of Maku belonged to Kapet gens. She therefore stood in the same relationship to *pwoitchon* as did *topwal;* but as the wife of Maku, when classified (metaphorically) as the child of Papi-Talipwoitchalon, is a woman out of a man, whereas *pwoitchon* is a man out of a woman (as child of Nyalel), the wife of Maku and *pwoitchon* are terminologically brother and sister, not cross cousins. This is dependent upon the peculiarity of the Manus kinship system which classifies a man's mother's brother's daughter as a sister.

mother of one of them, died for their sins. Let the mother of the other now die also for their sins.'

"Then *pwoitchon* went and abused *nyalel.* He said, 'This talk of yours about killing the wife of Maku for the obscenity and scandal between the dual wives is not good. When all the ghosts and all the mortals first heard that obscenity and scandal, all the ghosts, the ghost of your brother, the ghost of your mother, the ghost of your father said you should die. You died. But now you strike down a mortal for what? Only if her brother, if her mother, if her father say she should die, should she die. If they say she should live then should she live. It is not for you to interfere. Who are you? Hand the soul stuff over here.'

"She gave it to him. He gave it to me. I have thrown the soul stuff into the water."

The oracle here made unusual use of a common dogma. It is a common usage to say in a seance. "If Sir Ghost of his says he must die, then die he must; if his Sir Ghost says he must live, then he must needs live." By conventional statement a person's own Sir Ghost or own family ghosts are responsible for his life or death. By conventional usage, moreover, a person's own Sir Ghost or own family ghosts are usually held responsible for chastising him or her with sickness.

In the above case the medium avoids the conventional usage, picking out as the angry ghost the sick woman's daughter's co-wife's mother's ghost, a far cry from the conventional family ghost. She then uses the convention to overcome the angry ghost as selected, on the ground that the ghost is trespassing outside its field. So the sick person is recovered.

By conventional usage a Sir Ghost is not normally held responsible for a ward's death as we have seen. That may happen, but the tendency is to pick rather upon a malicious ghost. The oracle in her above seance does not reckon with this fact. She is using rather the oft-repeated dogma as voiced in hundreds of seances, "If his Sir Ghost says that he shall die, he dies; if that he shall live, he lives," a dogma not fully observed in practice, the real practice not being formulated.

The medium is using a convention in an unconventional way. I do not know whether she was aware of it or not. Naturally she could not tell me as she was ostensibly inspired, and prepared to swear to inspiration to the end. But I believe that the oracles acquire the conventions that are customary in such an easy and loose impressionistic manner that they may possibly be unaware of such innovation as the above. Of course they are not at all unaware of the use of native police ghosts instead of ghostly dogs in ghost intimidation; Man of Lorengau was not unaware of the great changes that his proposed reform of the holding of seances would entail; everyone was aware that the idea of a death such as *topwal's*, for capturing a foreign woman as prostitute, would not have been raised in the old days of war, and free capture of such prostitutes. Indeed everyone professed an awareness that the ghosts had not been interested in the maintainence of any kind of sex morality at all in the preceding generation. But this on examination turned out to be a mythical Golden Age.[132] The young men put it in the generation of their fathers. But when I examined some old men of that generation still living they in turn put it in the generation of their fathers. And when I found an old man or two of that generation still alive they also put it in the generation of their fathers. I do not know how far it might have gone back had it been ascertainable. It had become a tradition, but there is one fact in its favour as possible fact at some stage of the past. All the surrounding tribes settled breaches of sex morality by expiatory payment somewhat in the Manus manner but without thought of ghosts. Their ghosts were concerned only with unmade funerary feasts or with marriages of widows. Now we have detailed evidence showing that a change in secular custom, the abolition of war and of securing prostitutes by war, led to the ghosts punishing the taking of the last prostitute in Peri (after the Government edict against it) upon the person of one,

[132] Of free rape within the community itself, not rape of war captives from other communities. This Manus idea resembles some of the ideas in our own culture about "Cave Men."

Topwal, who became *topwal* for it. So it is possible that the mere presence of the old secular custom of expiatory payment for sex offence may have been subject to an innovation of attributing ghostly anger at sex offence. Presumably there always had been mortal anger.

However, that may be, there can be no doubt that the system is elastic. The oracles do not learn rules to follow; they gather impressions young, then as full blown oracles later they act upon their impressions of the traditions. But they do not feel bound to act upon precedent. I thought I was well used to Pikaro, the above medium, but in the above seance over the wife of Maku she made two unusual moves. First she made one ghost act without a shadow of reason. Secondly she applied an old dogma in a new fashion, using it in the same essential spirit as when the mediums sometimes use ghostly dogs, or native police ghosts to collect soul stuff.

33. *In Economic Difficulties*

The following two seances illustrate further the other type of seance than that over illness. A man called Pigs-a-Hundred came from Patusi village to consult Isole and her control, *tchemilo*. His one and only domestic pig had broken away, gone wild and been lost in the jungle on shore for thirty days now. He had tried to cut sago, but he had found his sago palms without good pith. Finally his son had just returned from working for the white man, but, with all his pay, he had not come to his father. He and his pay had gone to his mother and to his mothers' brothers (father and mother being divorced and of different villages).

Through Isole *tchemilo* told Pigs-a-Hundred that he should have moved his house seawards with the others. Patusi village at this time was in a state of upheaval. A large part of it was moving from a place of bad luck (*i.e.*, of ghostly displeasure) close inshore to a new site further out. Pigs-a-Hundred was apparently slow in moving. At least *tchemilo* represented Pigs-a-Hundred's Sir Ghost to that effect.

The unfortunate man replied, "Yes, but I must have sago to barter for tobacco wherewith to purchase labour to make possible my house-moving, and my sago palms are cursed by you (*i.e.*, his Sir Ghost) so that I cannot move my house. Then you cause my pig to run away and be lost. Send back my pig, if only instead of the pay I should get from my wife's people because they have my son and his earnings. And make my sago palms good so that I may move my house."

In short the man represented himself as so cursed by his Sir Ghost that he was almost ham-strung in all capacity to remove the cause of offence, a common plea.

34. *No House, No Fish!*

Nyapo's fishing became so bad at one point that he had a seance to determine why. The oracle quickly told him. Nyapo, without a house of his own, stayed with Pomalat of Pontchal early in my stay in Peri. Soon the wife of Pomalat and the wife of Nyapo quarrelled over dogs' teeth division. Nyapo [133] then went to Kampwen's house. Kampwen fell ill and the oracles said it was because Kampwen's Sir Ghost objected to having Nyapo's Sir Ghost in his house. So by the month of May Nyapo was staying in an old previously deserted ramshackle house. The oracles said Nyapo's Sir Ghost was disgusted with him for not sheltering him in a good new house. Nyapo had not been quick about house building. So his Sir Ghost was spoiling his fishing.

Nyapo replied that he had a pig and stores of oil ready towards paying for a new house. But he needed fish to barter for taro and tobacco, also necessary for paying for a new house. How could he give his Sir Ghost what he wanted if his Sir Ghost frustrated the necessary means to that end?

As is clear from the above two seances the Sir Ghost in causing bad luck economically can usually be answered back, and usually is answered back, in a manner that is not so relevant in cases of illness. The Sir Ghost is so strongly an

[133] Nyapo had recently come to Peri village. He was a comparative outsider with no close kin in Peri. His alliances with Pomalat and Kampwen were merely the alliances of men who were friendly in a common poverty and comparative insignificance. He was theoretically related to Kalaat gens, which he never lived near, or made any claims upon. This relationship was through his wife, but it was not close relationship even to her.

upholder of economic soundness, and of debt paying, house building and the like that when he paralyses his ward's economic affairs, his ward can point to double-faced behaviour, or at least to ghost imposed hindrance to ghost desired ends. Perhaps it is because of this logic vested in the sinner that the resort to the oracle for diagnosis of Sir Ghost caused economic hindrance is not frequent. The economic set-back has to be very serious indeed before such resort is made. It is not popular and it is not very satisfactory to anyone. Slight economic set-backs do not lead to seances, as slight illnesses often do—if one may compare degrees of seriousness.

35. *A Sister Does Not Help Her Brother*

Pwentchiam, a woman, fell ill in the house of Pokenas. Pwentchiam usually stayed in Patusi village into which she was married. This was her only appearance in Peri village during my stay. Her mother's (but not her father's) son was Pokenas. The wife of Pokenas acted as medium.

The mother of Pwentchiam (or of Pwentchakup, as the daughter was also named) by her first marriage, to a man of Mbunai village, bore a son, Poitchapet by name. By her second marriage, to a man of Lopwer gens of Peri village, she bore Pokenas, a son, and Nyambulel, a daughter. Nyambulel was now married to her fourth husband, Talikai. We have told that Talikai had two wives, Lomot, who was living with him, being one. Nyambulel, who was not living with him, but who had retired to the house of her mother, was the other.

By her third marriage this mother of Poitchapet, Pokenas and Nyambulel, bore Pongi, a son, and Pwentchiam, a daughter. The mother also bore others who died as infants whom we may neglect here; an account of the causes of their deaths appeared in the list of the believed causes of infantile mortality. The father of Pongi and of Pwentchiam was of Patusi village, but Pongi lived in a ramshackle house in Peri village with his mother and his half sister, Nyambulel. Poitchapet was dead now, and as *poitchapet* was Sir Ghost to Pongi, his half brother through a common mother. Thus *poitchapet* was not a Sir Ghost in his own proper patrilineal line.

The wife of Pokenas opened the seance over Pwentchiam by ordering her control to summon *poitchapet* on the plea that her daughter (and Pokenas' daughter), Kamutal, was ill. (This Kamutal must be kept distinct from the elder Kamutal who was the mother of Paliau. The wife of Pokenas was barren and this Kamutal was her adopted daughter.) When *poitchapet* appeared he was asked why he struck down Pwentchiam, his half sister (a fact probably known already from divination). The ghost *poitchapet* immediately declared that the control had summoned him here by a lying pretext. Kamutal was not ill at all. But he proceeded to tell what was required of him.

Pwentchiam and Nyambulel had joined forces and food supplies to give away as a gift for which a return of dogs' teeth would be made; *poitchapet* objected to Pwentchiam helping Nyambulel, her half sister, instead of Pongi, her full brother. Pongi kept *poitchapet's* skull and looked after it. Dogs' teeth should come into the house of Pongi and beneath the eye of *poitchapet.* Pwentchiam should help her own house, not another's.

In reply Pwentchiam said "Pongi is not rich or strong. He is lazy, and he does not help us women in our affairs." The ghost *poitchapet* was inexorable, however. He knew Pongi was lazy. He knew Pongi had made no move towards gathering food to contribute himself, as Nyambulel had. But Pongi looked after his skull, and he looked after Pongi, and Pwentchiam was Pongi's full sister. So he struck down Pwentchiam. But now he would rub the soul stuff in the water. If only he had known that the control wanted him for Pwentchiam he would not have come. His presence was obtained by a lie of the control's, pretending that it had been Kamutal who was ill.[134]

36. *A Medium's Self-Interest*

Selan's two months' old infant fell ill. Selan himself as medium discovered that his Sir Ghost and control was angry

[134] This trick of the medium, the wife of Pokenas, comes into agreement with her general use of tricks such as languorous voice, and appearance of remoteness and difficulty, not generally used by other Peri mediums.

at him for not building fast enough the new house he had in project. Pokenau, who like Selan was of Pontchal gens, had been cutting and working sago to give to Kalaat (Turtle) gens in an economic exchange that was pending. The exchange was mainly between a part of Pere gens and Kalaat, Pokenau being involved by distant relationship only. Pokenau had cut into two palms that had proved to be deficient in sago pith. He asked Selan, as medium, at the close of the above seance, to ask *sori*, his Sir Ghost, why his sago palms yielded next to nothing. To this *sori* answered that Pokenau was cutting his sago with the project of entering into a gift to Kalaat, when he should have been thinking to devote his sago to help his gens "brother," Selan to provide the feast to pay for the communal work preparatory to Selan's projected house building. As soon as he began to cut sago for the right purpose his sago palms would prove to be good. Accordingly next day and for some days thereafter Pokenau was at work cutting his sago to help with Selan's project. And Selan gained a point from the illness of his infant, and his seance over it.

37. *Custody of Children*

Songan, an old man of Kalo gens, and probably the oldest man in Peri, fell ill. His sister, Itong,[135] acted as medium. She diagnosed his case as due to the fact that Songan's son's daughter, a child, had gone to live with Songan's son's divorced wife, when the child should have continued to live with its father, as it had before. We have met with this type of diagnosis several times before. Songan's Sir Ghost, the ghost of a dead son, was protesting for the rights of his living brother by acting upon Songan. I do not know whether the child was recovered by the father or not in this case. An illness brings strong pressure to bear upon the offender, when it is represented that the illness is caused by the offence. But

[135] This was the mother of Bonyalo, the dependent of Paliau. She had two controls, *polum* and *pokamitch*. In some of her seances one only appears, in other seances, the other. Theoretically *polum* was supposed to recover soul stuff on the air or on land, *pokamitch* soul stuff to get which the control had to dive underwater; further *polum* was the ghost of a white person, *pokamitch*, the ghost of the medium's own son.

small children and divorced mothers are sometimes notoriously hard-hearted. In any case Songan recovered quickly.

38. *Lapse of Kin Duties, and a Quarrel*

The wife of Maku fell ill again and Maku with her this time. Pikaro was summoned in as medium. She said first that Maku and his wife had neglected to help Selan in his activities directed towards the building of his new house. Selan's Sir Ghost, *topwal*, was striking them for it. Selan had recently slept in Maku's house while his wife had born a child in Selan's house, looked after by her brother who had taken over Selan's house for the time. In the second place Maku and his wife had not gone overseas to obtain coconuts necessary for a feast to release *tchokar's* widow from her year of mourning for *tchokar*, whereas many others had already done so; for this neglect *tchokar* was striking them. It appeared that Maku and his wife had slept in the house of *tchokar* after *tchokar's* death. Maku was related to *tchokar* through his wife. This *tchokar* who had adopted Selan (and also Poiyo at one stage) was an ancestor of a part of the group that now form Pontchal gens, but were, in their ancestors' generations, of Pere gens. Maku's wife was of Kapet gens, but she was resident in the house of one of her former husbands who was of Matchupal gens. Her mother had been of Pontchal gens and a sister to *tchokar*. Her residence in Matchupal gens territory made her a functioning member of Pontchal gens, if of any, as the territories of the two gentes adjoined, and most of the members of both gentes had been associated in the act of making a Usiai affinal relative of Korotan a captive prostitute (the act which led to the splitting of Pere gens into Pere and Pontchal gentes). Thus Pontchal and Matchupal often worked as a unit, so that a woman living in a Matchupal house whose only relative of the territory had been a mother of Pontchal gens was indubitably Pontchal, since the wife of Maku took her mother's affiliation before that of a former husband (although she and her present husband lived in her former husband's house).

As for Maku, he came from another village and lived in his

wife's place. So he was functionally of Pontchal also. As both Maku and his wife were old and poor they had not contributed much weight to the exchanges for *tchokar* at the death. So *tchokar* struck them for neglect.

It may be noted that the spiritualistic system here acts as a reminder to persons such as Maku and his wife that they actually have some kin affiliation and some kin duties. The pair had almost slipped out of any kin affiliation, since Maku was away from all of his kin permanently, while Maku's wife's kin of Kapet gens were no longer in Peri village, having all moved out to other villages, and she lived in a former husband's place, where she had no kin, except for the accident of close union based on neighbouring residence between Pontchal and Matchupal.

Both Selan and Pokenau were present at this seance. Both of them immediately became nervous, for they also were related to *tchokar*, and they also were involved. Neither of them had gone with those who had made the trip overseas to buy coconuts. Selan and Pokenau both pleaded pressure of work on Selan's projected house building, and *tchokar* through the control through the medium accepted their excuses and restored the soul stuffs of Maku and his wife. But Selan as *tchokar's* adopted son, and Pokenau as a member of a close paternal collateral line were really far greater sinners than the unfortunate, almost decrepit couple, Maku and his wife.

Word came to Peri of the illness of Paka, an important man of Mok village, between thirty and forty miles away; I rarely received details of illnesses or deaths in other villages, but concerning Paka I acquired fairly full information.

Some years before many of the present Mok villagers had lived near Tokumal Island, in the sea shallows adjoining that otherwise uninhabited island. Under the leadership of one, Pomat, they left that site for Mok. Now, about two and a half years after Pomat's death, his son, Paka leased the island with its coconut palms to Leu, a Chinaman, for a hundred sticks of tobacco. The others of Mok were furious with Paka, thinking incorrectly that he had sold the freehold outright. To appease them Paka divided the tobacco amongst them. Almost immediately after he fell ill.

The medium represented his Sir Ghost, *pomat*, as saying: "Previously when you gave Tokumal Island to Leu all Mok maligned you. They prosecuted you in the white Court and lost their case. But you distributed the tobacco amongst them. You were afraid of them."

Paka: "So! I was not afraid. But I said they should all have the tobacco."

Medium representing *pomat*: "You gave the tobacco to them. So now I am angry. I strike you for it. Let all that tobacco be returned to you and I will let you recover."

The recipients actually gave Paka back all the tobacco. There was one more count in the seance. The medium represents *pomat*, Paka's Sir Ghost, as saying: "The people of Rambutchon sent word to you that you should sail there. I am angry at the idea. I strike you in order that I may forbid it. Last time you and I sailed there a gale struck us, and we two drifted before it."

Paka: "So. Well, give me health, and if later on you say we may go, then we'll go. If then you say again we must not go, then we shall not go."

Medium representing *pomat:* "So. There is only a son of our line left in Rambutchon. There is not one cross-cousin of ours left there, not one mother's brother or one mother's brother's son. Only the one mother's brother's grandson. Only he wept over our drifting before the gale, only he came to you. So when this word came for you to sail again I was against it."

Paka: "Yes. All our relatives there are dead. And when we drifted we got no sympathy from the others. All right, you strike me to prevent my going again. Now make me better."

Medium representing *pomat:* "Yes. I will recover you."

Paka: "So, a village of ghosts, a village of sickness of white origin (*i.e.*, a time of illness is on the village). Only if you wish to travel do I travel." (Overseas trips are deprecated as dangerous when there is much sickness or death in the home village; then such voyages are not usually undertaken.)

Medium representing *pomat:* "Yes, maybe later on I shall say that you may go."

Paka duly recoverd, later news came, relieving some anxiety felt by some relatives of his in Peri.

39. *A Family Affair*

The fishing baskets of a man called Pomalat caught no fish. His wife, Nyamasim, acted as medium. The medium's control [136] disclaimed all knowledge of the identity of the ghost that had taken the spirit of the fishing baskets, and advised Pomalat to ask his Sir Ghost. The Sir Ghost [137] at first denied any hand in it. Pomalat told him he lied. Then the Sir Ghost admitted having taken it because Pomalat had not paid fish, taro and betel nut to Ngandaliu, a payment that Pomalat was planning to make, but had not made yet. Pomalat told his Sir Ghost again that he lied. At this the Sir Ghost admitted that Pomalat was right. Ngandaliu had not called for that debt. It was not due yet, as Pomalat said. He had not taken the spirit of the fishing baskets at all. The Sir Ghost of Ngandaliu [138] had taken it (no reason given—evidently perseveration in the medium's mind). He would go to the Sir Ghost of Ngandaliu, get the spirit, and restore it. This was done, and Pomalat's Sir Ghost advised Pomalat that the matter was righted. He should fish again tomorrow and see if it was not righted.

A weak medium this, and a worsting for her, on the whole; however, from the Manus view, a worsting of a Sir Ghost rather than of a medium. This seance appears to have been rather more indecorous than most. However from one aspect it was a purely domestic affair and therefore quite fitting in its lack of decorum.

40. *Ghosts and Fish*

Pomaleu, more generally known as the son of Paliau (*i.e.*, son-in-law of Paliau) speared a turtle, but lost the turtle,

[136] *nouna* by name.

[137] *katoli* by name.

[138] The Sir Ghost of Ngandaliu was of Pontchal gens, of which gens Pomalat was a member. Ngandaliu, himself, was of Pontchal gens or of Lo gens as he felt inclined, his brother Selan having been adopted into Pontchal, and he himself into Lo gens.

spear and all. He summoned in the medium, Pikaro, and consulted his Sir Ghost, *kialo* [139] to say why this sad thing had occurred. His Sir Ghost did not even bother to disclaim responsibility, saying only, "Who knows; it's just the way of fish." Not a word more could be got from *kialo* except a recommendation to Pomaleu to go back and look in the spot of the spearing again next day, a recommendation without a promise attached, however.

41. *Magician's Method*

Patalian, the magician, as a bachelor, almost made a bachelor's simple living out of his magic alone these months. He performed exorcism over Alupwai's new-born infant, then later in Alupwai's subsequent illness twice over Alupwai. Now Alupwai's sister, Lawa was newly delivered of an infant, and Patalian exorcised the infant. Because of his feud with Kalo gens, Kalo having refused him a wife that he had partly paid for in advance and kept the payment, he collected fees for his exorcism in that quarter. He could not approach Lawa herself, as she was the woman he had been foiled of marrying. The infant was taken into another house away from its mother temporarily to allow Patalian access to it for his exorcising. Then over and above these retainings, resulting from an old quarrel, Patalian in April had two retainings of a more general nature. Two youths, who had been working on a white plantation on the mainland of New Guinea, returned to Loitcha village, just beyond Patusi. They, although well and healthy, were still afraid of the New Guinea sorcerers, and they asked for an exorcism of any sorcery that might be in their bodies. Then later in April an open threat of attack by sorcery was made by Korotan to Selan, and Selan briefed Patalian to protect him. I had opportunity to observe Patalian's exorcising method several times. He began by taking ginger, an aromatic herb (*ku*) and a piece of bark that smelt like cinnamon (*moso* by native name) and chewing them with betel nut and lime. Then he intoned:

[139] The same *kialo* that afflicted Alupwai and Sali, according to oracles friendly to Paliau, and friendly to Pomaleu or Son-of-Paliau.

A little of the "medicines" (lit. herbs)
of the magic of *sobalabalue*,
it was of the shore of the West,
it came down to me from there.
it came out of Kwimborokol
(a place of *tchinal* spirits)
it climbed out of that cavern
it came out of Pwalikiu
(a place of *tchinal* spirits)
Amusim of Pwalikiu
carried his ginger, his *ku*, his *moso*
stood in the entrance of his house.
He made his magic with it.
The children new from their mothers died
of it, the sons died of it,
the daughters died of it.
One watched the morning star;
at its rising he washed his son in
coconut milk
at its rising he washed his daughter in
coconut milk.
Tidings of it went to Palitaui.
The chief of Palitaui went up,
went to the cavern of Pwalikiu
wishing to acquire the magic of *sobalabalue*.
The chief of Pwalikiu offered him food.
He refused it; offered him water;
he refused it; offered him betel nut;
he refused it; offered him wind magic;
he refused it; offered him magic of the stone;
he refused it; offered him love magic;
he refused it.
The Chief of Pwalikiu said, "What do you want?
"I want the magic of *sobalabalue*."
He gave him one piece of ginger
(as earnest of having given him the magic with it)
He took it and went to his place, to Palitaui.
He directed it against women.
Their infants remained well.
The chief of Palitaui cursed him;
"Let him copulate with his mother,
let him copulate with his sister;
he deceived me over the magic;
he did not give me the magic in reality
it still rests in its original place in Pwalikiu."

PLATE IX

A BRIDAL CANOE

Tidings of it went.
The chief of Meli went up
wishing to acquire the magic of Pwalikiu.

(Then follows a repetition of what happened to the chief of Palitaui. It appears, from the only variation in wording, that the power of the magic is conveyed from one person to another by the old owner giving the new owner a piece of ginger which should be a piece of the "original" ginger that first held the charm. For the deceitful giving is phrased in this second case, "He gave him a wrong, non-sacred piece of ginger." Patalian claimed to use a piece of the original ginger in his own charm, not ordinary ginger, but a fetish piece.)

Following two failures by two men to get the magic, the speaker told how his grandfather got it.

"My grandfather went to the cavern of Pwalikiu.

"The chief of Pwalikiu gave him betel nut, he refused it. (And so also water, food, coconuts, wind magic, love magic etc.)

"'Well what do you want?'

"'I want the magic of *sobalabalue*.'

"The chief of Pwalikiu said:

"'You have not been in unseemly haste to acquire it.'

"He gave the magic to my grandfather. My grandfather purchased it with good dogs' teeth, good shell money, good wooden bowls.

"He took it to Nouna Island.

"He worked with it on all the infants of Nouna.

"He acquired dogs' teeth, shell money and wooden bowls thereby.

"Many men asked him for the magic.

"They offered dogs' teeth, shell money and wooden bowls. He did not give it away.

"My mother bore me. I was yet small. I stayed yet upon my mother's thighs.

"He gave me ginger, *moso, ku*

"He pressed my body to his, and sent his magic firmly into me.

"I came in time to Manus,

"I exorcise the infants of all women with it,

"When the (evil of the) magic is broken by fees of dogs' teeth, shell money and wooden bowls.

"All break (the evil effects of) my magic so.

"So our village becomes well."

Patalian recited the above history before exorcising an infant. The original owner of the magic was of Pwalikiu. Now Pwalikiu never was a place of human habitation. It was spiritually inhabited. When Patalian spoke of his grandfather going and getting it from the magic's owner there, after others had failed, he usually called the owner, "the chief of Pwalikiu." But sometimes he called him Amusim, a familiar figure in the myths. Only he did not always stick to Amusim. At another exorcism he mentioned Elau, another familiar figure in the myths, as the "chief of Pwalikiu."

The history varied also when he exorcised an adult, rather than an infant. It was still the same history, and the same magic, only the references to the "infants new from their mothers," sickening from the magic and recovering from the exorcism, were not made, nor the references to "all women, their sons and daughters." The remark about the "washing in coconut milk as the morning star rises" was not made in other reference either. It referred to the custom of pouring green coconut milk over the body of an infant in the exorcism of it. When an adult was exorcised the replacement of the references omitted was:

> He said (*i.e.*, the giver of the magic)
> magic shall not hurt you;
> *kussi* (a type of black magic) shall not hurt you;
> *melo* (another type of black magic) shall not hurt you;
> you will be able to walk anywhere
> in the midst of everyone.
> Do but chew this ginger
> and go freely unhurt.

This was spoken with due repetition, of course.

The actual exorcism of infant or adult was done in the general manner already described for other magicians than Patalian. Thus in exorcism of an infant the magician chewed betel nut, ginger, etc., and called upon the names of the familiars that were his exclusive property. He spat the herbal mixture into coconut milk and commanded the familiars to come out on top of that liquid concoction which was then poured over the infant in a kind of baptism. Then the *tcheritcheri* painting of the infant in certain parts of the body followed. Then the familiars were summoned to come out on top of the pay for the ceremony, and to come away with the pay and the magician.

In the exorcism of an adult the magician chewed a betel nut, ginger, etc., called on the name of his familiars, commanded them to come out on top of the betel nut, ginger, etc. mixture which he then spat on to the seat of illness or supposed seat of illness. He then swept away the familiars from the seat of illness with *ti* leaves. The magician then usually calls the familiars' attention to the pay and tells them to go on top of it and come away with it. Patalian did this.

The above acts are stereotyped, coconut milk for infants, but sweeping away with *ti* leaves for adults, for example. What I learned from watching Patalian was that exactly the same magic was used for infant as for adult exorcism, with a slight variation in the words of the history and of the exorcism itself to make it appropriate. Moreover the magician takes full liberty in wording his exorcism, so that he may make it refer to a purely individual idiosyncrasy of an individual case and occasion, if he so wills.

The theory of the use of betel nut, ginger and other herbs, aromatic or hot, of the conveying of these herbs partly masticated to the patient's body seems to be the enticing of the familiars out of the body concerned; for the familiars are supposed to be in the body doing damage there prior to exorcism. But apart from the local theory, the practice goes where that particular Manus theory does not. I know it in the Massim, as an example.

Generally speaking a magician is supposed to be able to exorcise his own familiars only, so that the man whose magic did the damage must be the one to remove it. This is a dogma generally bowed to, but on occasion it is ignored for practical reasons—as, for instance, when Patalian exorcised the two youths who believed that they had influences of New Guinea mainland sorcery in them, and who wanted some exorcism, any that it was practicable to obtain; and again when Patalian exorcised Selan because Korotan threatened in a public rage and fury to sorcerise Selan to death, and the village knew that after the exhibition he gave he could not publicly relent for a year or two at least. Certainly he could not pronounce an exorcism immediately, and meanwhile Selan must have some protection from him. A sorcerer who has gone to the last length, fully aware of the seriousness of his expressed intention, cannot be asked a day or two after for an exorcism, nor compelled to give it—not in Manus. No exorcism is ever secured by threat of violence against the sorcerer. For the man who deliberately shouts out that he will sorcerise another to death simply courts violence, if any is offering. If it is not offering, then he for his part is content to use the supernatural weapon only. And his opponent must break the usual dogma and practice by briefing another than the causer of damage or of potential damage as the curer and exorcist of it. Apparently the usual dogma and practice have been broken on such occasions before I saw it so broken in Manus. Aversion to violence causes it to be broken in Manus, as propensity to theft (but not aversion to violence) causes the same usual dogma and practice to break down on occasion in Dobu, as I have shown elsewhere in my account of the Dobuans.

Beyond the general similarities of Manus magic as practised by different magicians, differences will be noted. Man of Lorengau names as the fetish object of his magic, "The Wooden Bowl of the *Nam*," Patalian names a special piece of magically consecrate ginger "of the *Sobalabalue*." Another magician's (Songan's) fetish was a stone.

The herbs are generally the same, betel nut, ginger, and a green coconut or *tï* leaves, but other herbs, *ku*, *kawe*, *moso* (all aromatic) may or may not be added.

Man of Lorengau had some special uses of his own—the sea weeds, star fish, sea anemone, *paris* and *endros* leaves used in his magic concoction, and the feast of special foods that had to be made before he would complete his work. In this latter connection I may add that the other magicians knew of special foods that should be dealt with as a conclusion to their magic, Man of Lorengau had a giant crab and *pongapong* fruit; Korotan had a special species of fish called *karawin*, and the ceremony was called *karawin tchariti*, or "cutting up *karawin*," but Korotan never had this ceremony performed and was vague about it. I could not even be sure that it was a concluding feast, as with Man of Lorengau's giant crab, but it might have been. Other magicians had their special species of fish, but they were as vague as Korotan also. Each of these magicians warned his patient to refrain from eating the special food connected with his magic for a week or two after the exorcism. What was a feast enforced on his patients with Man of Lorengau was a taboo enforced on patients with other practitioners. But the other practitioners all said that there should have been a ceremony with the food to close the exorcism, only they had never insisted upon it, and they were not sure of its nature now. An examination of the histories of the magic already discussed shows that Patalian's came from his grandfather who was a native of Nouna Island, an outlying western island of the archipelago with a Matankor population (Patalian had been adopted in Manus as a child captive taken in war, but had visited Nouna subsequently twice); Pope's magic was from a man of Lolomondru, an Usiai place; Man of Lorengau's magic was from his mother's brother who was an Usiai, who had it from a Ndrukul man (of an Usiai tribe of the north); Korotan's magic was from his cross-cousin, who had it from his father (both Manus) who had it from a man of Ndrombut, a Matankor place. Thus no magic discussed, as yet, claims anything more than a recent arrival in Manus possession from either Usiai or Matankor sources. The case is such for all the magic practised in Manus. An Usiai magician can give a longer history, sometimes thirty names and places of previous possessors being cited. But the origin and the majority of the possessors are normally Usiai, some being Matankor. A survey of the histories shows that the Manus natives know what they talk about when they say that

Manus magicians borrow Usiai or Matankor magic. Even although the statement is often made with derogatory intent, that intent uses fact, not fiction. The magician is not normally held in great respect by the Manus, although they use him. They admit the magic as a practice, but as theory they insist that the practice is imported, and Usiai or Matankor origin is of course a slur when it is insisted upon by non-magicians. I cite these facts because they may have some bearing on the disuse of ceremony by some Manus magicians. Man of Lorengau, alone of them, was half Usiai by blood and fluent in the Usiai language and customs. So it was reasonable that he should conduct his magic with more style than the others.

42. *A Blind War Leader Hounded and at Bay*

Korotan, as we have said before, was blind, stone blind now for two years past, and he had already fallen disastrously from his former proud place as an economic leader. His old position as head man and former war leader of Peri, meant little to him now that he was forced to eat up his capital and even to eat up wealth that came to him through ceremonial gifts, which he was later bound to repay, but certainly would not be able to repay to the full satisfaction of his creditors.

It had not been assumed at once that he was, at a stroke, deprived of his leadership. Such was the case, but it had not been realised. His former partners in exchanging wealth gave him gifts on credit after his blindness as before. Since credit in Manus is maintained largely by abstemiousness and frugality, the honest man passing on his assets, for which he is indebted, in order to pass on the burden of meeting his debts, as often as he feels capable of "tightening his belt," credit there depends on a matter of psychology at bottom. It was therefore not necessary that Korotan should have abused his credit. His son's fishing might have kept him from day to day, and his continued prudence might have kept his economic credit strong. Blindness, however, may affect psychology, and Korotan's prudence went with his sight. Maybe also his son's fishing was not enough. However it began, Korotan had now eaten pigs that were his on credit only, and had failed payment.[140] He had failed Paliau over eighteen months ago. When dunned for payment and dunned with insulting charges of economic discredit, the blind man had turned at bay and threatened Paliau with his sorcery. For eighteen months Paliau had not been near Korotan. Now a reconciliation had been effected by a white trader who was friendly with both men,[141] a reconciliation as far as being both in the trader's presence at the same time went. And Korotan exorcised his sorcery from Bonyalo's infant, Bonyalo being Paliau's henchman, as we have seen.

One afternoon of the third week in April Selan and Ngandaliu, each in his own canoe, began dunning Korotan for his debts to them, shouting across the water at a distance to Korotan in his house, the longest and highest house in the village with its extra and specially privileged set of piles, a privilege of only the headman of Peri. Korotan came out on his house verandah bearing a bundle of sticks such as are used to record the count of the turtles a man has killed and the count of the men he has killed in war. Korotan had a great sized bundle on this latter count. He sidetracked the point of his debt almost immediately. He was insulted by loud public dunning of a debt he could not pay, as he was intended to be insulted by it. He cried: "Am I not your elder? Am I not a man of rank?"

Ngandaliu: "No! You are a backslider from your debts."

Korotan: "I have made my *metcha*. When did you make a *metcha?*"

Ngandaliu: "When did you pay Paliau what you owed him? When did you pay Tchawan? When will you pay us? You ate the pigs you cannot pay for. You are nothing but a stomach."

It must be understood that this dialogue was conducted in loud shouting, with much stamping of the floor and of the

[140] Korotan's blindness was probably only a final killing stroke. His fall had begun when he had lost his dependents (some years before his blindness) because they had captured as a prostitute an Usiai woman who was related to Korotan's Usiai wife.

[141] A trader, my friend, Mr. Krämer, visited Peri about once a month.

canoe respectively to punctuate it, and in the whitest rage, and that this continued, working up in intensity.

Korotan: "Come, come, come, come capture these sticks, this wood. Come let fly (inviting violent attack and thinking of war with spears). Come match their count if you can do nothing else."

Selan: "We two are not up to that. You were with those of old who made war. But you boast there with those sticks (count of men killed in war). We have none because the whites have stopped war in our time. But my father when he died, died not from ghosts, but in war. You took the results of my father's wars. He died. Those counting sticks you boast over there are not really yours. They are not the count of what you did with your hand. But the counting sticks of the work of my father's hand you have there."

This incidentally was true. Korotan, as war leader, kept the count of all the enemies slain by his party—all of the Peri men. It was not his individual count that he kept.

Selan: "Now individual count to individual count I will break stick for stick of the counting sticks for turtle and for dugong with you."

That is Selan offers a contest in the count of turtles and dugong killed, confident that he has killed more than Korotan.

Korotan: "I do not go fishing."

Selan: "You talk of contesting the count of men killed in war with me. But since the Administration prevents it I have not killed a man in war."

Korotan, insultingly: "Your father, did he build a house?"

Selan: "My father built a house."

Korotan: "You will not build your house."

Selan: "I am able to build."

Korotan: "What (wealth) have you to do it with?"

Selan: "I have sufficient."

Korotan: "Did you make a *tchinal?*" [142]

[142] *Tchinal* in this sense is a feast. The giver offers betel nut ceremonially to all those who are related to him (and to his gens relatives) by marriage. The gift of betel nut obligates the giver to give oil and dogs' teeth to the recipients of betel nut later. And they, by receiving the betel nut, are obligated to give food of various valuable kinds against the oil and dogs' teeth to come. Each nut

Selan: "No, you are the elder and we the younger so that we have not yet made our *tchinal*. But when you offered betel nut was not some taken, but much left in the wooden bowl?" (*I.e.*, were there not many of your relatives-in-law who refused to enter into dealings with you, so making your *tchinal* a small affair.) "We playing our part within your *tchinal* had all the betel nut we offered accepted." (*I.e.*, Korotan "farmed" out the betel nut amongst his village too so that the relatives-in-law of others also might take it—as was the custom.)

Korotan: "Liar! May your spirit go out (*i.e.*, may you die). You are but war captives, slaves, and you wear a dogs' teeth girdle from shoulder to hip with pendant Ovalis shells.[143] (*I.e.*, you usurp the privilege of rank, and a particular privilege of only two or three families of rank.) You were taken in war from the place of your father and grandfather."

Selan: "Your betel nut, you liar! The father of us two was not a captive. He was a ranking man of Taui. He made feasts, he made a *tchinal*. The 'spirit of dogs' teeth' Ngandaliu does not wear from shoulder to hip. He was unwilling to do it. (*I.e.*, the privileged way of wearing dogs' teeth that is in dispute is called 'the spirit of dogs' teeth.') But I wear it from shoulder to hip, with its pendant Ovalis shells attached to the string ends. It is a right of the house of Talikoumoto, the father of us two. My father wore it. I wear it. Now you wear it. But did your father wear it? (*I.e.*, have you a real hereditary right to it, or do you usurp the right?) If he did, come tell it me! I would like to hear it. You lyingly usurp it. You do but imitate wrongfully a right of another house. It is no right of your house. You, yourself, made it out lyingly to be yours." [144]

given and received entails a certain fixed value and fixed amount of wealth to be given as future gifts.

[143] Called *mana*.

[144] This is vulgar abuse. All persons who are *lapan* (of rank) and not *lau* (commoner) have the right to wear dogs' teeth on the body from shoulder to hip. At least nearly all *lapan* do so. On occasion one *lapan* denies the justice of the right in another *lapan*, but this, I think, is merely quarrelsomeness. One other *lapan* had once tried to induce a white Court to make Korotan abandon what he

Korotan: "Faeces your backside! I shall talk to you two. My wood here. Counting sticks for men killed in war lie on top. Counting sticks for the gifts I have made lie on top. And within are the counting stics for the evil (*i.e.*, men killed by my sorcery). If I talk out now, Ngandaliu, Selan, what will become of you? Ndraki dared my sorcery fetish (or 'wood') and the fetish (or 'wood') consumed Ndraki. Now as to you two there" (spits viciously in the direction of the two).

Ngandaliu (spits back viciously in Korotan's direction)! "Your sorcery will stay with you only. It will afflict your child. It will afflict your women folk. It never did damage anyone else. It is like your war record. Your part was to take canoe crews and charm them with magic and then let them do the fighting. You made war that way. You did nothing with your own arm."

Korotan: "I shall do it now. I shall hurl my sorcery at you (holding his bundle of sticks high in the air and stamping resoundingly. Korotan's son comes up behind him unobserved by the blind man and knocks the precious bundle of sticks from his hands into the sea).

Korotan (weakly and softly): "I am weak. I cannot get my wood. I cannot see it. Why did you knock my wood from me?"

Selan (dancing with rage with his arm extended as if about to throw a spear): "He did but hurl your wood away. Why, you ask him? You deceived him. You said that you would buy his bride with two thousand dogs' teeth that you would bind to the trees of Rambutchon. So saying you deceived your son."

(Korotan had not made the gifts for his son's marriage that he had promised the bride's people. The son had now been married over a year, and the gifts by Korotan were not made.)

Korotan: "Let Selan show that he can pay for the bride of his own son."

Selan (dancing with rage): "Let me at him. You, you,

held to be a usurpation of *his* own family right. Korotan was the greatest *lapan* of Peri village by paternal succession without doubt, or shadow of doubt. But emulative quarrel in such matters is common.

you! Pay for the pigs, the taro and the sago of the men of Lo, the food that they and we have given you. You said that you would pay the bride price to them and to us and to Rambutchon when your son married the daughter of Pwailep.[145] We gave you gifts, and you got them by lies to us. You have few dogs' teeth. I have few dogs' teeth also, but I pay that which I have promised."

Korotan, overcome by his son's turning against him and publicly striking from his hands his bundle which recorded all his former deeds that he prided himself on, went inside his house, broke down and cried. But only his own household saw him break down.

Selan and Ngandaliu drew off to the latter's house, and shortly afterwards night fell. Despite the more or less involved terms of the dialogue used, the contestants had touched each other on the sorest points that they could lay upon. One man can insult another most woundingly in Manus in terms of his economic or war-like achievements that his opponent cannot parallel, or by impugning his honesty in business affairs and his credit. And the entire quarrel had been conducted with such shouting, temporary loss of articulate speech, stamping, and dancing in rage with the right hand drawn back as in spear-hurling position, as I never saw before or after. The pitch of real rage reached by both parties had been great in intensity, and might easily have proceeded into violence. Korotan's debtors would have sued him in the white Courts and obtained some justice, had he not been blind. Now they knew that they could not hope for judgment against him as he would have the magistrate's sympathy in his blindness. They themselves believed in a harder justice than they hoped for from any white court. I may add that a white magistrate settling native affairs is apt to interpret the law on the side of benevolence in cases the parallel of which might not

[145] Ngandaliu, elder brother of Selan, had been adopted by Kali, father of Nane, of Lo gens. So Ngandaliu and Selan had been associated with Lo gens of Peri village and others of Rambutchon village as the party of the female, on behalf of Korotan's son's bride. This bride on her father's side was of Rambutchon village, but her mother was of Lo gens of Peri village, and, as usual, the bilateral kin were the party of the female, whose gifts, in this case, Korotan, had not repaid.

secure any such benevolence in a white community. Usually such interpretation suits native ideas. But the Manus are not any more benevolent than we in economic affairs, and they have as firm an idea of justice though the heavens fall, as we. This one case of threat of sorcery that occurred in Peri during my six months' stay there, arose through native knowledge of what seemed to them an over humanitarianism of the white law, and a failure of justice from it. They had not tried the law, I believe. They merely regarded it as hopeless from what they already knew of it.

Early next morning at about six a.m., I was awakened by shouting from Korotan's house. I was up in a moment and out on my verandah watching. There stood Korotan, white and drawn, but erect on his house verandah. Out of spear range Selan stood in his canoe, at him again. Selan was now gathering all his economic resources towards building himself a new house. House building is not a light matter in Manus. It is ceremonial. A man must build by making great expenditures ceremonially given to others, who buy the actual materials from the land people and do the labour required. The house itself is regarded as sacred. Objection to an old house, orders for building a new come from a Sir Ghost, who must be fittingly housed by his ward. The different prestige of different families is expressed by the different sizes of their houses, and a man must keep up the standard set by fathers before him. Selan needed the repayment of his previous outlays to Korotan, and would not let the man alone. I did not hear what Selan had said. As I came out Korotan was calling out in deadly earnest and with a kind of awe:

"You shall not build your house. Before your first validating feast for it your spirit will go from you. You shall die with your hair (*i.e.*, young as you are now). Remember Ndraki. He dared me. I vowed death to him, and immediately afterwards he died. So now you will die. My sorcery consumed him. Now it will consume you. I talk no longer now. I act."

Selan: "Your spirit go from you! May you die. You will die before me."

The words used were brief and to the point. Korotan went into his house, and Selan went to seek out Patalian. He had Patalian exorcise him. It was whispered about in some quarters that Korotan had been awake all night and had been heard spell binding from within his house before dawn that morning. Paliau in his house nearby had overheard it.

Selan went about the village smiling gaily and with jaunty air. He showed no fear whatever, and admitted none, either in speech or in behaviour. He pointed out that Korotan had done the same thing to Paliau, and all that happened was that eighteen months afterwards Bonyalo's infant's ailing was credited to Korotan's sorcery. But all new-born infants ail. Sorcery being about can hurt infants and always does. But Usiai or Matankor (scornfully) magic is only strong enough to hurt new-born infants. Korotan's magic was stronger in Korotan's youth when Ndraki died. Now Korotan was old, blind and feeble and his magic was old, blind and feeble with him. That was the way of it. A man and his magic were strong or weak together. He was being exorcised by Patalian's magic and Patalian and his magic were strong and lusty.

This quarrel gave me the final evidence regarding the use of sorcery in Manus. Quarrels over debts that did not lead to such extremes as the above quarrel had occurred with great frequency, during my stay in Peri. They were marked by shouting and stamping, and by recriminations over past events, by challenges from one that the other match his past economic record in this particular or in that; but not one of them led to threat of sorcery. At the same time I knew that sorcery was not expected to follow secretly after them. What was expected was that there would be a sickness from the ghosts, due to non-payment of debt, and then the matter would be adjusted by the oracles, if not by mortal agreement before that happened. Now it was clear that sorcery was not suspected after the general run of quarrels, simply because it had not been threatened. Manus is a culture that stresses openness and public revelation, and avoids the maintenance of secrets. And sorcery was, by convention, even more open than sin, open at its inception as sin was not.

43. *The Remarriage of a Widow and Death Resulting*

Patalian, the practitioner in magic, and Tuwain, the eldest son of the senior family line of Kalo, were still firm friends, despite the quarrel between Patalian and the rest of Kalo gens. As it subsequently transpired, Songan, the oldest man of Kalo, although not of the senior family line, was in sympathy with Tuwain and Patalian.

About the time of Patalian's exorcising of Selan after the latter's quarrel with Korotan, Patalian came regularly to my house to be treated for ringworm. These treatments continued daily. After three weeks of this Patalian told me of his secret design that inspired his project of ridding himself of ringworm. The widow of *pwanau* looked favourably upon him as a future husband. He had found an opportunity or two to talk to her for a moment or two unobserved, and they were making plans for a marriage. This was a dead secret as yet. I was not to utter a word to anyone. Patalian commented with a Manus lover's delight upon the widow. She was a good worker and a good business woman. And her kin were good financiers such as would be a profitable connection for him. The affair went forward with all the secrecy that we think of as characteristic of high romance. But the secrecy was really because the widow had promised to give her work and her business assets to Paliau until such time as Paliau had completed the final funerary feast for his titular father, *pwanau;* and because many persons in the community would prevent the widow's remarriage if they could, since *pawnau's* possible circle of more or less vicarious vengeance might include them. To add to the thrill in Patalian's proposed move the final funerary feast for *pwanau* was not yet accomplished. This was a consideration that could hardly promote a greater need for secrecy, for that need would be absolute apart. But it would add to the public horror at the event of the marriage, if it succeeded; and it would add fuel to *pwanau's* anger, even if more fuel could hardly make that anger much hotter.

As I found later not only had I been Patalian's confidant before the act, but Tuwain and Songan had been also. The confidant of the widow of *pwanau* was the wife of Pondramet, an undistinguished woman of Kalo. Thus three members of Kalo were the confidants of the scheming pair.

These three of Kalo were doing what they considered a justice to Patalian. The latter had paid some little wealth for Lawa of Kalo, Ndrantche's daughter, and had been foiled by Ndrantche. Patalian had paid one axe, one large fish-net, one canoe, five fathoms of shell money and one hundred dogs' teeth to Kalo. Only the shell money and the dogs' teeth had been returned to him, Patalian having declined to receive the rest in return. The widow of Pwanau (or of *pwanau*, as he was now as Sir Ghost to his heir, Paliau) was of Lopwer gens. Lopwer gens consisted of only four adult persons, the others being Ndrantche, Pokenas and Poli.[146] Subsequent upon Ndrantche's marriage to the leading man of Kalo, now dead, Lopwer and Kalo gentes worked together in economic matters (probably long subsequent upon the initiation of the marriage).

The widow of *pwanau* in her former life as the wife of Pwanau had not, however, had her marriage validated so much by her own gens, Lopwer, as by an outside person. Lopwer and Kalo had not been as united then as they were now, after a long connection by Ndrantche's marriage, a marriage which set them apart in separate economic exchanges at first, before uniting them now, as it had after the death of Ndrantche's husband of Kalo. Mbosai financed the wife of Pwanau, Pokenas of Lopwer helping him. Mbosai as a rich financier, usually confined himself to financing the members of his mother's gens, Matchupal, and the members of his father's gens, Kalaat. His financing the wife of Pwanau had been a move of his to exchange with a financial equal, Pwanau, who had been richer than anyone in Lopwer or in Kalo. Mbosai's mother and the mother of the then wife of Pwanau had been elder and younger sister respectively, a relationship that Mbosai had used in order to initiate exchange with Pwanau, and a relationship only sporadically used in Manus society.

[146] As usual any absolute statement on gentile affiliation is misleading. Poli had been adopted by Songan of Kalo gens, and was functionally fully Kalo, although Lopwer by blood. Ndrantche, as widow of a leader of Kalo, was now virtually Kalo. Nyambulel, the run away wife of Talikai, and Pokenas' sister, was Lopwer also, however; but she lived in a house in another territory than that of the adjoining Lopwer-Kalo territory.

Patalian had not paid any wealth to Mbosai or to Pokenas. He had not been treating with them for the widow of *pwanau*. Previously Patalian had made pre-economic overtures. Before he had made overtures and economic payment for Lawa of Kalo gens, and been frustrated, he had tentatively approached Mbosai and Pokenas for the widow of *pwanau*. His approach had been declined outright. He was no economic match in exchange for Mbosai and Pokenas.

Now those three of Kalo, Tuwain, Songan and the wife of Pondramet, who were in the secret plot for Patalian to elope with the widow of *pwanau* were really aiding Patalian to make an illegitimate contract. Paliau, heir of *pwanau's* goods and financial place, heir of *pwanau's* widow's economic services, guardian of *pwanau's* children, whom he trusted the widow of *pwanau* to tend under his custody, Mbosai and Pokenas, legal guardians and former financiers of the woman (when she and her guardians had been obliged to exchange wealth with Pwanau and Paliau), and all of Ndrantche's faction of Kalo that were at odds with Patalian had to be kept completely ignorant of Patalian's and the widow's scheme. If it were effected, any one of them, or any one of the two principals or the three accessories to the conspiracy, might be stricken by *pwanau*. I except myself as a fourth accessory, although I was, I suppose, exceedingly guilty. For since Paliau had built my house on an old site of his, *pwanau* was conventionally considered the guardian Sir Ghost of me and of my house as well as of Paliau's. And Patalian had had the impudence to confide his scheme to me under *pwanau's* own roof built on *pwanau's* own territory. I often had native children, and now and again an adult or two, sleeping in my house, a fact only permitted since my house had a spiritual guardian; that is in terms of native psychology. But Patalian's carelessness of that fact was another facet of native psychology—an example of the fact that the natives extended their own categories to my intrusive and strange presence or contracted them from my presence according to their most imperative need. I except myself as an accessory then; for I was not suspected subsequently, despite a general rage of suspicion.

With this air of conspiracy and ignorance of conspiracy in the village I had to leave it for a time on an expedition to a neighbouring culture—for my time was coming to a close. When I returned I found the deed accomplished. Patalian and the widow had chosen for their day of flight a day when most of Peri village were due to go to Mbunai village for a great economic exchange. They had separately lied their way out of going with their usual companions, and, behind the unconscious backs of their absent associates, they had decamped to Patusi village, where the house of a friend of Patalian's received them.

On the same day Songan went to the temporarily deserted house of Paliau. There he performed a charm over *pwanau*, a charm intended to devitalise *pwanau* as a ghost, and particularly as a ghost liable to take vengeance for his widow's remarriage.

The widow of *pwanau* had left her two children behind. They were now with Paliau. Patalian and his new wife were absolutely cut off from all contact with any one of Peri village. Their confederates were dissembling acquaintance with the affair, Songan included. His act of magic was not yet traced to him. Paliau, on his return, had found expectorated betel juice left on the house, and about the skull bowl, as the mark of the magic, and he realised what had been done, but had only suspicion of who had done it. I found a general fear of *pwanau* hanging over the village. For that fear no one would go near Patalian and the widow. The pair were generally regarded as if they were a source of the most dangerous contagion.

I went to see Patalian in Patusi. He appeared shy then, but two days later he came from Patusi boldly up to my house. I had to tell him to leave or all my servants would leave me. He understood and left immediately. I could have as easily entertained a leper as my guest at a party of my own people as Patalian then in my Peri house. He came and went quickly by dark, but with some of the tobacco the need of which urged him. Perhaps also a need of some relief from the Peri ostracism urged him. If so I could not afford to give it him.

He did not attempt to visit anyone else in Peri, but punted quickly back to Patusi.

The same night Paliau in a rage pierced Salikon's ears without ceremony. Salikon was the elder daughter of the widow of *pwanau* by Pwanau. Had all proceeded as previously planned Salikon's ears would have been pierced ceremoniously by Mbosai and Pokenas, her mother's financiers. Paliau would have feasted the two for their services. By traditional usage the real or titular kin of the mother's side should pierce a child's ears, and be feasted ceremonially for it by the kin of the father's side. By traditional usage Salikon's ears should have been pierced by Mbosai and Pokenas regardless of how Salikon's mother behaved to her dead husband's heir. But Paliau was no respecter of tradition as such. And he obtained some outlet for his feelings by preventing the ceremony; Mbosai and Pokenas were as innocent as he, and they were additionally outraged by insult as well as by double injury, both from the widow and from Paliau. Paliau suspected Pokenas of complicity.

Pokenas immediately went to his friend and relative-in-law, Sanau of Kalaat gens. Sanau was financing the girl, Kiteni, in her arranged marriage to *pwanau's* son, whom Paliau was financing, the lad himself being away working for a white man at the time. Pokenas induced Sanau to say that he would break off the contract of marriage. Paliau heard of the threat, and said that it was unlikely that Sanau could fulfill any such threat. He had paid dogs' teeth and shell money as bride price for Kiteni. If Sanau could collect that price which had now been handed over by Sanau to X, by X to Y, by Y to Z, and by Z to A, and return it to Paliau, then Sanau was stronger financially than he had understood. The threat was empty. So Paliau lorded it as he usually did. He had too many debtors to be unable to break a tradition or two at will without fear of consequences.

The next night Paliau sent word by a Patusi woman to the widow of *pwanau*. "You have run away. Now the affair passes into the hands of the ghosts. They are angry and they will exact revenge. But I, for my part, have pierced Salikon's ears." So Paliau sent word of his insult to the widow. The widow sent back insult by threatening play on Paliau's fears of *pwanau*. "I will come back to you and bring any revenge from *pwanau* upon your house." Paliau, thoroughly alarmed and even angrier, sent word: "If you come near me I will beat you till the blood runs from your body." The affair was the more galling to Paliau because Patalian had once been suspected of seducing Sain, Paliau's wife. Patalian, in anger, had rebutted the suspicion by himself taking the affair to the white Court and obtaining a magistrate's opinion that the charge was scandalous libel. But Paliau and Patalian had been cool to each other ever since.

It soon was suspected that all Kalo gens had been Patalian's confederates, Paliau suspecting Pokenas also. Songan was almost certainly the guilty magician, as Kalo's one magician. How the suspicion first fell on Kalo, I do not know. Possibly someone whispered something somewhere. Possibly it became known that a box of Patalian's effects were in the keeping of the wife of Pondramet. When the suspicion first became assured I do not know. In any case much was known shortly afterwards when a disaster occurred in Kalo, and brought all knowledge into public. Somehow Tuwain escaped suspicion, despite the fact that he was one of the three of Kalo who were genuine confederates of the pair,[147] and others of Kalo, Ndrantche and her faction, were falsely suspected.

This air of suspicion partly true, partly untrue, only privately canvassed and only privately surmised was soon clarified by the pointed and direct action that soon came from other than the mortal plane. The oracles' previous private detective work had prepared them for diagnosis of ghostly action, and the latter followed so directly that none of the results of the private detective work was wasted.

The wife of Pondramet was pregnant, and childbirth was now overdue. It was known by some that several months before she had tried to procure abortion by tight lacing without

[147] The ghost of Tuwain's dead wife had been married by the ghost *pwanau*. So Tuwain was delighted to score off *pwanau* in revenge. But Tuwain had been in favour of Patalian's proposal to Lawa, and so was not a confederate merely to score off *pwanau*.

success. Then later she had been ill following the exposure she suffered in the sea disaster of the Kalo canoe. Now she was ill again. Now that suspicion of complicity with the widow of *pwanau* and Patalian had fallen upon her, her indisposition assumed a more serious aspect from the supernatural view, but not from the natural view.[148] She had no fits of unconsciousness nor betrayal of any other startling symptoms.

The 20th of May was the sixth day after the runaway marriage. The newly married pair were still in ostracism. Isole, staying away from Peri that night, held a seance in Tchalalo village. Her husband and one or two other diviners there had heard, they thought, the sound of distant drums beaten by the ghosts. Isole held seance to discover what it was about. For a long time her control professed ignorance. Then at last he said that Mbosai had asked *pwanau* [149] to kill the wife of Pondramet, and *pwanau* had been beating a drum to convene a ghostly council to decide on the request.

Then suddenly next day the wife of Pondramet fell into an agony and died almost without a struggle. There had been no seance over her, summoned by her kin for her benefit; Isole's seance had been a private affair held afield. Without more than a few hours' warning she died. As she died the diviners made three different oracular statements. The Sir Ghost of Mbosai had struck her down because she had assisted the widow of *pwanau* to desert Paliau; whereupon Paliau had prevented Mbosai from piercing the widow's daughter's ears, and from the ceremonial honour of ear piercing. The Sir Ghost of Mbosai, avoiding Paliau or the former widow her-

[148] The wife of Pondramet was cross-cousin both to the widow of *pwanau* and to Patalian, therefore an ideal go-between, according to regular kinship function of usage of privileged liberty in sex affairs.

[149] Mbosai was not *pwanau's* ward by any view. But Mbosai was economic backer of the widow of *pwanau*, and he was represented as inciting the ghost of the leader of the party of the male to which he had been opposed as leader of the party of the female formerly. Such inciting of a ghost is not a function of ward in relation to Sir Ghost, however. It is a case of brothers-in-law or their functioning representatives, the leaders of party of the female and party of the male, being accustomed to co-operate to keep a woman in her place, faithful if married, if a widow faithful in not remarrying.

self, had blamed the now dying woman. Further *pwanau*, associated with two other Sir Ghosts of Pere gens men at *pwanau's* instance, had stricken her for helping to arrange the widow of *pwanau's* remarriage. Finally Patalian, before running away had left a chest of his effects in the charge of the wife of Pondramet. It was with her still for all to see now in the publicity of her death bed. The chest contained dogs' teeth, shell money and the fetish herbs of a magical spell. The magical familiars of the spell had thought, "this woman likes us too much." So they had gone inside her stomach to kill her. Patalian had warned her not to handle the chest because of the magic in it. But her curiosity as to the dogs' teeth wealth and shell money within had been too strong for her. Patalian's leaving the magic with the wealth had had as its object the preventing of such curiosity and the safe-guarding of his wealth naturally.

Before night came to allow a seance to be held the wife of Pondramet was dead. There was no time for expiatory payments following divination, or for a subsequent seance to confirm the divining results, and to collect the soul stuff in return for the expiations. The normal system depends for its operation on some forewarning of death, some time of resistance by the patient.

The ostracism of Patalian and his new bride by Peri villagers was now completely justified, and probably prolonged. The pair were still in Coventry with their sole friends in a Patusi village house, when a fortnight later I left for Australia; and from what I heard their time of infection with the contagion of possible death to anyone of Peri associating with them or speaking to them would probably last for at least two months.

The same day as that of the death, the Government assistant medical officer of the district came on his visit to Peri, and inoculated everyone against hookworm. During the inspection the wife of Pomo fainted. The inspection and inoculation occurred later in the afternoon than the death of the wife of Pondramet. Now it so happened that Pomo and Pondramet and their respective wives had occupied the one house between them, the men being both too poor and ineffectual to have each his own house. The faint was thus very conspicuous, and evidently related to the death of the early afternoon.[150]

Talk of the way in which the wife of Pondramet had been neglected before her death was rife in the village. She and her husband were persons of little account, but there was some shock at the way in which death had stolen upon her without public attention having been first focussed upon her. And one individual was blaming another for neglect. Even one eight-year-old girl remarked of the ten-year-old adopted girl of the dead woman as the latter cried over her mother's corpse, "Yes; when her mother was alive she ran away to play on the islands; now she's dead she stays at home and cries for her."

In the seance held that night over the faint of the wife of Pomo the new ghost of the wife of Pondramet was credited with having struck her former house mate. The new ghost said: "Yes; before I died no one came to see me or pay attention to me. The wife of Pomo here paid no attention to me. But when I died everyone suddenly took an interest in me. Why? Perhaps to see whom I would strike down. Well then, I struck her down."

In other words, the ghost attributed the sudden interest in her to her accession to power as a ghost, since it was not an interest of any genuine mortal friendship. She was correct in this, I may add, in so far as a ghost can be correct. The medium was shrewd in her judgment.

There followed the formalities of the ghost restoring the soul stuff by putting it in the water, and the medium bathing the wife of Pomo with it. The medium, the wife of Pokenas, then continued to communicate ghostly advice regarding the death of the day.

Control through medium: "But the ghost of the wife of

[150] Pondramet by an earlier marriage had born to him a daughter who became the wife of Pomo. Pomo was of Matchupal gens; so was Pomo's wife, Pondramet being a Matchupal man. They all lived in the one house, and by some legal quibble Pomo's marriage was denied to be incestuous. The quibble was based on ignoring blood or ignoring adoptive ties according to convenience. Pomo's convenience was not everyone else's. So others might dub his marriage incestuous.

Pondramet became a ghost for the fault of the widow of *pwanau*. For that fault she died. She will not strike the wife of Pomo again, but she will strike the widow of *pwanau*."

Pokenau: "Let us hear what *sori* says."

sori through control through medium: "I talked to *pwanau*. I said, 'My cross-cousin, that one (Patalian) has married your widow; but he was not from his mother's womb. His so-called mother adopted him when he was taken a captive child in war. What he has done to you is evil. You are angry at your widow. You mourn for your two daughters that are now left motherless. I am angry also. As for that one who stole your widow he is not with me, he is with others.'

Patalian had been brought up as a child with Sori and Pokenau. Sori and Pokenau called him brother, and he called their parents father and mother. Now as a ghost *sori* dissociates himself from Patalian on the ground that Patalian was not a blood brother. Blood ties are not generally reckoned in Manus as closer than the ties resulting from early adoption, and *sori's* ground for disclaiming relationship would dissolve a great proportion of the fully functioning relationships in Peri; while if blood relationships were reinstated in place of these adoptive relationships, a large number of completely non-functioning relationships would suddenly become functioning. The conflict between blood and adoptive ties is never a real conflict, but only a device that enables a person or a ghost to claim or to disclaim a given relationship based on either blood or adoption at will, simply by stressing the non-functioning relationship. In the case of *sori*, Pokenau, and Patalian, the non-functioning relationship happened to be blood.

Of course if Pokenau had come out aggressively in Patalian's favour, the medium could not have represented *sori* as she did. She was merely making explicit through the words of *sori* (avowedly) what was implicit in Pokenau's behaviour. And Pokenau, pressed publicly, would have agreed.

This same device of claiming or disclaiming relationship at will is ever present and often used in economic association or refusal to associate. It presents an equal appearance of full motivation whether a man uses it so to protect his idea of his economic interest, or whether a medium uses it to read attitudes into another family than her own. The wife of Pokenas, with Pokenas, was affronted by the loss of the ear piercing ceremony and by the lack of good faith shown by her husband's financial ward, the widow of *pwanau*. It gave her some satisfaction when as medium she could represent *sori* as disclaiming his brother, Patalian (also virtually disclaiming *sori's* ward, Pokenau). Pokenau and Patalian had always worked together and been friends, as well as close relatives. It must have been pleasing to this particular oracle to make explicit the present rift between Patalian and Pokenau, and, if possible, to exacerbate it, and at the same time to be a sincere oracle in doing so. Whether the legalistic use of what is no real conflict as if it were a real conflict of ties in economic affairs arose from the oracles' somewhat malicious use of it to make conflict in other families (for oracles represent freely the Sir Ghosts of other families), or whether an economic interest in fickleness in reckoning kinship was primary, providing an idea for the oracles to use, is of necessity indeterminate. Either is comprehensible as a primary motivation. Of course there may be individual reluctance in relinquishing a child when a child is handed over to another family in adoption. But there is no cultural conflict such as might make a blood tie more highly esteemed than an adoptive tie, or might advantage the one and disadvantage the other.[151] Women ordinarily pretend that adopted children are from their own wombs,[152] but the men do not pretend to any false biological fatherhood, although they understand physiological fatherhood. They simply do not consider physiology important. They would be as reluctant to lose an adoptive child as another, and they may, of course, make either renunciation as a favour to one whom they feel they have need of favouring. As the culture is patrilineal it is the men's view that is cul-

[151] There might be a greater social solidarity if there were some decision in this matter—the case of Lomot giving away secrets to Paliau concerning Isole's seance accusing *pwanau* will be recalled.

[152] Margaret Mead, "Growing Up in New Guinea," p. 77 et seq.

turally significant. The women's view however is all that Manus has of the idea that blood is all important. And, as a woman's view in a patrilineal culture, it is without institutionalised effect, and is a mere impotent figure of speech that the men do not hesitate to show up as such where the facts contradict a pretense; and one woman will often show up a pretense of another, even if less readily than the men.

To continue the seance:

sori through control through medium: "Wait a little, while I talk to *tano*" (*sori's* father).

After a due wait *tano* through control through medium: "Yes, *pwanau* is a true cross-cousin of mine. His father, the man, my mother, the woman (*i.e.*, his father was brother to my mother). The *metcha* of my mother became the *metcha* of his father. Were we two mortal now we would be betrothing our respective children. But I died, and he died. You all do not understand betrothal obligations. I bore you, *sori* and Pokenau, from my loins. And your mother nourished and fed this other one who has done evil. And I am ashamed for it. He was nourished and fed by me and by my wife. Now he has done evil to a cross-cousin of mine between whom and me there should be betrothals of our respective children and exchange of wealth.

"I said to *pwanau;* 'My cross-cousin, listen to my words. Pondramet and his wife aided your widow to remarry. Now I shall marry the (ghost of the) wife of Pondramet. She shall make good the loss of your widow.'"

So the oracle not only made the relationship of the *tano*, *sori* and Pokenau family to Patalian appear of no account, but she gave the relationship to *pwanau*, and so to Paliau. The real spirit in which Manus relationship is reckoned lies in the phrase "the *metcha* of my mother became the *metcha* of his father." That is, the dogs' teeth and shell money of an important gift that was made by the speaker's (Tano's) father's kin group to the speaker's (Tano's) mother's kin group, was used by the latter group as a similar gift to the kin of the wives of their men, one of those men being Pwanau; the speaker's (Tano's) father made a gift that was so passed on by Pwanau's father, each to their respective wives' kin group. The terminology does not express this explicitly, for "metcha of my mother" means "metcha given to my mother's kin in her name," and "metcha of his father" means "metcha given by his father to his mother's kin in her name." Even apart from this terminological twist the idea of stating the fact that a speaker's mother was another's father's sister in such terms may seem to be a trifle involved. But relationship in Manus is explained more readily and more often in terms of the economic duties proper to a relationship than in any other way. He who performs the economic duties proper to a certain relationship thereby assumes that relationship. That fact is common usage. But the assumption of such duties may be founded in blood ties or it may be founded in ties of long standing adoption, or it may be founded in ties of such temporary adoption as may be taken up by a financier who has wealth to invest beyond his circle of ties by blood and long adoption. There is some terminology to express relationship without going into details, since it is sometimes felt that the details of why the relationship function was discharged by so and so for so and so are not of great subsequent importance, as well as being possibly involved. So phrases such as "the *metcha* of my mother became the *metcha* of his father" are frequently used. They express the facts of kinship by reference to the facts of economic obligations performed. They measure kinship by a single standard instead of by three standards. And as phrases they perform the function of giving a definition of kinship that no one can dispute. There can be none of "he is my brother because he came from my mother's womb" (one day) and "he is not my brother because we were not brought up by the same parents" (next day) a slippery fickleness that is rendered possible by the women's trick of stressing blood of their own children where the men do not—as a consistent usage for each sex—and by its established economic and oracular uses by both sexes. Either the *metcha* of my mother became the *metcha* of his father, or it did not, and everyone knows the facts. Moreover in Manus, kin is as kin does, and economic doings are all important. So the phrases of kinship function fulfilled are the genuinely strong phrases.

I make this point in order to show clearly how the medium in the above instance proceeded. She placed the relationship of *sori* and *tano* to Patalian on a slippery basis, and then proceeded to place the relationship of *tano* and *pwanau* on a non-slippery basis. Her action was arbitrary enough. Patalian had performed economic duties enough to his family, and they constitute relationship *de facto* as generally reckoned.

The talk of Tano's children marrying Pwanau's children was the chatter of kinship merely. As cross-cousins they, in theory, would betroth their children, Tano's son to Pwanau's daughter. As a matter of fact Pwanau produced no daughter that would have matched Sori or Pokenau in age, and had he produced such he might not have chosen such a match on economic grounds. The medium makes *tano* ascribe the lack of a match consummated to the deaths of himself and of *pwanau*, which deaths had nothing to do with the case; but match consummated or not, such talk is a way of expressing kin solidarity.

As a ghost *tano* wished to marry *pwanau's* revenge victim avowedly to compensate *pwanau* for the loss of his widow. The theory here is apparently as follows: "We are closely related; so if I gain from your loss that makes all well." It may also comprehend some notion that marriage is a form of revenge. "You killed her; I am in sympathy with you; now I'll marry her, and that should console you." The medium was a woman who had been raped, it was said, by a number of men, and who subsequently married Pokenas.

It was not stated at first that *tano* had succeeded in marrying the ghost of the wife of Pondramet. News of *tano's* intention only came on the night of the death. Next day it was rumoured that the Sir Ghost of Man of Lorengau had the same intention; also that the ghost of a youth long ago betrothed to her as mortal had the same intention. This youth had never married her. Before the due date for his marriage, his betrothed had been captured in war by a war party of Manus men from Mok. She had been held there as a public prostitute for three years, before Korotan succeeded in retaking her and bringing her home again.

Where news of the intention of *tano's* two rivals came from I do not know exactly, nor did those who told me know. The gaps between the carriers of news were too many to bridge. Probably there had been seances elsewhere, very likely in other villages. After the burial, on the fourth day after death, it was generally agreed that *tano* had married the ghost of the woman. Again the origin of the general decision was obscure. But in all probability it came from a diviner whose decision was accepted.

The third evening after the death there was an angry public quarrel. Kalo gensmen came up and indignantly charged Paliau that during a seance he had asked *pwanau* to kill all Kalo with a hatchet. The charge was not that he had asked *pwanau* to kill the wife of Pondramet only, but all Kalo. It included a charge of responsibility for the death of the wife of Pondramet, of course. Paliau spoke briefly in reply pointing out that he had been sleeping in my house since the ear-piercing episode, so that he had not been present at any seance; this was, I believe, true. The commotion died down rapidly.

The case of the death of the wife of Pondramet is interesting, because charges that mortals try to influence the ghosts were made. First it was true that Songan of Kalo had used magic on Paliau's house, in Paliau's absence, on the day of the run-away marriage, this magic being intended to prevent *pwanau's* revenge. Then later Isole, the medium, said oracularly at Tchalalo village that Mbosai had asked his Sir Ghost to kill the wife of Pondramet, on the night before the death. Finally Kalo, probably ignorant of Isole's seance in Tchalalo village, but probably depending on some seance of their own that I did not hear about, charged Paliau with urging *pwanau* on to kill all Kalo. In no other case did I ever hear of such belief in mortal interference with the other plane. And I can state categorically that it is not suspected and therefore certainly not done. But the remarriage of widows is a special case. Ghosts of former mortal husbands are believed to punish remarriage of widows as drastically as Sir Ghosts punish sexual misconduct or non-payment of economic obligations. Unfortunately for steadfast perpetual widowhood, ghosts are not believed to punish the remarriage of widowers equivalently. Sexual misconduct by man or by woman is equally punished. The single standard keeps the system on a firm basis here. But the Sir Ghosts are males, and female ghosts are not often credited with potency, not nearly as frequently or with as much conviction as the Sir Ghosts. In consequence widowers remarrying go scot free as a general rule, free from fear of the ghosts of their dead former wives. The system of child betrothal removes the young girls from widowers' attentions. So the widowers normally turn to the widows. And the widows normally remarry. It is true that when a man marries a widow he, as well as she, and his friends, as well as her friends, are believed to be open to attack from the ghost of the former husband. But it is also true that the widow and her group are held most culpable, the ghost of the former husband is believed to be far more dangerous to her and her group than to the man and his group. Vengeance is executed by ghost, not by Sir Ghost; and ghost lacks the fine impartiality of Sir Ghost and the idea of even handed justice associated commonly with Sir Ghost. It becomes very much a matter of vengeance done upon the living spouse by the conventionally empowered sex amongst the ghosts. Manus is more strongly patrilineal on the other plane than on this plane. But this decision is a support to the men upon this plane.

Public opinion is steadfastly puritan against sexual misconduct, steadfastly indignant against economic failure or dishonesty, but decidedly non-moral about widow remarriage. The men's attitude about a widow is usually a questioning one, as to who will get her and when. Her husband's heir and the financiers interested in her alone profess a moral horror at the idea of her remarriage, because meanwhile she works for them. And if she leaves them her children are left motherless with them. The children should stay with the patrilineal gens of their father. It is felt admirable that a widow should stay with her children and work for those who will be most intimately concerned with her children in the future. But that is hardly expected as an enduring status.

Probably because of a double standard for widows and widowers, and because of child betrothal, the remarriage of widows is the general custom in a way that sexual misconduct or economic back sliding is not the general custom. I wish to urge this because here we have an element in the Manus spiritualistic system that does not function perfectly. The implication of the unpleasantness that follows remarriage of a widow is clearly that widows should not remarry, as they do not in the Amphlett Islands of the Massim area for example. But a double standard that goes with the idea of ghost punishment, incompatible with the different idea of Sir Ghost punishment, prevents the implication from realisation except in unpleasantness. This unpleasantness might be expected to lead a widow to devote more time than she would otherwise to remaining single and caring for her children herself. Perhaps that is true.

We have shown that widow remarriage is not effectually prevented by former husband's ghostly revenges or by public opinion. Here we meet with the comparative disrespect which distinguishes the concept of ghostly malice so clearly from the other concept of Sir Ghostly enforcement of justice with the attitude of comparative respect that is given it. And parallel with this we meet here also the idea of manipulation of the other plane. The respected Sir Ghost as enforcer of justice is not manipulated by his ward. He manipulates his ward. But a ward may stand in relation to his Sir Ghost as an egger on of the Sir Ghost to act as a malicious ghost towards his widow or her friends when she remarries.[153] I do not know that Mbosai or Paliau actually acted so. But charges were made here as never elsewhere.

It is customary to act as Songan did with magic to prevent a ghost from vengeance for his widow's remarriage. Such

[153] As we have seen, the malice of ghosts is especially directed against women, while the idea of Sir Ghostly enforcement of justice is especially used in connection with men.

magic is entirely regular, and is sometimes performed with a ward's consent to his Sir Ghost. Pokenau, for example, had consented to having *sori* so charmed at *sori's* death. But the widow of *sori* was still a widow. Paliau had not consented to the magic being performed over *pwanau;* hence Songan did it by stealth on the crucial occasion. Charmed ginger is put between the teeth of the skull of the ghost to exclude it from vengenace upon his widow. This magic is used only in these circumstances. It differs from the ordinary exorcism over the grave, the exorcism which keeps the ghost from harming his own relatives and which is customary.

Evidently if mortal efforts to lay a ghost's vengeance upon his widow are not effective, there is suspicion of mortal counter measures such as the instigation of a Sir Ghost by a ward. This suspicion may precede knowledge of a ghost's vengeance, as Isole attributed such to Mbosai before the wife of Pondramet's sudden attack, before Songan's magic on *pwanau* had proved ineffective.

Instigation of a Sir Ghost to act as a malicious ghost by the Sir Ghost's ward is then peculiar to the remarriage of the ghost's widow. It is not a general characteristic to suppose that whenever ghostly malice has been bruited there has been mortal instigation. It is only here where the interests of a family or two of one gens are concerned with keeping the widow unmarried, where the interests of various odd widowers of other gentes are in making a marriage, and where there is no strong public opinion to decide between the conflicting interests involved, that active manipulation of the Sir Ghost (to one party) of the ghost (to the other party) occurs.

Such manipulation is, according to the usual English definition, the border of magic. As long as the Manus native feels of his Sir Ghost, "Thy will, not mine," as he usually does, his belief is essentially religious. But when he feels "You must do this for me," his belief begins to be magical. It is interesting to note that within the general Manus system the religous attitude towards the Sir Ghost or even towards malicious ghosts flourishes where there is general agreement in the code which men follow; whereas once a double standard comes forward to intensify conflicting interests, rather than to decide clearly between them, the magical attitude usurps the religious. Sir Ghostly justice is accepted religiously because all men know what justice is and respect it; ghostly malice is accepted somehow when all men are subject to it alike. But when widows get special malice and widowers none, so that the interest of one sex is not that of another, and when there is further conflict between a group interested in keeping a widow unmarried, and with her children who belong to their group, and outside groups interested in an incompatible aim, then the issue becomes so confused that there can be no general forceful agreement on a general issue; not unless the religious system with its double standard in this particular issue is discarded entirely in making an agreement, or reworked into such form as will allow a single standard. I would suggest that the Manus facts show that a rift in the general application of a code in Manus society may actually promote magic. It is hard to say, "Thy will not mine," when there is no general will. Instead we find, "Do this my will."

I suggest that this is true of magic generally in Manus. Only in one other instance are the family ghosts used or manipulated. That is when the female descent line has exclusive and absolute magical power to use these ghosts to make fruitful the women, and fruitful or barren the wives of the men of the male descent line, without reciprocal power—the *tandritanitani* used either peaceably, or in anger as the case may be. And here of course we have a traditional allocation of power to one of two lines that are respectively empowered, and denuded of special privilege in certain specific ways, the *tandritanitani* being but one of them, others being inheritance and succession. It is not impossible theoretically that there may be some connection between magic in this instance, and magic in the widow remarriage instance. The fact that widows are subject to special ghostly malice, widowers to none such, is a facet of patriliny as it appears in Manus, so that magic on behalf of widows is not unrelated to magic on behalf of the female descent line.

I illustrate my argument with cases where the ghosts are used aberrantly, magically or semi-magically; not with cases of the regular magic of familiars and herbs. The magic on behalf of widows and their remarriage is a border line case where magical herbs, commonly used on familiars, are used on a ghost, against a ghost. The half-magic against the remarriage of widows is instigation of a Sir Ghost to do his ward's will in causing death, a rare cultural form in Manus, and one confined to countering the magic on behalf of widows. The *tandritanitani* has been already described as one descent line's exclusive and compulsive power over the family ghosts for certain ends. All these three are aberrant magic, that show clear signs of connection with the religious cult of ghosts, and that would appear to be the result of aberrant handling of the religious forms commonly used in a very different spirit. My object is to trace the social conditions of this aberrant handling. It is suggested that in Manus it is associated with conflict of interest.

Any Manus native will say that true magic, that is magic that employs familiars and herbs, "belongs to quarreling" (*pati tundrun*). Such magic is regarded as the regular resort of an injured man against one who has stolen from his trees, opposed the completion of a marriage in which validating wealth has been exchanged, or otherwise personally interfered with his plans. It would appear that where there is social conflict, deep founded in the system, there has grown up social custom of magic at the expense of handling the religious system in an aberrant magical spirit. Assimilation of religion to magic appears to have taken place here. If this is a true judgment it would appear to be a case of social conflict promoting the use of magic beyond its more normal limits, which lie outside the ghost cult. The *tandritanitani*, in a variant form, is found also in Tikopia and in Samoa, and I give here only the Manus facts.

Even before the death of the wife of Pondramet the widow of *pwanau*, now the wife of Patalian, had sent word by a Patusi woman to Paliau: "Patalian put bad magic on me, and so I ran off with him. He put bad magic on me and caused me to forget my children. But Paliau was good to me. I want to go back and help him make his *metcha*. Others have remarried and gone back. I want to go back. I want to see my two daughters. If I cannot see them I will go to far off Nouna Island with Patalian and never come back." Paliau had merely said, "She never intended to come back; she lies." The ostracism continued, but according to usual custom the widow of *pwanau* came to mourn over the corpse of the wife of Pondramet. No Coventry is so stern as to prevent such ceremony in Manus. But Sain, the wife of Paliau, and Molong, the wife of Paliau's brother, although as closely related to the wife of Pondramet as the runaway widow, Sain even closer, were in doubt whether to go to mourn over the corpse or not. They were under *pwanau's* care, and he might object to their going near the widow. Their husbands waited in the greatest suspense to see if their wives would go or not. "If they think of their sister (the corpse) they will go; if they think of their children (*i.e.*, their children's safety) they will not go." The pair did not go. But half an hour before the burial the corpse was taken out of the Kalo house, where it had rested, to a Matchupal gens house where Sain and Molong could mourn over it, without danger from the Sir Ghosts of Kalo (who might revenge Kalo upon *pwanau's* heirs' wives) or danger from *pwanau* for their going near his widow (who did not intrude upon them).

The widow's younger daughter cried because she wished to see her mother. But Paliau would not allow it. "Remember once before when your mother wanted to marry [154] how Salikon (the elder daughter) fell ill. Now this time your father is so angry that if you speak to your mother you will surely die. Your mother is evil. She has gone, and now you and Salikon will become ill."

[154] An event before the beginning of this diary.

CHAPTER V

THE FUNCTIONING OF RELIGION IN MANUS

1

THE Manus ghostly cult is fluid and amorphous. It has form, but it is a wide, loose form that follows the recurring accidents of existence. It is a system adjusted to deal with the passage of the individual through time, but in contrast with Manus *rites de passage*, which deal with the steady, healthy progress of the individual life cycle, it is adjusted to emergencies and disasters. There is no ritual in Manus that is daily, weekly or annually regulated, except that which is evoked by the recurrence of the high tide which seasonally sweeps the spawning fish over the barrier reef. The ritual that exists in Manus is not shaped by any concept of human need of constant or calendrically periodic response to a super-humanity that demands such response.

Religion which is cast in this episodic form functions in a very different manner from a religion which is regulated calendrically. Take a hypothetical period of time in a small Manus community. Assume that during that time fishing is good. Assume that during that time no one is at a stage in the life cycle that must be met, according to convention, by a *rite de passage*. Then there would be no religious practice whatever, other than a little divination as to the direction in which fish shoals or turtle or dugong are to be found, or jesting divination as to whether an old woman will catch her pig before it reaches that sand bank yonder or not. This is not a hypothetical assumption. An approximation to such periods occurs in every Manus community at times. Only the large size of most of the villages and the extension of relationship tend to break up such periods of religious unconcern before they have long continued.

In Manus there is no ritual commerce until a mortal falls ill, or until one of the female line makes *tandritanitani* over the male line, or until at an important economic occasion there is a more or less perfunctory invocation and throwing of a handful of taro at the house front. But it is equally true that in Manus there is constant daily interrelation with the supernaturals. It is the endeavour to keep the moral code.

The Manus are probably as honest and fair-dealing a people as exist anywhere. They have no inclination to depart from the truth and they have as keen a sense of aim as men can have. With the rarest exception, their delinquents are feeble-minded or psychopathic, and if a person is of normal intelligence he is utterly reliable. In describing the oracular forms in Manus I have dwelt on sin after sin, including all the present sin and much of the past sin of more than eighty living adults and a considerable number of dead, all of whom were still, or had been, engaged in an endeavour to keep a very stringent code with a very great measure of success. The endeavour to maintain sexual purity as such purity is conceived, and the endeavour to work up to, and often beyond, the fair limits of endurance are by far the most exacting commands. Speech free from scandal and obscenity and the demand for humility and confession of sin in the face of public exposure are also exacting. Hard work is exacted up to the limit. The Manus take very few siestas, except after all-night fishing. They are always up and doing in a torrid climate; they always "have work." And an observer cannot help but think that they die young, as they do, because of the speed and constancy of the work they do; which, in turn, is kept up by the heavy blame that falls upon a man who has rested for a very brief while, as a man accused of causing illness in his house.

The virtues of the Manus are essentially those which we know as belonging to a puritan and Christian strain of the strictest type amongst ourselves, as that in our past history. They have never formulated a code of commandments for the teaching of morals. But from the preceding chapter of this study we derive the following moral code:

I

Thou shalt not have sexual intercourse with any but thy legally married spouse; excepting, in past history in the case of a man with a prostitute woman captured from an enemy people.

II

Thou shalt not fail to meet thy economic obligations on the pre-arranged date; thou shalt not fail to co-operate economically with thy kin in their economic exchanges; thou shalt not fail to recognise by economic exchange thy affinity to families that are connected with thine by marriage, even upon the other plane.

III

Thou, being a woman, shalt not resent thy husband's economic solidarity with the women of his kin by making charges of incest against him (*sobalabalate*) and them.

IV

Thou, being a woman and a widow, shalt not desert thy children and remarry; if thou breakest this law thou shalt not take thy children to thy new house, for they belong to the house of their father and to the surviving kin of that house.

V

Thou, being a junior, shalt not disobey the elder of thy kin.

VI

Thou shalt not use obscene language except to thy cross-cousin, excepting thou be a woman, in which case thou canst use obscene language only to thy male cross-cousin. Thou shalt not use obscene gesture except with the same allowance.

VII

Thou shalt not thieve.

VIII

Thou shalt not fail to observe meticulously the last rites over thy dead or fail in thy funerary economic obligations.

IX

Thou shalt not consume much wealth or use much wealth to validate an affair of one of thy kin to the present detriment of the validation of an affair of another of thy kin without first seeking thy Sir Ghost's decision. Thou shalt not decide for thyself disputed questions, such as consumption of wealth versus use in economic exchange, or use in one exchange versus use in another.

X

Thou shalt not allow thy house in which thy Sir Ghost is sheltered to fall into disrepair.

XI

Thou shalt not go to a place where the blood of thy ancestors was shed.

XII

Thou shalt not go to a house of which a person has been recently killed or in which a person is being held ill by thy Sir Ghost or by thy husband's Sir Ghost or by the Sir Ghost of one of thy near kin, a house towards which that Sir Ghost is acting as malicious ghost—at peril of reprisals.

XIII

Thou shalt not take a *pwitch* fish (a large species of king fish).

XIV

Thou shalt not break thy gens taboo (on food, or fish, or bird).

XV

Thou shalt not refer to past breaches of these laws that led to illnesses or deaths except, as oracle, thou mayst refer to them when present events flow from them.

XVI

Thou shalt not keep secret any present breach of these laws; thou shalt not make false charges of any breach of these laws.

I could have arranged the whole discussion of religious events in Manus, as given in Chapter IV, under the heads of these various commandments. I have not done so, for the diary form allows the reader more freely to make his own deductions, or to follow different lines of interest. It is clear, however, that these commandments are implicit in the practices of the Manus religious cult.

In practice the articles of the Manus code are not all equally realised in fact. The dead of the paternal line make claims on the living of their line towards certain conformities, and these are decisively in the paternal interest. Thus the claim of the patrilineal line to the custody of the children, against the mother's claim after the death of the father is supported by the Sir Ghost (see illustrations in sections 26 and 27 of the diary in Chapter IV). From the facts of section 43 of the diary—regarding remarriage of widows—and sections 26 and 27—regarding custody of children—we formulated as one commandment of the moral code:

"Thou, being a woman and a widow, shalt not desert thy children and remarry; if thou breakest this law thou shalt not take thy children to thy new house, for they belong to the house of their father and to the surviving kin of that house."

In writing of the custody of the children, Margaret Mead says: "When a man dies the widow is often permitted to keep the children, to take them away with her to her own village, where they are ultimately adopted by some male of the mother's kindred or by a subsequent husband of the woman. This is most likely to be the case if children have not yet been betrothed. If one or more members of the father's gens, or maternal relatives of the father who are resident in the father's village, have made betrothal payments on behalf of the children, they are likely to claim the children. But even here, if the widow is a member of the same village, girls will be permitted to go with their mothers, only returning to their paternal kin for ceremonial occasions upon which expenditures of property are necessary. There is not the sense that children belong to their own gens which in so many parts of the world accompanies strict unilateral organisation . . .

rather children belong to their parents, but more importantly to the father than to the mother. The mother's claim is always subsidiary." [1]

The fact that widows do often secure custody of children is without a doubt. But it is also a fact that there is a feeling that children should belong to their father's heir. The Sir Ghost will be diagnosed as making his heir ill, if his heir fails to secure custody of the children. In this way there does exist a feeling that children belong to their own gens, rather than to their parents (and hence to the widow as surviving parent). This feeling is not always effective in fact, whereas the feeling that children belong to their parents—hence to the widow as surviving parent—is often effective in fact.

It is apparent that the Sir Ghost cult functions for certain ends that are not infallibly secured. It does express and promote the interest of the gens or paternal clan in its unit constellation of the clan. But in the writer's experience clans are often of this nature—rigidly propounded in religion, law, morals, native codification of social organisation; and yet the rigidity is not adhered to in practice. The Dobuan matrilineal clan is an exception. Usually, however, the family bulks more and more, the clan less and less in practice, however strong the religious formulation in the interest of the clan. Manus is a case in point; Dobu is an example of an opposite sort, where the clan interest makes the family interest exceedingly insecure.

Another case in which the Sir Ghost cult supports the interest of the unilateral paternal side is in the Sir Ghostly displeasure of a wife's jealousy because her husband devotes time and gifts of fish to his sister (for illustration see section 15 of the diary). This case has been formulated in the moral code as: "Thou, being a woman, shalt not resent thy husband's economic solidarity with the women of his kin by making charges of incest against him (*sobalabalate*) and them."

In point of fact, women, as wives, are definitely jealous of their husbands' allegiances to the women of the paternal side, to women as sisters. This jealousy is not always ex-

[1] Mead, Margaret, "Kinship in the Admiralty Islands," pp. 288–89.

pressed in the Sir Ghost-prohibited bad language of *sobalabalate*, but it exists nevertheless. Take for example the work done by a man's wife for the man's sister when the latter approaches child-bearing. Dr. Mead, visualising the brother's wife's view point, says:

"Whether the first weeks or so are spent in her own house, or in the house of her sister-in-law, they are weeks of extra work, much coming and going of relatives, irksome observance.[2] At the same time her husband is harried by the necessity to provide the sago for the birth feast. This means that all the fish which can be spared from the household must be traded for sago—and this at the time that there is an extra mouth to feed. Nor can she supplement the household fare by shell-fish, because she must remain in constant attendance on the new mother. Altogether it is a wearisome non-reciprocal obligation, because when she herself bears a child the same obligation will be discharged by her brother's wife in much the same spirit."[3]

There is thus a regular toll of labour exacted from women as wives of brothers by women as sisters—a non-reciprocal toll.

The curse of *sobalabalate*, as when a woman says to her husband, "Your sister is my co-wife, I see," is a wife's reaction against her husband's devotion to his female relatives, usually against his giving his sisters the best of his fishing catch and bringing little home to his wife and family. It is in context with the toll of labour upon the brother's wife in the interest of the brother's sister at the latter's time of approaching childbirth. Nevertheless the actual use of the bad language of *sobalabalate* is rare. Dr. Mead writes:

"This *sobalabalate* situation seems to occur in the case of women who are unusually anxious to make their marriages into important relationships, when this desire on the part of the wife coincides with an extra affection for a female relative on the part of the husband."[4]

[2] The pregnant mother is debarred ritually from many ordinary acts, which have to be done for her. Her food must be cooked specially apart at a special fire, etc.

[3] *Ibid.*, pp. 305–6.

[4] *Ibid.*, p. 305.

The case of Sir Ghostly correction of *sobalabalate* occurs once only in the diary—in section 15—and the above reading of the fact suits the case.[5] It is certain that the suppression of jealous *sobalabalate* is the suppression of jealousy in the family interest, against the clan unit interest. The instrument in the suppression is the Sir Ghost cult, which works for the unilateral interest.

While, in practice, the custody of children is not always secured to the gens by the Sir Ghost cult provision in its favour, the suppression of *sobalabalate* is secured fairly well on the whole. The Sir Ghostly code is not equally successful in enforcing its various provisions. But then nothing of importance is gained by cursing, and something substantial is gained in custody of children.

It is noteworthy that both in widows' custody of children and in wife's *sobalabalate* we find family encroachment on clan, encroachment on the unilateral interest, which the Sir Ghost, of the paternal line, is made to resent. Nevertheless, the family encroachment is on unit of clan, not on clan as a wide body. And the unit of clan is never really a strict clan unit. Thus, Dr. Mead, discussing sisters-in-law further, says:

"Nor can women go to their brothers' houses with the same freedom that their brothers come to theirs. For the women are the cooks; a woman can feed her brother in her husband's house, where her position as mistress of the hearth is undisputed; but she may refuse to cook for her husband's sisters. Her husband has no redress, except an open quarrel which would send her off to her brother's house. Here again, she exercises a formal right of entry and residence which her brother's wife cannot dispute." [6]

What is meant here is that a brother may go casually and freely to his sister's husband's house. But a sister goes to her brother's wife's house with the probability of more or less impotent protest from her sister-in-law, and in consequence does not do so casually and freely, but only after a quarrel

[5] A past case is also referred to in section 14.

[6] *Ibid.*, p. 306.

with her husband. Sisters-in-law are not normally on good terms, as brothers-in-law are. This fact effects a difference in house entry, although the rights of a brother to enter the house where his sister is wife, and the rights of a sister to enter the house where her brother is husband are formally equal—as rights. In practice brothers drift equably and good humouredly and frequently into sister's houses, whereas sisters only come into brother's houses with their limbs bruised from their husband's beating, or their tempers equally frayed.

So, on the whole, the wives, the potential users of *sobalabalate*, do not exercise their right. They manage to keep their husbands' sisters out of the house, except when these rivals for gift of the husband's fish have been beaten, badly abused or made pregnant as a result of their own family concerns. The family on the whole triumphs generally. A brother meets his sister most often in his sister's house, where she lives with her husband and children. He often does something financially for one or two of his sister's children. Looking for brother and sister in company in Manus, one sees often brother and sister and sister's children, as if the clan were matrilineal, and not patrilineal. One does not see as often the patrilineal clan unit of sister, brother and brother's children. And when a father's sister does perform rites for her brother's children, she does so in company with her mother and daughter and daughter's daughter —not a clan function.

The Sir Ghost cult provisions also represent the family interest, in the commandments against pre-marital unchastity and against adultery. Here no kinship tie avails to protect a kinsman who has sinned. A brother may nearly kill a sister for her unchastity (see section 8 of the diary for an instance). Thus a married woman's infidelity is resented equally by her kinsman and by her husband. The Manus contrast to Dobu here is extreme. In the strong clan group of Dobu, a kinsman takes a kinsman's or a kinswoman's part in such matters. In Manus, the strength of the family is more apparent, and may be enforced by the effective cooperation of brothers-in-law as well as by the sanctions of the religious cult.

If we examine the Manus moral code, as derived from the operations of the Sir Ghost cult, we see:

1. Provisions of the code which are supported secularly, as well as by the oracles representing Sir Ghost, are more effectively enforced. For example, brothers-in-law combine to punish adultery in wife and sister, and it practically never occurs. The punishment is immediate violence without waiting for the oracles, who also visit sex lapse with a more delayed punishment of Sir Ghostly origin (illness or death). Similar violence (by a brother) may be used against sex lapse in an affianced sister.

2. Provisions of the code which are not supported secularly, but which are left to oracular punishment, such as an heir's failing to secure custody of the children from the widow, are not as effectively enforced as those of class 1; but it would be an error to suppose that there is any single provision of the oracular code which is without some secular support.

2

Manus religious forms are well adapted to sanction their code of morality. An extreme contrast to the smooth-working Manus scheme I have already described in "Sorcerers of Dobu," another island of the New Guinea littoral. Certain aspects of the functioningof Manus religion may be clearly seen by comparing them with Dobuan practice.

Both Manus and Dobu use supernatural sanctions to enforce correct and lawful behaviour toward neighbours. In both, sickness is interpreted as convicting the sick person or his kin of social breach, such as not having paid due debts or the like. The sins are not by any means the same in detail, but have some features in common. In both it is held that reparation of the sin should cure the sickness. If it does not, and death occurs nevertheless, the ground of indictment of sin of the sick or of his kin is shifted to an indictment of malice exercised by supernatural agencies.

In Manus when a man is ill an oracle comes in from the

PLATE X

KOROTAN, THE BLIND WAR LEADER

village and makes enquiry of the sick man's ghostly father why he is punishing his son. The oracle obtains an answer which is always in terms of the sick man's sins or the sins of his close kin. The kin of the sick make reparation for this towards the person they have offended, nearly all the common sins being practical offences against neighbours. The reparation is done in good spirit. Submission to the will of the ghostly father is keenly expressed in Manus sentiment, and the sentiment is not socially wasted. It is quickly converted into submission to the social code, which is actually given as from the dead, by the oracles. If after indictment and a confession and reparation of offences, the sick person does not recover, but dies, the contretemps is not socially serious. The malice of some unrelated person's ghostly father is indicted by an oracle, and this unrelated person avoids the dead's kin for some months as a precaution against their ghostly father returning malice upon his person, but, as a rule, without dangerous malice between the living persons concerned.

In Dobu the contrast to the Manus system is extreme. A diviner is summoned from far away to state the sin or offence of the sick. He divines the person's identity who, within the locality, is venting a legitimate grievance upon the sick man by the use of sorcery or witchcraft; and states the legitimate grievance. Since the provenience of sorcery and witchcraft is the locality, and the unknown plaintiff with a grievance operates in person, the diviner, to be above the battle, must come from without. One result is that he usually is ignorant of the locality affairs where he divines, although he is conversant with his own locality affairs where he does not divine. He is often driven to surreptitious conversations with young children of the locality which engages him to divine as a necessary preliminary to his solemn divination. Again, he is often driven to avoiding pronouncing a clear issue, but to giving out hocus pocus, or what his employers feel to be hocus pocus. In Manus the fact that the oracle, diviner or medium, works in his or her own home, avoids this disadvantage of oracles' crass ignorance of affairs.

In the second place, when the Dobuan diviner *does* know the affairs of another locality which employs him he does not necessarily operate freely. He may know in the first place that the sick person is ill from no justly exercised magic, the right being not with the offended sorcerer or witch who is active, but with the sick person. In such case the diviner refuses to act. He may be prevented by an initial presupposition that is not possible with the Manus use of the ghostly father instead of the Dobuan use of the infuriated magician.

In the third place, the Dobuan reparation to the offended person who has a legitimate grievance correctly stated by the diviner is not made in good spirit. There is nothing corresponding to the Manus sentiment of a clean submission to the will of the ghostly father, which is converted into an equally clean submission to the rights of the social code. Instead there is a magician's pride in a mastery of the elemental forces, which displaces a sense of submission and a sense of humour. There is only crestfallen chagrin at the failure of one's magic (which would have protected the wrong-doer if it were powerful enough). There is a disposition to wish for revenge upon the successful magical plaintiff. And the law of right and wrong suffers greatly from having been personally executed by the personal magic of the plaintiff instead of by some comparatively impersonal factor, such as the Manus ghostly father. This atmosphere embarrasses the diviner, and makes his work difficult. If he makes a mistake in his facts he enkindles sheer unmitigated enmity between the sick and the person he names, resulting in no good and no reparation whatever.

In the fourth place, if reparation of offences has been made and the sickness does not mend, but death intervenes, the social contretemps is most serious. The sorcerer or witch is, as in cases of illness, still within the locality but evidently malicious, and not acting judicially. No diviner will touch the case. The kin of the dead summon the people of the locality to come to mourn and watch the mourners divine the guilty person themselves. Then they set to work on counter-malice and vengeance, again in terms of magic. The result is an absence of trust in the locality.

It will be clear from a comparison of these two cases that a supernatural sanction used to enforce correct and lawful behaviour towards neighbours may be well or badly adapted for the purpose. The Dobuan variety is so badly adapted that it defeats its own purpose, probably more than it aids it. According to Spencer and Gillen, the Central Australians divine the sorcerer or witch responsible for illness and death in a far-off country where their habitual enemies in warfare live. The Dobuans have their far-off habitual enemies in warfare, and might well dispose of their troubles there—instead they must have two different sets of troubles. They use sorcery and witchcraft in a praiseworthy attempt towards a worthy social object within the home locality—but the instrument defeats the ends of its wielders. The form is not fit for the function which is attempted.

Very different institutions may be used in an attempt towards the one and the same social function. Where one institution is adaptable, and is well-adapted in fact to this social function, another is most refractory. In either case the system continues.

It is apparent that the forms of institutions may allow or constrain their usefulness for the social purpose to which they may happen to be put. The Manus religious forms are better adapted to the sanctioning of morality than the Dobuan magical forms. It has been suggested to the writer that the Manus want an orderly society, and they have institutions which make for order. The Dobuans may want other values and possess institutions which perpetuate those other values. This is no doubt true in part. The Manus want health, long life and good fishing from their ghosts. The Dobuans want health, long life, but also personal power from their magic. They possibly want personal magical power at the expense of their fellows, more than they want good government. Nevertheless, this view is true but in part. To a certain extent no community gets what it wants. Different peoples are subject to different accidents of locality and of general culture area in the general forms of their institutions. Thus the Dobuans do in fact want good government, and do try to use sorcery in the interests of justice. This might be accomplished more easily by a political head, such as a king or chief, who had exclusive control of specialist sorcerers, than it can be democratically, without the secular forms of government in chieftainship or kingship. The difficulty of the form may be indicated by the rarity of the moral sorcerer in the known cultures of the world, as well as by the Dobuan attempt in fairly evident difficulty.

We are used to the idea of morality enforced by religion from our own cultural pattern. And so prominent is the same idea in the Manus system that one is easily led into making the Hebrew and Christian analogies. They are definitely analogies—Manus religion is not influenced by Christianity.

Sir Edward Tylor in writing of primitive religion from a thorough knowledge of all that was available in his time said:

"To some the statement may seem startling, yet the evidence seems to justify it, that the relation of religion to morality is one that belongs in its rudiments, or not at all, to rudimentary civilization . . . the popular idea that the moral government of the universe is an essential tenet of natural religion simply falls to the ground. Savage animism is almost devoid of that ethical element which to the educated modern mind is the very mainspring of practical religion. Not, as I have said, that morality is absent from the life of the lower races. But these ethical laws stand on their own ground of tradition and public opinion, comparatively independently of the animistic beliefs and rites which exist beside them. The lower animism is not immoral, it is non-moral. The essential connection of theology and morality is a fixed idea in many minds. But it is one of the lessons of history that subjects may maintain themselves independently for ages, till the event of coalescence takes place." [7]

It must be remembered that Tylor had postulated three

[7] Tylor, E. G., "Primitive Culture," Vol. II, pp. 359–61, First American Edition.

levels of religious evolution from lower to higher stages: (1) ancestor cult, (2) polytheistic cult, (3) monotheism. The presumption was that these levels were from ancient and lowly to modern and high. The Manus natives anticipate evolution, according to this theory, by two stages. They remain in the ancestor cult stages, but remaining at that "most primitive level," without trace of polytheism or monotheism, they yet parallel the major innovation of the "most modern and highest level," the innovation of a coalescence between religion and morals, the innovation that stood behind Tylor's assurance that monotheism was the "highest level"—savage animism being "almost devoid of that ethical element which to the educated modern mind is the very mainspring of practical religion." Tylor is entirely correct in stating that in most primitive regions of the world religion and morality "maintain themselves independently." Primitive religion generally enjoins, as the correct means of setting man right with the supernatural, ritualistic acts such as sacrifice, libation, the proper rites over the dead, and the keeping of a variety of taboos and more or less aesthetic ceremonials.[8] The Manus religion stands out against this background in clear and bold relief. It is a concentration on setting man right with man as the way of setting man right with the supernatural. It does not go directly about its apparent business. It does not concentrate on direct attention to the supernatural. It embodies a belief that setting man right with man sets him right also with the supernatural. "The educated modern mind" of Sir Edward Tylor's day held the same belief. Manus religion exemplifies on the lowest level of ancestor cult the thoroughgoing coalescence of religion and morality that has been characteristic also of the Christian religion.

[8] This is true even of the Admiralty Islands tribes neighbouring to the Manus tribe.

APPENDIX

WHO'S WHO IN CHAPTER FOUR[1]

Alupwai: a woman of Kalo gens married to Tunu of Pere gens. Her record of sexual sin with Pwaliap and Pwanau is made public as a result of her illness after child bearing. Her sins of theft and trespass in conjunction with Tunu are exposed also. Her sister Lawa's offences—obscenity used to her mother-in-law and raking up of scandal with her cross-cousin, Nyakareu, about Nyakareu's husband's sins—are also re-exposed. The sins of the men of Kalo gens, her brothers by blood and also her brothers of gentile range, are not exposed in connection with Alupwai, for she has married away from her gens, as has Lawa also.

Bonyalo: the son of a man of Pere gens, now dead, and of a mother of Kalo gens still living. Bonyalo is very stupid indeed and he works for Paliau, who attends to Bonyalo's affairs. Itong, the mother of Bonyalo, is a widow and a medium, but Paliau does not use her as a medium in his affairs, possibly because such action might give her a hold on her son greater than his own. Itong is of a different family of Kalo gens than that of Alupwai and Lawa. Bonyalo is the ward of the ward of *pwanau* (*i.e.*, indirectly under Paliau's Sir Ghost).

Ghizikup: the leading man of Mbunai village, corresponding to Korotan in Peri, and Liankor in Taui village. He holds the native office of what was war leader of the village, an office called *Luluai*.

Ilan: a woman of Kametatchau gens, a gens now almost extinct in Peri. Many of her mother's relatives of Pontchal gens still survive however. She is the wife of Topaz, a man of Matchupal gens, who is very fond of visiting his mother and sisters in Kalaat gens. Ilan's new-born infant falls ill and

[1] Names of mortals only, with but one or two exceptions; names of ghosts are without initial capital letter and are in italics.

she is indicted by Itong, the mother of Bonyalo, as medium, for scandalously charging Topaz with incest because he neglects her for his mother's kin in Kalaat gens.

Isau: the father's sister of Pokenau of Pontchal gens. She is a widow who lives in Pokenau's house. The record against her is laziness in not getting firewood for Pokenau's house, for which Pokenau's Sir Ghost made her ill.

Isole: sister of Korotan and Talikai of the leading family of Peri village. She is of Pere gens and she lives in her own place, having brought her husband there and kept him there despite his being a solid citizen and not at all the type of poor man who more often lives in a wife's place. Isole is very forceful indeed and very intelligent. She is a medium, and has no record of past sin against her. When she falls ill she is charged only with not having obeyed her control's expressed desires that she shall confine her activities as medium. Isole's control is *tchemilo;* her Sir Ghosts, the *talipolalau.*

Itong: the mother of Bonyalo, Paliau's retainer. She is of Kalo gens and sister of Songan, an old man of Kalo. Her son is a moron, and her mother was unsound in intelligence. The mother of Itong, Semean, had five children, one of whom was said to have been insane. The grandchildren, Itong's brothers' and sisters' sons, I knew. Three of them had very pronounced exhibitionistic perversions and others were stupid. Itong's strain was very unbalanced. Itong herself was the only medium noted for adhering to the convention of using spirit dogs to collect soul stuff in preference to the new convention of using the ghosts of members of the native constabulary. Her controls were *polum* (for land and overhead work) and *pokamitch* (for under-water diving work).

Kali: an old man of Lo gens, the father of Nane. He was a rich man in his day, which was now over, and over honourably. He was nevertheless convicted of the sin of surreptitiously selling a *pwitch* fish to the Usiai, a sin contributory to the death of his grandson, Popwitch. For most of his life he had dealt openly in this way with *pwitch* fish, however, as the taboo on dealings with *pwitch* fish was a new thing. He was the ward of the ghost of his dead son, *malaut.*

Kampon: a woman of Matchupal gens. Her mother, the wife of Maku, was resident in Kampon's father's house, the father now being dead, and Kampon's mother remarried to another man named Maku. Kampon as a girl had been seduced by Selan, and became pregnant out of wedlock. The infant died. An effort had been made to marry Kampon to Selan, but Selan ran away. Kampon was seduced next by Poiyo, also of Matchupal gens. Her kin brought the pressure of white Government upon Poiyo to make him marry her. This was effected to the great indignation of Poiyo's first wife, Nyakareu, and in the end much obscenity, scandal and death resulted.

Kamutal: formerly the wife of Potek who adopted Pwanau and Paliau, now generally known as the mother of Paliau. After being widow of *potek* for some time she married Ndroga, who was Pwanau's blood father's blood brother's son, but unrelated to *potek*. She was of Matchupal gens, and a medium. Her control was *nyandros*.

There was another Kamutal in Peri village, who was an adolescent girl, adopted daughter of Pokenas and the wife of Pokenas, Nyambula.

Keah: a poor man and a moron of Kametatchau gens married to a woman of Kalo gens who suffered from pathological and insane jealousy. She was a medium who never found employment except by Keah.

Kemwai: a rich man of Lo gens, and the son of Kali's elder brother. He was virtually the leading man in Lo gens, but he lived in his wife's place, Isole, his wife, being far more than his equal in wit and in influence, and of *lapan* rank, whereas he was *lau* (common). Kemwai was a prominent diviner, and a law-abiding person in temperament. His Sir Ghosts the *talipolalau*, are also (and by blood) Isole's.

Kialo: the present husband of Lawa of Kalo gens. He is of Patusi village.

On occasion *kialo* of Matchupal gens of Peri village is also written Kialo, in reference to a time when he was still alive. This *kialo* is the ghost of the former husband of Lawa, and so becomes involved with his living namesake of Patusi village.

Kiteni: an adolescent girl of Kalaat gens.

Korotan: war leader of Peri village, now blind. He had the right to build a house of larger size and with more house posts than anyone else in Peri. He outranked all other *lapan* (men and women of rank). His blindness led to his not being able to meet his debts. Like other *lapan* and rich men he had once had dependents to work for him, but owing to a large group of his young dependents having taken captive an Usiai woman who was an affinal relative of his and used her as a prostitute, he had lost his dependents. He had cast the young men off so that they even obtained from white Administration political recognition of their separation from the rest of Peri village (after their term in gaol where Korotan had caused them to be sent).

Some years after the loss of his dependents Korotan's Usiai wife died. Korotan behaved as no Manus man does by custom. He wept, and he kept her skull, hung it in honoured place in his house and talked to her ghost often. Because he wept for his wife's death he went blind—so report explained his blindness which followed almost immediately after.

Following the loss of his dependents, then of his sight, he no longer could meet the debts he owed. He was hounded by his debtors.

Kukun: a rich man of Patusi village.

Lawa: a woman of Kalo gens, and blood sister to Alupwai. Lawa had been married to Kialo of Matchupal gens in Peri village. Kialo died, partly because Lawa used obscene abuse upon his mother, partly because she raked up scandalously the very real sins of Poiyo of Matchupal gens, Kialo's titular father. Lawa, after Kialo's death, was sought in marriage by Patalian, the head of her family, Tuwain, agreeing to Patalian's suit. The rest of the family were against Patalian, because he had once seduced their mother, mother also of Tuwain. The family quarrelled seriously and split. Then Lawa was helped by a woman of Kalo, the wife of Pomalat of Pontchal, to marry a man also called Kialo, but of Patusi village. This made another split, most of Kalo gens viewing this successful move with an equal enmity as to Patalian's unsuccessful move. Many men of Kalo gens were stricken by *kialo* (ghost of the former husband) for this remarriage of Lawa. The Kalo wife of Pomalat was still not on speaking or meeting terms with most of Kalo gens during my time in Peri village (see Nyamasim).

Lawian: the unmarried daughter of Isole and *kemwai* of Lo gens who was seduced by Noan of Lo gens.

Liankor: war leader of Taui village.

Loloan: sister of Keah, the poor man of Kametatchau gens. She was married into Pomatchau village.

Lomot: the wife of Talikai; a woman of Patusi village and a gens relative of Pwanau (now *pwanau* and Sir Ghost to Paliau) by blood.

Luwil: a dependent of Paliau. He was called a brother of Paliau. Actually he was a son by blood of Paliau's adoptive father. Luwil was adopted into Matchupal gens whereas Paliau was adopted into Pere gens. If Luwil's Matchupal gens adopter had lived to keep Luwil his dependent, Paliau would have had no claim upon Luwil.

Main: the sister of Kemwai and the loose woman of the village. All her sins were in her past however. She was now growing old. She was stupid.

Man of Lorengau: a magician of Mbunai village; a versatile linguist speaking German, some English, nearly all the languages of the Admiralties, some Bismarck Archipelago dialects, and a little Samoan. He was born of an Usiai mother and of a Manus father; an innovator and an experimentalist, very upset at criticism at his not being radical enough; he liked to try internally medicines (European) usually used externally, in order to discover the effects, and similarly with everything; a male medium as well as a diviner. He had had five wives, and had a great reputation for love magic. He was a friend of Nane, and like Nane, had many friends on the north coast, where dugong is to be fished. More than anyone else he practised face-painting as protection against ghosts whenever he traveled. He attempted radically to alter the conventions of the ghost cult during my stay.

Mbosai: a rich financier of Kalaat gens who was financially interested also in the members of his mother's gens, Matchupal. He was a prominent diviner. He was very fat and strongly resembled the ideal picture of a European capitalist. He was among the three or four richest men in Peri.

Mwe: a son of Nane of Lo gens.

Nane: the son of Kali; a rich man of Lo gens. He was a great fisher of turtle, and he held the hereditary magic as the castrator of all the boars born in the village (none were born, or sows either, during my stay).

Nḍralina: a lad of Taui village.

Ndrantche: the mother of Tuwain, Sali, Alupwai and Lawa; formerly seduced by Patalian; subsequently the wife of Papi-Talipoitchalon of Kalo gens and now his widow.

Ndrapol: a poor man of Pontchal gens.

Ndroga: a man of Patusi village married to Kamutal, the former wife of Potek. He lives in his wife's place. Kamutal has no house, but lives in Ngandaliu's house, Ngandaliu being (in one of his several manifestations) of the same gens as Kamutal. Ndroga was a long lean man, otherwise inconspicuous.

Ndroi: a lad of Kalo betrothed to Lawian. Lawian was of the best stock in Peri, Ndroi of the worst. Lawian was seduced by Noan, a thief and a moron. She was engaged to a boy who had sex perversions and who, shortly after Lawian's seduction, was lodged in gaol for breaking into a white man's house by night (Ndroi being away at work at the time).

Ndroso (or Ndrosal): the brother of the wife of Pokenas, less of a personality than his very manly sister. The pair are of Peri gens, and born of a father who by other marriages begat Korotan, Talikai, Nyakareu, Pwoikaton and Pikaro.

Ngamasue: a dull man of Kalo gens. He had adopted Ndroi and was therefore head of the party of the males who were to validate Ndroi's engagement to Lawian, daughter of Kemwai and Isole.

Ngamel: a rich financier of Peri gens whose dependents' work provided for his household. He had paid a medium well to consecrate him as a diviner. But from the beginning his back would not itch at all in connection with divining. He never practised in consequence. He was a realistic man. His wife was not a medium.

Ngandaliu: a constant fish trap maker and fisherman, who was energetic enough, but who cultivated no dependents, and preferred to do his own work. He was decidedly individual in this. He had been adopted by Kali but was of Pontchal and of Matchupal gentes as well as of Lo gens according to which suited him. By blood both he and his more aggressive brother, Selan, were of Taui village, not of Peri.

Noan: a thief and a moron, son of Pope; seducer of Lawian; black-listed from work for any white man; a former school boy specially educated in a Government boarding school.

Nyakareu: the first wife of Poiyo. She was of Pere gens, and a daughter of Korotan's father by another mother than Korotan's. She was also called Ponyama which means liar. She was always shouting obscenity at Kampon, Poiyo's other scandalously acquired wife.

Nyamaka: the mother of that Kialo who was the former husband of Lawa of Kalo, the Kialo now dead. She was a widow, of Pontchal gens. Her last husband, the dead *kialo's* father had been of Matchupal gens.

Nyamasim: a woman of Kalo gens married to Pomalat. She had arranged the marriage of Lawa of Kalo to Kialo of Patusi village after Lawa was the widow of *kialo* of Matchupal gens of Peri village. This act brought Kalo gens out with spears against Pontchal gens (into which Nyamasim had married), but as the event turned, no blood was shed. She was a medium, and her husband a diviner.

Nyambula: see Wife of Pokenas.

Nyandatelun: the mother of Bonyalo who has been discussed under her other name, Itong.

Nyapo: a man who had deserted his own place and kin of Loitcha and come to live a comparatively solitary life in Peri village.

Paka: a man of Mok village.

Pakob: the son of Ngamel, a small boy, not to be confused with the ghost of the same name.

Paliau: a financier and capitalist of Pere gens, and a highly intelligent and ambitious man. He was adopted by Potek, to whom Pwanau succeeded as heir. Paliau succeeded Pwanau. By birth Paliau and Tchawan were brothers from Mbuke village. Tchawan was adopted differently from Paliau in Peri village and came to comparatively nothing. Paliau was formerly one of the native army organised under the former German Administration to police unsettled territory not yet under control.

Patalian: like Paliau, Patalian had been a member of the native army used in the German Administration to put into unsettled territory in New Guinea. In Peri he was a war captive, taken as a child from his own people of Nouna Island. He was adopted by the grandparents of Pokenau and Sori, and was thus of Pontchal gens. He had difficulty in finding a wife, and as he was a magician, his magic made trouble for those who put difficulty in his path. He had one eye damaged by a gun explosion.

Pepi: a small son of Pokenau.

Pigs a Hundred: a man of Patusi village and cross-cousin to Pokenau.

Pikaro: a "sister" of Korotan of a collateral line which was also a collateral line to that of Pokenau. After the split of Pere gens into Pere and Pontchal she was equally related to either party. She lived in her sister's daughter's husband's house sometimes (Tchawan's), and sometimes in her dead husband's brother's son's house (Pomat's); both of these houses were Matchupal gens houses. She was a widow, and a frequently employed medium.

Poiyo: a man of Matchupal gens with marks of former leprosy on his body. He had two wives, one being of his own gens (Kampon), the other and first wife being Nyakareu, half-sister of Korotan, and, like Korotan, of Pere gens. Poiyo had only one ramshackle old house, and was in constant trouble from the ghosts for his and his wives' sins. He was having a new house built during my time in Peri, but it was taking him more than six months to validate the finishing of it by the necessary feasts to the builders.

Pokenas: a man of Lopwer gens whose house was managed for him by his wife. Pokenas was a diviner, his wife being a prominent medium, as well as an intelligent and a forceful business woman.

Pokenau: the native constable of Pontchal gens, a poor business man; a somewhat lazy man in trade, but very active mentally. With Paliau and Patalian, he was one of my best informants. He had been a diviner, but had given it up, except for divining the whereabouts of fish. His wife was not a medium, so he had less need to divine (in order to anticipate his wife in the making of decisions) than had some other men such as Kemwai and Pokenas whose wives were mediums.

Pokus or Son-of-Nyapo: a financier of Taui village.

Poli: a man of Lopwer gens by birth; he was adopted by Songan of Kalo gens, and so became Kalo. He was a diviner, but not very important in economic affairs. His father Songan had a magical charm which he gave several times (with its fetish stone) to Poli, but which he had taken back several times because he fell ill shortly after. The dogma is that bequeathing magic kills off the person bequeathing. Songan and Poli played with the dogma to see if it could be defied, and found that it could not be defied.

Pomalat: a man of Pontchal gens by birth; he had also some alliance to Matchupal gens as he had been adopted by a Matchupal man. He was assistant native constable of Pontchal. He was cross-cousin to Paliau of Pere gens through Paliau's Matchupal mother. The pair had been in a jesting relationship until for the second time Pomalat sent Paliau on a long canoe voyage by giving deceitful information as a jest. The second time Paliau cursed Pomalat with *tandritanitani*. Pomalat was a diviner.

Pomaleu or Pomele or son of Paliau (*i.e.*, son-in-law of Paliau): a man of Matchupal gens and the younger brother of Poiyo. But effectively he functioned as a retainer of Paliau, his father-in-law, of Pere gens. He was the ward of *kialo*, the son of Nymaka, the younger brother (and therefore titular son) of Poiyo, the same *kialo* that, as mortal, was the husband of Lawa of Kalo, the sister of Alupwai.

Pope: a man of Lo gens. His father was not of Lo, but despite the theoretical patriliny of Manus, Pope was effectively of his mother's gens of Lo. Pope was a moron, and subject to occasional cataleptic fits. He was the father of Noan, the seducer of Lawian. He is not to be confused with the ghostly *pope*, who is one of the two controls of the wife of Pokenas.

Pomat: a man of Matchupal gens and an economic dependent of Mbosai. Pomat was *lapan* (of rank), not a commoner, and should therefore have been independent. But somewhere his patrimony had been exhausted, the commercial credit of his line damaged, so Pomat worked for a rich man, and never worked effectively enough to achieve independence.

Popwitch: the son of Nane of Lo gens who died during my stay in Peri, and who is not to be confused with the ghosts, *popwitch* senior and *popwitch* junior.

Pwanau: now a ghost, *pwanau*. The name written as Pwanau refers to the mortal span of *pwanau* in past history—and only in past history. Pwanau was the adoptive son of Potek, as Paliau was also. Pwanau was older than Paliau. Apart from their having the one adoptive father, Pwanau and Paliau were unrelated. Pwanau succeeded Potek, and Paliau, Pwanau. In my time in Peri *potek* was out of the social structure, having been dropped completely, but *pwanau* was Sir Ghost to Paliau.

Pwentchiam: a woman of Lopwer gens and the full sister of Pokenas. Pwentchiam was married into Patusi village.

Pwiseu: a rich man of Pere gens; he was of a collateral paternal line to that of Ngamel, with whom he cooperated often on an equal footing.

Pwoikaton or Talikawa: a poorer man of Pere gens. He was not very old yet, not old enough to be certainly settled in poverty. He was of the same father as Talikai, Korotan, Nyakareu, Nyambula (the wife of Pokenas) and Ndroso. Pwoikaton and Ndroso were the poorer offshoots of their father.

Sali: the younger brother of Alupwai and Lawa of Kalo; the son of *papi-talipoitchalon* (as mortal) and Ndrantche. Tuwain was the eldest male of this biological family.

Salikon: the eldest daughter of Pwanau and the wife of Pwanau, who was adopted by Paliau after Pwanau became *pwanau*, and still tended also by the widow of *pwanau* until the latter made a run-away marriage with Patalian, after which Paliau kept Salikon.

Sanau: a quiet man of Kalaat gens, but independent and sufficient.

Selan: the only male medium in Peri village except when Man of Lorengau (properly of Mbunei Bunai village) also practised as a male medium in Peri. Selan was a functioning member of Pontchal, Matchupal and Lo gentes, and was not by birth of any Peri gens. He had been adopted by Tchokar who as a very rich man had found need to function in the same three gentes in order to invest his savings completely.

Songan or Taliposala: an old man of Kalo, the adoptive father of Poli, the brother of Itong (the mother of Bonyalo), a magician.

Tali Katin, Son-of-Katin: a man of Taui village (his wife's village).

Son of Nyapo or Pokus: a financier of Taui village.

Talikai: a half-brother of Korotan, the war leader of Peri village; of Pere gens, and Korotan's probable successor (Talikai being the younger of the two). Talikai officially had two wives, but he tried to keep the two in his house and failed. One went to her mother's house, and Talikai, unlike Poiyo, declined to make arrangements to live with one wife in one house, and with another wife in another house. This was because Talikai was proud. His affairs in consequence raised no scandal while Poiyo's did.

Talilona: a former war leader of Patusi village, now dead. The daughter of Talilona, Ile, was also dead (and properly *ile*). The ghost of a dead brother of Talikai (*pwoitchon*) on the ghostly plane married *ile*, and the economic validation of the marriage was conducted by mortals related to the dead who were so married (for the first time as dead, in a manner different from that of their mortal marriage).

Taliposaala or Songan: see under Songan.

Tchawan (also called Tchaumutchin): an elder brother of

Paliau by blood. Tchawan and Paliau were born in Mbuke village, however, and all their real ties in Peri village, where they lived, were adoptive. Tchawan was adopted by a rich man of Matchupal gens but not made his heir. Paliau was adopted by a rich man of Peri, and after the death of an elder brother, Pwanau, became his heir. So Paliau dominated Tchawan, and Tchawan often worked for Paliau.

Tchokal or Manawei: a man of Patusi who had left all his kin and come to live with Pwiseu, whose wife was of Patusi.

Tcholai: the son of a dead brother of Korotan, now adopted by Korotan.

Topaz: a young married man of Matchupal gens who kept up strong ties with his female kin on his mother's side (of Kalaat gens) and gave fish to them to the great annoyance of his wife, Ilan, who was of Kametatchau gens on her father's side, and secondarily linked to Pontchal on her mother's side.

Tunu: by blood the son of Potek. Pwanau, adopted by Potek, was Potek's heir, then Paliau, also adopted by Potek, was Pwanau's heir. Tunu worked for Paliau. Tunu's wife was Alupwai of Kalo gens. Tunu was still of Pere gens, his blood father's gens. Another son of Potek by blood, Luwil, by name, had been adopted by a man of Matchupal gens, but nevertheless was equally an economic dependent of Paliau.

Tuwain: the eldest son of the eldest family line of Kalo gens. Tuwain's father (now dead) called Papi, or Talipoitchalon or Papi-Talipoitchalon was the former leading man of the gens. Tuwain is elder brother to Alupwai, Lawa and Sali.

Village Constable of Taui.

Widow of *pwanau:* this widow, the mother of Salikon was of Lopwer gens, and Pokenas of Lopwer was one financier of her former marriage validation, Mbosai (of Kalaat and of Matchupal) being the other by a relationship through female ancestors only. The widow of *pwanau* contributed her work to Paliau's household (Paliau being the ward of *pwanau*) after the death of Pwanau. The widow of *pwanau* outraged

Pokenas, Mbosai and Paliau by marrying Patalian by elopement.

Wife of Keah: a woman of Kalo who was subject to delusions founded in pathological jealousy, and not controlled by any intelligence, she being of low mentality generally.

Wife of Maku: a woman of Kapet gens, all the other members of which had left Peri village or died off (some the one, some the other). She was resident in a former husband's house, it being near Pontchal gens territory, the gens of her mother (who was now long dead, the wife of Maku herself being an old woman).

Wife of Pokenas: a woman of Pere gens who was very intelligent (by name Nyambula). Pokenas, a good business man and an intelligent medium, the husband, did as he was told. When he objected Nyambula called in her brother, Ndroso, who lived opposite, to deal with Pokenas. A woman affronted by her husband usually runs for refuge to her brother's house. The wife of Pokenas always struck first, and, if Pokenas objected, called her brother into Pokenas' house. Her particular invention worked perfectly in her favour and she never had the slightest fear of having to take refuge in her brother's house.

Wife of Pomo: the daughter of Pondramet, a poor man of Matchupal gens. Pomo, her husband, was also of Matchupal gens. The couple and Pondramet and his wife lived in a poor ramshackle house, and conducted an obscure existence for the most part.

Wife of Pondramet: a woman of Kalo gens; she was not the mother of the wife of Pomo, although her husband, Pondramet, was the father of the wife of Pomo. The Pondramet pair and the Pomo pair had lived in one house. The wife of Pondramet was cross-cousin to the widow of *pwanau* and cross-cousin to Patalian, and she acted as secret go-between for the pair in their scheme to dare *pwanau* and marry. Immediately after the runaway marriage *pwanau* got the wife of Pondramet, who died suddenly.

Frequently mentioned ghosts are:

pwanau, Sir Ghost of Paliau.

sori, Sir Ghost of Pokenau.

tchemilo, control of Isole.

the talipolalau—brothers ghosts, Sir Ghosts of the brothers Korotan and Talikai, with Korotan's son, Tcholai, and Korotan's and Talikai's sister, Isole.

GLOSSARY OF MANUS TERMS

arakeu: built up coral rubble platform adjoining which only men of rank may build a house; the platform was used for ceremonial exchanges and meetings.

drengen: the relationship between two persons who exchange with each other in an affinal exchange; the two persons who so exchange *kawos;* all exchange of goods from barter to ceremonial exchange.

komambut: the dogs' teeth, shell money and bead belts given by the bilateral kins of the parents of a boy to validate the boy's betrothal.

kussi mburror: sorcery used on adults.

lapan: a man or a woman of rank.

lau: a commoner.

lom kamal: the male line proceeding from a brother.

lom pein: the female line proceeding from a sister. (In either male or female line a person of the opposite sex is admitted only as brother to a sister of the female line, or as sister to a brother of the male line.)

luluai: war leader and man of highest hereditary rank in a village.

mamandra: the confinement of a girl just before her marriage; the gift-giving by her kin at the close of her confinement.

matangongo: gift of pots and grass skirts given by the bilateral kin of the girl to be married the day after their receipt of the *komambut.*

matiruai: repayment of *mwelamwel* and *mamandra* gifts after the consummation of the marriage *metcha;* gifts like *komambut* given late in a marriage by the kin of the husband to the kin of his wife.

molua: the soul.

mwandrin: a house of mourning.

mwelamwel: gifts on the person of the bride given with her by her bilateral kin on her marriage day.

mwere rang mwere palit: between the mortals between the ghosts, *i.e.*, a medium's control.

palit am mbwaro: magic to damage infants and child-bearing mothers.

patandrusun: tabooed food or other object of a female descent line.

pataran: the relationship between the principals of either party in an affinal exchange of wealth.

patieyen: father's mother, and the female line through females proceeding from her (applied to females only).

pwokean: rich, strong in body, aggressive, hard working.

sobalabalate: the form of language in which a wife charges her husband with incest.

sorosor: magical charm to cause illness placed upon private property in trees to protect them.

tandritanitani: the magical power which the *lom pein* have over the *lom kamal.*

tchinal: a familiar of Usiai-derived magic; also represented as an ogre in Manus legends.

MAP OF THE ADMIRALTY ISLANDS

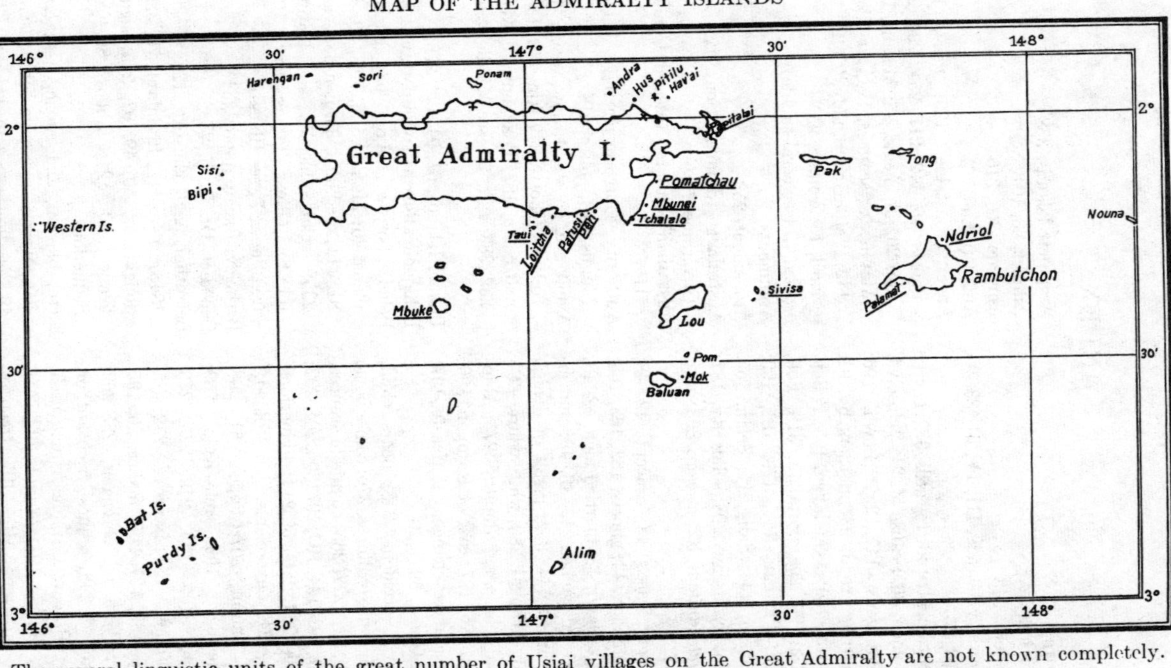

The several linguistic units of the great number of Usiai villages on the Great Admiralty are not known completely. Villages underlined are present or former Manus Villages. + Mission Stations. ● Government Station.

INDEX